Globalizing Linkages

The Global Story of Christianity Series
History, Context, and Communities

Seven One-Volume Books

SERIES EDITORS
Emma Wild-Wood & Mark A. Lamport

SERIES ASSISTANT EDITOR
Gina A. Zurlo

SERIES INTRODUCTION
Dana L. Robert

BOOK EDITORS
Mitri Raheb *(Middle East)* | Amos Yong *(Asia)* | Wanjiru Gitau *(Africa)*
Alex Ryrie *(Europe)* | Raimundo Barreto *(Latin America)*
Upolu Vaai *(Oceania)* | Christopher Evans *(North America)*

SERIES EDITORIAL ADVISORY BOARD
Edwin Aponte *(Louisville Institute)*
Elias Bongmba *(Rice University)*
Arun Jones *(Candler School of Theology/Emory University)*
Brett Knowles *(University of Otago)*
David Maxwell *(University of Cambridge, UK)*
Elizabeth Monier *(University of Cambridge, UK)*
Dana L. Robert *(Center for Global Christianity*
and Mission/Boston University)
Nelly van Doorn-Harder *(Wake Forest University)*
Stephanie Wong *(Valparaiso University)*

SENIOR EDITORIAL CONSULTANT
Joshua Erb

Series Concept

The Global Story of Christianity Series is designed as a set of accessible introductions for those who wish to understand the emergence of the Christian faith and its global church presence today. The concept of "story" will be the featured motif and is reflected in fifteen chapters spread over three main subheadings in each book:

> **Section One:** The Story of Christianity Narrated in Historical Context
>
> **Section Two:** The Story of Christianity Expressed in a Grand Church Family Mosaic
>
> **Section Three:** The Story of Christianity Encounters Twenty-First Century Issues

The Global Story of Christianity Series

Book Title	Year of Release	Editors
Surviving Jewel: The Enduring Story of Christianity in the Middle East	Book 1: 2022	Mitri Raheb *(Dar al-Kalima University College, Bethlehem)* & Mark A. Lamport
Uncovering the Pearl: The Hidden Story of Christianity in Asia	Book 2: 2023	Amos Yong *(Fuller Theological Seminary)* & Mark A. Lamport
Globalizing Legacies: The Intermingling Story of Christianity in Africa	Book 3: 2024	Wanjiru M. Gitau *(Palm Beach Atlantic University, West Palm, Florida)* & Mark A. Lamport
Entangling Web: The Fractious Story of Christianity in Europe	Book 4: 2024	Alec Ryrie *(University of Durham, UK)* & Mark A. Lamport
Engaging Coloniality: The Liberative Story of Christianity in Latin America	Book 5: 2024	Raimundo César Barreto Jr. *(Princeton Theological Seminary)* & Mark A. Lamport
Restoring Identities: The Contextualizing Story of Christianity in Oceania	Book 6: 2023	Upolu Vaai *(Pacific Theological College, Fiji)* & Mark A. Lamport
Expanding Energy: The Dynamic Story of Christianity in North America	Book 7: 2024	Christopher H. Evans *(Boston University)* & Mark A. Lamport

Globalizing Linkages

The Intermingling Story of Christianity in Africa

EDITED BY
Wanjiru M. Gitau
AND
Mark A. Lamport

CASCADE *Books* • Eugene, Oregon

GLOBALIZING LINKAGES
The Intermingling Story of Christianity in Africa

The Global Story of Christianity Series 3

Copyright © 2024 Wipf and Stock Publishers. All rights reserved. Except for brief quotations in critical publications or reviews, no part of this book may be reproduced in any manner without prior written permission from the publisher. Write: Permissions, Wipf and Stock Publishers, 199 W. 8th Ave., Suite 3, Eugene, OR 97401.

Cascade Books
An Imprint of Wipf and Stock Publishers
199 W. 8th Ave., Suite 3
Eugene, OR 97401

www.wipfandstock.com

PAPERBACK ISBN: 978-1-6667-3265-8
HARDCOVER ISBN: 978-1-6667-2659-6
EBOOK ISBN: 978-1-6667-2660-2

Cataloguing-in-Publication data:

Names: Gitau, Wanjiru M., editor. | Lamport, Mark A., editor.

Title: Globalizing linkages : the intermingling story of Christianity in Africa / edited by Wanjiru M. Gitau and Mark A. Lamport.

Description: Eugene, OR: Cascade Books, 2024. | The Global Story of Christianity Series 3. | Includes bibliographical references and index.

Identifiers: ISBN 978-1-6667-3265-8 (paperback). | ISBN 978-1-6667-2659-6 (hardcover). | ISBN 978-1-6667-2660-2 (ebook).

Subjects: LCSH: Christianity—Africa—History. | Africa—Church history.

Classification: BR1360 G60 2024 (print). | BR1360 (epub).

VERSION NUMBER 04/12/24

Scripture quotations are from the Authorized (King James) Version. Rights in the Authorized Version in the United Kingdom are vested in the Crown. Reproduced by permission of the Crown's patentee, Cambridge University Press.

For *Wanjiru—Ogbu U. Kalu*, author of *African Christianity: An African Story*

For *Mark—Athanasius* (Alexandrian bishop/apologist, 296-373), *Samuel Ajayi Crowther* (Nigerian linguist/bishop, 1808-91), *Bengt Sundkler* (Swedish-Tanzanian historian/professor, 1908-95), *Vincent Donovan* (American missionary to East African Maasai, 1926-2000), *Leslie Newbigin* (British missiologist/theologian, 1909-98), and *Lamin Sanneh* (Gambian scholar of missions and world Christianity, 1942-2019)

Contents

List of Figures and Tables | xi
Series Introduction—Dana L. Robert | xiii
List of Editors and Introducers | xxiii
Preface—Gina Zurlo and Mark A. Lamport | xxv
Acknowledgments | xxxiii
List of Contributors | xxxv
List of Abbreviations | xxxix

Book Introduction—Mark Shaw | 1

Section One
The Story of Christianity Narrated in Historical Context

1. Antiquity: African Christian Connections within the Mediterranean Region—Kyama Mugambi and Rudolf K. Gaisie | 13

2. The Beginnings of Christianity in Sub-Saharan Africa: Kingdom of Aksum and the Christian World of Late Antiquity —Stanislau Paulau | 28

3. European Pioneers to Tropical Africa—Fohle Lygunda li-M | 43

4. Christianity and Slavery in Africa—Akintunde E. Akinade | 58

5. The African–Black American Missionary during the Missionary Era —Uchenna D. Anyanwu | 73

Section Two

The Story of Christianity Expressed in a Grand Church Family Mosaic

6. Connections and Collaborations among the Nubian, Coptic, and Ethiopian Churches—Joshua Robert Barron | 93

7. The Catholic Church and the Network of Evangelization —Stan Chu Ilo | 108

8. Protestants Working Together—Modisa Mzondi | 125

9. Salvation in African Pentecostalism—Joseph Bosco Bangura | 142

Section Three

The Story of Christianity Encounters Twenty-First-Century Issues

10. New Kinships and Identities in Christ in Africa—Harvey Kwiyani | 161

11. Christianity and Nation-State Formations —Tharcisse Gatwa | 175

12. Christianity, Wars, and Ethnic Challenges —Georges Pirwoth Atido | 193

13. Christianity and International Connections: Ecumenism, Development, and Advocacy Organizations—Kudzai Biri | 209

14. Christianity Encounters the Gospel of Health and Wealth: A Ghanian Case Study—Sampson M. Tieku | 226

15. Transtemporal Connections: African Christian History as Intellectual History—Wanjiru M. Gitau | 241

Timeline: Africa—Brett Knowles | 256

Index of Subjects and Names | 293

Figures and Tables

Figure 1. North/South Distribution of Christianity, 33–2050 CE | xxvi
Figure 2. Christianity in Africa | xxx
Figure 3. Four Different Mission Mechanisms | 75
Figure 4. Early and Medieval Christian Sites in Northeast Africa | 95
Figure 5. Medieval Nubia | 95

Table 1. Religions over 1 Percent in Africa, 1900–2050 | xxvii
Table 2. Christianity in Africa by Region, 1900–2050 | xxviii
Table 3. Christianity in Africa by Country, 1900–2050 | xxix

Series Introduction

The Global Story of Christianity

History, Contexts, and Communities

DANA L. ROBERT

WHAT DOES IT MEAN *to tell the story* of global Christianity? Storytelling is important for personal identity, for community life, and for shared humanity. When people tell their own stories, both individually and as communities of faith, they share who they are and who they hope to become. When people make friends, they swap stories. They introduce themselves. They discuss their work, or where they went to school. They might talk about the sports teams they support, or what activities they enjoy. As people get to know each other better, they exchange stories about their families, or politics, or other important issues. Friends do things together—and the being together creates memories that launch new stories they recall when they see each other again. In listening to each other, people's stories merge and create a common basis for relationships—even across boundaries or divisions.

Global Christianity is the story of a huge extended family. Christians are rooted in a common ancestor, Jesus Christ. For two thousand years, the followers of Jesus of Nazareth have traced their spiritual lineage through him to the God of ancient Israel, as spoken through the prophets and written in the Bible and celebrated in worship and outreach. Christianity is now the world's largest religion, encompassing one-third of the world's peoples. During the twentieth century, the family of faith burst out of European frameworks and began growing rapidly in Africa, Asia, and Latin America. By 2018, Africa had become the continent with the largest number of Christians, followed by Latin America, and Europe, with Asia soon to become second in numbers.[1] Christianity as a global story reminds me of the chatter at a giant family reunion, where the relatives get together and reminisce about their distant family history, and the departed saints that

---

1. Zurlo, "Who Owns Global Christianity?"

they remember—and the old family arguments that never seem to end. For better or worse, whether or not they know each other personally, the people who call themselves Christians are spiritual brothers, sisters, and long-lost cousins. Shared family history connects them.

And yet, nobody has only *one* story. This book series on the global story of Christianity embodies many stories that have unfolded across two thousand years of time, and which inhabit wide-ranging geographic and cultural spaces. The sheer size and complexity of the global Christian family means that a shared history is composed of multiple memories, from thousands of contexts. Being part of a community means organizing the stories into a convincing whole and claiming a common identity through them. Communities can be direct sets of relationships, such as families, neighborhoods, sports clubs, therapy groups, and local churches. They can also be "imagined" and thus composed of people who may never meet in person, but whose groups—including ethnicities, cities, political parties, and even nations—share common interpretations of experiences. For Christians, both personal and imagined faith communities use shared narratives to organize their spiritual realities. And yet, the meaning and identity of faith communities also changes over time, depending on the context. Depending on one's purpose or needs, different parts of one's story become more important than others. I am reminded of a friend who was the new pastor of a small church. Each week, no matter how hard he tried to get the old-timers to move, nobody would sit in the front section of the church. Finally, in frustration he asked one old man why he wouldn't move toward the front of the church. "I've been sitting in this pew for forty years," he replied. "It is not my fault that the people who used to sit in front of me have died or moved away." In his mind, the old man was still sitting in his imagined community made up of previous generations of friends and neighbors who had composed his church. But the new minister, looking out every week, saw nothing but empty front pews, waiting to be filled with new faces and new stories. Because the context had changed, the church community had changed; and because the community had changed, the context had changed—even though the old man had not moved anywhere at all. And yet, until the old man shared his story, the history of his community, the new minister couldn't understand the old man's resistance to his request.

History, contexts, and communities—all these pieces are important frameworks for organizing the many stories that together paint a global picture of Christianity. The connection among history, contexts, and communities was beautifully expressed by the late Andrew Walls, Scottish historian and expert on African Christianity, and a founder of the field of "world

Christianity."[2] Walls asked his readers to imagine a visitor from outer space, a professor of comparative religions, who visits Earth for fieldwork every few centuries, to observe the practices and beliefs of representative Christians. First the space man visits the original Christians in Jerusalem, a few years after the death of Jesus. He finds that they are Jewish and follow Jewish customs, including offering animal sacrifices, worshiping on the seventh day, and reading old scrolls in Hebrew. They identify the Messiah, Son of Man and Suffering Servant, with their teacher who just died, Jesus of Nazareth. They live in close-knit families and eat meals together in each other's homes. When the visitor from space next returns to earth, he observes a big church meeting of church leaders around 325 CE, in Nicaea (now in Turkey). Hardly any are Jewish and most are unmarried. To them, sacrifice means a ritual meal of bread and wine and they worship God on the first day of the week, not the seventh. They talk about Jesus, but they are debating whether the Greek words *homoousios* or *homoiousios* better characterize his nature. They argue a lot about theology.

Walls goes on to describe the space visitor's next field visit, Ireland in the 600s. There monks are gathered on a rocky coastline reciting the psalms. Some are going into a small boat with a box of beautiful manuscripts heading toward nearby islands to ask the inhabitants to give up worship of multiple nature divinities. Other monks sit alone in caves, denying themselves food. Upon examining the manuscripts, he finds they are the same writings he saw on his last visit, and he hears the monks recite the same basic statement of belief or creed he heard at Nicaea in 325. Yet these monks seem much more interested in being holy than in debating theology.

Next the space visitor returns to earth in 1840s London. He finds a convention of mostly white Christians hearing speeches about the desirability of promoting Christianity and trade in Africa. To eliminate the slave trade, they are planning to send missionaries, lobby the government, and promote the education of black Africans. He sees many people carrying printed Bibles and finds out they accept the creed of Nicaea. They talk about holiness but would be shocked at the thought of praying alone in a cave. Rather, they are well fed and committed to political activism.

Finally, the space visitor returns in the 1980s to Lagos, Nigeria, in time to see a white-robed procession of people dancing and chanting through the streets. They are inviting people to come with them and experience the power of God. They talk about healing and driving out evil

2. Walls preferred the term "world Christianity" to what this book series is calling "global Christianity." On the use of the terms "world" versus "global," see Robert, "World Christianity"; Sanneh and McClymond, "Introduction," 4–6; Johnson and Kim, "Describing the Worldwide Christian Phenomenon."

spirits. They say they accept the creed of Nicaea, but they are not really interested in theological creeds or in political activism. They do care passionately about personal empowerment through prayer, preaching, and healing. Back on his own planet, the professor must figure out what it all means. He notes that the location of the Christian heartland has shifted each time he has visited. How does he conclude what it means to be a Christian? Is there any coherence across time? What do Christians around the world have in common, despite the visible differences in culture, race, locations, ethnicities, and practices that he observed?

Andrew Walls's fantasy about the space visitor illustrates the complexities of telling the global story of Christianity. What each era had in common was its historical connection. Like links in a chain, history connected the different communities to each other. Jews from Jerusalem preached to Greeks and led to the events of Nicaea in 325. Emissaries from the Mediterranean planted the seeds that became Irish Christianity. Celtic missionaries launched what became the religion of London in the 1840s, and the British evangelical lobby sent the messengers who energized churches in Africa. To bring the story up to the present, today Nigerian churches send missionaries around the world, including to London. In fact, some of the largest churches in Europe have African pastors. Other historical connections involve a "continuity of consciousness" across time.[3] In each group's story, Jesus Christ "has ultimate significance." They use the "same sacred writings," though in different formats and languages. Writes Walls, "Each group thinks of itself as having some community with the others," continuous with ancient Israel, even though they are no longer Jews.[4] These elements of continuity, however, are embedded in very different contexts, ranging from the Middle East to West Asia, to Europe, Africa, and beyond. In each context, the space visitor found worshipping communities, ranging in form from house churches to bishops' gatherings, from monasteries to conferences and popular processions. The shape of the Christian communities and what they do differs according to their local cultures, politics, and historical period. And yet, taken together, the many stories echo the shared memory of Jesus Christ, passed down through the ages.

About This Book Series

To tell the global story of Christianity, each book in this series is organized into a common format. If we think about what goes into telling our stories,

3. Walls, "Gospel as Prisoner," 6.
4. Walls, "Gospel as Prisoner," 6–7.

the elements are common to the books in the series. The *first* thing to notice is that the books each cover a different *geographic region*. In other words, they are organized by "neighborhood." This organization allows the editors, who come from each region, to explore the "historical context" and to answer the questions: Where are we from and how did we get here? Who are the people who brought Christianity? How did the Christian story change in each part of the globe, and what difference did it make? How are the followers of Jesus in that region anchored in his heritage? What is the testimony of the people of each region about their Christian identity, and how did they become part of the global story of Christianity? There are a range of answers to questions like "Where are we from and how did we get here?," including stories of migration and mission, slavery and coercion, violence and resistance, joy and struggle. Analyzing where they have come from also allows the editors to build toward where they think their region might be going.

The *second* section of each book in the series talks about the kind of *faith communities* found in each geographic region, and the issues they face. Communities reflect group identities shaped by such factors as theology, ethnicity, language, or persecution. In the case of the volume on Asia, a vast continent with thousands of different ethnic groups, the communities described are organized by subregion. The North America volume discusses some of the fundamental theological and organizational issues behind different groups of North American Christians. In Christian parlance, faith communities shaped by shared theologies and histories are often called "denominations," organized groups of Christians that recognize each other as brothers and sisters but have different stories to tell about how they got to be where they are today. Some faith communities are rather like private clubs, with high membership fees and strict rules as to who can belong. Others are more like groups of sports fans, open to anyone who feels like supporting the team and participating in its activities. In all cases, the discussion of different communities shows how their identity reflects both its local context and its participation in the global story of Christianity. Communities each have their own special saints, prophets, and leaders—people who have guided them and symbolize their identity to the world. They have their own favorite religious practices. Conversations internal to each community spill into the outside world, and sometimes attract others to join them. Contexts shape communities, and communities shape contexts. Faith communities are where the global story of Christianity forms church families and creates spaces in which they build a home.

The *third* section of each volume discusses *global issues* that are important to each region today. This is where the urgency behind each volume becomes clear. What are the passions that drive the communities in context?

What problems do they face? What political and social issues are vital to their well-being? Some of the volumes explicitly discuss what churches call "ecumenism," churches cooperating and joining together to pursue shared ideals and common goals. Important twenty-first-century issues such as climate change, racism, interfaith relations, war and peace, gender, church-state relations, and religious persecution are global issues that affect people on every continent. It is often these pressing issues that connect Christians in solidarity with others across geographic boundaries.

Elements of a Global Story

Although each book in the series stands alone, putting them into dialogue with each other paints a bigger picture of what is called "global (or world) Christianity." As already mentioned, Christianity in the twenty-first century has become a multicultural religion practiced by one third of the world. The fact that it exists nearly everywhere means that to tell the story of Christianity in one region affects the story of Christianity in another region. To think of Christianity as a global story requires seeing each region as connected. In scholarly terms, this idea is called "entanglement," an important concept in global history. The idea of historical entanglement means that each region is shaped by its relationship to the others. To think of Christianity as a global story means looking for ways in which the local and the global are entangled—all mixed up together, influencing each other, and not easily separated. As people in each region embrace what they see as the universal story of Jesus Christ, the way they practice their faith affects the nature of the religion as a whole. To be "global" means that regional stories are linked, with and through their Christian faiths.

Looking for interconnections among the regions is a way to trace how the assumption of entanglement creates a global story out of what are usually thought of as separate stories. As you read the different books in this series, also zoom out and look for common themes that bind the regions together to create a global story, though from different perspectives and angles. What follows are three major themes that intersect all the volumes—movement, translation, and public theologies:

- *Movement* is central to the global story of Christianity. Without new people entering old spaces, or people on the move, Christianity could not spread from one place to another. The New Testament journeys of Paul throughout the Mediterranean modeled how Christians moved from place to place in spreading their faith. Migration and "global diaspora" are features of the global Christian story, especially today when more people are on the move than ever before. When people deliberately cross boundaries to spread their faith, they are often called missionaries. During the era of colonialism, Europeans sent missionaries around the world. Today missionaries go from everywhere to everywhere, including especially from Korea, Brazil, Nigeria, and North America.[5] Sometimes movement to new areas causes migrants to embrace Christianity as a new way of life. Although migrants typically seek economic security over religious change, sometimes the act of moving to a new place can inspire them to launch missions of their own: Central Americans moving to North American cities, and Africans moving to Eastern Europe, have started numerous churches. Forced migration can also spread Christianity. In a monstrous crime against humanity, over ten million Africans were sent to the Americas as slaves. Many of their descendants became Christians and reshaped the faith into a vehicle of resistance. Migrating people—whether forced or by choice—bind together their places of origin with their destinations and change both places in the process.[6]

- *Translation* is another theme that makes Christianity a global story. In literal terms, translation of the Bible into thousands of languages has been the foundation of Protestant missions for centuries, and the basis for faith-sharing across linguistic and cultural boundaries. Once people have the Bible in their own language, they interpret it according to their own cultural norms and needs.[7] During the twentieth century, many indigenous prophets—equipped with the Bible in their own language and inspired by dreams and visions—launched new Christian movements in Africa, Asia, and Latin America. Studies of conversion show how new Christians translate the Christian faith into their own personal contexts, or use it to revitalize their surroundings.[8] At a more theoretical level, translation can refer to cultural processes of hybridization, of adopting the Christian message and reframing it to fit new contexts and to energize Christian communities.[9] Since all communication comes packaged in particular cultural forms, the process of translation is necessary for sharing the Christian faith across all kinds of ethnic, cultural, and geographic barriers. As Christians encounter

---

5. Robert, *Christian Mission*.

6. See Frederiks and Nagy, *Religion, Migration, and Identity*; see also Hanciles, *Migration and the Making*, and Hanciles, *Beyond Christendom*.

7. Sanneh, *Translating the Message*.

8. Kling, *History of Christian Conversion*.

9. For a postcolonial analysis and typology of historical religious encounters, including syncretism and selection, see Lindenfeld, *World Christianity and Indigenous Experience*, 1–30. See also Jones, *Christian Interculture*, and Gruber, *Intercultural Theology*.

- *Public theologies* also shape the global story of Christianity. In the modern West, people often think of faith as a private matter, separate from politics or social life. But the idea that religion is a matter of personal choice, irrelevant to community life, is a fairly recent cultural innovation that itself assumes a public theology of secularism.[10] In most of the world, in most periods of history, religion carries practical implications for how people live in community. Christianity shapes people's attitudes toward authority, power, nature, gender relations, and human rights. Such ideas as "the doctrine of discovery," or the "priesthood of all believers," or "one nation under God" express the relationship of Christianity to peoples, politics, and land. The global story of Christianity consists of theological flows that spread around the world through migration and social media.[11] Public theologies require analyzing flows of power, including the supernatural and spiritual power embedded in Christian belief itself, the unequal political and economic power of Christians who use faith to justify control of others, and the tenacious power of resilience by Christians who are suffering or persecuted. By the late 1900s, evangelicalism, liberation theologies, and Pentecostal practices were all vehicles for political power, especially in Africa and the Americas. Christian charitable outreach through nongovernmental organizations remains a major social factor throughout the world, especially in poor communities. Half of all Christians are Roman Catholics, a worldwide faith network with a central teaching authority lodged in the pope and the Vatican. Public theologies—the globalization of religious ideas, institutions, power, and practices—are a key feature of Christianity as a world religion.

Conclusion: From Local Stories to Global Story and Back Again

To tell the global story of Christianity requires reconstructing the entangled histories of communities down through the ages, in different regions. It requires retracing their historical contexts and learning how communities

10. Casanova, *Public Religions in the Modern World*.
11. Schreiter, *New Catholicity*.

respond to the urgent issues of the day. As this series shows, only as different Christian communities tell their own stories—and listen to the stories of others—can the global story of Christianity be glimpsed in all its fullness.

For Further Reading

Casanova, José. *Public Religions in the Modern World*. Chicago: University of Chicago Press, 2011.
Frederiks, Martha, and Dorottya Nagy, eds. *Religion, Migration, and Identity: Methodological and Theological Explorations*. Theology and Mission in World Christianity 2. Leiden: Brill, 2016.
Gruber, Judith. *Intercultural Theology: Exploring World Christianity after the Cultural Turn*. Göttingen: Vandenhoeck & Ruprecht, 2018.
Hanciles, Jehu J. *Beyond Christendom: Globalization, African Migration, and the Transformation of the West*. Maryknoll, NY: Orbis, 2008.
———. *Migration and the Making of Global Christianity*. Grand Rapids: Eerdmans, 2021.
Johnson, Todd M., and Sandra S. Kim. "Describing the Worldwide Christian Phenomenon." *International Bulletin of Missionary Research* 29 (2005) 80–84.
Johnson, Todd M., and Gina A. Zurlo. *World Christian Encyclopedia*. 3rd ed. Edinburgh: Edinburgh University Press, 2019.
Jones, Arun, ed. *Christian Interculture: Texts and Voices from Colonial and Postcolonial Worlds*. University Park: Pennsylvania State University Press, 2021.
Kling, David. *A History of Christian Conversion*. New York: Oxford University Press, 2020.
Lindenfeld, David. *World Christianity and Indigenous Experience: A Global History, 1500–2000*. Cambridge: Cambridge University Press, 2021.
Robert, Dana L. *Christian Mission: How Christianity Became a World Religion*. Hoboken, NJ: Wiley-Blackwell, 2009.
———. "World Christianity as a Revitalization Movement." In *World Christianity: History, Methodologies, Horizons*, edited by Jehu Hanciles, 17–18. Maryknoll, NY: Orbis, 2021.
Sanneh, Lamin, and Michael J. McClymond. "Introduction." In *The Wiley Blackwell Companion to World Christianity*, edited by Lamin Sanneh and Michael McClymond, 1–18. Malden, MA: Wiley-Blackwell, 2016.
Sanneh, Lamin O. *Translating the Message: The Missionary Impact on Culture*. American Society of Missiology Series 42. Maryknoll, NY: Orbis, 2009.
Schreiter, Robert J. *The New Catholicity: Theology between the Global and the Local*. Faith and Cultures Series. Maryknoll, NY: Orbis, 2004.
Walls, Andrew. "The Gospel as Prisoner and Liberator of Culture." In *The Missionary Movement in Christian History Studies in the Transmission of Faith*, 3–15. Maryknoll, NY: Orbis, 1996.
Zurlo, Gina A. "Who Owns Global Christianity?" https://www.gordonconwell.edu/blog/who-owns-global-christianity/.

Editors and Introducers

Wanjiru M. Gitua (PhD, Africa International University) is Assistant Professor of Practical Theology and World Christianity at Palm Beach Atlantic University and is author of *Megachurch Christianity Reconsidered: Millennials and Social Change in African Perspective* (2018); *The Kingdom of God in Africa: A History of African Christianity* (with Mark Shaw, 2020); and *Becoming Cosmopolitan: Unfolding Two Centuries of Mission at VTS* (with Bill Sachs, 2023).

Mark A. Lamport (PhD, Michigan State University) has been a professor for nearly forty years at theological schools in the United States and Europe. He is coauthor of *Nurturing Faith: A Practical Theology for Educating Christians* (2021); coeditor of the seven-book series *The Global Story of Christianity*; coeditor of *Emerging Theologies from the Global South* (2023); *Christianity in the Middle East* (2 vols., 2020); *Encyclopedia of Christianity in the Global South* (2 vols., 2018); *Encyclopedia of Martin Luther and the Reformation* (2 vols., 2017); *Encyclopedia of Christianity in the United States* (5 vols., 2016); and *Encyclopedia of Christian Education* (3 vols., 2015).

Series Introduction

Dana L. Robert (PhD, Yale University) is William Fairfield Warren Distinguished of Professor of World Christianity and History of Mission, and Director of the Center for Global Christianity and Mission at Boston University School of Theology. She is a member of the American Academy of Arts and Sciences, and in 2017 received the Lifetime Achievement Award from the American Society of Missiology. Recent books include *Faithful Friendships: Embracing Diversity in Christian Community* (2019) and *African Christian Biography: Stories, Lives, and Challenges* (2018).

Book Introduction

Mark Shaw (ThD, Westminster Theological Seminary) studied world Christianity at the University of Edinburgh and is Professor of Historical Studies and Director of the Centre for World Christianity at Africa International University in Nairobi, Kenya. He is the author of several books, including *Global Awakening: How Twentieth Century Revivals created a Religious Revolution* and *The Kingdom of God in Africa: A History of African Christianity* (with Wanjiru Gitau).

Preface

AFRICA HAS AN EXTREMELY important role in our understanding of trends in global Christianity. Already by the year 1980, most of the world's Christians lived in Africa, Asia, Latin America, and Oceania, and today that figure is 67 percent (fig. 1). The entire field of world Christianity partly owes its origin to scholar-missionaries studying new forms of Christianity in Africa, such as Harold Turner, Bengt Sundkler, Marthinus Daneel, and David Barrett. They identified new forms of Christianity completely driven by African realities, where African Christians—both women and men—asked African questions and provided African answers. Other scholars observed these trends and subsequently searched for them elsewhere worldwide, giving rise to many of the core aspects of world Christianity studies today: contextual theology, intercultural hermeneutics, ethnodoxology, gender studies, and migration studies. As a result, Africa is, in many ways, the new "center" of world Christianity both demographically but also perhaps epistemologically.

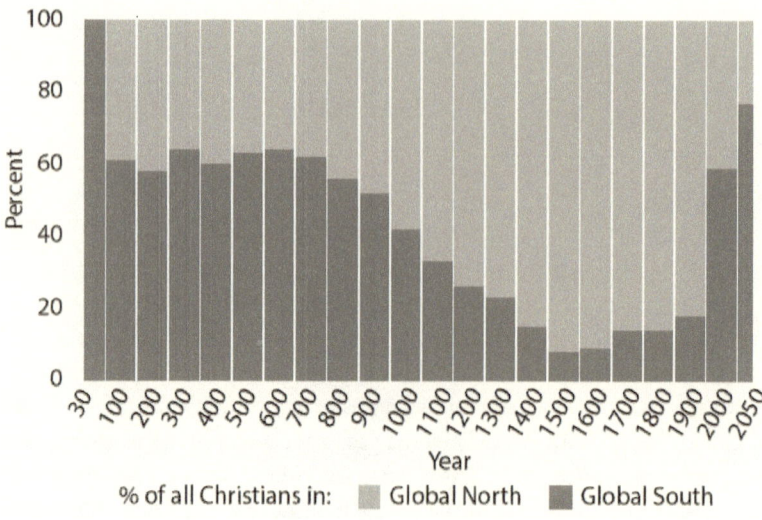

Figure 1. North/South Distribution of Christianity, 33–2050 CE

Source: Todd M. Johnson and Gina A. Zurlo, *World Christian Encyclopedia*, 3rd ed. (Edinburgh: Edinburgh University Press, 2019), 4. Used by permission of the authors.

Table 1 shows the diversity of religion in Africa from 1900 with projections to 2050. Africa has always been an extremely religious continent: still 99 percent religious in 2020. Yet, it experienced a profound religious transformation in the twentieth century. From just 9 percent Christian in 1900, it grew astonishingly to 49 percent Christian by 2020, mostly at the loss of traditional religions, which declined from 58 percent to 8 percent over the same period. Islam also made tremendous gains, increasing from 33 percent in 1900 to 42 percent in 2020. Looking forward to 2050, it is likely that together Christians and Muslims will encompass 93 percent of the continent's population. Building positive relations between these two major world religions remains critical for the continent. Yet, at the same time, some of the world's most egregious religious violence occurs across the African Sahel, where Muslims in the north meet Christians in the south.

Year	1900	%	2000	%	1900-2000 %p.a.	2020	%	2000-2020 %p.a.	2050	%
Religious	107,800,000	100.0	813,413,000	99.3	2.04	1,351,671,000	99.3	2.57	2,467,842,000	99.3
Christians	9,640,000	8.9	384,290,000	46.9	3.75	664,051,000	48.8	2.77	1,286,487,000	51.8
Protestants	2,204,000	2.0	150,581,000	18.4	4.31	258,107,000	19.0	2.73	473,823,000	19.1
Catholics	1,890,000	1.8	129,929,000	15.9	4.32	234,985,000	17.3	3.01	488,750,000	19.7
Independents	40,000	0.0	81,490,000	10.0	7.92	128,395,000	9.4	2.30	230,012,000	9.3
Orthodox	4,324,000	4.0	35,531,000	4.3	2.13	56,564,000	4.2	2.35	102,633,000	4.1
doubly-affiliated	0	0.0	-32,628,000	-4.0	16.18	-41,365,000	-3.0	1.19	-41,587,000	-1.7
unaffiliated Christians	1,182,000	1.1	19,387,000	2.4	2.84	27,365,000	2.0	1.74	32,856,000	1.3
Muslims	34,999,000	32.5	345,655,000	42.2	2.32	566,564,000	41.6	2.50	1,019,929,000	41.0
Ethnic religionists	62,472,000	57.9	78,536,000	9.6	0.23	113,612,000	8.3	1.86	146,930,000	5.9
Total population	**107,808,000**	**100.0**	**818,952,000**	**100.0**	**2.05**	**1,360,677,000**	**100.0**	**2.57**	**2,485,136,000**	**100.0**

Table 1. Religions over 1 Percent in Africa, 1900–2050

Data source: Todd M. Johnson and Brian J. Grim, eds., *World Religion Database* (Leiden/Boston: Brill, accessed Oct. 2022). Used by permission of the authors.

African Christianity has always been tremendously diverse, with a large presence and long histories of all major Christian traditions: Orthodox, Catholic, Protestants, and independents. Protestants are the largest with 19 percent of Africa's population, and an estimated 44 percent of all Protestants in the world live in Africa. Catholics are next, with 17 percent of the population, and are steadily growing. African Christianity is marked by a tremendous movement of African independent (or initiated, or indigenous) churches, which formed either as breakaway movements from Western-founded denominations or emerged separately from Western Christianity altogether. The largest of these denominations is the Church of Jesus Christ on Earth by His Special Envoy Simon Kimbangu (Democratic Republic of the Congo, 12 million members), Zion Christian Church (South Africa, 5.5 million members), and the Celestial Church of Christ (Nigeria, 4 million members). Independents were 9 percent of Africa's population in 2020. The smallest major tradition, but also the oldest, are the Orthodox (4 percent), found primarily, in order of size, in Ethiopia, Egypt, Eritrea, and Kenya.

A major feature of African Christianity is its Pentecostal/charismatic theology, worship, beliefs, and practices. Africa has always been important in the history of Pentecostalism, dating to movements and revivals in the early twentieth century. In 2020, 36 percent of all Pentecostal/charismatics worldwide lived in Africa, and it is anticipated this will increase to 44 percent by 2050.

Region	Pop. 1900	% Christian 1900	Pop. 2020	% Christian 2020	Pop. 2050	% Christian 2050
Eastern Africa	4,640,000	15.7	294,009,000	65.4	573,808,000	67.8
Middle Africa	193,000	1.1	153,512,000	83.2	347,635,000	85.5
Northern Africa	2,278,000	8.5	11,905,000	4.7	15,039,000	4.0
Southern Africa	2,056,000	37.1	55,268,000	82.2	69,053,000	80.7
Western Africa	472,000	1.7	149,357,000	36.6	280,952,000	36.3
Africa	**9,640,000**	**8.9**	**664,051,000**	**48.8**	**1,286,487,000**	**51.8**

Table 2. Christianity in Africa by Region, 1900–2050

Data source: Todd M. Johnson and Gina A. Zurlo, eds. *World Christian Database* (Leiden/Boston: Brill, accessed Oct. 2022). Used by permission of the authors.

Africa's diversity is not just religious and ecclesial, it is also most certainly ethnic and linguistic. With roughly 4,040 different people groups and 2,090 languages on the continent, African Christians showcase the translatability of the Christian message and the ability for the gospel to adapt to any culture, anywhere. Regionally, Christianity is found in the highest proportions in Middle Africa (83 percent Christian), followed by Southern (82 percent), Eastern (65 percent), and Western (37 percent) (table 2). North Africa remains majority Muslim and just under 5 percent Christian in 2020, although the region was nearly 9 percent Christian in 1900. Sub-Saharan Africa has changed its religious makeup dramatically; Middle Africa, for example, grew from just 1 percent Christian in 1900 to 83 percent by 2020.

Country	Pop. 1900	% Christian 1900	Pop. 2020	% Christian 2020	Pop. 2050	% Christian 2050
Algeria	563,000	12.2	128,000	0.3	375,000	0.6
Angola	17,000	0.6	31,084,000	93.0	68,281,000	94.4
Benin	7,300	1.2	5,503,000	43.5	12,729,000	50.4
Botswana	17,100	14.3	1,787,000	70.2	2,914,000	79.2
Burkina Faso	0	0.0	5,021,000	23.3	13,542,000	33.4
Burundi	100	0.0	11,410,000	93.4	23,109,000	95.5
Cabo Verde	69,300	99.0	553,000	94.9	683,000	93.9
Cameroon	9,500	0.4	15,811,000	59.7	32,647,000	63.7
Central African Republic	50	0.0	3,910,000	73.2	9,675,000	83.9
Chad	0	0.0	5,865,000	35.2	13,188,000	36.2
Comoros	100	0.1	4,400	0.5	8,400	0.7
Congo	13,500	2.5	5,093,000	89.3	9,381,000	90.4
Congo DR	125,000	1.4	88,187,000	95.0	208,488,000	95.9
Côte d'Ivoire	700	0.1	9,613,000	35.9	18,995,000	37.0
Djibouti	100	0.5	12,000	1.1	14,100	0.9
Egypt	1,552,000	14.8	9,685,000	9.0	12,391,000	7.7
Equatorial Guinea	6,500	5.4	1,409,000	88.3	2,463,000	88.3
Eritrea	194,000	44.1	1,660,000	46.7	2,735,000	45.9
Eswatini	800	1.0	1,032,000	87.4	1,506,000	91.0
Ethiopia	2,871,000	38.0	69,218,000	59.1	134,691,000	62.7
Gabon	20,900	7.5	1,942,000	84.7	3,162,000	84.2
Gambia	3,700	4.2	112,000	4.4	283,000	6.1
Ghana	103,000	4.7	22,885,000	71.1	38,668,000	74.0
Guinea	1,800	0.2	465,000	3.5	771,000	3.3
Guinea-Bissau	4,800	4.0	261,000	13.0	540,000	15.7
Kenya	5,000	0.2	42,108,000	81.0	71,702,000	84.1
Lesotho	33,800	11.1	2,077,000	92.1	2,726,000	94.1
Liberia	32,800	10.6	2,097,000	41.2	4,296,000	48.3
Libya	10,000	1.3	35,600	0.5	34,900	0.4
Madagascar	1,010,000	39.2	16,397,000	58.1	31,409,000	60.9
Malawi	13,500	1.8	15,365,000	79.3	29,467,000	79.3
Mali	690	0.1	475,000	2.2	1,191,000	2.5
Mauritania	50	0.0	10,500	0.2	14,700	0.2
Mauritius	127,000	33.5	429,000	33.1	381,000	31.1
Mayotte	30	0.3	1,400	0.5	1,500	0.2
Morocco	30,100	0.6	31,400	0.1	40,600	0.1
Mozambique	16,700	0.6	17,402,000	55.8	40,481,000	64.2
Namibia	12,400	8.7	2,267,000	91.1	3,455,000	91.4
Niger	0	0.0	63,200	0.3	124,000	0.2
Nigeria	176,000	1.1	96,446,000	46.3	178,204,000	47.2
Réunion	90,000	52.0	838,000	87.5	971,000	86.2
Rwanda	100	0.0	12,030,000	91.5	21,349,000	92.7
Saint Helena	3,000	100.0	5,200	95.8	3,600	93.9
Sao Tome & Principe	1,300	3.1	210,000	96.1	349,000	95.2
Senegal	18,400	1.8	845,000	5.1	1,675,000	5.1
Seychelles	18,700	97.1	99,900	94.7	110,000	93.9
Sierra Leone	46,800	4.6	964,000	11.7	1,447,000	10.6
Somalia	600	0.1	4,300	0.0	3,100	0.0
South Africa	1,992,000	40.7	48,106,000	81.8	58,453,000	79.5
South Sudan	100	0.0	6,398,000	60.3	11,294,000	64.7
Sudan	2400	0.1	2001000	4.5	2178000	2.6
Tanzania	92,000	2.4	34,146,000	55.3	76,363,000	58.8
Togo	4,000	0.9	4,039,000	47.8	7,787,000	50.3
Tunisia	120,000	7.5	23,800	0.2	18,100	0.1
Uganda	180,000	6.8	37,495,000	84.4	73,866,000	84.3
Western Sahara	100	0.7	860	0.2	1,500	0.2
Zambia	2,000	0.3	16,182,000	85.5	32,562,000	86.9
Zimbabwe	19,000	3.8	12,809,000	81.7	23,292,000	88.1
Africa	**9,640,000**	**8.9**	**664,051,000**	**48.8**	**1,286,487,000**	**51.8**

Table 3. Christianity in Africa by Country, 1900–2050

Data source: Todd M. Johnson and Gina A. Zurlo, eds., *World Christian Database* (Leiden/Boston: Brill, accessed Oct. 2022). Used by permission of the authors.

The countries with the most Christians in Africa are Nigeria (95 million), the Democratic Republic of the Congo (85 million), and Ethiopia (67 million) (table 3). The diversity of African Christianity is on full display in just those three countries: Nigeria's largest denomination is the Catholic Church (with the Anglicans a close second); the DRC's is also the Catholics, followed by Kimbanguists; and Ethiopia's is the Ethiopian Orthodox Church, followed by the Word of Life Evangelical Church (which is Baptist).

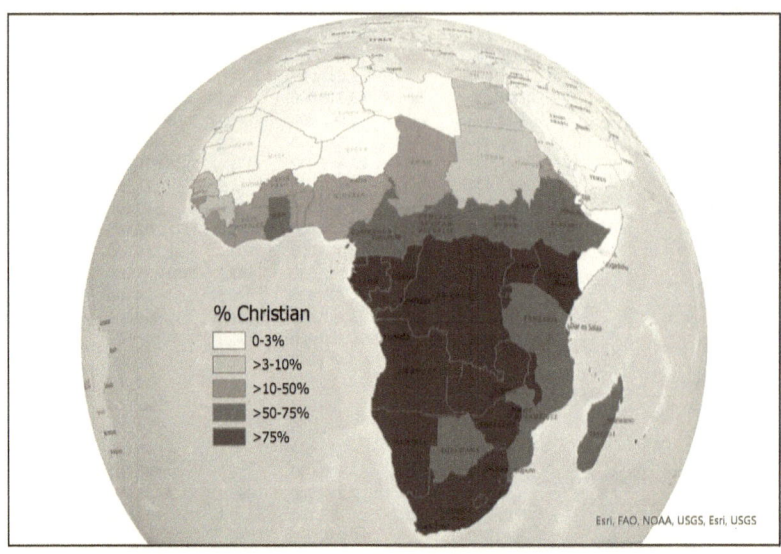

Figure 2. Christianity in Africa

Data source: Todd M. Johnson and Gina A. Zurlo, eds. *World Christian Database* (Leiden/Boston: Brill, accessed Oct. 2022). Used by permission of the authors.

Given current trends, it is all but assured that the future of World Christianity is African, but more specifically, female and African. Women have made tremendous contributions to the growth of Christianity in Africa, as indigenous evangelists, founders of independent movements, and spiritual leaders of their communities. Women make up the vast majority of most congregations, perhaps upward of 75 percent. They are remarkably resilient against cultural, societal, and theological obstacles that try to relegate them to second-class status. Instead, African women are making important contributions to indigenous theology and are advocates for gender rights, girls education, HIV/AIDS prevention and care, peaceable societies, and a host of other issues.

Gina A. Zurlo and Mark A. Lamport

Acknowledgments

THE GERM OF AN idea pollinated into a book-length treatment of the history, plight, and experiences of the multifaceted expressions of Christianity celebrated in the global church. We have been more than a little assisted by the comments, guidance, and perspective of sensational scholars Philip Jenkins, Erica Hunter, Wafik Wahba, Harold Suerman, Akram Khater, Jonathan Swift, Deanna Ferree Womack, and Michael Ghiz. Special appreciation goes to Brian Stanley and Emma Wild-Wood, both at the Divinity School, Centre for the Study of World Christianity, University of Edinburgh. Thanks one and all for your friendship and collegiality in the spirit of collaboration.

Conceptualizing on the angle for the book titles and their intended appealing splash came from the fertile minds of Rachel Baker, Jean Van Horn, Gary Camlin, Bill Engvall, Alayna Baker, Aaron Lamport, Jay Ellis, Amy Grubbs, Zachary Grubbs, and Michelle Lamport.

The following were instrumental in shepherding the contents of the book into production-worthy copy—Joshua Erb (senior editorial consultant), Philip Bustrum, and Mel Wilhoit for tremendous skill and detail in indexing the contents.

Further, we are beholden to Michael Thomson, acquisitions and development director for Wipf & Stock Publishers. He tracked Mark down in the produce aisle of a large grocery chain in Grand Rapids and proposed the first book in the series to him! Emma Wild-Wood and Gina Zurlo filled out the team nicely. Soon thereafter Mark came back to Michael and pitched the remaining six to fill out this seven-book series: *to tell the global story of Christianity*. Michael is at once analytical and spontaneous, perceptive and intelligent, exacting and gracious. We are pleased that an additional large international edited book is also in process under Michael's guidance describing "emerging theologies from the global south" (Cascade 2023). Thank you for cheering on our vision.

Finally, we feel great respect for Christians in the Africa and wish to tell their historic, unique, and inspiring story of Christianity. There is good evidence that the most dynamic growth and creative trends will be revealed in the coming years from Africa, as missiologists consider it "the center of Christianity."

Contributors

Akintunde E. Akinade (MPhil, PhD in ecumenical theology from Union Theological Seminary, New York City) is Professor of Theology at Georgetown University in Qatar. He studied with both James H. Cone and Kosuke Koyama. Akinade serves on the editorial boards of *The Muslim World, Religions/Adyan, Trinity Journal of Church and Theology, Journal of Interreligious Dialogue,* and *The Living Pulpit.*

Uchenna D. Anyanwu (PhD, Fuller Theological Seminary) serves with Calvary Ministries (CAPRO) and volunteers as a Mission Advocate with Frontier Fellowship. He is the author of *Pathways to Peacebuilding: Staurocentric Theology in Nigeria's Context of Acute Violence.*

Georges Pirwoth Atido (PhD, Africa International University) is the Rector of the Shalom University of Bunia in the Democratic Republic of Congo. Recent publications include "Church Revitalization in Congo: Missiological Insights from One Church's Efforts at Glocalization" in the *International Bulletin of Mission Research* (2017).

Joseph Bosco Bangura (PhD, Evangelische Theologische Faculteit, Leuven, Belgium/Vrije University Amsterdam) teaches missiology and intercultural theology at the Evangelische Theologische Faculteit (Belgium) and Protestant Theological University (the Netherlands). He is the author of *Pentecostalism in Sierra Leone* (2020).

Joshua Robert Barron (PhD, Africa International University) is a missionary in Kenya with the Association for Christian Theological Education in Africa (ACTEA). He has taught at Community Christian Bible Training Institute in the Maasai and Turkana communities as well as at the Maasai Discipleship Training Institute. He cowrote a text designed to equip local congregations for biblical understanding published in Maa, kiSwahili, and Nga Turkana (2016).

Kudzai Biri (DPhil, University of Zimbabwe) is Associate Professor at Alexander von Humboldt Stiftung, Bamberg University, Germany. Her recent publications include *The Wounded Beast? Single Women, Tradition and the Bible in Zimbabwe* and *African Pentecostalism: The Bible and Cultural Resilience*.

Rudolf K. Gaisie (PhD, Akrofi-Christaller Institute of Theology, Mission and Culture [ACI], Akropong-Akuapem, Ghana) is Research Fellow and Director, Centre for the Study of Early African Christianity (CESEAC) at ACI. Recent publications include *Jesus Christ as Logos Incarnate and Resurrected Nana* and *Ancestor: An African Perspective on Conversion and Christology*.

Tharcisse Gatwa (PhD, University of Edinburgh) is Research Professor of Ethics and Missiology, Director of Research at Protestant University, Rwanda (PIASS). Recent publications include *Memory Work in Rwanda: 25 Years after the Genocide against the Tutsi*; *Home Grown Solutions: A Legacy*; and *African Christian Theologies and Reformation Impact*.

Stan Chu Ilo (PhD, University of St Michael's College/University of Toronto; PhD, University of South Africa) is Research Professor of World Christianity and African Studies at the Center for World Catholicism and Inter-Cultural Theology, DePaul University, Chicago, and Coordinator of the Pan-African Catholic Theology and Pastoral Network. He is the editor of the *Handbook of African Catholicism*.

Harvey Kwiyani (PhD, Luther Seminary, Minneapolis) is a Malawian theologian serving as CEO of Global Connections in England. He teaches mission and leadership at the Church Mission Society (CMS) in Oxford, where he leads a Master's Program in African Diaspora Christianity. He has authored several books, including *Sent Forth: African Missionary Work in the West* and *Multicultural Kingdom: Ethnic Diversity, Mission and the Church*.

Fohle Lygunda li-M (PhD, North-West University, South Africa) is Extraordinary Researcher in Missiology at North-West University, South Africa, and Director of Africa Center for Interdisciplinary Studies, Kinshasa, DRC. Recent publications include *Transforming Missiology: An Alternative Approach to Missiological Education* (2018).

Kyama Mugambi (PhD in theological studies-world Christianity from Africa International University) is Assistant Professor of World Christianity at Yale Divinity School. He is the author of *A Spirit of Revitalization: Urban Pentecostalism in Kenya* (2020).

Modisa Mzondi (DLitt and DPhil, University of Johannesburg) is Senior Lecturer and Supervisor at South African Seminary, and Master of Divinity Program Coordinator. Recent publications include "John L. M. Dube's Leadership: Evaluating Frank Chikane, Kenneth Meshoe, and Mmusi Maimane as Leaders" in *Conspectus* (2021).

Stanislau Paulau (PhD, University of Göttingen), originally from Belarus, is Professor of Global History of Christianity and Orthodox Christian Studies at the Martin Luther University Halle-Wittenberg, Germany. He is the author of the book *Das andere Christentum: Zur transkonfessionellen Verflechtungsgeschichte von äthiopischer Orthodoxie und europäischem Protestantismus* (2021).

Sampson M. Tieku (PhD candidate, Asbury Theological Seminary), originally from Ghana, is a doctoral student. His passion is to investigate critical issues pertaining to African Christianity, which was nurtured at Princeton Theological Seminary where he concentrated on world Christianity for his MTh.

Abbreviations

AACC	All Africa Conference of Churches
ABCFM	American Board of Commissioners for Foreign Mission
AEA	Africa Evangelical Mission
AEAM	Association of Evangelicals in Africa and Madagascar
AIC	African-initiated church/African independent church
ATR	African traditional religion
BMS	Baptist Missionary Society
Circle	Circle of Concerned African Women Theologians
CMS	Church Missionary Society
CWME	Commission on World Mission and Evangelism
DRC	Democratic Republic of the Congo
EATWOT	Ecumenical Association of Third World Theologians
EFZ	Evangelical Fellowship of Zimbabwe
GMC	General Missionary Conference
HvTSt	*HTS Teologiese Studies/Theological Studies*
ICT	Institute for Contextual Theology
IMC	International Missionary Council
LIM	Livingstone Inland Mission
MTSR	*Method & Theory in the Study of Religion*
NAAMC	National African American Missions Council
RES	*Répertoire d'épigraphie sémitique*
SACC	South African Council of Churches
SPG	Society for the Propagation of the Gospel
UMCA	Universities' Mission to Central Africa
WCC	World Council of Churches

Introduction

Africa by the Numbers: The Rule of Three in African Christianity

MARK SHAW

IN A WORLD AWASH in statistics, one might tell the story of African Christianity with four numbers. The numbers are 21, 8, 685, and 3. The first number is about the age of African Christianity. The second number is about its recent past. The third number is about where it is today. The fourth number is the most enigmatic of them all and is about what lies beneath.

The first number refers to the twenty-one centuries of African Christianity. Christianity on the continent did not come with missionaries or settlers in the nineteenth century. The movement entered Africa through Alexandria in the first century and has never left. Through the fluctuations of time African Christianity has endured for over two thousand years, making it one of the oldest forms of Christianity in the world.

The second number, 8, refers to how many millions of Christians were probably on the continent in 1900. This number, which may seem large if taken in isolation, must be contrasted with the number of Muslims and African religionists on the continent at the beginning of the twentieth century. Muslims were at 14 million and African religionists at 118 million, respectively. Christianity began well behind the pack.

The third number is 685. This refers to an estimated 685 million Christians in Africa today. That number is projected to rise to 761 million by 2025 and 1.3 billion by 2050. African Christianity has moved from the back of the pack to what is now the most statistically dominant faith on the continent.[1]

The fourth number is 3. Though this is the smallest of the four numbers, it is the one I would like to focus on for the remainder of this introductory

---

1. My numbers are drawn from the Center for Global Christianity: https://www.gordonconwell.edu/center-for-global-christianity/wp-content/uploads/sites/13/2020/12/Status-of-Global-Christianity-2021.pdf.

essay. The number refers to a trio of underlying factors that help us explain the reason for Christianity's dramatic growth in the last century-plus.

Christianity has continually reinvented itself over the last two millennia by embracing three intersecting principles. The practice of these principles, however crudely, helps explain why some churches grow and revive and why others do not. These principles are the translation principle, the indigenous principle, and the contextual principle.[2]

The translation principle is the most well known, associated as it is with the names of Andrew Walls and Lamin Sanneh. This principle enables the gospel to transform the worldview and value system of a new person or a new group. The translation principle is more than Bible translation. It is a process of *inculturation* when the gospel overcomes the resistance of traditional beliefs and takes up residence in the heart of an individual or culture.

The second principle, the indigenous principle, is about the transfer of power. It had early champions in Henry Venn and Rufus Anderson. Later missiologists would call this process *indigenization*. Venn and Anderson spoke of the need for self-governing, self-propagating, and self-supporting churches as the great priority in missions. Under indigenization the marginalized became empowered activists, and new groups and new generations were brought to the front lines of the three-self process.

The contextual principle, or *contextualization*, was first articulated in modern times by Taiwanese theologian Shoki Coe.[3] For Coe, contextualization was the process of applying the gospel to injustices in the culture and systems surrounding the church. It was primarily a term for Christian social reflection and action to show the love and justice of God.

Contemporary missions studies have attempted to roll these three principles into one, using the term *contextualization*. There seems to be no loss of momentum in this trend, but this important word has been stretched so thin that it now bears a half a dozen competing definitions.[4]

For this reason, I believe in the number three when telling the African story. I'd like to illustrate the value of the three principles and their interconnections by briefly looking at three African cities, separated from one another both by many centuries and many kilometers. We want to travel to nineteenth-century Freetown in Sierra Leone and twentieth and twenty-first-century Accra in Ghana. We begin in Egypt in the city of Alexandria and with one of the most remarkable leaders of the African church, Athanasius.

---

2. I discuss these three principles at length in Shaw, *Global Awakening*.
3. Wheeler, "Legacy of Shoki Coe."
4. Bevans, *Models of Contextual Theology*.

Alexandria: Athanasius against the World

How does the rule of three apply to the emergence of Coptic Christianity in the fourth century? At the center of this story was a young Egyptian who straddled both the foreign faith of the Greek-speaking Eastern Empire and the local faith of Coptic-speaking rural Egypt. The Christian revolution of which he was a part was more than theological but included new views of power and new views of contextual mission.

Translating Truth

Athanasius is remembered in history as the father of orthodoxy for his defense of the deity of Christ in the Arian controversy that rocked the Eastern Empire for much of the fourth century. Leaders and movements that translate truth, transfer power, and transform their world help explain how Christianity regains its vitality after periods of corporate decline. We start with the translation principle.

Arius, the renegade cleric who fought for the unity of God, reflected much of Hellenistic and Egyptian traditional religion by seeing the only real choices before him as monotheism or polytheism. Athanasius wrote his great work, *On the Incarnation*, to show that there was a third way. His biblical theology resulted in what Robert Jenson called the "evangelization of metaphysics."[5] Beyond the fight over *homoousios* and the language of Hellenistic philosophy was the great question of salvation. The truth of Scripture needed to be translated, even at great personal cost, into the depths of both Greek and Coptic language and thought. The result was not syncretism but the exaltation of Christ as "God from God, Light from Light, true God from true God, begotten, not made, consubstantial with the Father; through him all things were made" and who "for us men and for our salvation . . . came down from heaven."[6]

Transferring Power

From 325, while still in his twenties, Athanasius assisted his mentor, Bishop Alexander of Alexandria, in the Council of Nicaea in 325. The council met from May to July. By the next year Alexander was dead and his young deacon was selected as his successor, possibly still in his late

---

5. Quoted in Leithart, *Athanasius*, 20.
6. See the Nicene Creed.

twenties (since Athanasius's birthday is somewhere between 295 and 299). His enemies protested his appointment on the grounds of being under age. Five times under four emperors and for a significant percentage of his forty-five years in episcopal office, Athanasius found himself exiled from his church by the state.

He began to see power more in spiritual authority than merely in the holding of an office. When the young Frumentius, newly released from his servitude in Ethiopia, traveled not to his home in Tyre but to Alexandria to meet Athanasius and to plead that missionary bishops be sent to the Axumite kingdom, Athanasius consented by appointing him bishop.

Transforming One's World

Athanasius led a full-service church. The Alexandrian church, for all its infighting, was the center of welfare, education, health, hospitality, and social justice. One of his central duties was the regular distribution of grain to the needy. Prayer and piety were mixed with practicality and social commitment.

The greatest contextual challenge Athanasius faced was not Arianism but *Romanitas*, the ideology of empire that saw Caesar as lord and Christ and his church as servants of the state. This had all happened under Constantine (and his sons), with their collective vision of one God, one emperor, and one church, although not always in that order.

So hostile was Athanasius to this politicization of the church that he was frequently exiled for his refusal to obey imperial demands, such as the restoring of Arius after the Council of Nicea when there clearly had been no repentance on the latter's part. His *Life of Anthony* not only popularized his model of charismatic leadership but served as a protest to the co-opting of the church by the state. Athanasius spoke Coptic and spent many weeks with Anthony, the famous hermit. Anthony emerges as the prototype of the new charismatic leader, willing to enter the fray of church politics for the sake of the gospel but far more interested in winning victories over himself and over the demonic powers that assaulted him daily. The life of Anthony became a fourth-century bestseller, fueling the monastic movement and playing a role in the conversion of many, including the great Augustine of Hippo.

Freetown, Sierra Leone:
Samuel Crowther and the Liberation of West Africa

The story of Christianity in West Africa in the nineteenth century is, to large degree, a story of "revival Christianity" in Freetown, Sierra Leone. Andrew Walls has called Christianity in Sierra Leone "the first part of Africa, one of the very few areas anywhere in the world to see a mass movement towards the Christian faith, where a whole non-Christian people became Christian."[7] As a movement, its practice of the three principles were integral to its spread.

The Translation Principle in Sierra Leone

The message of the gospel that came to the people of Sierra Leone was one of liberation both within and without. Abolition in England was an enthusiastic cause of many Evangelicals and was seen by prominent Evangelicals like William Wilberforce, Granville Sharp, and the Venn family as driven by the gospel of new birth. H. R. Niebuhr describes this new understanding of the gospel: "To be a member of this kingdom is to be one who sees the excellency and the beauty of God in Christ, and so loves him with all his heart for his own sake alone."[8] The new birth, more than creed or custom, became the defining feature of evangelical revival and of the gospel proclaimed to recaptives. A new eschatology accompanied the new birth teaching, postmillennialism, which proclaimed that through evangelical revivals the great majority of the world's peoples would experience such a personal transformation that every area of society would be transformed.

Transferring Power

The gospel of the new birth had implications for leadership and power structures within the church. If the experience of new birth made one a true Christian, then it was also necessary for church leaders. How can one be ordained or elevated to leadership in the church if unregenerate? The case of Samuel Crowther illustrates both the vitality and the limits of this charismatic view of leadership.

Crowther was a recaptive. His slave ship had been intercepted by the Royal Navy, operating on the 1807 law that outlawed the slave trade, and

---

7. Wall, *Missionary Movement*, 102.
8. Quoted in Shaw and Gitau, *Kingdom of God*, 154.

he was freed in Sierra Leone, becoming one of the eighteen thousand freed slaves in Freetown by the year 1825. That number would rise to sixty-seven thousand by 1840. Crowther converted to Christianity soon after his arrival, a pattern that was emulated by thousands of other receptives. As Jehu Hanciles has written: "Their conversion to Christianity in large numbers represents one of the most spectacular achievements in modern mission history" and the "first mass movement to Christianity in modern Africa."[9]

Crowther attended Fourah Bay College and was eventually ordained in London as the first African bishop of the Anglican Church. He went to work among his native Yoruba in Nigeria and then became head of the Niger mission, which sought to combine commerce and conversion along the Niger river. After decades of moderate success, he and his African team were eventually challenged by a new generation of zealous evangelical missionaries from the UK, fresh from the Moody revival and Keswick conferences that taught a second blessing experience of complete consecration.

The new missionaries' zeal became incompatible with the older "Krio" model of Christian mission. The new birth was no match for second blessing. The humiliation of Crowther would lead to the rise of independent churches in West Africa and wave after wave of indigenous leaders, a reminder that the indigenous principle calls for generational change that can be disruptive.

Transforming One's World

Krio Christianity was not perfect. Like their language, Krio Christians mixed traditional practices, including ancestor veneration, with the new gospel of Christ within. They dressed like Europeans and preferred their version of English to their vernaculars.

From certain perspectives, one could argue that Christianity in Sierra Leone seemed too tied to foreign expressions of the faith than local issues. This judgment does not consider the tireless efforts of Krio Christianity to end slavery and poverty through the strategy of the day, Christianity and commerce. The passionate and prolonged application of this praxis brought change to many parts of West Africa, perhaps most notably the Niger River Delta and interior. Though Krio Christians may not have dressed as their African compatriots did, many gave their lives to promote abolition and end the interior slave trade in Africa by building an alternative economy.

---

9. Quoted in Shaw and Gitau, *Kingdom of God*, 166.

Accra, Ghana: Mensa Otabil and Neo-Pentecostalism

Our third case takes us to a third city. From Alexandria and Freetown, we travel to Accra, the capital of Ghana. Ghana's distinction in modern African history is as the first nation that achieved freedom from Britain (1957). Ghana, like the many new African nations that would follow her, preached a political gospel. The new nationalists promised everything. In 1962 Kwame Nkrumah, Ghana's liberator, had a statue of himself erected in central Accra with the inscription "Seek first the political kingdom, and all things will be added unto you." Nkrumah's regime ended in a coup in 1966 after years of corruption and autocracy.

The citizens of West African nations witnessed the collapse of this political gospel by the end of the 1960s. The political collapse in the 1960s and 1970s led to economic collapse in the 1980s. Africans were "generally 40 percent worse off in 1991 than in 1980. . . . The continent was slipping out of the Third World and into its own bleak category of Nth world."[10]

Young people become particularly disillusioned with the failed promises of their politicians. Many turned to religion. In the later 1960s and 1970s, a youth revival swept through Nigeria and surrounding countries. The revival acted as a bridge between the missionary Christianity of the 1950s and the Pentecostal and Neo-Pentecostal movements of the 1980s and 90s. The cluster of revivals sweeping through West Africa brought with them the forces of inculturation, indigenization, and contextualization.

Translating Truth

The youth revival centering in Nigeria in the 1970s changed the message of African Christianity once again. No essential feature of orthodoxy or of Evangelicalism was lost, but a new emphasis was placed on the ministry of the Spirit and deliverance from the powers of darkness. As Ogbu Kalu has written, the revival changed the Christian paradigm from a missionary Christianity to "a deep religious structure that undergirds all the varieties of African traditional religion, a religion with power."[11]

Alan Anderson has summarized the new message the youth evangelists and Pentecostal and Neo-Pentecostal preachers were proclaiming in the late twentieth century: "Pentecostals in Africa proclaim a pragmatic gospel

---

10. Shaw, *Global Awakening*, 163.
11. Quoted in Shaw, *Global Awakening*, 163.

that seeks to address practical needs like sickness, poverty, unemployment, loneliness, evil spirits and sorcery."[12]

In Accra, the new message from Nigeria circulated among the youth in the churches. It reached a young man named Mensa Otabil. Otabil had grown up in the Anglican church but by 1975 was drawn to the Power House Fellowship, where he was baptized in the Holy Spirit. In 1984 he founded his own church, the International Central Gospel Church. His vision for the new church was "lift up the image of the black man so that he can be a channel of blessing to all men."[13] He began to preach about "mental slavery" that imprisoned the African soul. Otabil's sermons became a book, *Beyond the Rivers of Ethiopia*.[14] Otabil and others called for a "realized eschatology" in which the new age of the Spirit brought the kingdom of God to earth in some measure.

Transferring Power

A "new light" message needs "new light messengers." The rapid spread of the new churches gave rich opportunities for marginalized groups to use leadership gifts. One of the fastest-growing churches in Africa and the world in the early years of the twenty-first century was the Redeemed Christian Church of God under the leadership of E. A. Adoboye. They claimed fourteen thousand branches in Nigeria alone and a presence in over 110 countries, including China, Pakistan, and Malaysia.[15] These new leaders were overwhelmingly young.

Transforming One's World

Education has, for over a century, been the narrow ladder that Africans used to climb out of poverty. The new churches of Africa were educational entrepreneurs, changing the educational enterprise from one of stifling government control to widespread recognition of the role that private Christian higher education needed to play in nation-building.

While it is too early to assess what long-term role they will play in political life in Africa, concern has been expressed that the new churches have not always been agents of democracy and have supported some

---

12. Shaw, *Global Awakening*, 173.
13. Shaw, *Global Awakening*, 168.
14. Otabil, *Beyond the Rivers*, 1993.
15. Shaw and Gitau, *Kingdom of God*, 171.

autocratic regimes. T. O. Ranger's conclusion on the question is that in direct and indirect ways Neo-Pentecostalism is more a catalyst of democracy than an inhibitor.[16]

Conclusion: Africa by the Numbers

We have looked at expressions of African Christianity in three very different cities, three very different centuries, and led by three very different individuals. They faced different crises. They spoke different languages. But they shared three principles. They translated truth to make it live in hearts. They transferred power and mobilized the marginalized. They transformed their world with new structures and movements they made it a better place to live and witness.

I remain in awe of the twenty-one centuries of African Christianity and the 8 million of 1900 becoming the 685 million of the 2020s. But for understanding the deeper story of African Christianity, there is no number quite like the number three.

Bibliography

Bevans, Stephen B. *Models of Contextual Theology*. Faith and Cultures Series. Maryknoll, NY: Orbis, 2002.
Leithart, Peter J. *Athanasius*. Edited by Hans Boersma and Matthew Levering. Foundations of Theological Exegesis and Christian Spirituality. Grand Rapids: Baker Academic, 2011.
Otabil, Mensa. *Beyond the Rivers of Ethiopia: A Biblical Revelation on God's Purpose for the Black Race*. Bakersfield, CA: Pneuma Life, 1993.
Ranger, Terence O., ed. *Evangelical Christianity and Democracy in Africa*. Evangelical Christianity and Democracy in the Global South. Oxford: Oxford University Press, 2008.
Shaw, Mark. *Global Awakening: How 20th-Century Revivals Triggered a Christian Revolution*. Downers Grove, IL: IVP Academic, 2010.
Shaw, Mark, and Wanjiru Gitau. *The Kingdom of God in Africa: A History of African Christianity*. Carlisle, UK: Langham Global, 2020.
Walls, Andrew F. *The Missionary Movement in Christian History: Studies in the Transmission of Faith*. Maryknoll, NY: Orbis, 1996.
Wheeler, Ray. "The Legacy of Shoki Coe." *International Bulletin of Missionary Research* 26 (2002) 77–80.

---

16. Ranger, *Evangelical Christianity and Democracy*.

— Section One —

The Story of Christianity Narrated in Historical Context

1

Antiquity

African Christian Connections within the Mediterranean Region

KYAMA M. MUGAMBI AND RUDOLF K. GAISIE

THE INTERCONNECTEDNESS OF EARLY Christianity in the Mediterranean region contributed essential components of global Christianity, which twentieth-century scholarly reflections have not yet sufficiently acknowledged. These contributions came out of early African Christians' deep commitment to the church catholic, and from their studious devotion to the sacred texts. We examine here the development of productive dialogue between regional scholars, which nurtured collaborative thinking about Christian orthodoxy. We look at how discourses among scholars in linked knowledge centers around the Mediterranean Sea yielded robust theological discourses on pertinent issues of their day.

Various dimensions of this interconnectivity in the region are evident. Geographical proximity with the Middle East and southeastern Europe afforded trade and political links that predated Christian theological engagement. Through commerce and conquest, cities like Cyrene, Carthage, and Alexandria became melting pots of Coptic, Berber, Punic, Greek, and Roman cultures.

Later on the introduction of the church brought together communities of faith under the common challenge of persecution. During this time and in the peaceful time thereafter, leading hubs within the region hosted intellectual centers in Alexandria, Cyrene, and Carthage. There convened important Christian thinkers. Christian expansion, amid these theological conversations, produced a network of vibrant ecclesial relations between the churches. These connections nurtured the formulation of Christian orthodoxy, which continues to define the nature of, and relationships between, global Christian communities today.

Historical and Geographical Connections

Northern Africa as a contiguous region is bounded in the north by the Mediterranean Sea and the Sahara Desert in the south. In antiquity, the port cities of this region sustained regular traffic with regions across the Mediterranean. Arabs, Phoenicians, Greeks, and eventually Romans, all facilitated the transfer of tradable goods from as far as India in the East to continental Europe in the West.

Important cities in the region were Alexandria, Cyrene, and Carthage. Alexandria came under Greek rule during the Hellenistic period. It was the most prominent of several cities Alexander the Great founded in his name. Established in 331 BCE, Alexandria lies west of the Nile Delta next to an ancient Egyptian trading village. It was the home of the Great Library—built in the third century BCE—dedicated to the Muses, the nine goddesses of the arts. The city grew and gained notoriety in the Greek world, both for its significance in trade and for the library.

Cyrene was the most prominent of five cities that formed the Pentapolis of Cyrenaica, in modern-day Libya. The others were Ptolemais, Euesperides (Benghazi today), Taucheira (Tocra today), and Apollonia (now Susa). These coastal cities sustained commercial dealings within seafaring routes in the Mediterranean Sea. Like other cities in the region, the Pentapolis came under Roman rule in the first century BCE. After the introduction of Christianity, the cities in Cyrenaica came under the Alexandrian bishopric. Authorities and the intellectuals of the day within Alexandria and Cyrenaica used Greek as their language of commerce and instruction. Local languages remained in use among the populace for official matters and for worship in the rural areas.

Carthage was an important city farther west (in modern-day Tunisia). Settlers from Tyre (modern-day Lebanon) established a trading colony there in the ninth century BCE. Rising from these Phoenician origins, Carthage became the center of the Carthaginian Empire in the fifth century BCE. After a series of three wars with Rome, Carthage came under Roman rule in the second century BCE. It is from the Punic Wars challenging Rome that Hannibal and the Barcid generals achieved notoriety for their skill and sophistication. A vibrant city with rich artistic and intellectual heritage, Carthage also produced philosophers, among them, Carnaedes and Clitomachus.

Carnaedes (214–129 BCE), a Cyrenian philosopher, became the leader of the New Academy in Athens. His pupil, Clitomachus (187–109 BCE), came from Carthage. Like his teacher, Clitomachus also gave leadership to the New Academy in Athens. He remained connected to his hometown in Africa, famously writing a consolatory letter when Carthage fell to Rome in 146 BCE.

Until the collapse of the Roman Empire in the fifth century CE, the Mediterranean Sea remained relatively safe for commerce and travel. Roman imperial forces controlled the cities all around what they called *Mare Nostrum* (our sea) with sufficient security to facilitate movement. A conducive environment resulted not just in the exchange of goods but of ideas as intellectuals traversed the sea to visit learning centers.

Christian Beginnings in Biblical Texts

It is from this interplay between trade and culture that northern Africa came to host a large population of Greek-speaking Jews. In Alexandria, Hellenistic Jews translated Hebrew Scriptures into Greek in the third century BCE. This body of texts, known as the Septuagint (commonly abbreviated as LXX), became the authoritative Scriptures in the Jewish diaspora and especially in Africa. This translation of the Old Testament thus provided a widely accessible translation for Hellenistic Jews and later Christian converts in the Mediterranean world.

The Septuagint was held in high esteem among Hellenistic Jews and Christians because of the accuracy of its translation. It derived its name from the legend that seventy scholars worked on the Hebrew Scriptures separately and arrived at the same translation. The document made the Hebrew sacred texts accessible for Jews who were not fluent in, or had lost knowledge of, ancient Hebrew. Jews in the first century BCE used the LXX in their writings.

Paul the apostle sometimes quoted from the LXX. Philo of Alexandria (20 BCE–50 CE), a Jewish philosopher and thinker, made extensive use of the Septuagint in his exploration of Jewish thought in conversation with contemporary Hellenistic ideas. He extensively used the allegorical method of interpretation.

Hellenistic Jews in Alexandria participated in the economic and political life of the city, making religion an integral feature of their existence. Some of the earliest evidence of Jewish places of worship outside the Holy Land is found here. At the center of their religious life and worship was the Septuagint, up to the time of Jesus's birth and ministry. Early Hellenistic converts into Christianity continued to use these Greek Scriptures together with the collection of Greek texts that later formed the New Testament. The inspired writers mention parts of Africa in these sacred texts.

In addition to featuring prominently in the Old Testament, Egypt receives a special mention in the Gospels when Jesus's family took flight to escape the Herodian infanticide. The narrative of Christ's passion in the Synoptic Gospels includes Simon from Cyrene. The Acts of the Apostles record that those who heard their languages spoken at the festival of Pentecost came from the entire Middle Eastern region. Egypt and parts of Libya near Cyrene represented Africa's presence there. This high point in the story of Christian expansion in Scripture is the connecting point between the Jerusalem sect and the wider region.

Chapter 8 of the book of Acts documents the conversion of an African (Ethiopian) proselyte who was an official serving in the treasury of the candace (the title of the queen regent of Nubia, the area of present-day Sudan). The official would likely have been familiar with Old Testament writings (possibly the Septuagint) as was common to Jews and proselytes in the region. The official may have come from the Nubian kingdom; though, given the scant details, it is difficult to ascertain with precision. The book of Acts refers to Apollo, an influential Jewish teacher who moved from Alexandria to Jerusalem. In the narrative, Apollos's knowledge of Christianity required corrective input from Paul's perspective. Apollos features prominently in the apostle Paul's letters. People from Cyrene worked together with those from Cyprus in evangelizing the Hellenistic world (Acts 11:20). Elsewhere, the narrative of Paul's travel in Acts, on an Alexandrian ship—bearing the figurehead of the twin gods (Castor and Pollux)—shows how early Christians mobilized mission through these established trade routes. Later on the Coptic Church tradition identified Mark the Evangelist as its founder.

Stories like these connecting Africa with the New Testament are difficult to prove, and their veracity remains the subject of debate. In the absence of corroborative evidence, we see from the inclusion of these important stories in the canon and tradition the connectedness of the church within the region. Subsequent literature demonstrates how Christianity in northern Africa grew increasingly connected with Christianity in Jerusalem and other areas of the Middle East. Early Greek noncanonical writings such as the Epistle of Barnabas, the Greek Gospels of Egyptians, and even material by early Christian "gnostics" collectively affirm the connection among early North African Christians. It is for the theological discourse resulting from the linkages that early African Christianity is best known. Activities of the Alexandrian Catechetical School provide useful insights about interconnectivity of early Christians through theological debate.

The Alexandrian Theological Tradition

The Alexandrian Catechetical School refers to both a physical location (the city) and the body of work associated with Christian scholarship found in that city. The school fostered a commitment to the study of Christianity and its sacred texts, using contemporary scholarly disciplines honed largely within ancient Greek intellectual traditions. Christian writers operating in this Egyptian "mission school" opened Christian teachings to the Hellenistic world of thought in ways similar to Philo of Alexandria connecting Jewish thought to the Hellenistic intellectual tradition. The Alexandrian school presented classes for both converts and non-converts and was prepared to engage with Christian heretics. Over time, the school developed a long line of distinguished teachers concerned with theology, morality, philosophy, and related disciplines.

While the rural Egyptians spoke their local languages in their daily activities, the school, situated in the urban setting of Alexandria, operated in the Greek language for its formal instruction. Use of Greek enabled people from all around the Mediterranean to engage with the important literature of the day through the teaching within the educational institutions. The rigor of the studies was well matched with the extensive writings of the school's prolific instructors. The quality of study not only raised the bar for successive generations of students, but also nurtured ever-growing lines of inquiry within theology and philosophy.

The school trained church leaders, bishops, and missionaries whose influence grew within Alexandria and beyond. Here, philosophical tools from Alexandria's older intellectual heritage were repurposed for application among Christian scholars within the Mediterranean region. Notable scholars from Alexandria include Pantaenus, Clement, Origen, Heraclas, Dionysius, Didymus the Blind, and Athanasius the Great. The school also hosted important theologians and church leaders from outside the continent. These include Gregory Thaumaturgus, Jerome, and Basil.

Clement (150–215 CE) found in Alexandria a home for his eventual vocation as a Christian pastoral scholar. His vast knowledge of Hellenistic philosophers, historians, and poets is evident in his critical appraisals of ancient learning as a Christian evangelist. An exemplar of Christian engagement with culture, he used the Hellenist frames of reference to highlight the Christian message. He was particularly keen to show that Christ, the Logos, was as active among the ancestors of Jews as he was among the gentiles. He taught how the Logos gave the law to the Jews and philosophy to the Greeks to prepare both for the incarnation.

Origen (185–253 CE) was possibly the most prolific of the early church theologians. An ascetic, Origen taught as a catechist at the school, taking over its leadership as a young man from his teacher, Clement. Clement's influence, directly or indirectly, on young Origen can only be deduced from Origen's literary output since he does not explicitly mention Clement in his extant works. Origen taught systematic study of biblical texts, producing his voluminous work the *Hexapla*. An innovative work of its time, the *Hexapla* consisted of different versions of the Old Testament in parallel columns for comparative study. In his numerous commentaries and treatises, Origen made critical use of an allegorical method of hermeneutics that would continue to influence the school after his departure. Ambrose, a wealthy intellectual nobleman from the city, and possibly others like him, supported Origen with stenographers or secretaries to aid the work of composition and copying.

While the *Hexapla* was a voluminous, important work in itself, it is the *Contra Celsum* (Against Celsus) that is considered Origen's most significant work. In it, Origen refuted objections to Christianity raised by Celsus, an influential pagan philosopher. Celsus dismissed Christianity as a religion for closed-minded, deluded, unpatriotic, and uninformed people. Origen methodically countered each of these assertions, forming a masterful study in apologetics emulated for centuries thereafter. Many of Origen's works formed essential reading, which shaped the course of theology as the works traversed the Mediterranean.

Several significant theologians, including Athanasius and the Cappadocian fathers, became his most devoted students. Though he did not become a bishop, he taught many who ascended to this office. Contemporaries and subsequent generations of Origen students made use of his reflections. It must be noted that his ideas were subject to debates about their fidelity to the tradition of apostolic teachings. This notwithstanding, Origen's stature as a pioneering theologian is best assessed within the circumstances of his own time.

One of Origen's mentees was Gregory Thaumaturgus (213–70 CE) who came from Neocaesarea (in the modern Black Sea region of Turkey). He met Origen while residing in Caesarea, and through Origen's friendly persuasion, he changed his career from law to service in the church. Gregory became a prominent churchman and theologian of his day, eventually serving as bishop of the region of Pontus. His epithetic Thaumaturgus (miracle worker) is apparently a testament to his fruitful labors in evangelistic work.

Heraclas (d. 248 CE), another of Origen's African students, became the bishop of Alexandria. He was the first bishop of Alexandria to be referred to as "pope" in the writings of his day. Heraclas followed Origen as head of the catechetical school. Dionysius "the Great" (d. 264 CE), a patriarch of Alexandria, joined the catechetical school after his conversion as an adult. He studied under Origen and Heraclas. Eventually Dionysius took over the leadership of the school in 231 CE.

One of the school's most distinguished leaders was Didymus the Blind (309–94 CE), who took over its leadership in 340. An astute Egyptian theologian, he was revered for his sharp theological mind and astounding memory. He was said to have committed large amounts of biblical and scholarly text to memory for use in his teachings. Didymus was Jerome's (342–420 CE) instructor at the catechetical school.

Jerome of Stridon (modern-day Albania) was a priest, theologian, historian, and translator. His greatest contribution to global Christianity was the Vulgate, an important Latin translation of the Bible. Jerome translated the Latin Old Testament using the Hebrew texts and not the Septuagint as many people did at the time. The Vulgate became an important translation for the Latin-speaking Western Church. Before this, however, there was evidence of some older Latin translations of canonical texts of the Bible, which might have been made in Carthage. Another of Didymus's students was Tyrannius Rufinus of Concordia (344–411 CE), a contemporary of Jerome and an Italian historian and translator. Tyrannius's major contributions were his Latin translations of Origen's important works.

Origen and other leaders of the Alexandrian school profoundly influenced the Cappadocian fathers, Basil of Caesarea (330–79 CE), his brother Gregory of Nyssa (335–95 CE), and their friend Gregory of Nazianzus (329–90 CE). Basil of Caesarea became bishop of Caesarea in Cappadocia (in modern-day Kayseri, Turkey). He supported what became known as Nicene orthodoxy as he fought Arianism. Basil contributed, together with Pachomius, an Egyptian monk, to the development of communal (cenobitic) monasticism. He was acquainted with Athanasius, the great Alexandrian teacher. Gregory of Nyssa, who served as a bishop in Nyssa in Cappadocia, was an erudite theologian, whose writings added to the discourse on the Holy Trinity and Nicene orthodoxy. Gregory of Nazianzus, bishop of Constantinople (in modern-day Turkey), contributed to pneumatology and developed an advanced rhetorical style in his theological work. Together, these theologians promoted the Nicene position on Trinitarian theology.

Athanasius and the Doctrine of the Trinity

One of the most important authors of what early churches accepted as the Nicene position was Athanasius (296–373 CE). He was a prolific Egyptian scholar mentored by Alexander (d. 328 CE), the bishop of Alexandria, and by Antony the Great (251–356 CE). Few theologians of the day could claim to have written, taught, and debated as much for theological orthodoxy as Athanasius did.

Athanasius was comfortable in both the Greek and Coptic worlds. He studied at the catechetical school and received instruction from Antony (Anthony). Antony was an influential monk who lived in the Egyptian desert. Antony's ascetic life drew the admiration of many Christians in Egypt. During this time, the Egyptian desert became home to many Christians, who like Antony sought piety through seclusion in the harsh environment. Pachomius (292–348 CE), a contemporary of Athanasius, also lived in the Egyptian deserts, and is credited with the growth of communal (cenobitic) monasticism in the area. It is from Athanasius we have a biography of the life of Abba (Father) Antony. Antony lived with devout piety outside the Greek academy, representing the best of a rural Coptic Christianity typical of his day. The intensity of Antony's devotion influenced Athanasius's spirituality profoundly.

Athanasius's contributions come to the fore because of his opposition to Arius about the deity of Jesus within Christian doctrine. Arius (256–336 CE), a presbyter in Alexandria, taught that Jesus (the Logos or Word) was a created being and therefore was not of the same essence as the Father. Together with his bishop and others, Athanasius argued from the Scriptures that Jesus was of the same essence as the Father and was not a created being. The controversy that reverberated across the Christian world at the time threatened to split the church (with some political implications within the Roman Empire). Emperor Constantine, having recently converted to Christianity, sponsored an ecumenical council in Nicea. He invited all available 1,800 bishops within the empire to deliberate the issue. Fewer than 500 bishops attended the council. These included, from Africa, Bishop Caecilian of Carthage (Latin speaking), Alexander of Alexandria, and Antiochus of Memphis, as well as others from Libya who sympathized with Arius, Theonas of Marmarica and Secundus of Ptolemais.

Athanasius attended the gathering as a young deacon with Alexander, supporting as he could or was allowed to. Athanasius fleshed out the theological position arrived at in Nicea with his writings and teachings from then on and through his eventual leadership of the church in Alexandria. The resulting position on the Trinity at Nicea was immortalized in the formulation of the Nicene Creed. This creed, with few modifications, remains a key confession for many historic denominations, among them Catholics, Eastern Orthodox churches, and various Protestant denominations. The creed served to unite the church at the time following the threat precipitated by Arian teaching.

Arian teaching had sunk deep roots into the region and did not disappear immediately. The ideas spread beyond Alexandria to the Middle Eastern region and even into Europe. Bishops gathered once more to deliberate on the matter in the First Council of Constantinople (381 CE) again affirmed Athanasius's position, issuing a more substantive teaching on the Holy Spirit's relationship with the Father and the Son. They concluded that the Holy Spirit, like the Son, was of the same essence and substance as the Father. The theological position arrived at modified the previous creed to bring about the widely used Nicene-Constantinople Creed, simply known as the Nicene Creed.

Athanasius eventually took over as bishop of Alexandria after Alexander's death. In this elevated position he continued his vehement rejection of Arian teachings. Athanasius's episcopacy was turbulent, with his being exiled several times among the Copts, away from urban Alexandria. Athanasius was also a significant contributor to a less-known initiative to maintain unity across Egypt and Cyrene. The letter to the African bishops, *Ad Afros Epistola Synodica* (362/3 CE), bore Athanasius's name and marks of his theology. The letter was a bold attempt to bring together ninety bishops of Egypt and Libya to deal with the aftermath of the Arian controversy. The letter affirmed the Nicene Creed while presenting a strong case against Arius. The letter advocated for unity within this community of African Christian leaders scattered across this part of North Africa.

Alexandria also maintained connections to the south in Nubia (upper Egypt and Sudan) and in Axum (modern-day Ethiopia). From the fourth century CE onwards, early Coptic Christians became instrumental in reaching southwards with trade and as facilitators of Byzantium's later interests in Nubian religio-political interests. For instance, Athanasius ordained the Tyre-bound Frumentius, and redirected him to new missionary efforts in Axum. Alexandria remained connected to the Ethiopian Orthodox Church from then to the twentieth century. Until 1959, Alexandria was responsible for appointing the *abun* (patriarch) of the Ethiopian Tewahedo Orthodox Church. Such was the influence of Alexandria on early African Christianity.

The coexistence of Athanasius's theological discourse in Greek and the indigenous Coptic faith of Antony, for example, illustrates the deep integration of Christian faith in the region during the patristic period. That Antony and Athanasius shared a common orthodoxy is instructive of the value of theological linkages between the academy and a local lived theology.

In the fifth century CE, Alexandria once again served the church by defending orthodoxy against Nestorianism at the Council of Ephesus in

431. Shenoute (348–465 CE), the leader of the White Monastery in Egypt, attended the council at the invitation of the bishop of Alexandria, Cyril (376–444 CE). Again, these contributions by Africans to the deliberations at the important ecumenical council were felt beyond Africa to the rest of the Christian world.

The Carthaginian Connection

Carthage nurtured a vibrant theological community of significant theologians. While the area did not have a school similar in nature to the catechetical school in Alexandria, theologians found here contributed a large corpus of works.

After the fall of the Carthaginian Empire, following the Punic Wars in the second century BCE, Carthage became the administrative capital of the Roman province of Africa. The Romans rebuilt it with new infrastructure to serve its growing population. The area was prosperous with various forms of agriculture and trade. Carthaginians comprised indigenous rural Berber people as well as people of Roman, Punic, and mixed origin. Latin eventually replaced the Punic language as the official language in the area around the refounded city while Berber and Punic languages continued in the rural areas. After the entry of Christianity in the first century CE, local languages did not find their way into liturgical use within the city in the same way Coptic did in Alexandria.

Evidence of early Christianity in this area comes from such documents as the second-century account of the Acts of the Scillitan Martyrs. This account describes the trial and eventual martyrdom of twelve Christians, five women and seven men from Numidia. Two of the twelve names were Punic while the others were Latin. While these names might not necessarily refer to the ethnicity of the martyrs, they indicate the cosmopolitan composition of the early Christians. Other documents exist that show the eager reception of Christianity in that part of Africa. The passion of the young women Perpetua and Felicitas in 206 CE, for example, bears the testimony of conversion, fervent faith, and martyrdom in that era.

A culture of theological inquiry complemented this demonstrated faith commitment of Carthaginian Christians. An outstanding example is Tertullian (155–220 CE), whose works proposed such words as "sacrament," "Trinity," and "resurrection" for use in theology. He was also among the first to use the word "Testament" for the Jewish (old) and the Christian (new) texts of the church. Tertullian was familiar with the teachings of Stoicism but was more critical of Greek philosophical thinking within theology than

Origen was. He argued, for example, that Athens had nothing to do with Jerusalem, implying that the academy had nothing to do with the church. In his writings, he documented his reflections on the Montanists, a movement within the church under the leadership of Montanus noted for the apparent overemphasis on the work of the Holy Spirit among its members. In due course, Tertullian's works found wide readership in Carthage. This connection shaped theology in Latin-speaking North Africa and across the Mediterranean. The context of these theological reflections in the third century CE was a time of great persecution.

Brutal widespread murder of Christians shook the Roman Empire under Decius (249–50 CE), Valerian (257–58 CE) and Diocletian (303 CE), endangering the lives of lay Christians, theologians, and church leaders. The persecution stemmed from the Christians' refusal to accede to the emperor's demands to sacrifice for the empire and his own well-being. The increasing number of Christians relative to other religious adherents in the Roman Empire exacerbated this dire situation. The consistent and severe maltreatment of Christians affected the church in multiple ways, with Christians dying to defend their faith. This persecution also raised the question of what to do with those who compromised their faith in the face of persecution.

During the Decian persecution, Cyprian (210–58 CE), then the bishop of Carthage, went into hiding—in his view, to avoid potential implications of his death on a church with a diminishing number of leaders. Upon his return, he called for a solution to the issue of lapsed Christians because leaders were divided over the matter. There was also a question about the validity of sacraments offered by leaders who had lapsed. Cyprian wrote several letters and treatises in addressing the challenges of church unity during his bishopric after the Decian persecution. During the Valerian persecution, Cyprian defended his Christian conviction and was eventually martyred in 258.

Augustine, Donatism, and the Councils of Carthage

The Diocletian persecution of Christians in 303 was particularly vicious following an edict prohibiting Christian meetings and targeting sacred texts in the Roman Empire. There were those who regarded Christians who surrendered their Scriptures as religious traitors. Some Christians were arrested in Abitina (west of proconsular Africa, present-day northern Tunisia) and sent to trial in Carthage for illegally celebrating Sunday worship. The trial took place in 304 CE. While the group was in prison in Carthage, Mensurius, the city's bishop, and his deacon Caecilian, forbade some Christians from sending food to their imprisoned colleagues. When Caecilian became bishop of

Carthage, following Mensurius's death, many within and outside Carthage did not recognize his ordination. A political change in the empire affected the balance of power in the church in Carthage.

Constantine's rise to emperor in the western half of the empire (in 307 CE) and eventually to sole emperor (in 324 CE) brought relative peace for Christians. Constantine's Edict of Milan in 313 CE effectively ended official persecution of Christians. Constantine then called for a council in 314 at Arles (France) where he retained Caecilian as bishop. Some in Carthage saw that as imperial imposition. A rival bishop, Majorinus, was elected in Carthage. He officially supported the position that lapsed priests rendered sacraments invalid. Marjorinus died shortly after and was succeeded by Donatus Magnus, also known as Donatus of Casae Nigrae (the village of blacks, in Numidia). Donatus, who was of Berber origin, advanced Marjorinus's movement. Through his vigorous lobbying and written work promoting this position, the movement became known by his name, the Donatist movement.

By the time of Augustine's birth in 354, Donatism was a strong movement within the church that needed to be addressed decisively. Donatists contended that the surrender of Scriptures during persecution amounted to deserting the faith. They also questioned the validity of deserters' authority to issue the sacraments. Augustine's works provided the most effective response to the onslaught of Donatism on North African Christianity.

In 371 Augustine (354–430) went to Carthage for the first time to study oratory and to become a teacher. Early in his life, in 372, he fell in love with a young woman in Carthage who became his mistress and lover for at least fifteen years. They had a son called Adeodatus (gift of God). In 373, in Carthage, Augustine read the work *Hortensius*, by Cicero, a Roman lawyer and philosopher, which taught the renunciation of worldly pleasures to embrace the philosophical life contemplatively. This sparked Augustine's interest in philosophy. Augustine joined the Manicheans for nine years. This religious group, founded by Mani, mixed elements of Christianity and other religions such as Zoroastrianism. This did not satisfy Augustine's thirst for spiritual knowledge.

He left for Rome and eventually took a teaching position in rhetoric in Milan. His mother joined him in Milan and took him to a church where they heard Bishop Ambrose (339–97). Ambrose, a devout Christian and trained rhetorician, impressed Augustine with his sermons. During his spiritual quest Augustine heard of Athanasius's *Life of St. Antony*, which steered him towards his eventual conversion. In August 386, Augustine had a dramatic conversion encounter. The episode, described in his confessions, climaxed with the reading of Rom 13:13–14, when he heard a childlike voice that he understood to be instructing him to take the Scriptures and read. On Easter Sunday in 387, Ambrose baptized Augustine, his son Adeodatus, and friend Alypius. He returned to Africa, staying for while in his birth town of Thagaste. Thereafter he moved to Hippo Regius (in modern-day Algeria) in 391 where he started a monastic community. Augustine was active in Hippo following his ordination as a priest. He preached, wrote, and debated the Christian cause and its traditional (orthodox) teachings. In 395, he was consecrated bishop of Hippo Regius as successor to Bishop Valerius where he served in that capacity until his death in 430. Augustine left important theological works, biblical commentaries, sermons, and letters, many of which are central to the development of (Western) Christian thought. Augustine's piety and example as a pastoral theologian stands out among African Christian scholars.

In his important work *On the City of God against the Pagans* (better known as *The City of God*) Augustine laid foundational theological and philosophical arguments that shaped Western thought. The book was essentially an apologia in defence of Christians against accusations that they had brought about the decline of Rome. Augustine dealt with such themes as sin, suffering, evil, free will, and human history. His approach laid the groundwork for the work of significant theologians hundreds of years later. This list includes notable names such as Thomas Aquinas and Martin Luther the Reformer.

Augustine built on the teachings of other African churchmen such as Cyprian of Carthage and Athanasius of Alexandria. Amid varied Christian perspectives that divided the church, especially in North Africa, Augustine's works sought to promote unity by addressing some of the misunderstandings.

Though it was the birthplace of the Donatist movement, Carthage, in addition to nurturing theologians, continued to remain an important hub promoting ecclesial unity even to the time of Augustine. Between 345 and 419, the city hosted no fewer than sixteen councils on a wide range of matters relating to the church. Though the impact of each conference differed from the others, Carthaginian, indeed Numidian, leaders remained steadfast in their efforts to build consensus around important theological issues. Of these councils two stand out.

The Council of Carthage in 418 united the leaders against the growing influence of Pelagius. Augustine's arguments on the supremacy of grace in the Christian experience prevailed over the Pelagian emphasis on works. These objections to Pelagius presented key building blocks of Reformation thought a millennium later. The council of 419 was perhaps the most important one in this region. The attendees, including Augustine, affirmed the key canons of eighteen previous councils—sixteen in Carthage, one in Milevum (in Numidia, Algeria), and the other in Hippo. A running theme found in the council's canons is the sense of unity and cooperation envisaged among the leaders of the church spread all over North Africa. Such unity held together through the shared fidelity to orthodox doctrines of the church as presented in the resolutions of the Council of Nicea.

Conclusion

Through the ages, indispensable aspects of Christian thought have found some of their formative concepts in the first five centuries of early African Christianity. Social, commercial, and political interconnectivity in the region birthed and incubated priests, theologians, and missionaries to the known Christian world at the time. While persecution tested the fortitude of Christians' faith, it is the controversies that spurred theological debates that would refine orthodox teachings. In particular, the Arian, Pelagian, and Donatist issues provided the context for the highest points of early African Christian thought. An exhaustive inventory of all the important African theologians of the early church would elude any single study. This essay samples a few of those who were crucial in navigating these important milestones.

The linkages between the theologians came through their writings and interpersonal relationships. Some were mutual, collegial friendships while others were teacher-student relationships. All were made possible by the free flow of goods, people, and knowledge all around the Mediterranean. Doctrinal ideas on one side of the Mediterranean found resonance and refinement on the other side. Monastic life nurtured on the continent helped carry the knowledge through mission within the Mediterranean region and beyond. Language and cultures contributed in different ways to the discourse. In Egypt, for instance, Coptic languages found use in liturgical practices as Greek remained the language of instruction. In Carthaginian Christianity it was Latin that carried the day within the Christian academy. Echoes of grassroot Christian experiences can, for instance, be found in Athanasius's writing, and they reveal a lived faith among Africa's early Christians in their local languages. This is less the case in Carthaginian literature where Latin remained the primary liturgical and instructional language. Nevertheless, the Christian world still awaits substantial evidence of Berber Christian literature. In all, connections between Christian thinkers in the region produced a legacy of orthodoxy that still speaks to the Christian experience beyond the twentieth century.

Bibliography

Athanasius. *Athanasius: Select Works and Letters*. Nicene and Post-Nicene Fathers, 2nd ser., 4. Edited by Alexander Robertson. Peabody, MA: Hendrickson, 1999.

———. *Athanasius: The Life of Antony and the Letter to Marcellinus*. Translated by Robert C. Gregg. New York: Paulist, 1979.

Bantu, Vince L. *A Multitude of All Peoples: Engaging Ancient Christianity's Global Identity*. Grand Rapids: InterVarsity, 2020.

Deferrari, Roy J., ed. "*Life of St Anthony* by St Athanasius." In *Early Christian Biographies*, 15:127–216. Washington, DC: Catholic University of America Press, 2010.

Eastman, David L. *Early North African Christianity: Turning Points in the Development of the Church*. Grand Rapids: Baker Academic, 2021.

Faraji, Salim. *Roots of Nubian Christianity Uncovered: The Triumph of the Last Pharaoh*. Trenton, NJ: Africa World, 2012.

Gaisie, Rudolf K. "Scripture as Context and Augustine's *De Doctrina Christiana*: A Modern African Christian Perspective." *Journal of African Christian Thought* 23 (2020) 10–18.

Kalu, Ogbu. *African Christianity: An African Story*. Trenton, NJ: Africa World, 2007.

Oden, Thomas C. *The African Memory of Mark: Reassessing Early Church Tradition*. Grand Rapids: InterVarsity, 2011.

———. *How Africa Shaped the Christian Mind: Rediscovering the African Seedbed of Western Christianity*. Early African Christianity Set. Downers Grove, IL: IVP Academic, 2010.

———. *The Rebirth of African Orthodoxy: Return to Foundations*. Nashville: Abingdon, 2016.

Origen. *Origen: Selected Writings*. Translated by Rowan A Greer. New York: Paulist, 1979.

Schaff, Philip. *The Creeds of Christendom*. Vol. 1. New York: Harper & Brothers, 1877.

———. *The Teaching of the Twelve Apostles, or The Oldest Church Manual*. New York: Funk & Wagnalls, 1889.

Wilhite, David E. *Ancient African Christianity: An Introduction to a Unique Context and Tradition*. New York: Routledge, 2017.

2

The Beginnings of Christianity in Sub-Saharan Africa

Kingdom of Aksum and the Christian World of Late Antiquity

STANISLAU PAULAU

An African Civilization of Late Antiquity

THE TOWN OF AKSUM is today merely a small district center within the northern Ethiopian province of Tigray. In late antiquity, however, it belonged to the most important political and religious centers of the world. Aksum gave its name to a powerful kingdom that flourished during the first seven centuries of the Common Era and that played a decisive role in the early history of Christianity in sub-Saharan Africa.

The Aksumite kingdom owed its power in the first place to its far-reaching international trade networks and its position on the Red Sea, from where it could dominate both land and sea passages to the Indian Ocean. The kingdom's seaport Adulis was the main commercial center of exchange between the Byzantine Empire and the countries of the Mediterranean Sea and the Indian Ocean. The *Periplus of the Erythraean Sea*, a Greek text dating from the mid-first century, which served as a guide for merchants conducting business in the Red Sea and the western Indian Ocean, describes Adulis as a bustling center of trade, in which ivory, tortoise shell, and rhinoceros horn were exchanged for cloth, garments, tools, weapons, and iron from places as far afield as the Roman Empire and northwestern India.[1]

As the power and wealth of the Aksumite kingdom grew into the second and third centuries, so also did its political ambitions. Several inscriptions testify that Aksumite kings waged war against other peoples in Africa and, from about 200 CE, in southern Arabia.[2] Its links with other countries, whether through diplomacy, cultural exchange, trading enterprise,

---

1. Casson, *Periplus Maris Erythraei*, 52–53.
2. Hatke, "Aksumites in South Arabia," 295–305.

or military campaigns, made Aksum part and parcel of the international community of the late antiquity.³ The tongue of ancient Aksum, Geʻez (occasionally called Classical or Old Ethiopic in scholarship), was not only a spoken language, but was used also for writing, which supported the development of a unique Aksumite civilization. At the same time, Greek inscriptions on coins and multilingual inscriptions on monumental stone structures (written in three scripts: Geʻez, Sabean, and Greek) prove the early ties of the Aksumite state with the Hellenistic Mediterranean and south Arabian cultural realms.⁴

Before the arrival of Christianity, the northern Horn of Africa region appears to have had a polytheistic belief system similar—but by no means identical—to that found in southern Arabia for many centuries. At the same time, it was also subject to Egyptian influences via Nubia, and it was aware of the Greek gods. The principal Aksumite god of the pre-Christian period was the war god, known as Ares in Greek and Mahrem in Geʻez. He was associated with the moon and is represented on coins and inscriptions by a horizontal crescent and, above it, a disc. This god stretches back to the Sabean period, where he was known as Almaqah. Other important gods were Astar, Meder, and Beher, who can be identified as the gods of heaven, earth, and sea.⁵

The Aksumite kingdom brought together many cultural influences of diverse origin and incorporated them in its unique, locally rooted civilization, which was known and respected far beyond the Red Sea region. The third-century Persian religious leader Mani, founder of the Manichaean religion, is, for example, reported by his followers to have stated, "There are four great kingdoms in the world. The first is the kingdom of the land of Babylon and of Persia. The second is the kingdom of the Romans. The third is the kingdom of the Aksumites. The fourth is the kingdom of Silis [Chinese?]. These four great kingdoms exist in the world; there is none that surpasses them."⁶ This remark clearly illustrates how far the fame of Aksum had spread in the world of late antiquity.

The Advent of Christianity

Our knowledge about the coming of Christianity to Aksum and its early development in the region is based on a diverse set of sources: written texts

3. Phillipson, *Foundations of African Civilization*, 195–207.
4. Phillipson, *Foundations of African Civilization*, 51–56.
5. Munro-Hay, *Aksum*, 196–202.
6. Gardner, *Kephalaia of the Teacher*, 197.

originating outside the Aksumite kingdom, coins, and other archeological materials, as well as inscriptions from Aksum and related sites.

The primary account of the advent of Christianity to the kingdom of Aksum is contained in the *Ecclesiastical History* by Rufinus of Aquileia. The larger part of this work contains a translation into Latin of a Greek *Ecclesiastical History* by Eusebius of Caesarea, which covered developments up to the death of Constantine the Great in 337. Rufinus extended this account by adding two new chapters, devoted to the years 337–95. It is there (bk. 10, 9–11) that the story of the Christianization of Aksum is to be found.[7] Rufinus claims that his information derived from Aedesius of Tyre, who had been a prisoner and servant in the royal household at Aksum with Frumentius, the future bishop. There is, however, general agreement among scholars that Rufinus's work was largely based on a now-lost work written by another historian, Gelasius, Eusebius's successor as bishop of Caesarea, in the 380s.[8] Rufinus's brief account was repeated by several fifth-century church historians, such as Socrates Scholasticus, Theodoret of Cyrrhus, and Sozomen. All of them wrote Greek works entitled *Ecclesiastical History* and their narratives have been directly derived from that of Rufinus. Remarkably, also one of the most important literary sources regarding the Christianization of Aksum written in Geʻez, the *Homily in Honour of St. Frumentius*, has striking similarities to the narrative described by Rufinus. The text preserved in fourteenth-century manuscripts appears to be based on Greek sources and composed in the Aksumite period, between the fourth and the seventh centuries.[9]

Given its exceptional importance, the account of Rufinus about Christianization of Aksum is well worth quoting in full:

> A philosopher named Metrodorus, they say, penetrated to Further India[10] for the purpose of viewing the places and investigating the continent. Encouraged by his example, one Meropius as well, a philosopher of Tyre, decided to go to India for the same reason; he had with him two small boys whom as his relatives he was instructing in letters. The younger was called Aedesius and the older Frumentius. When therefore the philosopher had viewed and acquainted himself with the things on which his mind was feasting, and he had set out on the return voyage, the

---

7. Rufinus of Aquileia, *History of the Church*, 394–96.
8. Gelasius of Caesarea, *Ecclesiastical History*, xxxiii–xxxvii.
9. Haile, "Homily."
10. It is helpful to remember that *India* was a rather vague term that could mean not only subcontinental India, but also Africa east of the Nile or south Arabia. Therefore, the Greco-Roman sources often localize the Aksumite kingdom in "India."

ship in which he was sailing put in to some port to obtain water and other necessaries. It is the custom of the barbarians there that whenever the neighboring peoples announce that their treaty relations with the Romans have been disrupted, they kill all the Romans they find among them. The philosopher's ship was attacked and everyone with him put to death together. The boys, who were discovered under a tree going over and preparing their lessons, were saved because the barbarians pitied them and brought them to the king. He made one of them, Aedesius, his cupbearer, while to Frumentius, whose intelligence and prudence he could see, he entrusted his accounts and correspondence. From that time on they were held in high honor and affection by the king. Now when the king died and left as heir to the kingdom his wife and her young son, he also left it to the free choice of the youths what they would do. But the queen begged them to share with her the responsibility of ruling the kingdom until her son should grow up, as she had no one more trustworthy in the kingdom, especially Frumentius, whose prudence would suffice to rule the kingdom, for the other gave evidence simply of a pure faith and sober mind.

Now while they were doing so and Frumentius had the helm of the kingdom, God put it into his mind and heart to begin making careful inquiries if there were any Christians among the Roman merchants, and to give them extensive rights, which he urged them to use, to build places of assembly in each location, in which they might gather for prayer in the Roman manner. Not only that, but he himself did far more along these lines than anyone else, and in this way encouraged the others, invited them with his support and favors, made available whatever was suitable, furnished sites for buildings and everything else that was necessary, and bent every effort to see that the seed of Christians should grow up there.

Now when the royal child whose kingdom they had looked after reached maturity, then, having executed their trust completely and handed it back faithfully, they returned to our continent, even though the queen and her son tried very hard to hold them back and asked them to stay. While Aedesius hastened to Tyre to see his parents and relatives again, Frumentius journeyed to Alexandria, saying that it was not right to conceal what the Lord had done. He therefore explained to the bishop everything that had been done and urged him to provide some worthy man to send as bishop to the already numerous Christians and churches built on barbarian soil. Then Athanasius, for he had recently received the priesthood, after considering attentively and carefully what Frumentius had said and done, spoke as follows in the council of priests: "What other man can we find like you, in whom is God's spirit as in you, and who could achieve such things as these?" And having conferred on him the priesthood, he ordered him to return with the Lord's grace to the place from which he had come. When he had reached India as bishop, it is said that such a grace of miracles was given him by God that the signs of the apostles were worked by him and a countless number of barbarians was converted to the faith. From that time on there came into existence a Christian people and churches in India, and the priesthood began. These events we came to know of not from popular rumor, but from the report of Aedesius himself, who had been Frumentius's companion, and who later became a presbyter in Tyre.[11]

It is to be assumed that the rapid rise of Frumentius in the Aksumite royal service was predicated upon his ability to speak and write Greek, the lingua franca of trade and international relations in the Mediterranean and the Red Sea regions. Greek was therefore regularly used also in Aksum, as can be seen from inscriptions and coinage.

Rufinus indicates that Frumentius's initial activities were focused on the Greek-speaking merchants of the Roman Empire living in Aksum, some of whom were no doubt already Christian. Most probably, he especially had to facilitate their trading activities and enable practice of their religion by arranging places of worship for them. It has been speculated that already these congregations enjoying the official protection of the state in the guise of young Frumentius could become the cells of the gradual Christianization of the local population.[12] However, this process becomes historically tangible only after the ordination of Frumentius and the conversion of the Aksumite royal court to Christianity.

The account of Rufinus does not provide dates for the described events, which makes them a matter of scholarly debate. However, Rufinus situates his narrative "in the times of Constantine," who reigned from 306 to 337.[13] At the same time, we know that Frumentius's appointment must have taken place between 328, when Athanasius was elected to the See of St. Mark, and 335, when his first exile was enforced at the Council of Tyre. There is a wide agreement among scholars that the ordination of Frumentius and his return to Aksum as its first bishop is likely to have happened around the year 335.

---

11. Rufinus of Aquileia, *History of the Church*, 394–96.
12. Esler, *Ethiopian Christianity*, 34–35.
13. Rufinus of Aquileia, *History of the Church*, 394.

The ordination of Frumentius as the bishop of Aksum by Athanasius of Alexandria is supported by yet another historical source, a Greek letter that the pro-Arian Byzantine Emperor Constantius II (reigned from 337 to 361) wrote to the Aksumite King Ezana (Aizanas) and his supposed brother Sazanas. Since Constantius II favored Arianism, he had deposed Athanasius as bishop of Alexandria and replaced him with George of Cappadocia. Against this background, he asked the Aksumite rulers to send Frumentius to Egypt, so that he might be confirmed in his office by the new Arian bishop.[14] The letter could not have been written much after the—by that time already third—deposition of Athanasius in 356. It was an attempt at swaying the Aksumites towards the Byzantine emperor's religious policy, but it had apparently no effect either on Frumentius's own position or on the Aksumites' adherence to the Alexandrian creed as championed by Athanasius. Since Rufinus does not mention this letter, he was probably unaware of it. Therefore, it constitutes an independent source that endorses Rufinus's account about the consecration of Frumentius as bishop of Aksum by Athanasius. This letter is also highly significant, because it confirms that the place that Rufinus roughly identifies as "India" and for which Frumentius was ordained bishop was indeed Aksum.

Remarkably, the letter mentions Ezana as the leader of the Aksumite realm. Epigraphic and numismatic evidence permit no doubt that he was in fact the Aksumite king who first adopted Christianity. A prominent transition from paganism to Christianity that took place during the reign of King Ezana (from ca. 330 to 365) can be traced with the help of coins. In the period 330–350 there is a shift on the coinage from pre-Christian symbols such as crescents, disks, and stalks to crosses, which reflects the conversion of the Aksumite royal court to Christianity.[15]

This transition to Christianity is also exposed in stone inscriptions made during the reign of Ezana. The surviving pre-conversion inscriptions celebrate Ezana's military campaigns and describe him as "the son of the invincible Mahrem," who was a god of war, while mentioning also three other gods, Astar, Beher, and Meder.[16] Quite different, however, are the inscriptions narrating about Ezana's campaign against the Noba (the Nubians), which must be dated to the period after his conversion to Christianity. There is a long version in Geʻez and a shorter one in Greek. Already the opening lines of a Geʻez version refer to "the Lord of heaven

---

14. The letter survives in a work by Athanasius (the *Defense to Constantius*). For the text of the letter see Szymusiak, *Athanase d'Alexandrie*, 125–26.

15. Phillipson, *Foundations of African Civilization*, 181–94.

16. Munro-Hay, *Aksum*, 226.

who in the sky and on earth holds power over all beings" and reveal his new monotheistic views.[17] In the following lines the inscription contains a highly detailed account of the campaign and attributes the success to the might of the "Lord of the Land," or the "Lord of the Heaven," or "the Lord of All," without though mentioning any particular Christian terms.[18] However, the Greek version of the same inscription, which is extant for only the first thirty-two lines, is remarkably different. Here we find already a clear Trinitarian language and multiple references of Christ. Furthermore, the whole military campaign is depicted as a humanitarian intervention with the aim to help peoples oppressed by the Nubians.

> In the faith of God and the power of the Father, Son and Holy Spirit who saved for me the kingdom, by the faith of his son Jesus Christ, who has helped me and will always help me.
>
> I, Azanas, king of the Aksumites, and Himyarites, and Reeidan and of the Sabaeans and of Sileel and of Khaso and of the Beja and of Tiamo, Bisi Alene, son of Ella Amida servant of Christ thank the Lord my God, and I am unable to state fully his favours because my mouth and my mind cannot (embrace) all the favours which he has given me, for he has given me strength and power and favoured me with a great name through his son in whom I believed. And he made me the guide of all my kingdom because of my faith in Christ by his will and in the power of Christ, for he has guided me. And I believe in him and he became to me a guide. I went out to fight the Noba because there cried out against them, the Mangartho and Khasa and Atiaditai and Bareotai saying "the Nobahave ground us down; help us because they have troubled us by killing." And I left by the power of Christ the God in whom I have believed and he has guided me.[19]

The differences between the two versions of the Noba inscription, the Greek and the Ge'ez one, reveal an important feature of the Christianization of Aksum. It seems that the expressions used in the Ge'ez version allude to the worldview of the Aksumite pre-Christian religious tradition and at the same time aim at overcoming its polytheistic core belief. Whereas the notion of "the Lord of Heaven" alludes to Astar, and the notion of "the Lord of the Land" evokes Meder, the term "the Lord of All" reminds that these are but expressions of the power of the one Lord. It was, therefore, a cautious and culturally sensitive strategy leading the Aksumites from polytheism to

---

17. Munro-Hay, *Aksum*, 227.
18. Munro-Hay, *Aksum*, 227–28.
19. Munro-Hay, *Aksum*, 229.

monotheism by reassuring them that the one God whom they must now recognize encloses all the dimensions of the individual gods that they previously worshiped. One can indeed see this inscription as a fascinating example of early inculturation of the Christian message in the Aksumite context.

At the same time, the Greek version of the inscription, highlighting the particular Christian identity of the Aksumite king and his Trinitarian belief in Father, Son, and Holy Spirit, was aimed in the first line at a Greek-speaking elite in the country and at an international audience. This inscription illustrates that Christianization of Aksum was a gradual process, first taking place at the royal court and only later reaching further parts of the population.

The Second Christianization

While the origins of Aksumite Christianity are well documented, there is much less reliable evidence for the subsequent development and organization of the local church. Even though the area where the Christian communities were established in the fourth century might have been initially limited to the largest political centers of the state, the new faith was progressing and reached as far as the coastal areas of the Red Sea on the one side and such regions as Wag and Lasta on the other side. The influence of Christianity was felt also in more remote areas, first of all around the military outposts of the Aksumites and along the trade routes. Notably, already in the fourth century, Aksumite pilgrims began to appear in Jerusalem, where Jerome of Stridon noted their presence.[20] Several fourth-century Aksumite coins that have been recently found there and in Caesarea prove these connections.[21]

It can be assumed that, after an initial period in which Greek might have been the language of the church service, during the next two centuries basic service-books, including the psalter, must have been translated into Geʻez. Penetration of Christianity into extra-urban areas most probably took place in late fifth century. This period, in which Christianity starts to spread all over the northern region of Ethiopia, is also known as "the second Christianization." In Ethiopian traditional history these developments are linked with the arrival of the so-called Nine Saints, monastic figures from the "Roman" (i.e., Byzantine) Empire. The establishment of numerous important monastic centers and churches, primarily in the northern Ethiopian region of Tigray, is attributed to them. The tradition underlines their role as missionaries who propagated the faith and translated the Bible, as well as

20. Cerulli, *Storia della comunità etiopica*, 1.
21. Barkay, "Axumite Coin from Jerusalem."

other important religious texts. Furthermore, the Nine Saints are traditionally credited with the introduction of monasticism.

Several scholars have suggested that the arrival of the Nine Saints in the Aksumite kingdom in the late fifth-century was connected with the decisions of the Council of Chalcedon.[22] This council, which took place in 451, sought to address a strong disagreement that had arisen during the first half of the fifth century between those who considered that Jesus Christ's human and divine natures were distinct and those who believed that his humanity and divinity were indistinguishable in a single nature. The council condemned the second, miaphysite position, and consequently, its adherents were persecuted by the Byzantine state. The Aksumite kingdom, which had not adopted the decisions of this council, could potentially be an attractive destination for miaphysite Christians seeking a refuge. It has to be noted that it was the compromise adopted at Chalcedon—i.e., the dyophysite position—that was the innovation; those who rejected it, the miaphysites, simply preferred to retain their earlier belief.

However, no contemporary source could provide reliable evidence as to either the real aims of the coming of the Nine Saint or their identity. A series of works of hagiography written from the fourteenth century onward, i.e., long after the events described therein, provides a much later interpretations of the facts, transmitted through a medieval cultural background. The issue of the origin of the Nine Saints has long been a matter of debate. According to their vitae, they came from different provinces of the Byzantine Empire: Rome, Constantinople, Cilicia, Antioch, Caesarea, and Egypt.[23] It was, however, generally accepted that they came from Syria. This suggestion has been intensively debated and put into question by the recent scholarship.[24]

An impressive example of early Aksumite Christian manuscript culture, the Garima Gospels, located in the monastery of Abba Garima, is associated with one of the Nine Saints. These two manuscripts, written in Geʿez, are the earliest complete copies of the Four Gospels, as well as the earliest surviving complete illuminated Christian manuscripts still extant in the world. Recent radiocarbon analysis of the manuscripts dated them as fifth to seventh century at the latest.[25]

The Geʿez literature of the fourth to seventh centuries includes an impressive corpus of works belonging to Jewish literature of the Second

22. Brita, "Nine Saints," 3:1188.
23. Brita, "Nine Saints," 3:1188.
24. Cf. Marrassini, "Some Considerations."
25. McKenzie and Watson, *Garima Gospels*.

Temple age.[26] Texts like the Ascension of Isaiah, the Book of Enoch, Jubilees, 4 Ezra, and the Book of Baruch, all translated from Greek, give us a clue about the theological orientations of the groups of Christian believers living within the kingdom of Aksum. It is thanks to the Aksumite Christians that some of these texts—banned or abandoned in other Christian contexts—have been preserved until today.

King Kaleb and the Aksumite Expansion to South Arabia

By the early sixth century, during the time of King Kaleb (also known as Ella Asbeha), who reigned from ca. 510 until 540, Aksum had become a major Christian power of the late antique world.[27] The Byzantine traveler Cosmas Indicopleustes reports that in Aksum there were "innumerable churches with bishops, large Christian communities and many martyrs and hermit monks."[28] A clear manifestation of the role of Christianity as state religion is the campaign that King Kaleb is reported to have launched against the local southern Arabian ruler Dhu Nuwas of Himyar in modern-day Yemen, who had converted to Judaism and embarked on a policy of expulsion of local Christians in the 520s, culminating in the massacre of the major Christian communities in Zafar, Tihama, and Najran.[29] The exceptional echo of the persecution in a large part of the Christian world caused the Byzantine emperor Justin, through the patriarch of Alexandria, to formally ask Kaleb, the king of Aksum, to launch a punitive military expedition against Himyar and provided him seventy ships to ferry the Aksumite forces across the Red Sea. The subsequent invasion finally ended with the complete defeat of the Himyarite king and the conquest of south Arabia by the Aksumites in 525, who then governed it for some time. While staying in Yemen, Kaleb rebuilt and constructed new churches in the most important cities of Himyar.[30]

There are a number of firsthand reports as well as more literary developed texts about Kaleb's campaign in Arabic, Syriac, Greek, and Geʿez.[31] Among the main ones is a Greek hagiographical text, the *Martyrdom of Arethas* (the alleged head of Najran), transmitted in Arabic and in Geʿez, and later on translated into a number of other languages of the Christian

26. Cf. Piovanelli, "Adventures of the Apocrypha" and "Ethiopic."
27. Fiaccadori, "Kaleb."
28. Cosmas Indicopleustes, *Topographie chrétienne*, 504–5.
29. Hatke, "Aksumites in South Arabia," 308.
30. For more details about the campaign, see Bowersock, *Throne of Adulis*.
31. Bausi, "Nagrān," 3:1115.

East, including Armenian, Georgian, and Old Slavonic. A probable echo of the martyrs of Najran can be found in the Quran (85:4–9).[32]

Kaleb's reign had a lasting impact on the Aksumite kingdom and the fate of Christianity in the larger region. Although Aksumite rule of Himyar officially ended at some point between 531 and 540, Aksumites maintained a significant presence in south Arabia.[33] Importantly, Kaleb considerably strengthened Aksumite ties with the Christian world beyond its borders.[34] According to several sources, after his return to Aksum, Kaleb sent his crown to Patriarch John III of Jerusalem to suspend on the Holy Sepulchre as a thanksgiving for his victory. Furthermore, he is said to have abdicated in order to end his life as a hermit next to his monastic mentor, Abba Pantalewon (who is considered to be one of the Nine Saints), in a mountainous area closed to Aksum.[35] The figure of Kaleb, who is considered a saint in the Ethiopian Orthodox Church, perfectly exemplifies what became a dominant feature of Aksumite—and later on Ethiopian—Christian monarchy, namely a synthesis of absolutist power and piety rooted in monastic ethos.

Conclusion: Formation of a Distinct Identity

Since the ordination of Frumentius as first bishop, the Christian church in Aksum, set up as a single bishopric, was under the spiritual authority of the Patriarchate of Alexandria (which would subsequently become the Coptic Orthodox Church). Hence, only the patriarch of Alexandria was able to appoint the bishop—or rather, metropolitan—serving as head of the Aksumite Church and being able to ordain priests and deacons. This metropolitan, locally called *abun* or *pappas*, was nearly always a Coptic monk sent from Egypt, and he was explicitly forbidden from consecrating bishops or possible successors in the Aksumite kingdom itself. It seems this custom had its advantages for both the Alexandrine patriarchs and Aksumite kings. From the point of view of the Alexandrine patriarchs, it kept the Aksumite kingdom within the sphere of influence of the See of St. Mark. The patriarch retained the right, established by Athanasius's consecration of Frumentius, to select a bishop for Aksum's metropolitan see. As far as the Aksumite ruler was concerned, this meant that he had, as the local head of the church, a foreigner, probably almost completely ignorant of the conditions prevailing in the country, and even of its language; in

32. Bausi, "Nagrān," 3:1115.
33. Hatke, "Aksumites in South Arabia," 316–21.
34. Cf. Paulau, "Introduction," 1–3.
35. Fiaccadori, "Kaleb," 3:330.

short, one whose interference in local politics was likely to be minimal, and who could offer little rivalry to the king's decrees. It is not certain when this arrangement became institutionalized, but it was later "established" by an apocryphal canon attributed to the Council of Nicea.[36]

Although the Aksumite Church was headed by a Copt and indeed in many instances of Christian doctrine and practice relied upon literary transmissions from Egypt, it developed its own distinctive characteristics and a unique identity. An emblematic figure in this regard is Yared, a sixth-century priest, who is credited with the invention of *zema*, unique Aksumite sacred music and hymnody, which is still in use in the Ethiopian and Eritrean Churches.[37]

At the same time, the Aksumite rulers themselves largely contributed to development of a unique Christian identity in their kingdom. Since the fourth century, they heavily relied upon Christianity as a means of both self-fashioning and self-legitimizing. It is therefore not surprising that some kings sought to connect their country with events and prophecies mentioned in the Bible. Already King Ezana, in his long list of titles in a bilingual inscription,[38] used the word "Ethiopia" in the Greek version as the translation for *Habashat*, the local self-designation of the Aksumite kingdom. This appropriation of the term "Ethiopia" was of paramount significance. The Septuagint, the Greek version of the Old Testament, uses the word "Ethiopia" as an equivalent for the Hebrew *Kush*, that is, the area that modern geographers refer to as Nubia (roughly equivalent to today's Sudan). There are several references to Kush in the Bible, some of which allowed even a messianic interpretation. The most hallowed of these proof texts comes from the psalter, "Let Ethiopia hasten to stretch out its hands to God" (Ps 68:31). The messianic role that the Bible regularly ascribes to "Ethiopia" afforded an attractive and ready-made way for Aksumite elites and their successors to write themselves directly into the grand narratives of biblical history. Against this background, Aksumite Christian interpreters bestowed a long and prominent tradition, beginning with Kush, grandson of Noah, on their country.[39]

Furthermore, it is possible that the central theme of later Ethiopian Christian self-understanding, the idea of Israelite descent, has already Aksumite origins. A long-discussed question in this regard concerns the genealogy of a number of ancient Israelite customs and practices that have

---

36. Munro-Hay, *Aksum*, 204.
37. Brita, "Yared," 5:27.
38. Munro-Hay, *Aksum*, 224–25.
39. Voigt, "Aithiopía," 1:163.

become a distinct marker of Christianity in the Horn of Africa. Among them are circumcision, the observance of "the first Sabbath" (i.e., Saturday) together with "the second Sabbath" (i.e., Sunday), and a series of ritual and dietary regulations, as well as the identification of their *tabotat* (altar tables) with the ark of the covenant.[40] Whereas the exact development of these practices is still being debated, there is a wide scholarly consensus that at least some of them go back to the Aksumite times.[41]

By the seventh century, the power of the Aksumite kingdom had weakened considerably.[42] Aksum's role in Red Sea trade was long held to have suffered from political shifts caused by the expansion of the Muslim Empire in Arabia, the Eastern Mediterranean, and Egypt in the 640s. However, despite the decline of Aksum, Christian states persisted in the Ethiopian and Eritrean highlands. In particular, monasteries were able to withstand the political upheaval and continue to function. Monastic networks, made up of small, autonomous centers, were more resilient to historical disruptions. They could preserve the distinct Christian Aksumite identity, which became foundational for the revival of Christian kingship in the medieval period.

This specific Aksumite identity found its most profound articulation in the highly influential medieval treaties *Kebra Nagast* (Glory [or Nobility] of the kings)[43] that substantiated the claim of *translation imperii* from ancient Israel to Aksum in a twofold way: first, by creating a genealogical link of the Aksumite monarchy with Solomon, king of Israel, and the queen of Sheba; and second, by putting forward an elaborate narrative about the transfer of the ark of the covenant from Jerusalem to Aksum, which in its turn was interpreted as a visible sign of the divine election of the Ethiopians as God's new chosen people. Consequently, the idea of the superiority of the Christian Ethiopian kingship was inseparably bound to the monarch's claim for Zion, i.e., the ark of the covenant preserved in, and ultimately identified with, Aksum. Thus, even after its political decline in the seventh century, Aksum remained an important spiritual and symbolic center of Christianity in sub-Saharan Africa.

---

40. Cf. Ullendorff, *Ethiopia and the Bible*; Munro-Hay, *Ethiopia*, 13–68 and 159–73; Rodinson, "Question of 'Jewish Influences'"; Schattner-Rieser, "Empreintes bibliques."

41. Piovanelli, "Jewish Christianity."

42. Lusini, "Decline and Collapse."

43. Marrassini, "Kebrä Nägäst."

Bibliography

Barkay, R. "An Axumite Coin from Jerusalem." *Israel Numismatic Journal* 5 (1981) 57–59.
Bausi, Alessandro. "Nagrān." In *Encyclopaedia Aethiopica*, edited by Siegbert Uhlig, 3:1114–16. Wiesbaden: Harrassowitz, 2007.
Bowersock, Glen W. *The Throne of Adulis: Red Sea Wars on the Eve of Islam*. Oxford: Oxford University Press, 2013.
Brita, Antonella. "Nine Saints." In *Encyclopaedia Aethiopica*, edited by Siegbert Uhlig, 3:1188–91. Wiesbaden: Harrassowitz, 2007.
———. "Yared." In *Encyclopaedia Aethiopica*, edited by Alessandro Bausi, 5:26–28. Wiesbaden: Harrassowitz, 2014.
Casson, Lionell. *The Periplus Maris Erythraei: Text with Introduction, Translation, and Commentary*. Princeton: Princeton University Press, 1989.
Cerulli, Enrico. *Storia della comunità etiopica di Gerusalemme*. Vol. 1 of *Etiopi in Palestina*. Rome: Stato, 1943.
Cosmas Indicopleustes. *Topographie chrétienne*. Edited and translated by Wanda Wolska-Conus. Vol. 1. Paris: Cerf, 1968.
Esler, Philip F. *Ethiopian Christianity: History, Theology, Practice*. Waco: Baylor University Press, 2019.
Fiaccadori, Gianfranco. "Kaleb." In *Encyclopaedia Aethiopica*, edited by Siegbert Uhlig, 3:329–32. Wiesbaden: Harrassowitz, 2007.
Gardner, Iain. *The Kephalaia of the Teacher: The Edited Coptic Manichaean Texts in Translation with Commentary*. Nag Hammadi and Manichaean Studies 37. Leiden: Brill, 1995.
Gelasius of Caesarea. *Ecclesiastical History: The Extant Fragments with an Appendix Containing the Fragments from Dogmatic Writings*. Edited by Martin Wallraff et al. Translated by Nicholas Marinides. Die griechischen christlichen Schriftsteller der ersten Jahrhunderte 25. Berlin: De Gruyter, 2018.
Haile, Getatchew. "The Homily in Honour of St. Frumentius Bishop of Axum (EMML 1763 ff. 85v–86r)." *Analecta Bollandiana* 97 (1979) 309–18.
Hatke, George. "The Aksumites in South Arabia: An African Diaspora of Late Antiquity." In *Migration Histories of the Medieval Afroeurasian Transition Zone: Aspects of Mobility between Africa, Asia and Europe, 300–1500 C. E.*, edited by Johannes Preiser-Kapeller et al., Studies in Global Social History 39, Studies in Global Migration History 39, 291–326. Leiden: Brill, 2020.
Lusini, Gianfrancesco. "The Decline and Collapse of the Kingdom of Aksum (6th–7th CE): An Environmental Disaster or the End of a Political Process?" In *The End of Empires*, edited by Michael Gehler et al., Universal- und kulturhistorische Studien—Studies in Universal and Cultural History, 321–36. Wiesbaden: Springer, 2022.
Marrassini, Paolo. "Kebrä Nägäst." In *Encyclopaedia Aethiopica*, edited by Siegbert Uhlig, 3:364–68. Wiesbaden: Harrassowitz, 2007.
———. "Some Considerations on the Problem of the 'Syriac Influences' on Aksumite Ethiopia." *Journal of Ethiopian Studies* 23 (1990) 35–46.
McKenzie, Judith S., and Francis Watson. *The Garima Gospels: Early Illuminated Books from Ethiopia*. Oxford: Manar al-Athar, 2016.

Munro-Hay, Stuart C. *Aksum: An African Civilisation of Late Antiquity.* Edinburgh: Edinburgh University Press, 1991.

———. *Ethiopia: Judaism, Altars and Saints.* Hollywood, CA: Tsehai, 2006.

Paulau, Stanislau. "Introduction: Placing Ethiopian Orthodox Christianity into a Global Context." In *Ethiopian Orthodox Christianity in a Global Context: Entanglements and Disconnections,* edited by Stanislau Paulau and Martin Tamcke, Texts and Studies in Eastern Christianity 24, 1–13. Leiden: Brill, 2022.

Phillipson, David W. *Foundations of an African Civilization: Aksum & the Northern Horn 1000 BC–AD 1300.* Woodbridge, UK: Currey, 2014.

Piovanelli, Pierluigi. "The Adventures of the Apocrypha in Ethiopia." In *Languages and Cultures of Eastern Christianity: Ethiopian,* edited by Alessandro Bausi, The Worlds of Eastern Christianity 300–1500, 87–109. Farnham, UK: Ashgate, 2012.

———. "Ethiopic." In *A Guide to Early Jewish Texts and Traditions in Christian Transmission,* edited by Alexander Kulik, 35–47. Oxford: Oxford University Press, 2019.

———. "Jewish Christianity in Late Antique Aksum and Ḥimyar? A Reassessment of the Evidence and a New Proposal." *Judaïsme ancien—Ancient Judaism* 6 (2018) 175–202.

Rodinson, Maxime. "On the Question of 'Jewish Influences' in Ethiopia." In *Languages and Cultures of Eastern Christianity: Ethiopian,* edited by Alessandro Bausi, The Worlds of Eastern Christianity 300–1500, 179–86. Farnham, UK: Ashgate, 2012.

Rufinus of Aquileia. *History of the Church.* Translated by Philip R. Amidon. Washington, DC: Catholic University of America Press, 2016.

Schattner-Rieser, Ursula. "Empreintes bibliques et emprunts juifs dans la culture éthiopienne." *Journal of Eastern Christian Studies* 64 (2012) 5–28.

Szymusiak, Jan-Maria. *Athanase d'Alexandrie: Apologie a l'Empereur Constance; Apologie pour safuite; Introduction, texte critique, traduction et notes.* Paris: Cerf, 1958.

Ullendorff, Edward. *Ethiopia and the Bible.* Oxford: Oxford University Press, 1968.

Voigt, Rainer. "Aithiopía." In *Encyclopaedia Aethiopica,* edited by Siegbert Uhlig, 1:162–66. Wiesbaden: Harrassowitz, 2003.

3

European Pioneers to Tropical Africa

Fohle Lygunda li-M

Setting the Geographical and Historical Contexts

THE HISTORY OF AFRICAN Christianity in tropical Africa is considered here from the perspective of the evangelization movements led by Europeans from the fifteenth century. The concept of "tropical Africa" is sometimes confusing and requires some reframing to avoid misunderstanding in the delimitation of this chapter. Tropical Africa simply means the part of Africa located between the Sahara and equatorial Africa to the north, and between South Africa and equatorial Africa to the south, characterized by an important savannah and a cold rainy season. It is bounded on the southwest by the Atlantic Ocean and on the southeast by the Indian Ocean.

The evangelization movement in tropical Africa generally comprises two phases, that of the fifteenth century with the exploratory movements and that of the nineteenth century with the missionary movements. This chapter deals with the European pioneers in these two phases divided into three following periods. The first period (1482–1792) is that of explorations under Portuguese leadership, including the dark period of the slave trade until the missionary revival of the eighteenth century often attributed to William Carey. The second period (1792–1885) starts from the beginning of what Kenneth Scott Latourette describes as the century of mission until the historic conference in Berlin, Germany (Nov. 15, 1884, to Feb. 26, 1885).[1] The third period (1885–1910) covers the period after the Berlin Conference until the beginning of the twentieth century, marked by the Edinburgh Conference in Scotland of June 14–21, 1910. In any case, each of these periods was very decisive in the evangelization (even Christianization) of part of tropical

---

1. Latourette, *Great Century*, vii.

Africa. The discovery of pioneering works in each period will allow us to clearly identify lessons for our time and milestones for the future.

The Pioneers of 1482–1792

It is true that the evangelization of the continent from the fifteenth century onwards was due to the wave of explorations in which Portugal took the lead, with Diego Cao as the figurehead, for having discovered the mouth of the Congo River in 1482. The king of Portugal, who had somewhat hegemonic appetites, could use only his aura to engage in an expansionist drive. He sent explorers to the Atlantic Coast to discover the new world. Being Catholic, the king made Portugal a Catholic country, and the missionaries could be only Catholic. Thus, the first Capuchin missionaries headed to the West Coast of the African continent, precisely to the Kongo kingdom, at the request of King Nzinga. They arrived in 1490 and were accompanied by builders who constructed Mbanza Kongo, the capital of the kingdom, located in the north of present-day Angola. King Nzinga was thus baptized. His son, Afonso, was sent to Portugal for his studies.

It is important to note, however, that the Portuguese were not the only ones to spread Christianity in Africa. The Spaniards, Germans, and Dutch were also involved.[2] The Dutch, who were treated as Protestant heretics by the Portuguese (generally Catholic),[3] arrived in Angola in 1641. With the entry of the Dutch into the slave trade, the inhabitants of Soyo became more attached to them and developed trade with these newcomers. The kingdom disintegrated in 1665, giving rise to two capitals, Mbanza Kongo (a little closer to the current DRC) and Mbanza Soyo (a little closer to the current Angola).

The Capuchin missionaries, however, had a disagreement with the elite of the Soyo Empire about the sale of black slaves.[4] The missionaries refused to allow baptized slaves to be sold to English or other non-Christian merchants. For them, only Portuguese merchants (usually Catholic) had the right to do so. It should also be noted that the Portuguese had advanced to the south of the continent, to the Cape of Good Hope.

The missionary work during this period was not successful in the long run. The natives were almost abandoned after embracing the white man's religion. It was in this context that a twenty-one-year-old girl, Donna Beatrice, appeared as a prophetess clothed with the power of St. Anthony,

2. Adogame et al., *Christianity in Africa*, 53–59.
3. Sundkler and Steed, *History of the Church*, 63.
4. Sundkler and Steed, *History of the Church*, 56–58.

which the Capuchin priests also spoke of. She performed miracles of healing and preached against fetishes, asking people to abandon them and burn them. This spirituality led her to openly defy the king by asking the people to return to Sao Salvador. In response, the king and his council, supported by the Capuchin priests who considered her a heretic, decided to burn her and her companions alive on July 2, 1706.[5]

To the south, still along the Indian Ocean, a group of 126 Dutch led by Jan van Riebeck, who became their governor, settled among the Khoikhoi people in 1652, becoming a "symbol of good will. The natives were to be free with the right to wages in return for their services. Because of her linguistic prowess, a young girl, Eva, from the Khoikhoi group served as interpreter. Mrs. Van Riebeck taught her Christianity and she became the first indigenous Christian person in South Africa. She was baptized, and also taught her sister how to pray."[6]

The intentional missionary program of the Protestants was the work of a small community in northern Germany, the Moravians, who sent missionaries to many parts of the world, including South Africa. These missionaries passed through Holland to join the other Moravian community there in order to travel together to South Africa. One of them, George Schmidt (1709–85), arrived in Cape Town in 1737 to work among the Khoikhoi. Seven years later, he was driven out by Dutch Reformed preachers, being accused of being a heretic. He moved to the district of Swellendam (later Genadendal), still among the Khoikhoi. The contacts with his leadership in Europe were not easy, and because he was able to gather only twenty-eight people, Schmidt was consecrated through an official letter through an official letter dated August 27, 1741. He baptized at least five of them, but without using the catechumenate document of the Reformed Church. Thus, he was accused of being a heretic, in addition to the fact that the river in which he baptized the people did not belong to him. Therefore, all the baptisms he administered were simply cancelled and Schmidt was sent back to Europe. But before leaving, he gave his New Testament (Dutch version) to Magdalena, one of the converts.[7]

As we can see, the missionary movements followed the route of the Portuguese explorers who had not limited themselves to the west or the south. They had continued eastward to the Indian Ocean. Vasco da Gama arrived there already in 1497. In 1505, Portuguese merchants occupied the port of Sofala. From then on, Dominican and Jesuit priests marked their

---

5. Sundkler and Steed, *History of the Church*, 60.
6. Sundkler and Steed, *History of the Church*, 64.
7. Sundkler and Steed, *History of the Church*, 67.

presence from 1541 on the Indian Ocean coast to Mozambique. In the north, along the ocean, the presence of Catholics was noted in 1597 towards Lamu and Mombasa, in present-day Kenya. The same discussion about the sale of baptized slaves broke out with the Arabs. For the Portuguese and the priests, baptized slaves should not be sold to the Arabs, lest they be denied the door to heaven, it was said.[8] The affront benefited the Arabs who ended up occupying this eastern part of the continent in 1729.

This stage of the evangelization of Africa was somewhat ephemeral. Some authors attribute this state of affairs to several reasons, including the following five: (1) missionaries had concentrated only around the coastal part of the continent, focusing on the elite rather than all the people; (2) there were not enough funds for mission; (3) many missionaries could not accommodate the climatic conditions and the local political situation; (4) there was a common belief in many places in Europe that there was no need to convert Africans; and (5) there was an emphasis on economic interest rather than concern for the salvation of souls.[9] Until the end of the eighteenth century, the need and the task of establishing Christianity on the continent were still unfulfilled.

The Pioneers of 1792–1885

The missionary impulse of the previous period, essentially Catholic, was interrupted for several reasons, including the lack of local roots of the gospel in most places. In any case, the sixteenth and seventeenth centuries were in some ways a period of missionary silence, mainly because of the influence of liberalism in Europe and the slave trade on the African continent. The vision of the young English Baptist pastor William Carey (1761–1834), to see the Baptist Church engage in mission to the Indians, gave impetus to the missionary movements of the seventeenth and nineteenth centuries. From the missionary mobilization of William Carey in 1792, the Baptist Church of England set up a missionary society called the Baptist Missionary Society (BMS), which deployed its first missionary to India. This zeal for the evangelization of distant peoples gave impetus to missionary movements that went beyond India and the Baptist Church.

Thus, several other missionary societies, denominational and nondenominational, came into being, including the London Missionary Society (LMS, 1795), the Dutch Missionary Society (1797), the Church Missionary Society (CMS) of the Anglican Church (1799), the American Committee on

8. Sundkler and Steed, *History of the Church*, 68.
9. Adogame et al., *Christianity in Africa*, 11.

Foreign Missions (1810), Methodists (1813), Basel Missions (1815), Paris Missions (1822), Berlin Missions (1824), Scottish Presbyterians (1825), Swedish Missions (1835), German Lutherans (1836), North German Missions (1836), and Norwegian Missions (1842).[10] Many of these missionary societies were also active in Africa.

Therefore, it was evident that in the midst of the slave trade, many of these missionary societies sent missionaries to Africa, especially along the coastal part towards both the Indian Ocean, east and south, and along the Atlantic Ocean, west and south. It is important to note that this period comes before the Berlin Conference, which will have direct implications on the missionary movements. We will come back to this later.

The South Coast

The African continent in this period was first visited by European missionaries, mainly Catholics from France and Italy, almost everywhere on the continent.[11] The Protestants spread first from the south. The Indian Ocean on the southern side of Africa served as a gateway to the gospel through missionary initiatives from Germany. It is reported, for example, that between 1800 and 1827 the Berlin mission sent about eighty missionaries to West and South Africa.[12]

One of the leading figures was the Scotsman Robert Moffat (1795–1883) who arrived in Cape Town in January 1817 via Stellenbosch where he learned Dutch. He translated the Bible into Setswana. Another important figure, Moffat's son-in-law, was David Livingstone (1813–73), a Scottish physician who was also known as an explorer, geographer, and human rights fighter in his fight against slavery, but also as a preacher of the gospel. At a time when there was still a great debate about the relevance of doctors on the mission field, David Livingstone joined Robert Moffat's hospital established since 1941 in Kuruman, South Africa. According to Moffat's report, Livingstone's ministry was so successful that he was besieged by many patients seeking healing.[13] However, Livingstone was concerned that this medical work was drowning out the work of proclaiming the gospel to the point that he felt less useful for the conversion of souls, a priority activity for the missionary societies of his day. Indeed, he encouraged young doctors to use their profession at the bedside as a good opportunity to proclaim the gospel following

10. Sundkler and Steed, *History of the Church*, 110–16.
11. Sundkler and Steed, *History of the Church*, 100.
12. Adogame et al., *Christianity in Africa*, 12.
13. Hardiman, *Healing Bodies*, 13.

the model of the Great Physician, Jesus Christ. Beginning in the 1870s, the missionary vocation of physicians gained momentum because it was finally argued that among the pagan peoples of Africa, India, and China, religion and healing went hand in hand in the religious worldview. The missionary vocation of physicians was thus encouraged.

Livingstone's stay in Kuruman was short lived. He decided to start exploring the interior of the continent and to fight against slavery. Thus, he headed for Central and East Africa on the side of Lake Tanganyika at the crossroads of the present-day region between the Democratic Republic of the Congo (DRC), Burundi, and Tanzania. The British journalist Henry M. Stanley discovered him there in 1876.

The West Coast

Already in 1800, the missionary presence was noted in West Africa, but the work of the Anglican mission (CMS) flourished only with the arrival of the German Gustav Nylander in 1806 in Sierra Leone.[14] Around 1830, the Basler Mission targeted the Gold Coast (Ghana) with an abolitionist, i.e., anti-colonial, ideal, although its missionaries were obliged to collaborate with the colonial regime in place.[15]

In the midst of the African slave trade, the BMS launched a missionary work among the slaves of Jamaica in 1813.[16] These slaves were sold across the Atlantic Ocean from Africa. It is important to remember that the English Bill of 1807, which abolished the practice of slavery, did not come into effect until the reign of Queen Victoria in 1838. This law put an end to the slave trade. Being thus free and wanting to evangelize their countries of origin, the converted slaves formed the Jamaican Baptist Missionary Society, founded in 1842, and deployed several hundred missionaries in Africa, particularly in Cameroon. It is interesting to note that the first Protestant missionaries on the Atlantic Coast of the continent were freed former slaves from Jamaica. Two names are usually mentioned, namely Pastor Joseph Merrick and John Clark who arrived in Cameroon in 1841. Their objective was to preach the good news to the black brothers and sisters who, to some degree, were still suffering from the practice of slavery at the hands of certain kings and other wealthy natives.[17]

---

14. Adogame et al., *Christianity in Africa*, 12.
15. Messina and Van Slageren, *Histoire du christianisme*, 37.
16. Messina and Van Slageren, *Histoire du christianisme*, 27.
17. Messina and Van Slageren, *Histoire du christianisme*, 27–29.

Joseph Merrick was not only interested in the verbal proclamation of the gospel; he was also involved in teaching and literature. He was convinced that the work of evangelization should not be done only by missionaries from abroad. It was therefore necessary to train the natives to read the Bible. To do this, schools, a printing press, and a Bible translation program had to be established. In Bimba, also in Cameroon, Joseph Merrick moved into an old slave building that still bore visible signs of cruel actions, but he transformed it with a new spirit of humanity, peace, and justice. This was his way of intervening in social and political life. He made friends with the king of Bimba who helped him to open a school. He contacted the people to learn the local language, Isubu, a Bantu language into which he translated several books of the Bible, notably Genesis and Exodus (in 1844), the Gospel of John (in 1845), and the Gospel of Matthew (in 1846). At his death in England in 1852, he left manuscripts of the Acts of the Apostles and the Epistle to the Romans.[18]

During his lifetime, he had two companions, first John Jackson Fuller, a young evangelist who joined him in 1844. Fuller owed his pastoral training to Merrick even though he was not yet qualified to baptize new believers. With the arrival of Alfred Saker of the BMS of England, Saker became the head of the mission and consecrated Fuller to the pastoral ministry in 1859.

The East Coast

In twenty-six years (1863–88), seven missionary societies were established in East Africa, inspired by the work of two missionaries, Johann Ludvig Krapf and David Livingstone. Krapf was a German citizen, serving as a Lutheran missionary but employed by the Anglican mission (CMS). He traveled to many parts of East Africa between 1844 and 1853 because of his vision of establishing a chain of mission stations everywhere. Livingstone, on the other hand, proposed to proclaim the gospel while fighting the slave trade. We will come back to this in the next section.

It is important to note that along the Indian Ocean, in Tanzania and Zanzibar, Catholic missions (French-speaking to Madagascar and English-speaking to Tanzania) were predominant. The Protestants, through Berlin Missions and the CMS, invaded the whole region from 1887 onwards.[19]

---

18. Messina and Van Slageren, *Histoire du christianisme*, 32.
19. Sundkler and Steed, *History of the Church*, 526–28.

The Interior of the Continent

The Universities' Mission to Central Africa (UMCA) was founded in 1858 as a direct result of David Livingstone's alarming speech to the British Senate in Cambridge on December 4, 1857.[20] This Anglican mission worked in north Rhodesia, now Zambia, in places where there were no other missions. The missionaries of UMCA lived a life of solitude, having been encouraged twenty-five years after its founding to take a vow of celibacy. This allowed the missionaries to move easily from one village to another, a task they were expected to fulfil faithfully. They did not have family members to accompany them in the missionary work. Another argument was that the climate and living conditions were not conducive to brides and children, and that their care would be an additional and less necessary burden on the mission budget.[21] To this end, the most sought-after missionaries were priests (pastors), as well as teachers, in view of the importance placed on teaching rather than medical work. Since the medical work was not overly important, it could only suffer from a lack of financial support. It eventually became the field of action of the women (nurses), and the budget allocated to it could be reduced or eliminated at any time in favor of other missionary activities.

The harmony within UMCA suffered, because after all, some people who were married could join the mission with special permission from the bishop. This was the case with the Anglican priest Moffat and the nurse Gladys Salisbury who were stationed in Mapanza and decided to get married in 1915.[22] On the one hand, in practical life, married missionaries were not well regarded by those who were attached to the vow of celibacy. On the other hand, no precautions were taken to ensure the protection of people of the same or opposite sex who were subject to community life. Therefore, some people suggested that the bishop should not accept women (unmarried, of course) in the mission. Since the medical work had become more the domain of women, this aspect of the mission suffered. As time went on, the cohabitation between priests and nurses, members of the same missionary society, was not easy.[23]

Missionary efforts in the interior of the continent were carried out by David Livingstone, but also by several other missionary societies thanks to the report made by the journalist Henry M. Stanley after his meeting with Livingstone. On the one hand, Livingstone traveled much of the interior of

---

20. Kumwenda, "African Medical Personnel," 195.
21. Kumwenda, "African Medical Personnel," 195.
22. Kumwenda, "African Medical Personnel," 197.
23. Kumwenda, "African Medical Personnel," 197–99.

the continent, healing the sick, preaching the gospel, and learning about the geography of the continent. These efforts were echoed to a level until Livingstone ceased to be heard from. Stanley, who went in search of him, finally met him on the plain of Ujiji, along the shores of Lake Tanganyika, near the present-day city of Bujumbura, in November 1871. On his way back, along the Congo River, he was impressed by the wealth of the country and the navigability of the river. He began to spread this information worldwide, attracting the curiosity and desire of missionary societies. Thus, the Baptist missionaries based in Cameroon, George Grenfell and his friend, arrived in the Congo on an exploratory visit in January 1878 before returning to settle there in June of the same year.[24] For his part, British evangelist Henry Grattan Guinness established a nondenominational missionary society, Livingstone Inland Mission (LIM), in 1877, in response to Stanley's call. The first LIM missionaries arrived in the Congo in February 1878 and settled there immediately. In spite of all the difficulties encountered by some on the mission field, the reality is also that during this period Christianity spread in many places. One of the contributing factors was the spirit of cooperation between the missions, especially through interdenominational missionary societies. German missionaries could serve in the Anglican Church or in the Anglican mission, the CMS.

The Pioneers of 1885–1910

This period was marked at the beginning by the Berlin Conference, which divided the continent among the Western powers like a cake on a plate. Due to its root cause of sharing European colonization and trade, this conference was also known as the Congo Conference or the West Africa Conference during Germany's sudden emergence as an imperial power. This event is very critical in the history of Christianity in Africa because it inaugurated a change in the landscape of missionary work. If until that time missionary societies could work in different places and collaborate despite their origins, the Berlin Conference made missionary societies attached to the places colonized by their countries of origin. Thus, the Anglican missions were concentrated in the countries assigned to the English, the Dutch Reformed in the south, the Presbyterians in the English-speaking countries of the West, the Lutherans in the countries assigned to the Germans, the Baptists in the countries assigned to the English, etc. As a result, missionary societies established in a geographical area before the Berlin Conference were forced to leave the place and abandon it, on the

24. Messina and Van Slageren, *Histoire du christianisme*, 35.

grounds that their countries of origin were not masters of those countries or places. Missionary work was thus facilitated by patriotic belonging and sometimes assimilated to the colonization mission.[25]

Therefore, the pioneers of this period are to be identified on a case-by-case basis, a difficult exercise to do in the framework of this very limited work. However, it is important to indicate here the three categories targeted by the missionaries in this period.[26] The first category was that of the kings and chiefs of the villages. The identification of, or better still the comparison between, the missionary work and that of colonization could only facilitate the task. But this approach was not always a real evangelical success because conversions in such a context were more influenced by a motive of appearance. The second category was that of young people, especially young men. This was the trend among both Catholics and Protestants. Therefore, the ministry of school education was of great importance. Finally, the third category was that of the freed slaves, especially in the coastal regions. This category was more extensive during the previous period (with the abolition of the slave trade in 1809), a period that saw the involvement of missions initiated by Afro-descendants.

Afro-Descendant Pioneers

Daniel Abwa proposes to write and teach the history of the vanquished for an Africa that wins.[27] Of course, the history of the victors often reflects only the misfortune of the vanquished, obscuring any details that might celebrate their acts of bravery and other heroic deeds. Rereading or rewriting history from this perspective helps to understand the persistent misfortune of ignoring the contribution of blacks to the global mission.

For example, the history books in circulation are almost unanimous on the fact that the missionary enterprise would have been the result of white initiatives and that whites would thus have been the primary inspirers. Thus, the British Baptist minister William Carey has often been hailed as the father of modern missions. It is said and believed that apart from God, who has been recognized since the Willingen conference in 1952 as the initiator par excellence of missionary work, William Carey was the first human being of the eighteenth century to deserve such an honor. For the fact that in 1792 he proposed to his London Baptist church that they go on a foreign mission to India to save thousands of people who were dying without Christ, he was the

---

25. Adogame et al., *Christianity in Africa*, 9.
26. Sundkler and Steed, *History of the Church*, 85–90.
27. Abwa, *Écrire et enseigner*, 5.

father of modern missions. This impulse from England would have been the basis of the missionary craze known in the nineteenth century, which was described by the American historian Kenneth Scott Latourette as the great missions century. All historical mission books in circulation hold this information as the truth to be popularized in theological and other institutions.

The same is true in almost every mission field where the names of Western missionaries have been brought to the forefront, if not the center, of mission activities. The written and transmitted history often mentions only the Western missionaries, usually leaving unmentioned the various and sometimes indispensable contributions of the African natives. The *Dictionary of African Christian Biography* lauds this with great amazement by showing the various contributions of African men and women to the expansion of Christianity in Africa and outside the continent.[28]

Undoubtedly, the historical writings produced by the missionaries also served as marketing tools to attract and secure support (material, financial, and spiritual) for their ministries on the mission field. Their brave deeds as well as their sufferings endured in the name of the gospel sometimes had to be publicized in order to attract and maintain the sympathy of donors. The experiences of the natives both in terms of their achievements and sacrifices were curiously obscured. In any case, it could not be otherwise insofar as the history of the vanquished could not be written by the victors except to place them in the status of pitiful people to be civilized or humanized. Thus, it is customary in many training institutions in Africa to subject the vanquished (Africans) to the history of the victors (Westerners), thus making them accustomed to ignoring their own true history and to disregarding any attempt to revisit their history.

Two examples can be cited here, that of the black pastor George Liele (1750–1820) and Bishop Samuel Ajayi Crowther (1807–91). Historically speaking, George Liele, and not the English pastor William Carey, would be the father of modern missions, and the missionary zeal of the late eighteenth century would have started with the defeated rather than the victors. The *missio Dei* entrusted to the church is not realized first and foremost by strong human beings but rather by weak people who allow themselves to be abandoned into the hands of the Almighty God. This is the truth that emerges from the story of George Liele, the founder of the first black Baptist church in the United States and the first Protestant missionary in Jamaica,[29] the common ancestor of Protestantism in Cameroon (1841) and in the DRC (1878).

28. See www.dacb.org.
29. Kamta, "Mission chrétienne."

The same is true of Samuel Crowther, a Yoruba from Nigeria, who was captured and sold into slavery to the Portuguese at the age of twelve.[30] He was soon freed and taken to Sierra Leone, where he was converted in 1825. He studied at Fourah Bay College in Freetown, and his interest in languages (Latin, Greek, and African languages) led him to undertake the translation of the Bible into his native Yoruba in 1851. With his team, he completed the New Testament in 1862 and the whole Bible in 1884. Even before that, he visited England several times and became a pastor of the Anglican Church. He took part in expeditions to the interior of Africa, expeditions that had as their goal exploration and the establishment of trading posts, but also evangelization.

Such people, both men and women, originating from Africa, have marked the history of Europe's contact with Africa, as well as Africa's contact with Christianity.[31] As noted here and there in this chapter, many of them also served as pioneers in various parts of Africa.

For Future Historical Accounts of Christianity in Tropical Africa

In light of the above, several questions and concerns can be raised about the true nature of what can still be referred to as "Protestantism," including those related to its symbol, doctrines, practices, and pioneers in tropical Africa. In fact, it is rather a mosaic of aspects of Christianity as they have been perceived by some and others, considering their various spatial and temporal contexts. As proof, we can already see several Reformist currents in Martin Luther, John Calvin, Ulrich Zwingli, etc. Each person had his own perception of the church or of Christianity. As a proof, these different currents were in antagonism against each other. One can, without exaggeration, call these different currents "sects of Protestantism" known under the politically elaborate names of Lutheran, Reformed, Presbyterian, Baptist, Mennonite, Anglican, Methodist, etc.

Thanks to the missionary movements of the nineteenth century, many other sects of Protestantism were added to the list. These new currents are offshoots of those that came directly from the sixteenth-century Reformation. These offshoots are linked to the experiences of certain dissident or disbanded groups of these other groups. Thus, we speak of several types of churches: Lutheran (Evangelical, Wisconsin, Apostolic,

---

30. Kenmogne and Zogbo, *Traduction de la Bible*, 107; Sundkler and Steed, *History of the Church*, 225–29.

31. Sundkler and Steed, *History of the Church*, 120–23.

etc.), Methodist (Afro-Zion, Episcopalian, Wesleyan, United, Free, etc.), Baptist (Full Gospel, Southern, Cooperative, etc.), Protestant (Lutheran), Presbyterian (Calvinistic Reformed, Evangelical, American, Revival, Australian, etc.), Mennonite (Conservative, Brethren, Old Order, etc.), Free Church, Covenant Church, etc.

One can see through these second-wave groupings and denominations their attachment to the names of people, groups of people, or geographical locations that interpret the Bible in their own way regarding the nature, mission, and organization of the church according to their historical and geographical contexts.

The third wave of sects of Protestantism appears on the mission field. For example, in Africa, one can see churches formed by missionaries. In this group, we can identify those that emanate from interdenominational missions, formed by missionaries from different denominations or even countries. We can also see churches that come from divisions (and conflicts) between missionaries on the mission field, each missionary going to form his own new denomination that he may or may not attach to a church or association of churches in his country of origin. Many of these churches (or denominations) may bear traditional epithets (Methodist, Baptist, Evangelical, Covenant, Presbyterian, Mennonite, Lutheran, etc.) without really being carbon copies in terms of teaching, faith practice, and church governance.

After these first three waves comes the fourth wave of sects of Protestantism, consisting of churches initiated by Africans either because of dissension or because of a personal call to start a church planting movement independent of the original church (or denomination). These are initially non-aligned churches, but some end up integrating into existing larger groups. In the case of the DRC, for example, some of these churches join the Church of Christ in Congo (ECC), others join the association of revivalist churches, and still others remain non-aligned. So it is amazing to hear people say, "We are Protestants" or "We are not Protestants."

Today, notions of church, Christianity, Protestantism, and mission are no longer simplistic, but rather complex. Likewise, the related notion of "pioneer" is no longer simplistic but rather complex. It is safe to say that the ecclesiology taught in our theological faculties in Africa according to the old twentieth-century pattern is a mere theoretical and academic exercise that no longer provides practicality for the reality of Christianity today.

Conclusion

The evangelization of tropical Africa owes much to the men and women, European and American citizens, who decided to brave all kinds of difficulties to take the gospel of Jesus Christ to the Africans located in the geographical area selected in this chapter. In their book on the history of Christianity in Africa, Bengt Sundkler and Christopher Steed have shown that in the nineteenth century, many of the missionaries sent to Africa, both to the coastal regions and to the interior of the continent, were young people between the ages of twelve and twenty-six.[32] While some of the missionaries survived the vagaries of the climate and deadly diseases caused by mosquitoes, tsetse flies, snake bites, and the like, many simply paid with their lives. It is in this perspective that some authors speak of Africa as the tomb of the missionaries, some of whom died in the same week they arrived on the continent.

This chapter has also brought to light the other aspect of mission, often neglected in many historical accounts of mission, namely the contribution of blacks in the diaspora and those who remained on the continent. Speaking of the evangelization of the West Coast, it has been pointed out that the first missionaries were former slaves who came from Jamaica as early as 1841. Several hundred missionaries from across the Atlantic invaded the western part of the continent to proclaim the gospel of salvation, peace, and justice. Unfortunately, because of the Berlin Conference, which allowed the European colonists to divide Africa like a cake, all the contributions of these African descendants have been elided. As some authors have shown, this conference even played a serious blow to missionary work and Christian witness by sowing division between missions that had once worked together. This conference also caused the evangelization of Africa to take place against the background of colonial cartography, making de facto Catholic or Protestant Christian states.[33]

The same is true of the contributions of Africans living on the continent who participated in the evangelization of nooks and crannies of the continent, often where Western missionaries could not go. Their names are not often found in many mission history books, even though they were at the forefront of the proclamation of the gospel and the expansion of Christianity in Africa. They are ignored pioneers. A few names have been mentioned only in passing, since the chapter was about European pioneers in Africa. Justice would be done to them by devoting a chapter to the contribution of

---

32. Sundkler and Steed, *History of the Church*, 109-10.
33. Adogame et al., *Christianity in Africa*, 9-17.

African pioneers (those of the diaspora and those living on the continent) to the expansion of Christianity in Africa.

Bibliography

Abwa, Daniel. *Écrire et enseigner une histoire des vaincus pour une Afrique qui gagne.* Yaoundé: CLÉ, 2020.
Adogame, Afe, et al, eds. *Christianity in Africa and the African Diaspora: The Appropriation of a Scattered Heritage.* Continuum Religious Studies. London: Continuum, 2011.
Dictionary of African Christian Biography. www.dacb.org.
Hardiman, David, ed. *Healing Bodies, Saving Souls: Medical Missions in Asia and Africa.* Clio Medica 80. Wellcome Series in the History of Medicine 80. New York: Rodopi, 2006.
Kamta, Isaac Makarios. "Mission chrétienne en Afrique, entreprise africaine?" In *Histoire du christianisme: Quelques éléments,* edited by Ekom Dake Trimua, 131–46. Yaoundé: CLÉ, 2006.
Kenmogne, Michel, and Lynell Zogbo, eds. *La traduction de la Bible et l'église: Enjeux et défis pour l'Afrique francophone.* Yaoundé: CLÉ, 2006.
Kumwenda, Linda Beer. "African Medical Personnel of the Universities' Mission to Central Africa in Northern Rhodesia." In *Healing Bodies, Saving Souls: Medical Missions in Asia and Africa,* edited by David Hardiman, Clio Medica 80, Wellcome Series in the History of Medicine 80, 193–250. New York: Rodopi BV, 2006.
Latourette, Kenneth Scott. *The Great Century, A.D. 1800–1914: Europe & the United States of America.* Vol. 4 of *History of the Expansion of Christianity.* New York: Harper, 1941.
Messina, Jean Paul, and Jaap van Slageren. *Histoire du christianisme au Cameroun: Des origines à nos jours.* Yaoundé: CLÉ, 2005.
Sundkler, Bengt, and Christopher Steed. *A History of the Church in Africa.* London: Cambridge University Press, 2004.

4

Christianity and Slavery in Africa

AKINTUNDE E. AKINADE

With the antislavery campaign, something new and permanent was attempted in African societies, and that represented a significant enough break with the old political morality.

LAMIN SANNEH

The Slave went free; stood a brief moment in the sun; then moved back again toward slavery.

W. E. B. DU BOIS

You must resist the common urge toward the comforting narrative of divine law, toward fairy tales that imply some irrepressible justice. The enslaved were not bricks in your road, and their lives were not chapters in your redemptive history.

TA-NEHISI COATES

On the Enslavement of Africans

THE NARRATIVES CONCERNING SLAVERY in Africa are laced with perplexing complexities especially when it comes to engaging the role of Christianity in the unholy venture that reduced African people to mere commodities and chattels. The brazen commodification of the human body was a despicable denial of the divine principle of *imago Dei* that categorically affirms both the dignity and the divine spark within every human being. For all intents and purposes, slavery denies the divine right of human personhood. The practice and process of slavery raise pertinent questions about the raison d'être of the human person. Prophetic theologies categorically affirm that human beings were created by God and are meant for freedom, not bondage. God's utter and resounding creation of humankind in the divine image bestows an unequivocal sacredness upon human beings, and thus they can be called the children of God. Humanity also flourishes within the context of community. It is in the midst of viable and authentic community that human beings can flourish and be fully human. The bold affirmation of Irenaeus about *Gloria Dei vivens homo* (The glory of God is a man fully alive) was reduced to naught because the pernicious practice of slavery reduced Africans to chattels and commodities that could be pawned and pilloried with reckless impunity.

The transatlantic slavery that started in the sixteenth century commenced a season that has been aptly described by Orlando Patterson as "rituals of blood."[1] The resistance to these toxic rituals constitutes one of the indelible contributions of Christianity within the African context. This chapter maintains that this process of resistance against slavery was fueled by complex circumstances and constellations. It affirms that the subversive sounding of the sacred offered a veritable resistance to the process of anomie set in motion by the transatlantic slave trade. The responses of African pioneers, prophets, and priests to slavery offer a sound contextual appropriation of Christianity in Africa. The abolitionist impulse was anchored in core Christian and African values.

The linkages between African Christianity and slavery evince the lures of Evangelical Christianity, historical permutations, and personal convictions. This chapter examines the mighty deeds and indelible contributions of key personalities in the annals of African Christianity and the abolitionist campaigns in Africa and abroad.

The Imperative of Freedom

The Atlantic slave trade was fueled by the spirit of commerce and civilization. Once the process was set in motion, it stamped Africans with the stigma of nonbeing "from the beginning," to borrow an apt phrase by Ibram Kendi.[2] The conquered slave is thrown into a cesspool of wretchedness and he or she cannot return home anymore. The forlorn hope for a detour to the homestead slowly and inexorably becomes a pie-in-the-sky that is terribly out of reach. The tortuous and barbaric walk through the valley of death is visited with vistas of horrendous disappointments and

---

1. See Patterson, *Slavery and Social Death*.
2. See Kendi, *Stamped from the Beginning*.

dangers. The slave's infinitesimal sense and semblance of somebody-ness gradually fades into perpetual oblivion.

The images of enslaved Africans are stark and surreal. The gory pictures are saturated with horrendous cruelties and stupendous calamities. Africans were hauled together like cheap merchandise to be disposed of at will. The precarious journey on the tempestuous sea also intensified the horror associated with slavery. The litany of unfettered terror unleashed on African slaves was a far cry from Jesus's admonition for justice, mercy, and compassion in the Gospels. The commodification of African people was a blatant denigration of their humanity and autonomy. The cry for freedom from bondage within the belly of the beast, known as slavery, was strident and strong. In the midst of untold pain, the lamentation for liberation cannot be surreptitious; rather, it must be loud and clear. The lure of liberation can be likened to the balm in Gilead for the weary soul. The desire for freedom from slavery was fully encapsulated in some of the spiritual stirrings by Africans in the diaspora. This new world intensified the yearning to break free from the vile trade known as slavery. One of the spirituals and the blues was very adamant about freedom:

> Before I'd be a slave, I'd be buried in my grave,
> And go home to my Lord and be saved.[3]

The strident stirring of freedom was one of the persistent themes in the history and practice of slavery. This yearning called for a form of realized eschatology that is grounded on the circumstances that are related to the here and now. Rather than a futuristic eschatology that valorizes a by and by redemption, African slaves in the diaspora called for a new heaven on earth. The Lord's Prayer that boldly states "Thy will be done on earth as it is in heaven" was not an empty testimony to the will of God for the world, especially for the downtrodden. The story of the exodus of the Israelites from bondage into freedom was also a compelling narrative that provided a prophetic testimony to the power of God over slavery and human bondage. Eventually, light overcame darkness. God's glory shone forth in the midst of human machinations. The human capacity to suppress the truth was defeated by God's unequivocal affirmation of freedom and justice. The Christian tradition in Africa presented many compelling voices that opposed the practice of chattel slavery. These voices were persistent against the virulent subjugation of Africans.

It is very important to reiterate at this point that the dream for freedom was not a hopeless one. Although sometimes coded in a surreptitious

---

3. "Oh, Freedom."

manner, the cry for freedom was real and persistent. The cry was not characterized by a blurred vision; rather, the hope for a new day that was replete with justice and freedom was as clear as the day. The stigma associated with Western fallacies and misconstructions about race was subjected to prophetic scrutiny.

History and Memory: Slave Trade in Africa

Slavery in Africa evokes ancient history and antecedents. In Africa, the precise origins of slavery are shrouded in mystery, especially before written records. The inception of records tell the story of slavery as a common practice in African societies. For instance, about twelve hundred years ago, Arabic chronicles described how Arab itinerant traders from the north came to Africa south of the Sahara offering salt in exchange for slaves.

The trans-Saharan routes were full of caravans with abundant slaves from black Africa. Slaves were also taken during military raids; notable examples are those taken from Nubia, in the Sudan, and from Borno. The Arab writer Ibn Khaldun wrote in his *Prolegomena to World History*, in 1377 CE, that God made Africa a natural source of slaves, for "the negro nations are, as a rule, submissive to slavery, because (negroes) have little human and have attributes that are quite similar to those of dumb animals."[4]

The transatlantic slave trade can be understood as a narrative of enslaved people who endured a litany of horrendous events that separated them from their homes, family, and familiar terrains. The raids in the African interior, movement to the coast, sale to marauding slave traders, forced confinement on a slave ship, and enslavement in the Americas tested the rugged dream and spirit of African men, women, and children who persistently struggled to maintain their humanity and dignity in a New World dependent on free labor and continued coercion.

The statistics connected with this inglorious trade speak volumes. These are indeed telling facts, since numbers don't lie. For about 366 years, European slave traders loaded over 12.5 million African onto slave ships. Around 11 million survived the Middle Passage. The transatlantic slave trade lasted from the mid-sixteenth century until the 1860s. European slavers engaged in their trade along the African coast, from Senegambia to Angola, and from the Cape to Mozambique. However, the majority of captives were taken from West and Central Africa and from Angola. The trade was initiated and coordinated by Portuguese and Spanish traders.

4. Khaldun, *Al-Muqaddimah*, 1:304.

The settlement of sugar plantations in the Americas added more weight to the demand for free labor.

African Christianity as Anti-Structure and Dissent

The anti-slavery movement and the missionary conceived a new vision of society that was grounded on justice, mercy, and freedom. This campaign led to confrontations with chiefs, kings, and Western powers. The spirit and legacy of dissent are very rife in African Christianity. They actually contributed to the spate of independent religious movements in Africa in the nineteenth century.

The amnesty of grace propelled the people of faith to initiate religious assemblies and congregations that celebrate the effervescent power of God. Testimonies concerning God's miraculous deeds within these religious communities led to stupendous conversions. Enthusiastic people of the most High God were spellbound and in awe of the copious stories of the wonderful works of the Ultimate Reality. The word of God became the living fire that wrought amazing and telling miracles that confirmed the surprising character of God. Such glorious moments removed the veil of skepticism and engendered spectacles of praise and halleluyah. The song on the lips of multitude of people was: "Have you been to Jesus for the cleansing power?"

The wave and wind of religious renewal in Africa are mitigated by contextual realities and modernity. This "push and pull" process remains the constant source of religious creativity in Africa. The seeds of healthy religious innovation are watered by constant evaluation and critical engagement. The spirit of vigilance keeps the emerging plant steady and robust. The audacity for theological reassessment is a dominant leitmotif in African Christianity. The *Geist* of autonomy and self-reliance that was pervasive during this period provided the building blocks for a robust post-Western Christianity in Africa in the twenty-first century.

Divine ways are completely different from that of humanity. God can choose anyone to inaugurate God's plan and reign in the world. God decided to use Moses, who actually confessed that he was not an orator, to speak to and confront Pharaoh to release the people of Israel from captivity. Eventually, God's liberative design for his people prevailed in spite of Pharaoh's arrogance, stubbornness, and naivete. Independent religious movements in Africa stripped religious proclamations of the hocus-pocus of imperial piety and elevated the spiritual yearnings of everyday people. The voice and proclamations of the *Volk* became the solemn invitation that brought the people beyond to faith and God's throne.

Slowly but surely, charismatic initiative valorized African representation in the production of authentic spiritual experiences. Eurocentric structures and sensibilities in the expansion of the Christian message in Africa created concrete and deep discontent and displeasure within indigenous agencies. The conscious suppression of subalterns in the field and history of mission in Africa led to visceral responses from Africans with strong convictions concerning the need for independence and self-reliance in religious matters.

History serves as the veritable storehouse of spiritual surprises and stories. The emergence and expansion of African independent churches (AICs) belong to a fascinating compendium of Christian encounter and experience in Africa. These sanctified congregations were neither surreptitious nor nondescript; rather, they were bold expressions and distinctive expressions of religion in the public domain. These churches represent a bold and vibrant indigenization of Christianity through creative use of African symbols, indigenous worship modalities, and traditional healing ideas. They gave new forms to sentiments and ideas that were already in the air during the anti-slavery movements in Africa.

The Legacy of Bishop Ajayi Crowther

The nineteenth century was characterized by political uncertainties and social upheavals in many African societies. It was also a time when new political and theological parameters were introduced to many African communities. "It was the best of times, it was the worst of times . . . it was the epoch of belief, it was the epoch of incredulity," to borrow a famous line by Charles Dickens.[5] In this season of constant flux in political, social, and civic life, missionary initiatives flourished in many African societies. The CMS, which represented what Philip Jenkins calls "Protestant internationalism," was at the forefront of this spiritual revolution in Africa in the early nineteenth century.[6] However, the high handedness and hubris of some of the missionary agents cast a very dark shadow on an otherwise lofty enterprise in spiritual matters. Nonetheless, their racist attitudes were often tempered by local realities and resistance.

The spirit and shadow of Bishop Ajayi Crowther hover over any credible discourse on the power and persistence of abolitionist crusades in Africa. Crowther was arguably the most widely known African Christian in the nineteenth century. His own biography accentuates the power of providence

5. Dickens, *Tale of Two Cities*, ch. 1, para. 1.
6. See Jenkins, *Next Christendom*.

in human affairs. At the young age of thirteen, his village, Osogun, experienced an unprecedented carnage that was masterminded by Fulani and Oyo Muslims. Crowther grew up in tumultuous times. The breakup of the old Oyo Empire and the ravaging Islamic jihadists, who were canvassing for a new Fulani Empire in the north, added palpable tension to an already fragile and precarious context. Incessant raids and destructive warfare were the order of the day. These conflicts contributed to the fissiparous tendencies that made many parts of the Yoruba kingdom susceptible to marauding slave raiders and traders. A telling Yoruba proverb states: "A cracked wall provides an easy passage for crawling reptiles." A divided kingdom becomes an easy prey for debilitating assaults and raids.

In his biography, Crowther provides a gruesome account of the pillage that was characterized by the inferno, capture, and roping by the neck, the slaughter of those unfit to travel, and the agony of being torn from family. Crowther was captured, and he actually changed hands six times before he was sold to Portuguese traders for the transatlantic slave trade.

The hand of faith finally placed Crowther in Sierra Leone, which has been established as the bastion of anti-slavery campaigns by evangelical Christians. Their work was vigorously inspired by William Wilberforce and the Clapham sect. This abolitionist movement drew its inspiration from biblical precepts that affirmed the equality of all races and peoples. As fate would have it, he was rescued by the British Naval Squadron and relocated in Freetown, a settlement founded in 1787 for the primary purpose of settling freed slaves. From the time of resettlement, Crowther took on the role of an anti-slavery crusader. At Freetown, he enjoyed the mentorship of many missionaries. Within six months, he was able to read the New Testament. He was recognized by his peers as an unusually gifted man. The hallmark of his ministry and episcopate was grace. He was surrounded by the turmoil and savagery of the slave trade, thus he became an avid proponent of freedom and justice. He invoked the words of Prophet Isaiah to assail the deeds of slave traders: "For Zion's sake will I not hold my peace, and for Jerusalem's sake I will not rest, until the righteousness thereof go forth as brightness, and the salvation thereof as a lamp that burneth" (Isa 62:1 KJV). He championed the movement that sought to abolish the slave trade in Nigeria. He did this well into his eighties. Crowther's pioneering work as an abolitionist set the tone for his other projects in West Africa in the nineteenth century. Crowther returned to Nigeria to lead the anti-slavery campaign and to establish Christian communities in the grassroots.

Crowther's pioneering work as an abolitionist set the tone for his other projects in West Africa in the nineteenth century. He embarked on translation projects, which signaled an indigenous discovery of Christianity. At a time when Victorian practices were insensitive to other cultural norms, Crowther's vision of Christianity was colored by tolerance to certain aspects of Africa's indigenous worldview, Islam, and the Catholic faith. His Yoruba Bible of 1851 was the first one in an African language. A conception of Crowther as a patriot to the core is apt and appropriate.[7]

Crowther also led the Niger Mission that started in 1841. The main agents in the mission were Africans. Its overall purpose was to produce a self-supporting African pastorate, one that would foster cooperation between autonomous African churches and Canterbury. It carried on successful projects in the Niger Delta as well as at Lokoja and in other areas in the Upper Niger. The active partners in the mission were Africans, with a large contingent of Sierra Leoneans with Nigerian connections.

The role of Henry Venn in Crowther's story is very important. Venn was the honorary secretary of the CMS for thirty-one years (1841–72). He was very supportive of the efforts to create "self-governing, self-supporting, self-propagating" churches in Africa. Just like the CMS, his work grew out of two different movements: the evangelical and the humanitarian. Venn supported the abolitionist strategy to regenerate Africa by "the Bible and the plough." This was a tactic that depended on thousands of liberated Africans in Sierra Leone, West Indies, and Brazil. His proactive policy of development boded well for the church despite the fraught circumstances. In Venn's perspective, Crowther should spearhead the mission in the Niger, establish a coterie of devoted African church leaders, and in so doing, contribute to the realization of a euthanasia of mission. However, things did not turn out as he planned.

Crowther was the sacrificial victim on the altar of racial purity and power. His episcopal rights were curtailed by the powers that be, and the poor man was reduced to a mere shadow of himself. A financial committee chaired by the Rev. J. B. Wood was constituted by the CMS to investigate the activities of the Niger Mission. This was the coup de grâce in the effort to oust Bishop Crowther. Wood summarily dismissed the Niger Mission as a monumental failure without any concrete evidence and sources. He sent his report to the CMS in London, and that was the final nail in the coffin of Crowther's denigration and defeat. Crowther was denied his right to read the report. Crowther and his African agents were rudely assailed by overzealous CMS agents. Their worth and decency were impugned in reports they were not allowed to challenge. By discrediting the African agents, European missionaries were inexorably planting themselves at the helm of affairs for the Niger Mission. A group of young and ambitious European missionaries

7. See, e.g., Ajayi, *History of West Africa*.

condemned the Niger Mission as spiritually stale and too extravagant. Their motive was too obvious: they wanted Crowther and his associates out of the picture so that they could show the whole world the best modus operandi for proclaiming the good news in Africa.

In terms of the sullen denigration of the role of Africans in the mission field, the case of Bishop Ajayi Crowther stands out, and it was a bitter pill to swallow by careful observers of ecclesiological developments in Nigeria. In spite of Bishop Crowther's daring imagination, unequivocal fidelity, and unparalleled patriotism, his daring ambition was drastically annulled by intrepid and unrepentant purveyors of Eurocentric and racist ideals within the CMS. In spite of being afflicted with a mild stroke at the age of eighty-five, he continued to fret about the prospects of the church in Africa. The bishop was feeble and weak, but he continued to contend with the storm within the church. The church was dealing with a crisis of legitimacy; but on the surface, it was business as usual. One of the crucial issues at this period was the role of the "native ministry," that is the role of African church leaders in the churches established by missionary societies. The real bone of contention centered on the question of whether or not the experiment of consecrating Crowther as a bishop in charge of the Niger Mission was a monumental failure that should not be repeated. Crowther's story revealed the acute tension between the CMS and the so-called "native question."

The way events unfolded within this missionary structure was an ugly site to behold. They reduced the mighty Crowther to a mere marionette with its strings in the hands of imperial overloads and agents of a dominant empire. The events leading to his final debacle and disgrace were real and difficult to dismiss. Unlike the proverbial tree that fell in the forest without anyone hearing it, Crowther's final fall boomeranged throughout the CMS. The unmitigated fiasco related to this event fueled the spirit of independence and indigenous religious leadership within the Nigerian church. The theme of reversal and unexpected consequences are poignant and powerful in African Christianity. The effects of the great gaslighting related to Crowther's story generated many unexpected irruptions within ecclesiastical circles. In spite of the ugly and unfortunate hegemonic impositions of the CMS, Bishop Crowther's vision and efforts laid the formidable groundwork for a steadfast autonomy with the African church. When the conspiracies against indigenous initiatives and self-reliance eventually unraveled in the latter part of the nineteenth century, its reverberations were felt in many religious, social, literary, and political circles.

The Odyssey of Olaudah Equiano

Olaudah Equiano was a remarkable advocate for the unreasonableness and economic flaws of slavery. He presented sound arguments that connected piety with abolitionist sensibilities. His arguments were based on personal convictions as an African Christian and also on the pragmatic conclusions of a dyed-in-the-wool realist. According to him:

> The populations, bowels and surface of Africa, abound in valuable and useful returns; the hidden treasures of centuries will be brought to light and into circulation. Industry, enterprise, and mining will have their full scope, proportionately as they civilize . . . Torture, murder, and every other imaginable barbarity and iniquity are practiced upon the poor slaves with impunity. I hope the slave trade will be abolished. I pray it may be an event at hand.[8]

Olaudah Equiano, also known as Gustavus Vassa, was an Igbo man from Nigeria. He wrote a book about his experience as a slave, which was published in 1789.[9] He advocated for the abolition of slavery on the basis of its economic inefficiency. He opined that legitimate trade would garner greater profits for England than the paltry returns from an inhumane trade in human chattel. This theme featured prominently in the writings of missionaries in the nineteenth century. He also called for the extension of Christianity to Africa. The virtues inherent in this religious tradition would act as a veritable catalyst for societal transformation in Africa. He associated Christianity with the processes of progress in several contexts. Africa was poised for modernity, and Christianity would offer the impetus for this new age of concrete development in Africa. In this august dispensation, slavery stood out as a sore thumb. In order for Africa to reach greater heights, the continent needed to consciously harness all the positive and transformative values that Christianity had to offer. Ultimately, this faith would serve as the harbinger of modernization. He was spot on in identifying the blatant contradictions between slavery and development. For him, slavery was against God's divine purpose for the people of God.

On the horror and savagery of slavery, Equiano described the surreal experience after his slave voyage across the Atlantic from Africa got him to a Virginia plantation in 1757 still in chains. He was summoned to go and look after a sick slave master in his house. His remarks were poignant:

---

8. Quoted in Sanneh, *Abolitionists Abroad*, 22.
9. Equiano, *Interesting Narrative*.

> When I came to the house where he was I was very much affrighted at some things I saw, and the more so as I had seen a black woman slave as I came through the house, who was cooking dinner, and the poor creature was cruelly loaded with various kinds of iron machines; she had one particularly on her head, which locked her mouth so fast she could hardly speak; and could not eat nor drink. I was much astonished and shocked at this contrivance, which I afterwards learned was called the iron muzzle.[10]

Beyond the cloud of Western hubris and delusion, Equiano was able to confront and critique the slavery system. In a letter to the Lords Spiritual and Temporal and the Commons of the Parliament of Great Britain in March 1789, he wrote that:

> Permit me with the greatest deference and respect, to lay at your feet the following genuine Narrative; the chief design of which is to excite in your august assemblies a sense of compassion for the miseries which the Slave Trade has entailed on my unfortunate countrymen. By the horrors of that trade I was first torn away from all the tender connexions that were dear to my heart; but these, through the mysterious ways of Providence, I ought to regard as infinitely more than compensated by the introduction I have thence obtained to the knowledge of the Christian religion, and of a nation which, by its liberal sentiments, its humanity, the glorious freedom of its government, and its proficiency in arts and sciences, has exalted the dignity of human nature. . . . May the god of Heaven inspire your hearts with peculiar benevolence on that important day when the question of Abolition is to be discussed, when thousands, in consequence of your determination, are to look for Happiness or Misery![11]

This persuasive missive was able to unearth the terrible contradiction that is connected with the slavery: its affront to the dignity of human nature. As an African Anglican, Equiano spoke truth to power. William Langworthy, in his recommendation of Equiano's book, wrote: "The simplicity that runs through his Narrative is singularly beautiful, and that beauty is heightened by the idea that is *true*; that is all I shall say about this book, save only that I am sure those who buy it will not regret that they have laid out the price of it in the purchase."[12] Although the letter's introductory words were

---

10. Raboteau, *Slave Religion*, 181.
11. Quoted in Gates, *Classic Slave Narratives*, 5.
12. Quoted in Gates, *Classic Slave Narratives*, 9.

patronizing, nevertheless, the words demonstrated the veracity of abolitionist impulse in the eighteenth century. The description of Equiano's campaign as the truth as opposed to the rabid duplicity associated with slavery spoke volumes about the spirit of the time.

Equiano's memoir has remained a classic slave narrative since its publication in the late eighteenth century. In fact, eight British editions and one American edition were published during Equiano's lifetime. His narrative became the paradigm of the nineteenth-century slave narrative. The memoir is loaded with subtle messages such as the subtitle *Written by Himself* and the author holding an open Bible in his lap. The open Bible represented a prophetic gaze into the contextual horror of people's perfidy, especially in their endorsement and practice of slavery. The plot of the book is also very telling: from African freedom, to European enslavement, to African freedom. He confessed that it is difficult for those who publish their own memoirs to escape the "imputation of vanity."[13] By all accounts, it was a candid recollection of the slave trade along the coast that stretched 3400 miles, from Senegal to Angola and other kingdoms such as Benin.

Equiano wrote passionately about slavery as a human rights issue, arguing that ending the trade in humans will engender real transformation and change in Africa. He concluded:

> The populations, bowels and surface of Africa, abound in valuable and useful returns; the hidden treasures of centuries will be brought to light and into circulation. Industry, enterprise, and mining will have their full scope, proportionately as they civilize. In a word it lays open an endless field of commerce.... Torture, murder, and every other imaginable barbarity are practiced upon the poor slaves with impunity. I hope the slave trade will be abolished. I pray it may be an event at hand. The great body of manufactories, uniting in the cause, will considerably facilitate and expedite it; and as I have already stated, it is most substantially their interest and advantage, and as such the Nation at large. In a short space of time one sentiment alone will prevail, from motives of interest as well as justice and humanity.[14]

His plea led to a worldwide resurgence against the injustice of slavery. Ironically and interestingly, white agitators sympathetic to his campaign wished to lead it themselves and eventually managed to sideline him. His request in 1779 to be ordained and sent as a missionary to Africa was rejected by the bishop of London. In that request, Equiano amplified his leadership qualities

13. Equiano, *Interesting Narrative*, 137.
14. Quoted in Sanneh, *Abolitionists Abroad*, 22.

and aspirations and they were summarily dismissed by the powers that be in England. In 1783, in London, he enjoined Granville Sharp, the anti-slavery advocate and humanitarian, to raise awareness to the horror of the 130 Africans who were thrown into the sea from a slave ship so that the owners could claim insurance compensation. Equiano later aligned with another ardent ex-slave, the Fanti Ottobah Cugoano, who in 1787 wrote a book entitled *Thoughts and Sentiments on the Evil and Wicked Traffic of the Slavery and Commerce of the Human Species*, a bold condemnation of slavery and the people, especially of Westerners who promote this trade under the guise of Christianity. Cugoano described slavery as an injury and a robbery, saying that there was not a modicum of reason, justice, charity, or civilization in the trade. While they tend to embrace Protestantism, nevertheless, Westerners seem to be the worst perpetrators of evil. According to Cugoano, they are "the worst specimens of floggers and negro-drivers."[15]

It must be noted that prevailing circumstances gave Equiano and his black compatriots robust visibility of which the white anti-slavery movement was jealous and weary of at the same time. Of course, the abolitionist train had already left the station, and Equiano was an important voice in this drive and initiative. His book was an instant bestseller and his ideas were creative and from the heart. At this time, slavery was a stubborn menace and Equiano used many resources ranging from piety, personal conviction, collaborative efforts, moral appeal, and humility to raise people's awareness about the cruelty of the slave trade. Equiano's affirmation of Christianity enabled him to identify the contradictions between the dignity and sanctity of humanity as espoused by Christianity and the absurdities of chattel slavery. He wrote about the virtues of religion and the existential evils of real life.

Conclusion: Redeeming the Good News

The figures of Olaudah Equiano and Samuel Crowther represent salient issues in anti-slavery campaigns from Europe and America to Africa. The role of recaptive agency in the abolitionist campaigns cannot be overemphasized. At a time when Africa was still considered a forgotten continent by many Westerners, both Crowther and Equiano shed light on the promise of Africa. Although the conditions were precarious, their voices and vision represented a beacon of hope for the downtrodden and the wretched of the earth. Recaptive agency engendered a vision of enlightened mutuality between Europe and Africa. Lord Lugard described this reciprocity as the Dual Mandate.[16]

15. Sanneh, *Abolitionists Abroad*, 25.
16. Campbell, *Abolition and Its Aftermath*, 87.

The crux of the issue is that the relationship between Africa and Europe has been affected by toxic and selfish interests that have proven detrimental to Africa's development. The anti-slavery movement constituted an anti-structure because it represented a bold disruption of the prevailing situation and circumstances in multiple contexts. This movement contributed to the spirit of dissent in African Christianity. The spirit contributed to the retrieval of the redeeming power of the good news in Africa.

Bibliography

Ajayi, J. F. *History of West Africa*. London: Longman, 1974.
Asiegbu, Johnson U. J. *Slavery and the Politics of Liberation, 1787–1861: A Study of Liberated African Emigration and British Anti-Slavery Policy*. London: Longmans, 1969.
Barry, Boubacat. *Senegambia and the Atlantic Slave Trade*. Cambridge: Cambridge University Press, 1998.
Baum, Robert M. *Shrines of the Slave Trade: Diola Religion and Society in Precolonial Senegambia*. New York: Oxford University Press, 1999.
Bellagamba, Alice, et al., eds. *African Slavery/African Voices*. Cambridge: Cambridge University Press, 2011.
Campbell, Gwyn, ed. *Abolition and Its Aftermath in Indian Ocean Africa and Asia*. London: Cass, 2005.
Cooper, Frederick. *Plantation Slavery on the East African Coast*. New Haven, CT: Yale University Press, 1977.
Curtin, Phillip D., ed. *Africa Remembered: Narratives of West Africans from the Era of the Slave Trade*. Madison: University of Wisconsin Press, 1967.
———. *The Atlantic Slave Trade: A Census*. Madison: University of Wisconsin Press, 1969.
DeCorse, Christopher R., ed. *West Africa during the Atlantic Slave Trade: Archaeological Perspectives*. London: Leicester University Press, 2001.
Dickens, Charles. *A Tale of Two Cities: A Story of the French Revolution*. Project Gutenberg, 1859. https://www.gutenberg.org/files/98/98-h/98-h.htm.
Diouf, Sylviane A., ed. *Fighting the Slave Trade: West African Strategies*. Athens: Ohio University Press, 2003.
Equiano, Olaudah. *The Interesting Narrative of the Life of Olaudah Equiano: Or Gustavus Vassa, the African, Written by Himself*. N.p.: CreateSpace, 2015.
Gates, Henry Louis, Jr., ed. *The Classic Slave Narratives*. New York: Signet Classics, 2012.
Grace, John. *Domestic Slavery in West Africa*. New York: Barnes & Noble, 1975.
Jenkins, Philip. *The Next Christendom: The Coming of Global Christianity*. Oxford: Oxford University Press, 2011.
Kendi, Ibram X. *Stamped from the Beginning: The Definitive History of Racist Ideas in America*. N.p.: N.p., 2016.
Khaldun, Ibn. *Al-Muqaddimah: An Introduction to History; The Classic Islamic History of the World*. Edited and translated by Franz Rosenthal. 3 vols. 2nd ed. Princeton: Princeton University Press, 1968.

Klein, Martin. *Slavery and Colonial Rule in French West Africa*. African Studies Series 94. Cambridge: Cambridge University Press, 1998.

Klein, Martin, and Suzanne Miers, eds. *Slavery and Colonial Rule in Africa*. Studies in Slave and Post-slave Societies and Cultures. London: Cass, 1999.

Korieh, Chima J., and Femi J. Kolapo, eds. *The Aftermath of Slavery: Transitions and Transformations in Southeastern Nigeria*. Trenton, NJ: Africa World, 2007.

Lovejoy, Paul E. *Transformations in Slavery: A History of Slavery in Africa*. African Studies Series 36. Cambridge: Cambridge University Press, 2012.

"Oh, Freedom." Wikipedia, last edited Nov. 30, 2022. https://en.wikipedia.org/wiki/Oh,_Freedom.

Patterson, Orlando. *Slavery and Social Death: A Comparative Study*. Cambridge: Harvard University Press, 1982.

Raboteau, Albert J. *Slave Religion*. New York: Oxford University Press, 1978.

Sanneh, Lamin. *Abolitionists Abroad: American Blacks and the Making of Modern West Africa*. Cambridge: Harvard University Press, 1999.

Searing, James. *West African Slavery and Atlantic Commerce*. African Studies Series 77. Cambridge: Cambridge University Press, 1993.

Shaw, Rosalind. *Memories of the Slave Trade: Ritual and the Historical Imagination in Sierra Leone*. Chicago: University of Chicago Press, 2002.

5

The African–Black American Missionary during the Missionary Era

Uchenna D. Anyanwu

Henry Vedder, in his work *Christian Epoch-Makers*, outlined the various epochs of Christian missionary movements. This chapter discusses the modern Christian missionary era (1800s to the present time), wherein Ralph D. Winter identified three microcosmic eras: the first era, 1800–1910; the second era, 1865–1980; and the third era, 1935–present.[1] Winter's three eras focus only on Protestant Christian missions and do not include mission ventures of the Roman Catholic and Orthodox traditions. Nevertheless, prior to the emergence of Protestant mission, the Roman Catholics were in mission through monastic orders. Stephen Neil, for example, opines that the foundation of the Jesuit order in the middle of the 1500s and the 1600s was "perhaps the most important event in the missionary history of the Roman Catholic Church."[2] Thus, before "the much delayed conversion of Protestant Christianity to missions"[3] about three centuries following the Reformation, the Roman Catholic friars had their boots deep in missions.

The discussion here focuses on African–black American missionary contribution within the modern missionary era. The survey in this chapter is framed within Winter's three eras spanning from the dawn of the nineteenth century to the early decades of the twenty-first century. I argue that although there were African American followers of Jesus involved in missionary service during the early part of the modern missionary era, that involvement, however, dwindled over time; but despite that, the missionary God is doing something new—raising African immigrant American Christians to

---

1. Winter, "Three Mission Eras," 264–66.
2. Neill, *History of Christian Mission*, 126.
3. Winter, "Three Mission Eras," 264.

collaboratively work with African American Christians to create a synergy of participation in God's mission in our broken world.

African–Black American Missionary

The term *African American* is widely understood as Americans of African descent with particular reference to those whose forefathers and -mothers were brought to the Americas through slavery. With the global trend of south-north immigration, many African peoples—not descendants of African slaves in the Americas—have immigrated and obtained citizenship, particularly in the United States and Canada. This binary taxonomy is becoming more complex, given that American-born children of immigrants are culturally more American than they are African. In view of this complexity, I delineate two dominant categories of African–black American missionary, namely: African Americans and African immigrant Americans (referred to also as diaspora Africans). The United States Census Board uses a very broad category—"Black African-American"—which fails to distinguish between these categories.

Sociological factors birth another stratum that is currently demographically minimal—a category comprised of children of African Americans and African immigrant Americans born from cross-racial, cross-cultural, and/or mixed marriages.[4] Although this category remains numerically minimal insofar as the focus of the present discussion is concerned, we need to acknowledge nonetheless the complexity of hybridity that emerges through mixed marriages across different races. Without dwelling on this, therefore, I highlight the concept to frame my argument.

Ralph Winter put forth what he referred to as "four different mission mechanisms . . . : 1) going voluntarily, 2) involuntarily going without missionary intent, 3) coming voluntarily, and 4) coming involuntarily."[5] We can situate these four mechanisms into four quadrants as shown in the illustration below.

---

4. A few publications that show studies of this trend include Omi and Winant, *Racial Formation*; and DaCosta, *Making Multiracials*.

5. Winter, "Kingdom Strikes Back," 211.

	☞ Voluntary ☞	☞ Involuntary ☞
☞ Go ☞	Quadrant 1: Voluntary Go	Quadrant 2: Involuntary Go
☞ Come ☞	Quadrant 2: Voluntary Come	Quadrant 2: Involuntary Come

Figure 3. Four Different Mission Mechanisms, based on Winter, "Kingdom Strikes Back."

Winter argued that in every missionary epoch God is actively concerned in advancing his mission in the world "with or without the full cooperation of His chosen nation."[6] When God's chosen people are in cooperation with the Spirit of *missio Dei*, they "go" voluntarily in obedience to wherever the Spirit leads to serve as witnesses. When such is the scenario, they are in quadrant 1—"Voluntary Go." But when God's people are insensitive, reluctant, and/or disobedient, the Lord may orchestrate circumstances that disperse his people and, therefore, they "Involuntarily Go"—quadrant 2.

In some instances, the unreached people may "Voluntarily Come"—quadrant 3—to live in close proximity to God's people. Similarly, circumstances may force them to "Involuntarily Come"—quadrant 4—to places where God's people dwell. Whatever the scenario, the purpose of the God of mission is "that they should seek God, and perhaps feel their way toward him and find him" (Acts 17:27a KJV), for it is the Lord of mission who establishes the "allotted periods and the boundaries of their dwelling place" (Acts 17:26 KJV). Analytically, therefore, we could place each missionary movement in one of these four quadrants. My analysis is as follows:

1. The African American category falls within quadrant 4—"Involuntary Come." African peoples were taken to the Americas as slaves, having been forcefully and inhumanely displaced from their African homelands to North America to live in close proximity to those who ostensibly had the message of the gospel. Many of these African Americans

6. Winter, "Kingdom Strikes Back," 211.

came in contact with the gospel and to faith in Christ. What the devil and the human elements of slavery meant for evil, God turned around for good to *save* lives (Gen 50:20).

2. Conversely, the African immigrant American category voluntarily moved from their African homelands to North America. They experienced neither the pain of slavery nor the sociopsychological antecedents that slavery left on the descendants of their African American brothers and sisters. Some within this category may be classified within "Voluntary Go"—quadrant 1. They voluntarily came to North America for the purpose of bearing witness to the gospel cross-culturally.

3. The majority of these African immigrant Americans came to America not necessarily as missionaries. They came in search of either better educational or employment opportunities. Some in this category were already Jesus's followers in Africa before their voluntary move to North America. On arriving in North America, they realized that the missionary God had a greater purpose than their primary reason of immigration. They sensed the missionary implication of their immigration journeys. Hence, we could place these in quadrant 2—"Involuntary Go."

4. Those who were not in Christ before their move to America, and then came to faith in Jesus following their more, we may place in quadrant 3—"Voluntary Come." They voluntarily came to America, driven by either their search for a better educational opportunity or greener economic pasture, but while they were in America they encountered the gospel and came to faith in Jesus.

5. In yet another category are those who were forced to leave their African lands, immigrating to North America due to war and political instability in their African homelands. These are in the "Involuntary Come"—quadrant 4. They involuntarily moved to America, driven by war or political upheavals.

6. Lastly, there are some African immigrant Americans whose goal for immigrating to North America was primarily to provide their children better educational opportunities. Delineating these various categories to fit into the four missionary mechanism quadrants can be more complex. Children of African immigrants born in North America form another complex category.

With the above framework, I now discuss the Christian missionary contribution of the various groups of the African–black American Christians.

Contributions of African–Black American Missionaries

Some doctoral dissertations and published works outline African Americans' contributions in missions during the modern missionary era. A general overview here will be impracticable, thus I cast only a succinct cursory view.[7]

It is noteworthy to first highlight that manumitted African American slaves made significant contributions in Christian missions a decade before William Carey sailed for India (1793) and before the first white American missionaries sailed for Burma (1812). "By the time William Carey—often mistakenly perceived to be the first Baptist missionary [and also considered to be the father of modern mission]—sailed for India in 1793, Liele [an African American] had worked as a missionary for a decade, supporting himself and his family by farming and by transporting goods with a wagon and team. . . . By 1814 his efforts had produced, either directly or indirectly, some 8,000 Baptists in Jamaica."[8] George Liele (ca. 1750–1828), having been freed by his master, Henry Sharpe, in 1778, "indentured himself to Colonel Kirkland as a servant for the amount of money necessary to pay his transportation" to Kingston, Jamaica.[9] He sailed aboard Kirkland's ship with his family, arriving in 1783. After having served Kirkland to pay the debt of his transportation, he gave himself to preaching the gospel, which ultimately led to the establishment of churches in Jamaica.[10] Similarly, one Amos—another unsung African American missionary hero—served and preached in the "Bahama Islands, British West Indies where he established a flourishing Baptist Church."[11] These unsung African American missionary heroes played significant roles in global missions during the early epoch of the modern missionary movement.

A common thread during the nineteenth and twentieth centuries was that the majority of African American missionaries served in Africa.

---

7. The bibliographical information provided here points the reader to sources for a more in-depth review.

8. Neely, "Liele, George"; see also Holmes, "George Liele."

9. Woodson, *History of Negro Church*, 44–45.

10. See Woodson, *History of Negro Church*, 44–48; Holmes, "George Liele."

11. Woodson, *History of Negro Church*, 45n1; Liele et al., "Letters Showing the Rise," 83.

Even though African Americans were "brutally treated as slaves and denied equality as freemen [and -women] in the U.S., blacks were given much responsibility in mission work... the majority of black missionaries were sent to Africa by white missionary boards."[12] With the Thirteenth Amendment, slavery was abolished in the United States, but the abolition did not attenuate the oppression against African Americans.[13]

Slavery and the suffering of its victims stoked theological questions among African Americans who had embraced faith in Christ. Pivoting on the exodus narrative and Ps 68:31,[14] the emerging motif appears to have been that God probably permitted slavery of black Africans so "that a knowledge of the gospel might be acquired by some of their descendants, in order that they might become qualified to be the messengers of it, to the land of their fathers."[15] An unnamed African Methodist Episcopal minister viewed African Americans as "the instruments in the hands of God for the redemption of Africa, the subjugation of America, and for bringing the world unto God and his Christ."[16] Similar motifs combined with the fires of the Second Great Awakening stirred the hearts of some African Americans to leave the United States to Africa as missionaries.[17] Some African American missionaries "involuntarily" came to the United States and, having received the gospel, "voluntarily" went to Africa as bearers of the gospel.

Lott Carey—an African slave in Richmond, Virginia, who came to faith in Christ and who "purchased his freedom in 1813 and that of his two children for $850"[18]—formed the Richmond African Missionary Society. Carey's biographer attests that "the word of the Lord was like fire in his bones, and it could not be resisted. The struggle between worldly advantage, and an imperious sense of duty, was long and desperate."[19] Carey left to serve in Liberia, where he preached the gospel to African "immigrants from America and to slaves rescued by the British from slave traders and handful of natives."[20] In addition to teaching new believers the way of Christ, Carey also served as a "health officer and government inspector."[21] Although

---

12. Seraile, "Black American Missionaries," 26.
13. Raboteau, *Fire in the Bones*, 42.
14. Raboteau, *Fire in the Bones*, 37–55.
15. Raboteau, *Fire in the Bones*, 45.
16. Raboteau, *Fire in the Bones*, 55.
17. Jacobs, *Black Americans*, 7.
18. Sidwell, "Lott Carey," 48.
19. Taylor, *Biography of Elder Lott*, 15.
20. Sidwell, "Lott Carey," 49.
21. Taylor, *Biography of Elder Lott*, 35.

fraught with lack of funds and challenges in view of his alliance with the American Colonization Society among others,[22] he promoted "education in Monrovia among the colonists and the natives."[23]

Among missionaries sent by five major Protestant denominations in the United States (Congregationalist, Baptist, Methodist, Episcopalian, and Presbyterian)[24] were a few African Americans, some of whom either did not continue for such a period as to make significant contributions or died not too long after their arrival in Africa. The Southern Baptists "sent their first three missionaries to Nigeria in 1849—Reverend Thomas J. Bowen, accompanied by Harvey Goodale . . . and an Afro-American, Robert F. Hill of Virginia."[25] The Methodists sent an African American missionary to Liberia in 1837, but the venture failed because during that epoch "only white men were allowed the franchise in the church."[26]

In 1820, the African Methodist Episcopal Church sent Daniel Coker to Africa who later pioneered the first foreign branches of the denomination in Liberia. Before the end of the nineteenth century Henry McNeal Turner (1834–1915), bishop of the AME and a fervent proponent of the "Back to Africa" movement, had established a new AME church in South Africa in addition to organizing AME conferences in Liberia and Sierra Leone.[27] The mission societies of the Episcopal Church, the Presbyterian Church, the Seventh-Day Adventists, and even the Mormons were not left out in the trend of sending missionaries to Africa, some of whom were African Americans.

The Presbyterians worked among Coptic Christians and Muslims in Egypt beginning from the mid-nineteenth century. Besides the Presbyterians' impact in Egypt, they also sent William Henry Sheppard, an African American, to the Congo with Samuel Norvell Lapsley (a white Presbyterian). Both men arrived in the Congo in 1890, but Lapsley died in March 1892. Sheppard survived the disease-ridden and harsh, tropical African terrain and served from 1890 to 1910. He mobilized other African American Presbyterians to join the labor force in Africa, casting the vision upon

---

22. Taylor, *Biography of Elder Lott*, 17–21, 57–61; Stepp, "Interpreting a Forgotten Mission," 13–25.
23. Sidwell, "Lott Carey," 50.
24. Jacobs, *Black Americans*, 7.
25. Jacobs, *Black Americans*, 9.
26. Jacobs, *Black Americans*, 10.
27. Jacobs, *Black Americans*, 10.

southern black Presbyterians to volunteer as missionaries to Africa during his visit back in America in 1893.[28]

The contribution of African Americans in Africa was not an all-male venture. African American women, such as Lucy Gantt whom William Sheppard married and who joined in the work in the Congo, Lillian Thomas DeYamert, and Althea Maria Brown, and many more, labored and made their marks in mission, not only in Africa but also in non-African lands. The autobiographer of Amanda Smith, an African American woman whose walk and work of faith led her to Africa and India among others, chronicles Amanda's life journeys and service.[29] Fabian Tata's PhD dissertation provides a further insight into the role that African American missionary women played in Anglophone Africa between 1850 and 1950.[30] Tata maintains that "black women missionaries emphasized a 'holistic' approach to Christian faith with the priority being the physical, intellectual and spiritual empowerment of African women and children through good health, education, and high morals."[31]

Another contribution of African American missionaries is their direct or indirect role in establishing educational institutions in Africa and the influence they had on some Africans who went to America to receive higher education and then returned to impact Africa. African American missionaries "were successful professionals who had profited from American education and who now sought to use their talents for the benefit of their ancestral home."[32] Prominent Africans they influenced included James E. K. Aggrey (of Ghana), who in turn became an inspiration for Nnamdi Azikiwe who became the first president of Nigeria. Azikiwe was instrumental in the establishment of the University of Nigeria, Nsukka, which he modeled after the American system. Kwame Nkrumah of Ghana followed in Azikiwe's steps and studied at Lincoln University in Pennsylvania, from which Azikiwe had graduated in 1933. Similar to Azikiwe, Nkrumah became the first president of Ghana (1960–66).[33]

African American missionaries sent to Africa considered the evangelization of the land of their ancestors as their task. Having received the

28. Williams, "William Henry Sheppard," 142, 144; Phipps, "William Sheppard," 113; Phipps, *William Sheppard*.

29. Smith, *Autobiography*; Stevens and Johnson, *Profiles of African-American Missionaries*, 102–6.

30. Tata, "Blessed Mothers."

31. Tata, "Blessed Mothers," vii.

32. Howard, "Black American Missionary Influence," 99.

33. Hawley, "Alumni, Faculty, and Trustees"; Howard, "Black American Missionary Influence," 102, 108.

gospel while in America, they "believed they had been brought to America for slavery by 'providential design' so that they might be Christianized and 'civilized' to return to the 'Dark Continent' with the light of 'civilization.'"[34] The mission mechanisms of "involuntary come" and "voluntary go" were at play insofar as their contribution was concerned. The involuntary coming of Africans to America, placing them in close proximity to Euro-Americans who had received the gospel, later turned to produce a "voluntary go" mechanism, motivating some African American Christians to return to Africa as missionaries.

Despite the willingness of some African Americans to "voluntarily go" as missionaries, the belief in the American society of racial superiority of the white to the black hampered the missionary efforts of many African American missionaries. Painfully, the white American church was not exempt from such bias—hindering them from valuing their African American brothers/sisters without racial prejudice or sense of superiority. By and large, this hampered the support African American missionaries could have received to advance their ministries and contribution to global missions. There was an expressed trepidation that African Americans being sent to Africa could stoke political fires such that black missionaries in Africa could preach "the gospel of Africa for Africans"[35] [instead of] "the gospel of St. Matthew."[36] Furthermore, African Americans who wanted to "voluntarily go" as missionaries faced challenges finding mission boards willing to accept, send, and support them. For black American women who were ready to "voluntarily go," the discrimination and male bias against them fettered the potential impact they would have made.[37] In view of all these challenges, it would be unfair to assert that African Americans were unable to make more contributions beyond what they did during the nineteenth and first half of the twentieth centuries. Eddie Stepp's assessment of the African American missionaries of the Southern Baptist Convention in Liberia between 1846 to 1860 was that they "paid lip service to the necessity of evangelizing national tribes, but instead they focused their energies on the American settlers."[38] Stepp's assessment may be valid in regard to Liberia but it was certainly not the case in other parts of Africa.

34. Jacobs, *Black Americans*, 16.

35. The gospel of "Africa for Africans" was a concept put forth by Marcus Garvey (1887–1940), an African Jamaican political activist who advanced the black and Pan-African nationalist ideology, and whose ideology came to be known as Garveyism.

36. Seraile, "Black American Missionaries," 28.

37. Tata, "Blessed Mothers," 391.

38. Stepp, "Interpreting a Forgotten Mission," ii.

What might be the current trends beginning from the second half of the twentieth century up to the present (2022)? I turn in the following subsection to attempt a response to this question.

Current Trends in the African–Black American Missionary Movement

In her 2020 PhD dissertation, Linda P. Saunders highlighted the rich missional history of the African American church and "her journey from missionary pioneer to missionary obscurity . . . a journey of victory and defeat chronicling the history of people forced to adopt and adapt to a new identity which included a transformation from African to African-American." Saunders sums up the African American church's participation in global missions as one that "succumbed to an insular worldview in an effort to survive the harsh realities of racism and racial inequality in the United States." She maintains that "finding a way to re-engage the African American church in global missions is a daunting, but worthy task."[39]

A number of Africans in search of higher education found the United States one of their destinations. Some from Anglophone African nations who came to study in the United States remained to work after their studies. With the introduction of the diversity visa program, more Africans obtained legal permanent residency in the United States and, with time, also naturalized to become US citizens. The voluntary migration of freeborn Africans to the US gave rise to a totally different pool of Africans in the United States—the African immigrant Americans. Unlike their African American brothers and sisters, these "voluntarily came" to the United States.

In addition to those who came to study, obtained legal permanent residence, and ultimately naturalized, there were others who involuntarily came, having been forced out of their African fatherlands by war or political upheavals. They came as refugees or political asylees and also later obtained legal permanent residency and naturalized. Missiologists might then pose the questions: Insofar as global Christian missions is concerned, what role are followers of Jesus from the African immigrant American category playing, and how does their role intersect with that of African Americans in the black American churches? I explore here the role and contribution of the African Christian Fellowship and highlight the potentials that African churches planted in the United States by African immigrant Americans may possess in regard to global missions.

---

39. Saunders, "Laying an Historical Foundation," ix.

In his PhD dissertation, Stanley Nwoji sought to understand the degree to which "African Christians in diaspora [in the United States] participate in God's mission."[40] He delineates African Christians in diaspora as the "modern African Christians who voluntarily or involuntarily migrated from Africa after colonization . . . from the continent to other parts of the world to form stable communities of African Christians who live for Christ where they are, are involved in God's mission, and are still connected to the African continent."[41] Nwoji's scope was limited particularly to the "African Christian Fellowship, and African-led churches in the United States." His conclusion was that although there exists "a strong missional ethic and a . . . strong practical mission theology that could back their missionary programs [yet] the African Christian community has an overall weak missional status with a weak missional identity and weak utilization of diaspora networks for mission."[42] One of Nwoji's recommendations was the emergence of a "consultation of all African-led churches and parachurches in the United States among themselves and with the host and sending continents (countries) in order to discover how to improve missional identity, missional ethics, diaspora network factor, and the practical theology of mission. . . . The vision of the consultation would be on participation of the African Christians in diaspora in the United States in God's mission back to Africa, the United States, and the rest of the world."[43]

In 2018 (nine years after Nwoji's recommendation), Lloyd and Jan Chinn—African American missionaries who have been serving in Africa for over a decade and who currently serve as World Venture's international ministries directors for Africa—in collaboration with some African immigrant American Christians convened the first BRIDGE consultation in Houston, Texas. BRIDGE—Building Relationships Intentionally with the Diaspora for Global-Gospel Expansion—held another consultation in 2019, and in 2020 a virtual consultation owing to the COVID-19 pandemic.

Lloyd Chinn and the major stakeholders at the maiden BRIDGE consultation held in 2018 outlined their focus to include "collaborative partnerships among African Diaspora for effective engagement with the church in Africa, . . . creating partnership between African-American and Diaspora churches to spread the Gospel among the unreached in North America, . . . being mobilized to reach the Islamic areas in North Africa . . . [and] emulating the African response of obedience to the Great Commission to reach

---

40. Nwoji, "Missional Status," 6–7.
41. Nwoji, "Missional Status," 12–13.
42. Nwoji, "Missional Status," ii.
43. Nwoji, "Missional Status," 213.

the unreached around the globe."⁴⁴ The BRIDGE consultation reconvened in person in 2022, where they focused on: partnering with African indigenous missional movements, networking with African diaspora missional communities, mobilizing black women for global mission, and engaging unengaged immigrant communities, among others. The goal of the consultation is to encourage collaborative partnerships among missional African immigrant Americans to expand gospel movements in local communities, in Africa, and globally. Among the organizations involved are the African Christian Fellowship, World Venture, and CAPRO-USA. BRIDGE is organized under the auspices of the Movement for African National Initiatives.

No doubt, the BRIDGE initiative must be lauded. Nonetheless, one has yet to see the emergence of a similar initiative involving diaspora African-led churches to engage in global missions to unreached people groups. Most of the ministries of diaspora African-led churches remain confined to a large extent to their diaspora communities. A collaborative missional effort between such churches and African American churches is yet to be seen. Diaspora African-led churches have yet to intentionally and contextually expand their missional outreach beyond church planting for African immigrants in North America. Similarly, a missional outreach to unreached people groups who have either voluntarily or involuntarily come to the United States remains a horizon yet to emerge insofar as the ministries of diaspora African-led churches are concerned. Many of the church plants of these diaspora African-led churches are majorly composed of African immigrants in North America.

The task that the BRIDGE consultation seeks to accomplish is the mobilization of the African American church to actively engage in global missions and to do so collaboratively with their African immigrant brothers and sisters. In an interview, Lloyd Chinn said: "The whole purpose of BRIDGE is to try to establish some collaborative partnerships with the black [African American] church in the U.S. with the African diaspora, who are in the U.S. to engage in missions."⁴⁵ Chinn further maintains that "a current movement that [he and his collaborators] are trying to promote is to get more black American churches engaged and have an understanding that black folks have always been engaged in mission"—a fact that Linda Saunders underscores in her dissertation.

In another interview with an African American couple involved in missions—Ron and Star Nelson—the couple maintained that the dearth of

---

44. Email from Lloyd Chinn to stakeholders, June 21, 2018. I am indebted to Meshack Ilobi—one of the BRIDGE consultation stakeholders—for sharing this information.

45. Transcribed virtual interview with Lloyd Chinn, Aug. 16, 2022.

African American missionaries in global and cross-cultural missions motivated them to found Sowing Seeds of Joy, which seeks to mobilize African American Christians for global missions.[46]

Other organizations seeking to make contemporary marks in missions from within the African American communities include the Carey Lott Foundation and the National African American Missions Council (NAAMC). Bishop David Perrin founded NAAMC in 2011 with the vision "to see African Americans and multi-ethnic churches mobilized for global missions."[47] The organization is also engaging in:

- Year-round training events for African American and multiethnic churches
- Coaching for African American pastors looking to establish or expand missions in their congregations[48]

Another development pertains to the Frontier Fellowship effort to involve African Americans in its global frontier mission initiatives. In a concrete move to do so, George and Pamela Pendergrass—an African American couple—joined Frontier Fellowship and are passionate to mobilize African American churches within their network for cross-cultural/global mission engagement. The Pendergrasses visited the Middle East and North Africa region in 2021 where they spent three months with Frontier Fellowship partners. In an oral report to Frontier Fellowship in January 2022, they highlighted the impression of a local North African partner who said: "There are not many people of color that come to places like this [a country in North Africa]. But what you do not realize is how closely related your culture is to ours." George and Pamela hope to push against the fear that people (particularly African Americans) have about going to such places to live and serve. They are trailblazing new territories for Frontier Fellowship with their vision that people of color can make impact in frontier missions. Thus, what are the possible opportunities and challenges? I turn to this question in the concluding subsection.

---

46. See https://www.sowingseedsofjoy.org/.
47. See https://www.naamcevents.org/about.
48. Reeves, "NAAMC Transitions," para. 3.

Challenges, Opportunities, and Collaboration: Toward Effective Participation in God's Mission

Ron and Star Nelson highlighted apathy to global missions among African American pastors as a common challenge. In one occasion after passionately sharing the need for African American churches to send and support missionary effort, a group of ten to fifteen African American pastors said: "Ron, missions is important. But we just don't have a place for it." In another encounter with an African American pastor, the response received was: "Ron, that's good. I love your story, but, you know, missions is just not our thing."[49]

On his part, Lloyd Chinn said the main challenge pertains to lack of awareness of missions among African American churches. Chinn maintains that "people are not seeing enough of people who are actually engaged in missions . . . and the challenge to get a Christian education established in the local church and in black communities is a huge problem."[50] The lack of understanding of the role that the African American church can play in global missions stems from the lack of missional education. It echoes another perspective that Adrian Reeves, executive director of NAAMC, highlighted—an idea that appear to be pervasive among African-American congregations, that "missions is for other people and not for us."[51] In order for such a notion to be changed, a robust missional education and exposure is required. But, how can this challenge be overcome? Collaboration will be key.

The need for collaboration across ecclesial, racial lines between African American, African immigrant American, Hispanic/Latin American, and white American churches will revive missional interest in church communities that lack global missionary awareness. Missional churches collaborating with those that are not missional could kindle the missional fire or cast the vision where it is lacking. BRIDGE is seeking to do this. Lloyd Chinn, currently writing his dissertation for a doctor of missiology degree, is focusing his research on this theme. Chinn is asking the question: How do African identity and impetus for mission stimulate a collaborative engagement between the black church and the Nigerian American churches? What might the barriers for such engagement be, and what might be the common bridges that can connect the African American church to the African immigrant Americans? Chinn's perception is that some will have synergies that will enable and promote collaborative ministry.

49. Transcribed in-person interview with Ron and Star Nelson, Sept. 10, 2022.
50. Transcribed virtual interview with Lloyd Chinn, Aug. 16, 2022.
51. Hopkins, "Black Missionaries," para. 3.

The African Christian Fellowship is modeling collaborative engagement for African immigrant American Christians who want to be involved in cross-cultural missionary engagement in Africa. They are working collaboratively with a few African Americans through a Building Bridges initiative. From ACF's perspective, the "implementation of the *Building Bridges* strategic initiative via collaboration and partnership with African Americans will have [a] synergistic effect on world evangelism and missions by the African Diaspora. Collaborative missions by the African Diaspora on the continent of Africa alone have potential for a great harvest."[52] It is true that, currently, ACF's focus has thus far been primarily on sub-Saharan Africa. Countries north of the Sahara are, however, not outside their purview. The ACF is imagining the impact that "the empowerment of sub-Saharan African Christians to evangelize northern Africa" could have on global missions. There remains, however, a challenge for them to go beyond sub-Saharan Africa and embrace engagement toward global missions in countries north of the Sahara or even outside Africa.

Opportunities abound for African American Christians to enlarge in missions. Frontier Fellowship, for example, although originally a Presbyterian organization, has begun to enlarge its reach to go beyond the mobilization of Presbyterian congregations. The onboarding of an African American couple is a testament to that. It is hoped that through the ministry of this couple, more African American followers of Jesus will become involved in frontier missions.

Collaborative missional engagement should not be restricted to African immigrant Americans and African Americans working together. It must be enlarged to include collaboration with white American, Asian, and Latin American churches and mission organizations in North America. The racial chasm that has often separated these communities of God's people must be eliminated. The set time has come for Jesus's followers from every nation, tribe, language, and skin color to lay aside the differences that divide us in order to unite as one body and as people purchased by Jesus's precious blood to collaboratively share the burden and resources toward our participation in God's mission in our broken world.

Bibliography

Adeoye, Elijah, and Matthew N. O. Sadiku. "The African Christian Fellowship, U.S.A.: Strategic Links with the Diaspora and the World." In *African-American Experience in World Mission: A Call beyond Community*, edited by Frank E. Gainer et al., rev. study ed., 154–59. Littleton, CO: Carey, 2009.

52. Adeoye and Sadiku, "African Christian Fellowship," 155.

DaCosta, Kimberly M. *Making Multiracials: State, Family, and Market in the Redrawing of the Color Line.* Stanford: Stanford University Press, 2007.

Hawley, Scott W. "Alumni, Faculty, and Trustees of the University of Pennsylvania Who Have Served as Heads of State or Government." University Archives and Records Center, Aug. 2002. https://web.archive.org/web/20070205032053/http://www.archives.upenn.edu/histy/notables/political/pennheads.html.

Holmes, Edward A. "George Liele: Negro Slavery's Prophet of Deliverance." *Baptist Quarterly* 20 (1964) 340–51. https://doi.org/10.1080/0005576X.1964.11751160.

Hopkins, Rebecca. "How Black Missionaries Are Being Written Back into the Story." *Christianity Today*, Dec. 13, 2021. https://www.christianitytoday.com/ct/2022/january-february/black-missions-history-rewritten-protten-liele.html.

Howard, Thomas C. "Black American Missionary Influence on the Origins of University Education in West Africa." In *Black Americans and the Missionary Movement in Africa*, edited by Sylvia M. Jacobs, 95–127. Contributions in Afro-American and African Studies 66. Westport, CT: Greenwood, 1982.

Jacobs, Sylvia M, ed. *Black Americans and the Missionary Movement in Africa.* Contributions in Afro-American and African Studies 66. Westport, CT: Greenwood, 1982.

Liele, George, et al. "Letters Showing the Rise and Progress of the Early Negro Churches of Georgia and the West Indies." *Journal of Negro History* 1 (1916) 69–92. https://doi.org/10.2307/2713517.

Neely, Alan. "Liele, George." In *Biographical Dictionary of Christian Missions*, edited by Gerald H. Anderson, 400–401. Grand Rapids: Eerdmans, 1999. https://www.bu.edu/missiology/missionary-biography/l-m/liele-george-c-1750-1828/.

Neill, Stephen. *A History of Christian Mission.* London: Penguin, 1990.

Nwoji, Stanley. "The Missional Status of African Christians in Diaspora: A Case of the African Christian Fellowship and African-Led Churches in the United States." PhD diss., Asbury Theological Seminary, 2009.

Omi, Michael, and Howard Winant. *Racial Formation in the United States.* 3rd ed. New York: Routledge, 2015.

Phipps, William E. *William Sheppard: Congo's African American Livingstone.* Louisville: Geneva, 2002.

———. "William Sheppard: Congo's African American Livingstone." In *Profiles of African-American Missionaries*, edited by Robert J. Stevens and Brian Johnson, 107–21. Pasadena, CA: Carey, 2012.

Raboteau, Albert J. *A Fire in the Bones: Reflections on African-American Religious History.* Boston: Beacon, 1995.

Reeves, Adrian. "NAAMC Transitions from Annual Conference to Year-Round Organizational Resource." NAAMC, Nov. 4, 2020. https://www.naamcevents.org/post/naamc-transitions-from-annual-conference-to-year-round-organizational-resource.

Saunders, Linda P. "Laying an Historical Foundation to Examine the African-American Church's Relationship to 21st Century Global Missions to Create a Contextualized Missions Training Model for Future Generations of African-American Missionaries." PhD diss., Columbia International University, 2020.

Seraile, William. "Black American Missionaries in Africa: 1821–1925." In *African-American Experience in World Mission: A Call beyond Community*, edited by Vaughn J. Walston and Robert J. Stevens, rev. study ed., 25–29. Littleton, CO: Carey, 2009.

Sidwell, Mark. "Lott Carey." In *Profiles of African-American Missionaries*, edited by Robert J. Stevens and Brian Johnson, 47–51. Pasadena, CA: Carey, 2012.

Smith, Amanda. *An Autobiography: The Story of the Lord's Dealings with Mrs. Amanda Smith, the Colored Evangelist*. Wilmore, KY: First Fruits, 2017.

Stepp, Eddie. "Interpreting a Forgotten Mission: African-American Missionaries of the Southern Baptist Convention in Liberia, West Africa, 1846–1860." PhD diss., Baylor University, 1999.

Stevens, Robert J., and Brian Johnson, eds. *Profiles of African-American Missionaries*. Pasadena, CA: Carey, 2012.

Tata, Fabian Tah. "The Blessed Mothers: African-American Missionary Women in English-Speaking Colonial Africa, 1850–1950." PhD diss., Florida State University, 2002.

Taylor, James B. *Biography of Elder Lott Cary, Late Missionary to Africa*. Baltimore: Armstrong & Berry, 1837.

Vedder, Henry C. *Christian Epoch-Makers: The Story of the Great Missionary Eras in the History of Christianity*. Philadelphia: Griffith & Rowland, 1908.

Williams, Walter L. "William Henry Sheppard, Afro-American Missionary in the Congo, 1890–1910." In *Black Americans and the Missionary Movement in Africa*, edited by Sylvia M. Jacobs, 135–53. Westport, CT: Greenwood, 1982.

Winter, Ralph D. "The Kingdom Strikes Back: Ten Epochs of Redemptive History." In *Perspectives on the World Christian Movement: A Reader*, 4th ed., 209–27. Pasadena, CA: Carey, 2009.

———. "Three Mission Eras: And the Loss and Recovery of Kingdom Mission, 1800–2000." In *Perspectives on the World Christian Movement: A Reader*, 4th ed., 263–78. Pasadena, CA: Carey, 2009.

Woodson, Carter G. *The History of the Negro Church*. Washington, DC: Associated, 1921.

Section Two

The Story of Christianity Expressed in a Grand Church Family Mosaic

6

Connections and Collaborations among the Nubian, Coptic, and Ethiopian Churches

JOSHUA ROBERT BARRON

THE FIRST TIME I taught my Church History course to a group of Turkana church leaders in northwest Kenya, I learned that here in Africa, Christianity is frequently thought to be the *wazungu* religion, the non-African and maybe anti-African faith of Europeans and North Americans. In kiSwahili, *wazungu* means "light-skinned people" but conveys the ideas of "foreign" and "strange." In Africa, Europe, and North America, there are many who think that Christianity is somehow inherently European. Misguided modern attempts by some Western missionaries to proselytize Africans into accepting Western culture (in either its European or North American forms) and civilization, instead of trying to make disciples in a way that allows for actual Christian conversion, have strengthened that misconception. But by the end of my course, two of my students told me, "Now we know that Christianity is not a *wazungu* religion. Now we know that the Christian faith has deep roots in African soil. Christianity is not an exotic import here but is an indigenous plant."

The first two chapters of this book have demonstrated that Christianity is deeply rooted in Africa and is, in fact, considerably older than the English language and that African Christianity was civilized and literate with already old traditions when most of my ancestors still lacked a written language, painted themselves blue, and practiced human sacrifice. Kenyan theologian John S. Mbiti (1931–2019) has noted on several occasions that African Christianity is so old that it can rightly be described as an indigenous, traditional, and African religion. This chapter tells more of the story of that ancient Christianity, focusing on the family group of Coptic, Nubian, and Ethiopian Christianity. While it is appropriate to speak of these different national and ethno-cultural expressions of Christianity, I agree with Andrew F. Walls that the plural form "Christianities" is not appropriate. In Egypt, Nubia, and Ethiopia there was a single church, which worshipped the same Jesus.

Names and Maps

Egypt, Nubia, and what we today call Ethiopia and Eritrea compose northeast Africa along the Nile Valley and surrounding lands. In the Hebrew Bible, Egypt is known as *Mitzraîm*. In Nilotic languages to this day, this has become *Misiri*. Ethnic Egyptians are called *Copts*, and their ancient language is called *Coptic*. The ancient lands of Nubia are found today in the countries of Sudan and South Sudan. In English Bibles, the names Ethiopia and Cush refer first to Nubia—to what is now Sudan and South Sudan—and second to what are now Ethiopia and Eritrea, or more generally to Africa south of Egypt. In ancient Greek writings, Ethiopia means simply "land where people with dark skin live"; this could refer to the whole of "Black Africa" south of the Sahara, as well as what are now south India and Sri Lanka, and even to a region between the Black and Caspian Seas where retired Nubian soldiers had established a colony with their wives and children.

It was only in later centuries that Christians in the lands that are now Ethiopia and Eritrea appropriated the name *Ethiopia* to refer to their land, emphasizing their own importance in God's plans for redemption for the whole world. As we saw in chapter 2, the historical ancient core of what is now Ethiopia was known as *Aksum* (or *Axum*) at the time Christianity took root there. At other times those lands have been known as *Abyssinia* and as *Habesha*. During the Christian era, Nubia at times has been divided into as many as four different kingdoms or united into a single kingdom. In the first century, the Nubian kingdom of *Meroë* was the most important. Later, *Nobatia* (or *Nobadia*), *Makuria*, and *Alodia* were important. Under Roman rule, *Alexandria* was the principle city of Egypt. At some point after the Arabic Muslim conquest, *Cairo* was built by the conquerors and eventually became more important than Alexandria. As the site of the influential White Monastery of Shenoute, *Atripe* is also important to Egyptian Christian history. *Philae*, an island in the Nile River in the border regions between ancient Egypt and Nubia, was home to an important temple complex important to traditional Nubian religious life, which later became a Christian center important to both southern Egypt and to northern Nubia. In the Nubian kingdoms, *Silimi* (now *Qasr Ibrim*) and, later, *Pakhoras* (now *Faras*[1]) served as the capitals of Nobatia, *Dongola* was the capital of Makuria, and *Soba*

---

1. The Faras site is now at the bottom of Lake Nasser, created by the Aswan High Dam on the Nile River. For some centuries, important Nubian sites had been buried under the encroaching sands of the Sahara. Now they are also buried under the waters of Lake Nasser.

was the capital of Alodia. The land of Aksum was named for its capital city; Adulis was the important Red Sea port of this kingdom.

Figure 4. Early and Medieval Christian Sites in Northeast Africa. Hand-drawn by the author from multiple sources, with especial reference to Adams, *Nubia*, 14.

Figure 5. Medieval Nubia. Hand-drawn by the author from multiple sources, with especial reference to Shinnie, *Medieval Nubia*, unnumbered page.

Beginnings

In Acts 1:8, Jesus tells the apostles that they will become his "witnesses in Jerusalem, and in all Judea and Samaria, and to the farthest parts of the earth." In Acts 2, we hear that those who came to believe in Jesus on the day of Pentecost came not only from Judah (modern Israel), but also from all over what are now Italy and Greece in Europe, Turkey, Syria, Jordan, Iraq, Iran and Saudi Arabia in Asia, and Egypt and Libya in North Africa. Some of these may have stayed in Jerusalem enjoying the fellowship of the church there; others no doubt returned to their homes, taking the gospel with them. Soon persecution in Jerusalem and Judea scattered the believers, and they went everywhere, proclaiming the good news about Jesus as they went. That Greek was a lingua franca not only in Egypt, which had been ruled by the Greek-speaking Ptolemies for 275 years, but also in both Nubia and Axum[2] no doubt facilitated the spread of Christianity in northeast Africa. There is epigraphic evidence that there may have been a Greek-speaking Christian community in Aksum in the 500s, by which time Christianity was widespread among local Aksumites.[3] In Nubia, Greek, along with Coptic and Old Nubian, were used in church and government writings throughout its history.

Christian communities were established very early in Egypt. Mark (the writer of the Gospel) is said to have organized the church there. The predominately Greek city of Alexandria included a large Jewish population, and it was here that Christianity was first established in Egypt; Apollos was from the Jewish community in Alexandria (Acts 18–19). In the cities and on the northern coast, Greek was widely spoken, but in the countryside, Coptic (the traditional Egyptian language) was spoken. The first formal theological institute in Christian history was arguably the Catechetical School of Alexandria, which was led by such great thinkers as Pantaenus (died ca. 200), Clement (ca. 150–ca. 215), and Origen (ca. 185–ca. 253). But Christianity soon spread to the native Coptic population as well. The Bible was translated into the southern dialect sometime before 200. In the 200s, translations of portions of the Bible began to appear in other Coptic dialects. Eventually, Christianity was able to place such deep roots in the local culture that for hundreds of years in Egypt the very words "Copt" and "Coptic" would come to be synonymous with "Christian."

One of the most important developments in Christian history had its beginnings in the Egyptian deserts—the rise of monasticism. While he

---

2. Hatke, *Aksum and Nubia*, 75.
3. Phillipson, *Foundations of African Civilization*, 99.

was not the first monk, Antony (or Anthony) the Great (ca. 251–356) was perhaps the most influential. Ethnically he was a Copt and culturally an African villager rather than a cosmopolitan Greek.[4] His biography written by Athanasius, *The Life of Antony*, popularized the movement. Pakhom (292–348)—known in the West by the Latinized form of his name, Pachomius—was from the border region between Roman Egypt and Nubia. He may have been of mixed Coptic and Nubian ethnic heritage. Following Antony's example in taking up the monastic lifestyle, he eventually founded the communal form of monasticism. The monastic movement would fan repeated revivals across the centuries throughout the Christian world. It also provided important centers for learning and for training church leaders and missionaries. This was especially true in northeast Africa. Within Egypt, the early monastic movement can be described as "Coptic speakers caught up in a wave of mass conversion in the African countryside."[5] Throughout Egypt, Ethiopia, and Nubia, monasteries would provide leadership for the African Church.

Egypt was also particularly important in the history of Christian doctrine. It was in Egypt that the Arian controversy erupted. Arius (ca. 256–336) was a Christian from Cyrenaica (Libya) who came to serve as a presbyter in Alexandria. While there, he preached that "there was a time when Christ was not," undermining the existing (though admittedly not yet always explicitly expressed) Trinitarian faith of the church. The controversy over Arianism ultimately led to the articulation of the Trinitarian faith, which the church had already been believing, in the Nicene Creed (325) and the Nicene-Constantinopolitan Creed (381), with additional clarifications. Athanasius (ca. 296/298–373), then a deacon and the secretary of Alexander, the patriarch of Alexandria, would emerge as the champion of orthodox Christianity over the Arian heresy. He attended the Nicene Council in 325. After Alexander's death, Athanasius was appointed to serve as patriarch of Alexandria. Later, another christological controversy erupted between Cyril (ca. 376–444), the patriarch of Alexandria, and Nestorius (ca. 386–451), the patriarch of Constantinople. The arguments concerned whether it is proper to speak of the incarnate Christ as having two natures (the view of the Antiochenes and of Nestorius) or as having a united nature (the view of the Alexandrians, including Cyril).[6] The complexities of the story are told in many other books, but the Council of Chalcedon met in 451 to decide

---

4. Walls, "Cost of Discipleship," 436–38.

5. Hastings, *Church in Africa*, 7.

6. Another key argument was whether we should speak of Mary the mother of Jesus as Theotokos (God-bearer) or as Christotokos (Christ-bearer).

the issue. The christological Definition of Chalcedon states that Jesus Christ is "fully God" and "fully human," praised Cyril and condemned Nestorius, and adopted a dyophysite (two natures) Christology instead of Cyril's miaphysite (united nature) Christology. Churches that accepted the canons of Chalcedon were thereafter called Chalcedonian or Byzantine or Melkite.[7] But the Coptic Church of Egypt, along with many Syriac-speaking churches in Asia, rejected Chalcedon. Thus while seen in the West as the Fourth Ecumenical Council, the Council of Chalcedon has been fairly characterized by Andrew F. Walls as "the great ecumenical failure of the fifth century" and was a lasting source of division. Because of their close ties with the Coptic Church, the Churches of Nubia and Ethiopia would remain primarily non-Chalcedonian or miaphysite as well. The Coptic Orthodox Church of Egypt, the Ethiopian Orthodox Tewahedo[8] Church, and the Eritrean Orthodox Tewahedo Church maintain their loyalty to Cyrillian Christology to this day. This shared theological commitment was important to future relationships between the Churches of Egypt, Nubia, and Ethiopia.

By Acts 8, we read of a royal official of the Nubian kingdom of Meroë becoming a follower of Jesus. Luke, of course, refers to him as an "Ethiopian eunuch" but there "Ethiopian" refers to his being someone with black skin from what we know today as Africa, not to the kingdom of Aksum. "Candace," whom this new Christian served, was not the name of the queen of Aksum, but rather *kandaké* is the regnal title of the ruling queens of the Nubian kingdom whose capital was Meroë.[9] Of course the Ethiopian Orthodox Church claims this man as their own, and he may have later traveled to Aksum[10]—but that is more than Luke tells us. He certainly returned to Meroë as a baptized follower of Jesus. But knowledge of any Christian communities in the Meroitic kingdom have been lost to history, following the dissolution of that kingdom no later than ca. 370.[11] Contributing to the demise of Meroë were one or two military incursions of the Aksumite army in

---

7. *Melkite* means "of the king" or "the emperor's;" the term derives from the Syriac word for "king" or "emperor."

8. The Geʻez and Amharic equivalent of the Greek term *miaphusis* (the root of miaphysite in English) is *tewaḥido*. Western Christians often call the non-Chalcedonian Churches "monophysite" (one nature), thinking that they mean to deny the full humanity of Jesus. This, however, is both a misunderstanding and a slur.

9. To read more, see the brief discussion on this point by Werner et al., *Day of Devastation*, 22.

10. Ethiopian Christian traditions variously claim that this official of the Nubian court either was the first to bring the gospel to Aksum or was in fact ethnically Axumite and the first to evangelize the region.

11. There is debate regarding this timeline; I am using the proposed dating of Obłuski, *Rise of Nobadia*, 9.

the earlier 300s. Ironically, at least one of those invasions was led by Ezana, the first Aksumite king to become a Christian.

As already related in chapter 2, around the year 316, the Christian brothers Frumentius and Aedesius, from what is now Lebanon, were captured on the coast of Aksum. The rest of their fellow travelers were slain, but the brothers were taken as slaves to the court of the king. Even though they were slaves, they were free to live as Christians and to share the gospel with whomever they would. After the king died, his widow served as regent until their son Ezana should come of age. Frumentius and Aedesius served the queen mother in the royal court, which enabled them to strengthen and organize the Christians who were already present in the kingdom. Aksum had well-established links with the Mediterranean world, and Christian merchants had settled in cities such as Aksum and Adulis.[12] While Frumentius's long ministry proved decisive, he was able to begin his ministry in communities that had already begun to be Christianized.[13] After Ezana ascended to the throne, around the year 328, the two brothers were released from slavery. Aedesius returned home, but Frumentius went to Athanasius, the patriarch of the Egyptian Church, to report on the growing Christian presence in Aksum, asking him to ordain and send a missionary bishop to serve the believers there. "Who," Athanasius asked him, "would be better than you?" and sent him back to Ethiopia.[14]

The establishment of an ecclesial hierarchy for the Ethiopian Church by the Egyptian Church marked the beginning of a close relationship between the Coptic Church in Egypt and the Ethiopian Church. As the first *abuna*, or metropolitan bishop, of the Church in Ethiopia, Frumentius (*Frémnaṭos* in Geʿez) organized the churches and regularized their ministry. From that day until 1959, the Ethiopian Church was dependent upon the Coptic Church of Egypt for its leadership. While this at times proved detrimental to the health of the churches in Ethiopia, it served to tie the Christians in the different regions of northeast Africa closely together. The link between the Coptic churches of Egypt and the churches in Ethiopia became so strong that the only primary source that documents the replacement of Roman rule with Arab Islamic rule in Egypt in 641, which was written within living memory of those events, is today preserved only in Geʿez (Old Ethiopic),[15] the language of ancient Aksum.

---

12. Eshete, *Evangelical Movement in Ethiopia*, 16.

13. Sundkler and Steed, *History of the Church*, 36.

14. This took place probably sometime between Athanasius's consecration as bishop in 328 and his first exile in 335.

15. Zaborowski, "Coptic Christianity," 223.

In 494, a multiethnic missionary band now known as the *Nine Saints* traveled to Ethiopia. Supported by the Ethiopian king, Ella Amida, they planted churches in the interior of Ethiopia. They translated the bible into the Ge'ez language and established several monasteries that followed the traditions of Pakhom. Before their arrival, Axumite Christianity seemed to be primarily limited to Aksum, Adulis, and the main trade routes.[16] The ministry of the Nine Saints revived existing churches, took the Christian faith to new lands, catalyzed the flourishing of Ge'ez literature, and strengthened collaborative networks between Ethiopian and Coptic Christianity. No later than this time, the Rule of Pakhom and Athanasius's *Life of Antony* were translated into Ge'ez.[17]

While the official conversion of the Nubian kingdoms began around 540,[18] archaeological work has demonstrated the presence of Christianity in Nubia well before that time.[19] No later than ca. 370,[20] three separate kingdoms had emerged in Nubia: listed from north to south, they were *Nobadia*, *Makuria*, and *Alodia*.[21] Coptic sources make it clear that the formation of Christian communities in these Nubian kingdoms was underway no later than the mid-300s,[22] and by the 400s we can speak of the steady Christianization of Nubia.[23] Throughout the 300s and 400s, the church had begun to grow among the common people of the three kingdoms of Nubia. Rufinus (344/345–411), an early historian of Christianity, records that Christian monks were found in Nubia in his day.[24] By this time Egyptian monasteries were full of monks; many were Coptic Christians but others came from elsewhere in the Roman Empire or even from Syriac-speaking areas beyond Roman authority in western Asia. Unknown Christian merchants and various Coptic migrants were in Nobadia at least a century before the arrival of official envoys of Christianity in 543.[25] Egyptian Christians, both Coptic and Greek, undoubtedly entered Nubia as refugees

---

16. Tamrat, *Church and State*, 23.
17. Hastings, *Church in Africa*, 9.
18. Bowers, "Nubian Christianity," 8.
19. Shaw and Gitau, *Kingdom of God*, 71; see also Faraji, *Roots of Nubian Christianity*.
20. Obłuski, *Rise of Nobadia*, 9.
21. Nobadia is sometimes known as Noubadia (Greek) or Nobatia (Coptic); Alodia is also known as Alwa (Arabic).
22. Faraji, *Roots of Nubian Christianity*, 243.
23. Faraji, *Roots of Nubian Christianity*, 252.
24. Shaw and Gitau, *Kingdom of God*, 72.
25. Sundkler and Steed, *History of the Church*, 30.

fleeing persecution.[26] Without fanfare or missionaries known to history, the church had been spreading gradually and quietly south down the Nile River from Egypt into Nubia and, at least for the southernmost kingdom of Alodia,[27] northward from Aksum.

Whereas Christianity's establishment in Aksum began with the royal court, in Nubia Christianity first spread among ordinary people and the poor,[28] and was not embraced by the political elite until the sixth century. Archaeological excavations at *Faras* (*Pakhoras* in Old Nubian) have found a church building from the 400s with Christian inscriptions;[29] it was apparently built in a poorer section of the city.[30] King Silko of Nobadia, the first Nubian ruler to embrace Christianity, was an exception to this rule. His conversion took place perhaps before 450[31] but did not yet lead to the official adoption of Christianity by the kingdom. Setting aside the lost history of a small Christian presence in the Meroitic period, Salim Faraji proposes three stages for the Christianization of ancient Nubia: intermittent evangelism by Coptic merchants and traders in northern Nubia, King Silko's conversion, and the arrival of Justinian's Melkite and Theodora's miaphysite missionaries in the 500s.[32] We now turn to this third stage.

In the 540s, the Christian establishment of the Roman Empire took official notice of Nubia. The emperor Justinian, eager to expand the influence of the state church's Chalcedonian Christology—and also eager for Christian allies along the Red Sea trading routes to India and China to bypass Sassanid Persian control of the Silk Road land routes—sent a missionary to the Nubian kingdoms in 543. But his wife Theodora, a native Egyptian and a proponent of Cyril's Christology, sent her coreligionist Julian, an Egyptian (Copt) from Alexandria. Theodora instructed the governor of the southernmost region of Egypt to delay her husband's emissaries to ensure that Julian got a healthy head start in his journey. Thus when the emperor's ambassador arrived, there were no camels to be had for his caravan for several days. But when Julian arrived with his company in the night, they were quickly provisioned and sent on their way. Building on the existing processes of Christianization, Julian's ministry led to the conversion of the court of Nobadia to Christianity, marking the establishment of

26. Werner et al., *Day of Devastation*, 25.
27. Sundkler and Steed, *History of the Church*, 33.
28. Shaw and Gitau, *Kingdom of God*, 72.
29. Baur, *2000 Years of Christianity*, 32.
30. Werner et al., *Day of Devastation*, 25.
31. Obłuski, *Rise of Nobadia*, 36.
32. Faraji, *Roots of Nubian Christianity*, 261.

Nobadia as a Christian state. After providing catechesis (doctrinal instruction) to the king and his nobles and baptizing them, Julian stayed for only two years before returning to Constantinople. But one of his companions was Bishop Theodoros of Philae. He provided periodic pastoral care and guidance for the Nobadian Church for several years.

In 566 Theodosius, patriarch of Alexandria, commissioned Longinus (who was also from Alexandria) to Nobadia to serve as its first bishop, establishing both Egyptian ecclesial primacy over Nubia as well as cementing the natural ties between Coptic and Nubian Christianity. Due to imperial interference—as a miaphysite, Longinus was imprisoned by Emperor Justin II—it was three or four years before he reached Nubia (after several failed attempts and a final successful attempt to escape prison). His ministry built on the foundations laid by Julian and Bishop Theodora of Philae. During this time Nubian Christianity began to flourish in both Nobadia and Makuria. In 580, the southernmost Nubian kingdom, Alodia, requested Nobadia to send missionaries to teach the Christian faith,[33] and Longinus undertook the journey. Makuria, however, would not let him transverse their lands. In the 540s, Justinian's pro-Chalcedonian envoy had been turned away at Nobadia's borders. The envoy instead had gone as a missionary to Makuria, though we know little of his story. But Makuria officially converted to Christianity in 569, adopting a Melkite/Chalcedonian Christology, the official doctrine of the Byzantine Empire. Thus Melkite Makuria did not allow a miaphysite missionary bishop to enter their lands at this time. (Fine distinctions do not always translate well, and eventually Makuria adopted the miaphysite Christology of the other northeast African kingdoms.) Only a few days after his arrival in Alodia in 580, Longinus baptized the king and his court, and the kingdom quickly converted to Christianity. It is likely, however, that Christian traders and monks from the neighboring kingdom of Aksum had already begun to establish the Christian faith in Alodia,[34] and this had prompted the king's request for missionaries.

In the years following 550, the majority of the Nubian people embraced Christ. By 559, the Egyptian temple in Dendur in northern Nobadia was remodeled and dedicated as a church building,[35] the beginning of a trend. A number of cathedrals and smaller church buildings were built throughout the three kingdoms. After perhaps "one or two generations, to be Nubian meant to be a Christian."[36] The Nubian churches developed their own dis-

---

33. Sundkler and Steed, *History of the Church*, 33.
34. Sundkler and Steed, *History of the Church*, 33.
35. Werner et al., *Day of Devastation*, 27–28.
36. Werner et al., *Day of Devastation*, 35.

tinct and indigenous liturgy and iconography and translated at least parts of the Scriptures, as well as writings of the church fathers, into the Nubian language (although both Greek and Coptic continued in use). Before the Nubians had honored their human kings as being just a little less than gods. But now they exalted Jesus as King above all kings.

From the beginning, there were close connections between all parts of the Christian world. In the first three centuries of Christian history, we know of Christians from Galatia (Turkey) visiting or serving in Gaul (France), from Italy to Egypt, from Lebanon to Aksum, and from Egypt to India. This interconnectedness and polycentricity continued to be the norm for these churches in northeast Africa. Christian leaders in Alodia and Nobadia, and later in Makuria, corresponded with and visited each other as well as with the Coptic Church in Egypt and the Ethiopian Church.[37] We have correspondence between the Christian Axumite court and the Roman world regarding the Arian controversy—Constantius II, the son of Constantine the Great and Roman emperor from 337 to 361, favored the Arians, exiled Athanasius, and requested that the Axumite court send the bishop Frumentius (aka Abuna Frumentius Salama) to Egypt to be examined for theological loyalty; King Ezana flatly refused.[38] In Nubia, the large number of bilingual inscriptions in Old Nubian and Greek in Nubian churches, as well as the large number of Coptic language documents, point to the cosmopolitan and migratory nature of the Christian faith in this period. There was a long practice of correspondence between the patriarch of Alexandria and other Coptic fathers and the Christians in both Nubia and Ethiopia.[39] In 525, the Axumite king, Kaleb, crossed the Red Sea to the Himyarite kingdom (Yemen) to protect its (Arab) Christian population from persecution.

Continuations

In 641, calamity struck the world of African Christianity: Egypt fell to the invading Muslim armies. Henceforth, Christians in Egypt would have second-class status as *dhimmis*, and both Nubia and Ethiopia would be beleaguered and at times isolated. When the Arabs first conquered Egypt,

---

37. E.g., not long after his baptism, the first Christian king of Alodia wrote to the king of Nobadia. See Werner et al., *Day of Devastation*, 33.

38. Phillipson, *Foundations of African Civilization*, 202. It is interesting, however, that we do not know of official diplomatic contacts between Axum and the Roman world, including Egypt, regarding the christological controversies of the 400s that led to the Council of Chalcedon in 451.

39. Welsby, *Medieval Kingdoms of Nubia*, 97.

the majority of Egyptians were Christians. By the beginning of the modern era, the Christians were a shrinking minority. Because they held on to their Coptic culture and yet were willing to learn Arabic and provided church leaders for themselves, they survived. Sometimes Muslim rulers of Egypt would forcibly prevent collaborations between Copts and Nubians and Ethiopians, but those connections remained important. In 642, the Muslims attempted but failed to conquer Nubia. Perhaps motivated by this common enemy, no later than 707 Makuria and Nobadia merged into a single kingdom, at that time ruled by King Merkurios of Makuria. Merkurios was known in Nubia and Egypt as "the new Constantine" and was responsible for bringing his kingdom into the fold of the miaphysite patriarch of Alexandria.[40] From this time, kings of Nubia would often position themselves as protectors of Coptic Christians.[41] In 737, King Kuriakos actually invaded Egypt in order to protect the Coptic patriarch. In 836 a crown prince of Nubia successfully went to Baghdad to negotiate with the Caliph, receiving far better treatment than Latin Christians.

Between 750 and 1100, the church in Nubia was strong, and the Nubian people developed a culture that was authentically both Christian and Nubian. Their striking art was used to make pictures of the cross and illustrate biblical narratives. Often the Nubian king, powerful and wealthy, would abdicate to live in a monastery where he would devote the rest of his years to prayer and studying the Scripture. (There is some record of Ethiopian Christian kings doing this as well.) The Nubian Church's liturgy in worship was beautiful and well developed, and the churches worshiped in both Nubian, Coptic, and Greek.

In the 900s, a dispute between Cosmas III (patriarch of Alexandria from 920 to 932) and the Ethiopian king[42] began a seventy-year period in which the patriarchal see refused to ordain a new abuna for the Ethiopian church. Because only the abuna could ordain new presbyters and bishops, and only the Coptic patriarch could ordain an abuna, by the end of this period the Ethiopian Church was in dire straits. The then-current king of Ethiopia wrote to King Moses George of Makuria, asking him to intercede with Philotheos (*Filatéwos* in Ethiopian records, patriarch of Alexandria from 979 to 1003) so that the Ethiopian Church could receive a new abuna, restoring not only their ecclesial hierarchy but, due to their polity,

---

40. Obłuski, *Rise of Nobadia*, 200.

41. See Shaw and Gitau, *Kingdom of God*, 106; Baur, *2000 Years of Christianity*, 32; Ruffini, "History of Medieval Nubia," 763–64.

42. Abuna Petros took sides in a civil war, and the Ethiopian monarch sent him into exile and asked Cosmas to ordain a replacement. Because Petros was still alive, the patriarch refused.

Christian ministry in the country. The letter claimed that they had been "abandoned without a shepherd and our bishops and priests are dead, and the churches are ruined."[43] Moved by the plight of the Ethiopian Christians, George successfully interceded with Philotheos, who promptly sent a new abuna. Soon after this Al-Hakim, who ruled over Egypt as caliph of the Fatimid Dynasty (albeit under Mamluk Turkish suzerainty) from 996 to 1021, forbade the biannual exchange of letters between the Coptic Church and the Nubian and Ethiopian Churches; this prohibition was still in force in the 1100s.[44] But from the late 1200s, evidence of "strong links between Ethiopia and Christian Egypt" becomes increasingly abundant, with much Coptic and Arabic Christian literature being translated into Ge'ez.[45] While many of these works were translated in Ethiopia, many others were translated at Egyptian monasteries such as Saint Anthony's and the White Monastery of Shenoute, with which the (Egyptian) abuna of the Ethiopian Church maintained close links.[46]

In 1172, the Muslims of Egypt again tried to conquer Nubia. The Nubians remained undefeated, but were greatly weakened. In 1235, the patriarch of Alexandria was unable to provide bishops for Nubia. Under the harsher rule of the Mamluk Turks, who conquered Egypt in 1250, there was a steady exodus of Coptic monks from Upper Egypt migrating to monasteries in Nubia, as well as numbers of ordinary Coptic Christians who fled to Nubia as refugee migrants.[47] In 1315, the Mamluks appointed a Nubian prince who had converted to Islam as the king. While the church remained fairly strong until 1360, shortly after this their new bishop was martyred. By 1524, the northern Nubian kingdoms had finally fallen to the continuous Islamic assaults and only Alodia retained its independence and official Christian status. The Nubian Church in Alodia did not have any more presbyters, because it had been so long since they had a bishop, and only bishops were allowed to ordain presbyters. The Nubian Church used to get most of its leaders from monasteries. But monasticism was never as strong in Nubia as in Egypt and always had fewer monasteries, and thus few centers of strength.[48] Moreover, Nubian monasteries tended to house smaller numbers of monks.[49] With the disruption of church life due to the Muslim invasions, this source of leaders

43. Quoted in Tamrat, *Church and State*, 41.
44. Welsby, *Medieval Kingdoms of Nubia*, 97.
45. Bausi, "Ethiopia and Christian Ecumene," 234.
46. Bausi, "Ethiopia and Christian Ecumene," 235–36.
47. Welsby, *Medieval Kingdoms of Nubia*, 107–9, 256.
48. Baur, *2000 Years of Christianity*, 33.
49. Obłuski, *Monasteries and Monks*, 233–35.

had been lost. For many years the Coptic patriarch had been prevented from sending any bishops from Egypt to Nubia. So in 1524, the Nubian Church in Alodia sent a delegation to the Ethiopian Church to ask for a bishop so they could have some new priests ordained. But the Ethiopian Christians declined to help.[50] "How can we help you?" they answered, "We have to get our own bishops from the Coptic Church in Egypt." Another delegation of Nubians repeated the request in 1540, again to no avail.[51] In the 1700s, a Roman Catholic missionary traveled through the Sudan. He said that he found there were tribes there that were neither Jewish, Christian, Muslim, nor pagan, but that they wanted to be Christian. They remembered that they had once been a Christian people, but they had forgotten all Christian teaching and the stories about Jesus. They remembered only the names.[52] Other writers, however, testify to residual Christian communities in the 1700s—but by the 1800s these had disappeared.[53]

With the disappearance of the Nubian Church in Sudan, both the Coptic and the Ethiopian Church became increasingly isolated. In Ethiopia the coastal area (now Eritrea) was gradually lost by Ethiopia to Muslim invaders. African Christianity, which had once reached as far as Lake Chad and even areas of West Africa, was now struggling to simply survive. As a result, the Coptic and Ethiopian Churches seemed to lose their missionary vision. As they lost their vision for missions and evangelism, they became weaker . . . until new revivals arrived in the 1900s.

Bibliography

Adams, William Y. *Nubia: Corridor to Africa*. London: Lane, 1977.
Baur, John. *2000 Years of Christianity in Africa*. Edited by Silvano Borruso. Updated by Agostino Bertolotti. 2nd ed. Nairobi: Paulines Africa, 2009.
Bausi, Alessandro. "Ethiopia and the Christian Ecumene: Cultural Transmission, Translation, and Reception." In *A Companion to Medieval Ethiopia and Eritrea*, edited by Samantha Kelly, 217–51. Leiden: Brill, 2020.
Bowers, Paul. "Nubian Christianity: The Neglected Heritage." *East African Journal of Evangelical Theology* 4 (1985) 3–23.

50. Baur, *2000 Years of Christianity*, 34.

51. Welsby, *Medieval Kingdoms of Nubia*, 256.

52. Intriguingly, the Nilotic Maasai's migration from what is now Sudan to what is now Kenya and Tanzania began in the 1700s. In the 1900s, they told Christian missionaries that while they certainly knew about God (the Maasai name is *enkÁí*) and prayed to God, they did not really know God. Their ancestors had known God, they said, but had stopped telling the stories about God and so some of their knowledge about God had been lost.

53. Welsby, *Medieval Kingdoms of Nubia*, 256.

Eshete, Tibebe. *The Evangelical Movement in Ethiopia: Resistance and Resilience.* Studies in World Christianity. Waco: Baylor University Press, 2009.
Faraji, Salim. *Roots of Nubian Christianity Uncovered: The Triumph of the Last Pharaoh.* Trenton, NJ: Africa World, 2012.
Hastings, Adrian. *The Church in Africa 1450–1950.* Oxford History of the Christian Church. Oxford, UK: Clarendon, 1994.
Hatke, George. *Aksum and Nubia: Warfare, Commerce, and Political Fictions in Ancient Northeast Africa.* New York: New York University Press, 2013.
Obłuski, Artur. *The Monasteries and Monks of Nubia.* Translated by Dorota Dzierzbicka. *Journal of Juristic Papyrology* Supplements 36. Warsaw: Faculty of Law and Administration of the University of Warsaw, the Institute of Archaeology of the University of Warsaw, and the Raphael Taubenschlag Foundation, 2019.
———. *The Rise of Nobadia: Social Changes in Northern Nubia in Late Antiquity.* Translated by Iwona Zych. *Journal of Juristic Papyrology* Supplements 20. Warsaw: Faculty of Law and Administration of the University of Warsaw, the Institute of Archaeology of the University of Warsaw, and the Raphael Taubenschlag Foundation, 2014.
Phillipson, David W. *Foundations of an African Civilization: Aksum and the Northern Horn 1000 BC–AD 1300.* Woodbridge, UK: Currey, 2012.
Ruffini, Giovanni R. "The History of Medieval Nubia." In *The Oxford Handbook of Ancient Nubia,* edited by Geoff Emberling and Bruce Beyer Williams, Oxford Handbooks, 759–71. Oxford: Oxford University Press, 2020.
Shaw, Mark, and Wanjiru M. Gitau. *The Kingdom of God in Africa: A History of African Christianity.* Carlisle, UK: Langham Global Library, 2020.
Shinnie, P. L. *Medieval Nubia.* Museum Pamphlet 2. Khartoum: Sudan Antiquities Service, 1954.
Sundkler, Bengt, and Christopher Steed. *A History of the Church in Africa.* Studia Missionalia Upsaliensia 74. Cambridge: Cambridge University Press, 2000.
Tamrat, Taddesse. *Church and State in Ethiopia 1270–1527.* Hollywood, CA: Tsehai, 2009. First published 1972 by Oxford University Press.
Walls, Andrew F. "The Cost of Discipleship: The Witness of the African Church." *Word & World* 25 (2005) 433–43.
Welsby, Derek A. *The Medieval Kingdoms of Nubia: Pagans, Christians and Muslims along the Middle Nile.* London: British Museum Press, 2002.
Werner, Roland, et al. *Day of Devastation, Day of Contentment: The History of the Sudanese Church across 2000 Years.* 2nd ed. Faith in Sudan Series 10. Nairobi: Paulines Africa, 2010.
Zaborowski, Jason R. "Coptic Christianity." In *The Wiley-Blackwell Companion to African Religions,* edited by Elias Kifon Bongmba, 220–33. Wiley-Blackwell Companions to Religion. Oxford: Wiley-Blackwell, 2012.

7

The Catholic Church and the Network of Evangelization

STAN CHU ILO

THIS CHAPTER EXAMINES TWO important developments in the expansion of the Catholic Church from the second half of the nineteenth century to the beginning of the Second Vatican Council in 1962. These two developments are the missionary activities in Africa by Western Christians, and the impact of some papal mandates and initiatives, both of which defined the identity and mission of the Catholic Church in Africa before the Second Vatican Council. These two developments offer a road map for exploring the network of evangelization in African Catholicism within this period and have continuing consequences in the challenges and opportunities facing African Catholicism in this era of world Christianity.

The Twentieth Century: The Christian Century?

According to Brian Stanley, "As the twentieth century dawned, many Christians anticipated that the coming decades would witness the birth of a new era. Their expectation was that the accelerating global diffusion of Christianity from its Western heartlands to the rest of the globe will usher in the final phase of human history—the climactic millennial age of international peace and harmony."[1] At this point in time, "Christian" was understood by Pope Pius (in his encyclical *Il Fermo Proposito*, 1905) and many European ecclesial and political leaders as Western culture.[2] This view was clearly reflected in Hilaire Belloc's now-famous quote: "Europe is the faith and the faith is Europe." David Goldman puts it this way: "Hilaire Belloc's famous quip—'Europe is the faith and the faith is Europe'—is precisely correct," because Europe came into being because of Christianity

1. Stanley, *Christianity in Twentieth Century*, 1.
2. Pius X, *Fermo Proposito*, para. 3.

and Christianity in its form at the beginning of the twentieth century was indeed European through and through. According to Goldman, "Under the church and empire, nations owed fealty to a higher power by virtue of the authority of faith. Its common language was Latin, and its ultimate authority was the pope rather than the emperor."[3] Pius X rejected all forms of secular culture and proposed the subordination of all the laws of the state to the divine government of the gospel and urged "regaining the losses in the kingdom already conquered," so as "to restore all things to Christ."[4] Pius writes with so much optimism in these glowing words: "What prosperity and well-being, what peace and harmony, what respectful subjection to authority and what excellent government would be obtained and maintained in the world if one could see in practice the perfect ideal of Christian civilization" in the twentieth century.[5]

By the beginning of the twenty-first century, not only has the world not become more Christian, but the Christian cartography has changed so fundamentally. African Christianity, for instance, has taken on a life of its own and assumed its own unique character. Andrew Walls argues that with the "accession to Christianity in Africa along with the recent recession from it in the West, African Christianity must be seen as a major component of contemporary representative Christianity, the standard Christianity of the present age, a demonstration model of its character."[6] Understanding the historical factors in the expansion of Catholic Christianity from Europe to Africa, and how the work of evangelization from Europe to Africa was carried out through the network of missions under the direction of the Holy See, offers some important insight on the nature and identity of African Catholicism in the modern story of Christianity.

The Design for a Unitary Church from Rome to the African Hinterland

According to Adrian Hastings, "The ecclesiastical scramble for Africa coincided with the massive institutional revival of the Catholic Church worldwide in the post-Vatican 1 era on strictly ultramontane and Rome-guided lines. The contribution of Catholic missionaries was seldom a very creative one, but was highly disciplined and committed, it learned from Protestants

---

3. Goldman, *It's Not the End*, 353–54.

4. Pius X, *Fermo Proposito*, para. 5.

5. Pius X, *Fermo Proposito*, para. 5; quoted in Stanley, *Christianity in Twentieth Century*, 2.

6. Walls, *Cross-Cultural Process*, 119.

more than it would admit, and its ever-growing strength would prove decisive for the shape of African Christianity in the twentieth century."[7] The missionary strategies of the different European missionaries were diverse, reflecting the charism and identity of each group. However, even in the tension among European powers in the second half of the nineteenth century, the Church of Rome still had a strong influence in shaping the network of evangelization in Africa. Many factors contributed to this.

The first was nationalism in Europe, and the threats to papal power. The tension in Europe came from the wars and the fight for dominance in Europe among the European nations, as well as their rivalries and the balkanization of non-European lands in the south in pursuit of Western national interests, colonial territories, and missionary dominance. This tension raised questions about who the church is and the church's role in the movement of history, which was driven by the "triple g's" of God (Christendom), glory (empire), and gold (money). These factors were all significant in shaping the papal teaching in the later part of the nineteenth century. They formed the message and context of the proclamation of the papal documents written between 1870 and 1905 through which the papacy asserted its power and dominance particularly in the missionary congregations working in the non-Western world.

Two sets of documents were proclaimed at the end of the First Vatican Council (1869–70): *Dei Filius* (April 21, 1870) and *Pastor Aeternus* (July 18, 1870). These documents were written as a response to the great turmoil in the West, with the abolition of slavery; the ferments of *Kulturkampf* in Germany (1871–87) when Otto von Bismarck attempted to subject the Catholic Church to state control; the Franco-Prussian War; and the scramble and partition of Africa by Western powers that led to the Berlin Conference of 1884–85. Both papal documents, but particularly *Dei Filius* with its many anathemas, were designed as a reaction against rationalism, communism, secularism, and the rise of nation-states. This came as a direct response to the Italian Reunification that effectively led to the annexation and demise of the papal states in 1870. It was not surprising that Pope Pius IX threatened with excommunication any Italian Catholics who dared to participate in the elections following the unification of Italy.

Second was the anti-slavery movement. The contrast could not be sharper between the so-called uncivilized and miserable Africans who were being liberated from slavery—and who were being saved through Christianity and membership in the church—and the Western missionaries who were bearers of this new civilization that was offered to Africans. In

---

7. Hastings, *Church in Africa*, 419.

the two anti-slavery papal documents of the nineteenth century, Africans and blacks were referred to as wretched, and slavery as a curse. In a strong letter outlawing the participation of all Christians in the enslavement of black people and any other race for that matter, Gregory XVI's *In Supremo Apostolatus* (1839) refers to the African slaves as "these miserable people."[8] Leo XIII's *In Plurimis* (1888) speaks of the "dreadful curse of slavery."[9] He prays that through being liberated, and being baptized and welcomed into the Church, liberated black slaves "should acquire habits suitable to the Christian life," and the slaves now liberated from violence, sedition, and unlawful acts condemned by the Church can live as Christians by embracing the "virtue of the light of holy faith, and the character they received from Christ."[10] So strong was this characterization of Africans as benighted and accursed that at the First Vatican Council, Daniel Comboni (founder of the Comboni missionaries) as theologian of the bishop of Verona was quoted as having asked the pope to remove the curse imposed on blacks so that they could receive the blessings of Christ the Lord.[11]

Third was the birth of a new missionary movement that was still embedded in Christendom's ideals and had the goal of implantation of Western-type Catholicism, ecclesiology, education, and pastoral life in Africa. While mired in two destructive wars, there was a promotion of intense missionary activities through Benedict XV's *Maximum Illud* (1919) and Pius XII's *Mystici Corporis* (1943) and *Fidei Donum* (1957). Each of these documents offered some guidelines and foundations for understanding the nature of the Church, and the methods to be adopted for missionary work from Europe to the rest of the world. The methods being proposed were universally developed by the Vatican's *Propaganda Fide*, to advance and continue the uniformity of the Catholic Church and maintain Roman control over the churches in the Global South. However, the developments in post–World War II Europe, rising secularization, and greater tensions among the global powers came together through the law of unintended consequences in bringing about the emergence of African Catholicism in the twentieth and twenty-first centuries, after the Second Vatican Council that looked like and unlike the church the missionaries founded in Africa.

Finally, it must be noted that African Catholicism grew in the nineteenth and twentieth centuries through a cycle of dependency. Missionaries used financial resources from Europe to build the church in Africa, relying

---

8. Gregory XVI, "*In Supremo Apostolatus*," para. 1.
9. Leo XIII, *In Plurimis*, para. 20.
10. Leo XIII, *In Plurimis*, para. 9.
11. Lubov, "Pope to Combonians," para. 11.

on donations from European Christians. The image of Africa presented to European Christians, and which is still prevalent today, was that of a continent in darkness, dependent on Western resources and where people are dying and being enslaved, needing Western saviors. When in his encyclical against slavery, *Catholicae Ecclesia* (1890), Pope Leo XIII designated Cardinal Charles Lavigerie as the anti-slavery legate for Africa to the European nations, he also introduced an annual collection for Africa every Epiphany in Europe. Lavigerie worked hard in starting the anti-slavery movement in France and in the rest of Europe. He championed the liberation of African slaves and an end to illegal forms of slavery still taking place, in an impassioned speech denouncing "the continuing plague of slavery in Africa."[12] His speeches moved the hearts of many in France and Europe, including Pope Leo XIII himself who made a significant donation to support the missions in Africa. Lavigerie also went throughout the length and breadth of Europe, soliciting aid for African Catholics. Cardinal Lavigerie was the founder of the missionary congregation, the White Fathers in Africa, and later became the archbishop of Algeria.

His anti-slavery mission was taken to a new level by other people, particularly Monsignor François Cousepel du Mesnil who led the group from 1951 to 1957. Pope Pius XII in his encyclical "*Fidei Donum*: On the Present Condition of the Catholic Missions, Especially in Africa" captures what I think is very important in understanding the kind of dependent and paternalistic ecclesiology that was developing in the African missions in the second half of the twentieth century in the Catholic Church. He writes as follows in *Fidei Donum*: "There is every reason, therefore, why we should be subject to no small anxiety with regard to the fortunes of Catholicism in Africa. There is every reason to why all the Church's children should clearly realize their serious obligation to give more effective assistance to the missionaries. This they must do at the opportune moment in order that the message of saving truth may be brought to what is called "darkest" Africa, where some 85,000,000 people still sit in the darkness of idolatry."[13] Historian Elizabeth Forster notes that the document has the tone of "condescension and paternalism toward Africans."[14] The struggle even today in African Catholicism to extricate the local churches from dependency to Rome and Europe must be understood in the light of these developments. The African church was created in the age of mission through European generosity; how

---

12. Foster, *African Catholic*, 230.
13. Pius XII, "*Fidei Donum*," para. 20.
14. Foster, *African Catholic*, 248.

the missionary enterprise functioned in Africa offers us even a better understanding of the network of evangelization during this period.

Network of Evangelization in Africa: The Missionary Factor

The missionary factors that I shall highlight in this section refer to the extensive missionary activities in sub-Saharan Africa from the end of the transatlantic slave trade and the beginning of the partition of Africa in 1885, to 1914 when most of the foreign missions had taken hold in Africa. The World Missionary Conference in Edinburgh (1910) was a watershed because it unified all Protestant Christians in a concerted and systematic endeavor to achieve the goal of "evangelization of the world in this generation."[15] At the conference, there were delegates from China, India, Korea, and Japan, but there were meager indigenous African delegates except for expatriate missionaries and eight white South Africans. The noted British missionary Temple Gairdner wrote in his conference report that the only African delegate was "an unnamed negro of immense size glorying in his African race, from Liberia."[16] Adrian Hastings observed that "Edinburgh 1910 has much to say about Africa, but its mood was, only too clearly, patronizing rather than attentive."[17]

There was also a strong element of racism against people of African descent. Many missionaries in Africa found justification in an obscure passage of Scripture (Gen 9:18–27) which narrates Noah's cursing of Ham.[18] As David Goldenberg has argued so convincingly, Christian exegesis sometimes claimed that the devil was Ethiopian and black and the African was portrayed too as a sinner, an accursed person condemned to damnation and death in the valley of tears.[19] African theologian Benezet Bujo agrees here with Goldenberg based on evidence from some extant texts. This text of Genesis, he argues, was understood in Christian tradition to apply to black people, who were cursed because of the sin of their father Ham. In 1873 the Congregation of Indulgences published a prayer for the conversion of Ham's offspring in Central Africa, approved with a three-hundred-days indulgence by Pope Pius IX. Part of the prayer reads: "Let us pray for the most miserable Ethiopian peoples in Central Africa, who form a tenth of humanity, so that

15. Stanley, "Africa," 135.
16. Gairdner, *Edinburgh 1910*, 56.
17. Hastings, *Church in Africa*, 420.
18. Bujo, *Ethical Dimension of Community*, 135.
19. Goldenberg, *Curse of Ham*, 2–5.

God Almighty may take away from their hearts the curse of Ham and give them the blessings of Jesus Christ, our God and Lord."[20]

What emerged was that Africans joined the mission churches without fully embracing Christianity and without fully leaving their African traditional religious beliefs, worldviews, and mentality. According to Lamin Sanneh, the missionary method in this regard was very problematic:

> This concentration on missionary life as the model Christian life required converts to be dislodged from their cultural system and to be cast on the goodwill of missionaries. Converts suffered a double jeopardy. They were uprooted from their culture only to be cast adrift on the fringes of the missionary community as adopted clients. Suddenly and unexpectedly, converts found themselves bogged down in an untenable contradiction, for the very attributes missionaries fashioned for them denied their roots in the societies of their birth. It was as if a stranger entered your home to declare you an alien there.[21]

Price's summary of the motives of the missionaries in Africa is very revealing. According to him, some missionaries were inspired by pity for unbelievers doomed to hell for all eternity, who could be saved only if they knew of, and accepted, the person and work of Jesus Christ. Some were in revolt against the corruption and self-satisfaction of their fellow Christians in the West, and trusted that the new African Christians would display purity and primitive virtue. Some were artisans who sought a sphere in which they could do the work that they mastered, not for the profit of an employer but as an offering to the unseen Lord. And some, judging by their subsequent careers as traders, transporters, and administrators were seeking escape from the pressures of rigid convention and overcrowding in their own society as a result of the Industrial Revolution.[22]

There were missionaries who were driven by motive of pure Christian altruism to liberate Africa from a presumed darkness, suffering, poverty, and disease. This was why, as we shall see, many missionaries took part in liberating slaves and in a few instances went to war to fight with native rulers and some Islamic potentates in Africa who were still keeping slaves. "A series of tiny wars followed, leaving the missionaries to cope with the pathetic groups of people they had freed, and a horrified public in Britain to protest against missionaries engaged in organized warfare, whatever the cause."[23] Some

20. Goldenberg, *Curse of Ham*, 135.
21. Sanneh, *Disciples of All Nations*, 221.
22. Price, "Missionary Struggle with Complexity," 103.
23. Hastings, *Church in Africa*, 410.

of the missionaries, especially female religious congregations, were very involved in medical mission, building health facilities, and providing health education and community healthcare and other social services.

Dorothy Hodgson shows that missionaries were against women leadership in the mission fields of Africa and worked mainly to train the men. Whether this was due to the patriarchal mindset of the Western missionaries is not the concern of this chapter. However, what became obvious in many places in Africa was that as the missionaries began to reach the hinterland either directly or through African evangelizers, more women embraced the Christian faith than men, as was shown in a study of Maasai women.[24] The women Bible movement was strong in both East and West Africa as well as in southern Africa. However, it was in healthcare that the women missionaries and their African colleagues were most visible and more impactful.

One of the most prominent was the Medical Mission Sisters or the Society of Catholic Medical Missionaries, which was founded in 1925 by Anna Dengel. Other female congregations that had significant impact in Africa included the Maryknoll Sisters and the Missionary Sisters of the Holy Rosary, Missionary Sisters of our Lady of Africa, and Soeurs Agricoles et Hospitalière (Sisters for agriculture and hospitals), to name but a few. According to Barbara Mann Wall, "Women have been key players in the transformation of mission from one that expanded the Catholic Church and biomedical care to that of helping the poor to claim their rights and dignity within their own social systems. In the process, encounters between Africans and women from various religious congregations involved multiple negotiations that challenged a one-dimensional notion of a compliant indigenous population subjected to an overbearing Western presence. As Catholic sisters developed networks among those they served, they participated in various intercultural exchanges, and multidirectional movements of influence and ideas occurred."[25]

There are some historians who argue that the Catholic health mission work was not entirely without some other motives and that health outreach was subtly used to gain converts. According to Felix Ekechi, "As a condition for treating the children, the missionaries demanded that they be baptized first. Such a condition was imposed, they explained, in order that the children did not die in sin. The fact is that these missionaries hoped that these children would eventually become converts to the Catholic religion. The

---

24. Hodgson, "Engendered Encounters," 773.
25. Wall, *Into Africa*, 2.

Catholic missionaries fully recognized that the approach they had adopted was a 'powerful means of evangelization.'"[26]

There was no overarching singular motive of missionary work in Africa. Historians show that there are instances where the missionaries saw the colonial presence and pacification of indigenous peoples as part of divine providence to open the natives to the gospel and clear the way for a network of evangelization that would link Africa and the home country, while providing missionaries the security and support they needed for their work.[27]

In some instances, the missionaries saw the colonialists as impeding the cause of the gospel. Charles Lavigerie (1825–92), for instance, in his fight for abolition, aligned with European powers, but he sometimes "promoted independent actions by his missionaries, who were supported by coalitions with European civil society. Although Lavigerie lobbied the colonial governments, his missionaries demonstrated a tendency toward autonomous action and even establishing alternative sovereignties, contributing to the *sans frontier* character of missionary abolitionism."[28] When it comes to converting the people, Lavigerie was so worried that the French governor of Algeria would not allow his seminarians to study Arabic so that they could evangelize the Muslims that he appealed to both Napoleon III and Pope Pius IX. He resisted all attempts to stop the evangelizing mission of the White Fathers in Algeria and the rest of today's Francophone Africa. In the end, he prevailed and was able to send his missionaries to Zanzibar, Uganda, Tanganyika, Mali, and Burkina Faso.[29] However, there is a general consensus among historians that both the colonialists and the missionaries shared a common commitment to "civilizing Africa."

According to Chukwudi A. Njoku, the missionaries came to Africa at a time when the progressive epiphanies of the material culture of Western civilization translated into an unprecedented cultural pride and triumphalism among the citizens: "It is not surprising that the missionaries fully embraced the idea of a 'civilizing mission,' the idea of being heirs of a culturally superior people going out to share the riches and glories of their culture with people from cultures they generally assumed to be inferior to their own. Indeed, some of the rivalry between the various missionary groups working in the same missionary territories in Africa were hinged on cultural battles, namely, who was the more superior as

---

26. Ekechi, *Missionary Enterprise and Rivalry*, 75.
27. Hastings, *Church in Africa*, 408.
28. Gordon, "Slavery and Redemption," 584.
29. Calderisi, *Earthly Mission*, 105.

distinct civilization: the French? Or the German? Or the English? Or the Irish?"[30] Robert Calderisi was right in asserting that the missionaries and the colonial authorities did not always work in cahoots, but every attempt was made to establish a good working relationship so that each achieved its objectives in Africa without creating conditions that could antagonize Africans against the invaders. The same approach was also applied in the occasional rivalries among the missionaries between Catholics and Protestant. Just as the Western powers had scrambled and partitioned Africa, so too the missionaries had a different kind of scramble and partition of Africa, which was a mixed bag for Africans in the long run.

The Case of Algeria

The contention of this chapter is that the motivation of the missionary congregations in Africa in the network of evangelization from the second half of the nineteenth century to the second half of the twentieth century was not fixed or synchronous among them. This is true even for missionaries coming from the same Western country and working in the same African country. A good case study is the mix of empire and mission in Algeria. Darcie Fontaine proposes that it is important "to explore the role that Christianity played in the decolonization of Algeria and in particular how the complex relationship between Christianity and colonialism under French rule shaped the rhetoric and actions of Christians during the Algerian War of Independence (1954–1962)."[31] Fontaine demonstrates how the two contending narratives of the relationship between French colonialism and Christianity played out.

The first is the conservative position that saw the entrenchment and occupation of Algeria by France as "the reestablishment of Christianity in the former Roman homeland of St. Augustine."[32] In this quest, there was a good alliance between the conquering French imperialists and some missionaries who saw the entrenchment of Christian symbols in Algeria and the building of churches and Catholic schools and social agencies as a good way of reclaiming the Roman and Catholic heritage of Algeria. Added to this was a concerted effort at evangelization directed at the conversion of Muslims. This quest to convert Muslims was mostly unsuccessful. The appointment

---

30. Chukwudi, "Missionary Factor," 196–97. For an account of the rivalry among the Protestant and Catholic missionaries in eastern Nigeria, see Ekechi, *Missionary Enterprise and Rivalry*; and Kalu, *Embattled Gods*, 178–212.

31. Fontaine, "Treason or Charity," 734.

32. Fontaine, "Treason or Charity," 734.

of Cardinal Charles Lavigerie as archbishop of Algiers in 1866 gave a new impetus to the conversion of Muslim Arabs and Berbers in what he called "the barbarous continent of 200 million souls."[33]

Lavigerie promoted the "Kabyle Myth," which claimed that the Kabyles had "maintained vestiges of Christianity dating from the Roman occupation of North Africa."[34] However, the state's use of violence and oppressive method to "pacify" the people and the apparent support from some Catholics "was also a potential threat to the already antagonistic relationship between French colonizers and the Muslim Arab and Berber populations, whose religious integrity the French had guaranteed."[35] There were many elements of racism in the approach adopted by missionaries like Lavigerie, who became the linchpin of Catholicism, including regarding the Arabs as culturally backward and plagued with moral depravity, along with building mission orphanages with a view to "catch them young" as Catholics and a clear message of "civilization through conversion."[36] At the level of politics, a similar mentality prevailed in many quarters as the non-white peoples of Algeria were also regarded as being incapable of governing themselves and needing immersion in white culture in order to advance culturally and politically. Fontaine notes that the World Council of Churches (WCC), particularly at its 1954 international assembly in Evanston, Illinois, pledged their support to all people of Asia, Africa, and other regions under colonialism "to have equal relationship with Western Christians."[37]

According to Elizabeth Forster, there was an internal tension between the Vatican and some French missionaries who were inspired by the spirit of Archbishop Lefebvre, who was the pope's vicar for Franco-Africa on the mission and direction of the Catholic mission of modernity in Africa. Whereas most of the French missionaries wanted a greater convergence of the emerging "Franco-African Catholic world forged by conquest, colonization, missions, and conversions, and knit together by Catholic faith, Catholic education, Catholic press, and Catholic charities to the Metropole, the Vatican was open to reconciling Catholicism with African culture." This threatened to unhinge the dial of history spurred in France, some of whose missionaries would rather see Africa as the extension of the French version of Catholicism. The Vatican, on the other hand, had its own version of modernity in Africa which it was pushing forward rather than continuing

---

33. Quoted in Fontaine, "Treason or Charity," 737.
34. Fontaine, "Treason or Charity," 737.
35. Fontaine, "Treason or Charity," 737.
36. Fontaine, "Treason or Charity," 738.
37. Fontaine, "Treason or Charity," 740.

the "civilizing mission" in Africa by maintaining the firm relationship of Franco-African Catholicism to the Western heritage.[38]

The second approach in the network of evangelization that one could point to in Algeria was the more progressive one. This group embraced the new vision of the Sacred Congregation for the Propagation of the faith— "don't introduce them to our countries, just our faith."[39] This small minority of French people who embraced social Christianity were opposed to French imperialistic interest in Africa and were concerned with how Christianity could serve those at the existential peripheries. They were open to treating Muslims and Arabs with respect and dialoguing with them in finding common solutions to some of the challenging social problems that faced Algeria after the Second World War and beyond. Some of the Catholic organizations that worked in this direction included L'Association de la Jeunesse Algerienne pour l'Action Sociale and Le Service des Centres Sociaux, among other groups who worked in areas of social justice, education, medical services and joint service projects among Christian and Muslim young people. These groups had a common conviction that "Christianity itself needed to be 'decolonized' in order to have a future in postcolonial Algeria."[40]

Some of these so-called "progressivist Christians" were critical of the use of Christian message and values to defend the justification of "Christian Algeria" and were later arrested and placed on trial for treason either for abating the uprising begun later by groups like the National Liberation Front or for hiding some of the fighters in their homes to prevent their arrests by the agents of the state.[41] Missionaries from the Mission de France were from groups who saw their presence in Algeria as that of providing a different view of Christianity and Catholicism, in particular from the colonial entanglement of the churches. In the view of Fontaine, these groups "provided examples of Christian solidarity to the colonized peoples that both helped secure the place of Christianity in postcolonial Algeria and resonated far beyond Algeria's borders."[42]

The Network of Schools

Even though the goals of the missionary groups differed in many ways, one method that all of them adopted was the use of mission schools to promote

38. Foster, *African Catholic*, 7.
39. Quoted in Calderisi, *Earthly Mission*, 106.
40. Fontaine, "Treason or Charity," 735.
41. Fontaine, "Treason or Charity," 736.
42. Fontaine, "Treason or Charity," 737.

their agenda. Indeed, the schools offered the most complex scenario of the difficulty in separating the goal of the Christian missionaries and that of the colonial imperialist powers, because both goals synchronized in Western education. The African who went to the mission school was indoctrinated into the "Christian" way and the superiority of Western civilization. He or she assumed a higher place among his or her fellow Africans because he or she could understand the white man. He or she could gain access to colonial jobs, which offered a higher status and access to wealth.

On the one hand, good education made one a good Christian as well as a good agent for the colonizers. However, as history will show, some of the first people to be educated in these schools were to become nationalists who fought for the liberation of Africa. It is obvious that embracing Christianity and Western education offered some Africans a claim to power higher than their African brothers and sisters who still held on to African traditional religions (ATRs).[43] The functional and pragmatic nature of African conversion to Christianity through embracing Western education is well presented in this quotation by Ezeulu in Chinua Achebe's novel *Arrow of God*. Ezeulu, who was a chief priest of the Ulu deity, sent his son Oduche to the mission school and encouraged him to become a Christian while he himself remained a staunch adherent of ATRs. This was because according to him: "I want one of my sons to join this people and be my eye there. If there is nothing in it you will come back. But if there is something there you will bring home my share. The world is like a mask dancing. If you want to see it well you do not stand in one place. My spirit tells me that those who do not befriend the White man today will be saying had we known tomorrow."[44]

The Congregation of the Holy Ghost founded in France in 1703 was a very important player in the education of Africans among the Igbo of eastern Nigeria. The missionary strategy for the use of schools for missionary work was conceived by Bishop Joseph Shanahan who argued that no one was opposed to building a school. In the course of his missionary work, he built more than 1,360 Catholic schools in today's eastern Nigeria between 1906 and 1932 when he retired as a bishop.[45] The rationale for building schools by missionaries throughout Africa could be summarized in the words of an Alsatian missionary in Cameroun in 1914: "The tree of paganism is gigantic, with a thick trunk, many branches, and deep roots in

---

43. On the tension between African graduates from the mission schools, who were later to reject both Christianity and colonialism in the colonial period, see Ajayi and Ayandele, "Writing African Church History," 98–99.

44. Achebe, *Arrow of God*, 103.

45. See the title of ch. 5 of Calderisi, *Earthly Mission*, 95–98: "Africa: 'No One is Opposed to a School.'"

the lives of the people. It is not enough to attack it with an axe. We must dig deep beneath it to deprive it of its nourishing soil, so that it will fall on its own one day. Or we can light a fire inside it that will wear it down. That fire is already burning here in our schools and beginning to spread."[46]

Conclusion

By way of conclusion, there are two important points to be highlighted in order to understand the cultural process of the network of evangelization that developed during the era of Western missionary Christianity from the mid-nineteenth century to the early 1960s: the translation of the Bible into the vernacular, and the valorization of African agency in spreading the gospel. In Igboland in West Africa, for instance, the first Francophone missionaries to work among the people, according to Eddie Okafor, published three important reference books in the Igbo language, an Igbo grammar (*Grammaire Igbo*), Igbo-French dictionary, and English-Igbo-French dictionary.[47] Resources like these helped Africans to read the Bible in their own language. Lamin Sanneh sees this translation as offering the horizontal (African agency) and the vertical (Western missionary) of Christian expansion in Africa.[48] His argument is that translatability is the lifeblood of Christianity, which explains the success of Christianity across cultures. He holds that Christianity displays a huge diversity and pluralism because it is a cross-cultural process, which safeguards it from any monolithic tyranny or from the divinization of one cultural stream. Christianity promotes the idea that every culture is equal in the scale of divine providence.[49]

Thus, there was a transition in Western missionary activities in Africa, with the amazing positive consequences of the use of vernacular literatures, hymnody, and liturgy. Just as in Europe, so it was in Africa. In the West, the so-called barbarians abandoned their old pantheons and embraced the God of the Lord Jesus Christ, which merged with the highest expression of the good in the Greek philosophical tradition. In Africa, the God of the Lord Jesus Christ was also conceived in African names such as *Olurun, Chukwu, Nyame*, among Yoruba, Igbo, and Akan peoples of West Africa, among others.[50] When one considers that the Bible and the

---

46. Quoted in Calderisi, *Earthly Mission*, 99–100.
47. Okafor, "Francophone Catholic Achievements," 311.
48. Sanneh, "Horizontal and Vertical." This essay inspired his work *Translating the Message*.
49. Sanneh, *Translating the Message*, 51.
50. See Walls, *Cross-Cultural Process*, 42.

catechism were presented in over one thousand African languages within a period of less than fifty years, one can appreciate the cross-cultural impetus that the missionaries gave not only to African Christian religion, but also to the critical and constructive reformulation of African cultures, languages, and societies in general. It also shows the interior capacity of African languages and cultures for cultural experimentation and adaptation to meet changing needs and circumstances.

To a large extent the translation of the gospel and Christianity into African languages led to the valorization of African agency in the work of spreading the good news. Adrian Hastings gives several examples from Igboland, the Xhosa, Sotho, and Shonaland of the valorization of African agency: "The Christian advance was a black advance or it was nothing.... Whether in time a missionary did actually arrive might make rather little difference to the work of preaching, teaching, conversion, the brunt of which was almost always borne at primary level by black teachers. The missionary negotiation with chiefs and colonial authorities, arranged the building of houses, the translation and printing of texts, taught the teachers, punished irregularities, supervised the overall advance of the mission—all important functions but ones which by themselves do not at all explain the actual process of conversion."[51]

It is interesting to note that the most successful mission enterprises in Africa during the missionary period were those carried out by Africans, whether the pioneering efforts of African liberated slaves in Sierra Leone beginning in 1792 or that of William Wade Harris or Bishop Ajayi Crowther. The expansion of the Christian faith was also largely due to the fact that Africans could now become missionaries to their brothers and sisters. Even though this was a difficult process for Western missionaries to fully embrace, it was an inevitable process inherent in Christianity.[52] Thus, we find ourselves dealing with three cultural currents in missionary enterprise that affect the shape of contemporary Christianity in Africa: (1) There is a tension between those who still seek a synchronizing westernized church, especially within the Catholic tradition where there is an overarching influence of the Roman church on the nature and shape of local initiatives. (2) There is the indigenizing principle, which is robust in its claims and aspirations towards making Christianity an African project. (3) There is also the very strong current of rejection in Africa of even the most positive heritage of Christianity. This is often found in some reactionary

---

51. Hastings, *Church in Africa*, 437–38.

52. On the validation of the active African element and the impact of black missionaries in the shaping of African Christian religion, see Jehu, "Back to Africa."

theologies in many African churches, especially in the face of the secularization and culture wars, which have dealt mortal blows to Western Christianity and ushered in a post-Western Christianity and a post-Christian Western society in which Africa is now the main player.

Bibliography

Achebe, Chinua. *Arrow of God*. London: Heinemann Educational, 1974.
Ajayi, J. F. Ade, and E. A. Ayandele. "Writing African Church History." In *The Church Crossing Frontiers: Essays in the Nature of Mission in Honor of Bengt Sundkler*, edited by Peter Beyerhaus and Carl F. Hallencreutz, 90–108. Studia Missionalia Upsaliensia 11. Uppsala: Almqvist & Wiksells, 1969.
Bujo, Benezet. *The Ethical Dimension of Community*. Translated by Cecelia Namulondo. Nairobi: Paulines, 1998.
Calderisi, Robert. *Earthly Mission: The Catholic Church and World Development*. New Haven: Yale University Press, 2013.
Chukwudi, A. Njoku. "The Missionary Factor in African Christian Religion, 1884–1914." In *African Christian Religion: An African Story*, edited by Ogbu Kalu, 196–217. Pretoria: University of Pretoria Press, 2013.
Ekechi, Felix K. *Missionary Enterprise and Rivalry in Igboland 1857–1914*. Cass Library of African Studies. General Studies 119. London: Cass, 1972.
Fontaine, Darcie. "Treason or Charity? Christian Missions on Trial and the Decolonization of Algeria." *International Journal of Middle East Studies* 44 (2012) 733–53.
Foster, Elizabeth A. *African Catholic: Decolonization and the Transformation of the Church*. Cambridge: Harvard University Press, 2019.
Gairdner, W. H. T. *Edinburgh 1910: An Account and Interpretation of the World Missionary Conference*. Edinburgh: Oliphant, Anderson & Ferrier, 1910.
Goldenberg, David. *The Curse of Ham: Race and Slavery in Early Judaism, Christianity, and Islam*. Princeton: Princeton University Press, 2003.
Goldman, David P. *It's Not the End of the World: It's Just the End of You; The Great Extinction of the Nations*. New York: RVP, 2011.
Gordon, David M. "Slavery and Redemption in the Catholic Missions of the Upper Congo, 1878–1909." *Slavery & Abolition* 38 (2017) 577–600.
Gregory XVI. "*In Supremo Apostolatus*: Condemning the Slave Trade." Papal Encyclicals, 1839. https://www.papalencyclicals.net/greg16/g16sup.htm.
Hastings, Adrian. *The Church in Africa 1450–1950*. Oxford history of the Christian Church. Oxford: Clarendon, 2004.
Hodgson, Dorothy L. "Engendered Encounters: Men of the Church and the 'Church of Women' in Maasailand, Tanzania, 1950–1993." *Comparative Studies in Society and History* 41 (1999) 758–83.
Jehu, Henciles. "Back to Africa: Abolitionists and Black Missionaries." In *African Christian Religion: An African Story*, edited by Ogbu Kalu, 167–89. Pretoria: University of Pretoria Press, 2013.
Kalu, Ogbu U. *The Embattled Gods: Christianization of Igboland, 1841–1991*. Trenton, NJ: Africa World, 2003.

Leo XIII. *In Plurimis*. Vatican, May 5, 1888. https://www.vatican.va/content/leo-xiii/en/encyclicals/documents/hf_l-xiii_enc_05051888_in-plurimis.html.

Lubov, Deborah Castellano. "Pope to Combonians: Without Jesus, We Can Do Nothing." *Vatican News*, June 18, 2022. https://www.vaticannews.va/en/pope/news/2022-06/pope-francis-receives-comboni-missionaries-for-general-chapter.html.

Okafor, Eddie. "Francophone Catholic Achievements in Igboland, 1883–1905." *History in Africa* 32 (2005) 307–19.

Pius X. *Il Fermo Proposito*. Vatican, June 11, 1905. http://w2.vatican.va/content/pius-x/en/encyclicals/documents/hf_p-x_enc_11061905_il-fermo-proposito.html.

Pius XII. "*Fidei Donum*: On the Present Condition of the Catholic Missions, Especially in Africa." Vatican, Apr. 21, 1957. https://www.vatican.va/content/pius-xii/en/encyclicals/documents/hf_p-xii_enc_21041957_fidei-donum.html.

Price, T. "The Missionary Struggle with Complexity." In *Christianity in Tropical Africa: Studies Presented and Discussed at the Seventh International African Seminar, University of Ghana, April 1965*, edited by C. G. Baëta, 101–19. African Ethnographic Studies of the 20th Century 4. London: Routledge, 2020.

Sanneh, Lamen. *Disciples of All Nations: Pillars of World Christianity*. Oxford Studies in World Christianity. Oxford: Oxford University Press, 2008.

———. "The Horizontal and the Vertical in Mission: An African Perspective." *International Journal of Missionary Research* 7 (1983) 165–71.

———. *Translating the Message: The Missionary Impact on Culture*. Maryknoll, NY: Orbis, 1989.

Stanley, Brian. "Africa through European Christian Eyes: The World Missionary Conference, Edinburgh 1910." In *African Identities and World Christianity in the Twentieth Century*, edited by Klaus Koschorke, 116–80. Studies in the History of Christianity in the Non-Western World (Asia, Africa, Latin America) 10. Wiesbaden: Harrassowitz, 2005.

———. *Christianity in the Twentieth Century: A World History*. Princeton History of Christianity 1. Princeton: Princeton University Press, 2018.

Wall, Barbara Mann. *Into Africa: A Transnational History of Catholic Medical Missions and Social Change*. New Brunswick, NJ: Rutgers University Press, 2015.

Walls, Andrew F. *The Cross-Cultural Process in Christian History*. Maryknoll, NY: Orbis, 2005.

8

Protestants Working Together

Modisa Mzondi

Pre-Seventh-Century Christian Presence in Africa

According to *Britannica*, the continent of Africa and the adjacent islands occupy about 30.3 million km2; they cover 6 percent of Earth's total surface area and 20 percent of its land area.[1] Africa's estimated 2020 total population is 1,340,588,147; with different languages from the four language groups, namely, the Khoisan, Nilo-Saharan, Afro-Asiatic, and Niger-Congo. The latter, who emerged from West Africa (Bantu zone/area) is considered to be the largest language group on the continent and in the world. The Bantu occupy the largest part of the African continent, the eastern, central, and southern parts, and they speak more than two thousand languages. They are called Bantu because they all commonly use Bantu, which means "people."[2] Christianity reached North Africa before reaching these people in the sixteenth century prior to colonialism, and during colonial conquest and mission efforts.[3]

The spirituality of the Bantu differs from community to community and includes spirits, deities, and ancestors, commonly classified as ATRs. Bediako echoes what some earlier African theologians argued about Bantu spirituality, namely, that is *praeparatio evangelica* (preparation for the gospel), and recommends that African Christians and theologian should no longer see Christianity as a foreign religion.[4]

African Christian discourses emerged from two centers considered to be the home of Christianity, with dates spanning from the first century to the

---

1. McMaster et al., "Africa," paras. 2–3.

2. See https://www.worldometers.info/population/countries-in-africa-by-population/.

3. Barret, *Schisms and Renewal*, 76; Ruff, Review of *Savage Systems*, 91.

4. Bediako, *Christian Identity*; Young, *African Theology*.

fourth century, namely, Alexandria and Carthage. John Mark was born in Cyrene, a city whose ancient ruins are visible in the mountain cleft of Libya.[5] He is considered one of the prominent individuals associated with this region and he came to Egypt in 42 CE. He also authored the second Gospel.[6] Other prominent first- to fifth-century individuals associated with this region are Tertullian, Cyprian, Athanasius, Augustine, and Cyril.[7]

Augustine and Athanasius were involved in some of the theological disputes in this region. First, Augustine and Donatus provided interesting influential discourses flowing out of Africa, the former representing conformity to the Catholic church and the latter representing nonconformity.[8] Second, Athanasius disputed with Arius and upheld the view that Christ's nature was single instead of two, as Arius argued. Athanasius, the influential bishop of Alexandria, contributed to the spread of Christianity to Aksum and Nubia. Christian penetration in Aksum is dated to around the middle of the third century after the deployment of Frumentius as its bishop.[9] Rukuni and Oliver reiterate the involvement of Athanasius in the establishment of Christianity in Ethiopia,[10] while Mokhtar explains that Christianity penetrated Nubia later, and was placed under the supervision of Alexandria around the middle of the fifth century CE.[11]

Furthermore, Athanasius fostered "cooperation between Byzantine and Ethiopia to entrench Christian presence in Arabia implies common interest of Christian allies. The king's role in ecclesiastical matters was affected through the clergy, this being characterized by monastic dynamics."[12] Arguably, Athanasius's effort seems to point to the beginning of the earliest fifth-century CE cooperation in mission efforts in the Mediterranean region and North Africa. What follows next is an endeavor to chronicle historical cooperation of Protestants in missions after the mission efforts of the Roman Catholic Church in sub-Sahara.

---

5. Oden, *African Memories of Mark*, 17.
6. Mbiti, *Bible and Theology*, 1.
7. Kato, *Biblical Christianity in Africa*, 42.
8. Rukuni and Oliver, "Ethiopian Christianity," 2.
9. Mekouria, "Christian Aksum," 2:403–4, 406.
10. Rukuri and Oliver, "Ethiopian Christianity," 5.
11. Mokhtar, "Conclusion," 2:734.
12. Rukuri and Oliver, "Ethiopian Christianity," 4.

Global Mission Efforts

Global mission efforts occurred in the post-Protestant Reformation and the Enlightenment contexts because most mission agencies emerged between the seventeenth and the eighteenth centuries. The term "missions" originally referred to a theology of God the Father sending the Son and the Father and the Son sending the Holy Spirit; missions found its expression in the sixteenth century through the Jesuit movement's global outreach and was later associated with European colonialism in the sixteenth century.[13] Developments in the twenty-first century show Stroope's[14] objection to using the term "missions" by questioning its biblical relevance and appropriateness and instead suggesting the term "pilgrim witness."

Bosch opines that the following six paradigms characterized missions: (1) the apocalyptic paradigm of primitive Christianity; (2) the Hellenistic paradigm of the patristic period; (3) the medieval Roman Catholic paradigm; (4) the Protestant (Reformation) paradigm; (5) the modern Enlightenment paradigm; (6) the emerging ecumenical paradigm.[15] Lee and others argue that the Western paradigm has ended and advocate for a new paradigm.[16] This chapter focuses on Protestants working together in mission as expressed in Bosch's sixth paradigm, namely, the emerging ecumenical paradigm. This relationship borders the church and mission agencies debate with an emphasis that there is no biblical support for mission agencies.[17] It emphasizes that the church oversees mission work, while the opposite view promotes the agency in charge of mission work, that is, mission agencies are a reality.[18] The Roman Catholic Church and some Protestants churches advocate for the former position while some Protestant churches advocate for the latter position.

Past developments in missions in the eighteenth century in England contributed to the emergence of church-controlled mission work through parliament and were placed under the watch of the Church of England: (1) the Society for the Promotion of Christian Knowledge (founded in 1698), and (2) the Society for the Propagation of the Gospel (SPG, founded in 1701). In 1727, in Germany, the Moravian Church and Ludwig von Zinzendorf's

---

13. Bosch, *Transforming Mission*, 1; Kim, *Joining In*, 9; Smith, *Mission after Christendom*, 15.

14. Stroope, *Transcending Mission*, 355.

15. Bosch, *Transforming Mission*, 189–99.

16. Lee, "Rethinking the Nature," 125; Ma, "Millennial Shift," 20; Moon and Lee, "Globalization, World Evangelization," 264.

17. Neill, *Creative Tension*, 84.

18. Camp, "Theological Examination," 207.

efforts led to mobilizing missionaries to reach other parts of the world. In 1792, William Carey laid the necessary groundwork that argued for new approaches in missions that would use new structures. His argument birthed denominational mission agencies, namely, the BMS (1792) linked to the Baptist Church, the LMS (1795) linked to the Congregational Church, the Scottish Missionary Society linked to the Church of Scotland, the Glasgow Missionary Society linked to the Free Church. In addition, members of the Anglican Church founded the Society for Missions to Africa and the East (which later became the CMS) in 1799. Members of the Methodist Church formed the Methodist Church Missionary Society. Some years later, nondenominational mission agencies like China Inland Mission (founded in 1865; later called Overseas Missionary Fellowship) and missional denominations like New Frontiers International also emerged in England. In Europe, the Dutch Reformed Church, Protestant churches in Switzerland that founded *La mission Suisse dans l'Afrique du Sud* (Swiss mission in South Africa), and the Lutheran Church began mission work. Later, from South Africa, the Dutch Reformed Church, the Presbyterian Church, the Anglican Church, the Lutheran Church, the Swiss Mission in South Africa, and the Methodist Church engaged in mission work in several countries north of the Limpopo River and neighboring countries.

Developments regarding global missions in the United States of America brought the existence of the American Board of Commissioners for Foreign Mission (ABCFM, 1810) consisting of denominations (Congregational and others) who pledged to work together in mission work outside the United States of America. Unfortunately, some denominations broke away due to issues of control. The desire to shift from an emphasis on denominations in mission stirred John R. Mott to mobilize students for global missions. He subsequently established the Student Volunteer Movement (1888), which later merged with the Young Men Christian Movement to form World's Student Christian Federation (1895).

Mission Context in Africa

Mission efforts in Africa occurred prior to and post the 1884–85 Berlin Conference where European colonial powers agreed to share among themselves the colonized Africa and other parts of the world. These missionary efforts flowed from the Roman Catholic Church; the Protestant churches, consisting of the Anglican Church, the Scottish Church, the continental Reformed churches; and lastly, evangelical churches. The first is called the "Catholic Model of Mission"; the second is called "Classical Mission"; and the third "Faith Mission," comprised of those interdenominational groups that opposed European theological liberalism and nationalism.[19]

The Roman Catholic Church was the first to send its clergy in the eastern and western coastlands of the African continent to accompany Portuguese traders who established bases en route to India between the fifteenth and sixteenth centuries. The first base and mission efforts were established in Central Africa's kingdom of Kongo (1491), followed by Angola, Mozambique, and South Africa in southern Africa.[20]

The Africa Study Bible mentions free slaves were the first group to come as missionaries to Sierra Leone and Liberia.[21] Later, the first Protestant Reformed church–aligned mission agencies arrived in 1792 in sub-Saharan Africa.[22] These were followed by Scotland- and England-based missionary organizations who came to different parts of the African continent. Scotland's most popular missionary, David Livingstone (1813–73), reached Nyasaland (the current Malawi), South Africa, Angola, and south and north Rhodesia (current Zimbabwe and Zambia).[23] Four missionaries from the LMS began work in South Africa in 1799.[24]

The above developments reflect that mission efforts in Africa established three forms of Christianity in the continent, namely, the Roman Catholic Church, mainline churches, and evangelical churches. Another development is that of African-initiated mission efforts flowing from AICs.[25] Looking at the African context, Walls suggests that the presence of missionaries restricted the development of authentic African expressions of Christianity and that missionaries had to be forced to leave "by international warfare, political change, economic depression at home, or simply by schism—before the story could proceed."[26]

Global Ecumenical Movements

Mission agencies also strove for unity through establishing ecumenical structures aimed at promoting working together as noticed in the 1910 World Missionary Conference held in Edinburgh, Scotland, a conference

19. Fiedler, *Story of Faith Missions*, 320.
20. Choobe, "Encounters," 110–11.
21. *Africa Study Bible*, 1955.
22. Andriatsimialomananarivo, "Missiological Dimensions," 21–24.
23. Choobe, "Encounters," 112–13.
24. Jele, "United Congregational Church," 8.
25. Andriatsimialomananarivo, "Missiological Dimensions," 58–63.
26. Walls, *Missionary Movement*, 258.

that John Mott and others actively promoted.[27] Towards the end of the nineteenth century and the beginning of the twentieth, two earlier global Protestant mission conferences paved the way for the third historic mission conference held at Edinburgh in 1910. The first had been held in 1888 in London, and the second was in 1900 in New York. These two conferences had been held after William Carey suggested, in 1810, that a world conference on mission be held in Cape Town, South Africa. These conferences led to the establishment of the African Inland Mission (AIM, 1895), the Sudan Interior Mission (SIM, 1898), and the Sudan United Mission (1904). At this period England played an influential role in mission organization while the United States of America played an important role in mission revivals.[28] Subsequent developments in England caused the formation of the International Missionary Fellowship in 1941, followed by the Evangelical Missionary Alliance in 1958 (renamed Global Connection in 2000).

Although the ecumenical movement traces its origin primarily to the founding of the WCC in 1948, prior developments show several attempts to consolidate mission efforts among Protestants who belonged to the Evangelical Alliance (1846) and the new structure called the International Missionary Council (IMC) that emerged out of the 1910 Edinburgh Conference in Scotland. It has been noted that Edinburgh was characterized by an evangelical-pietistic-puritan spirit.[29] The IMC was integrated into the WCC in 1948 to establish the WCC's Commission on World Mission and Evangelism (CWME). However, some Evangelicals were suspicious of the merger and later joined together to form the World Evangelical Fellowship in 1951 (renamed World Evangelical Alliance in 2001). During these global developments, Christians from Africa did not feature in any of these mission efforts, as Africa and her inhabitants were regarded as part of the area that need to be evangelized.

African Ecumenical Movements

The rise of African nationalism and Pan-Africanism associated with independence from colonial powers, with Ghana being the first country to gain independence in 1956, created a basis for ecumenical movements to emerge on the continent in the mid-twentieth century. Although the emergence and spread of AICs throughout the continent is not negligible, the focus of this chapter is mainly on Protestantism and a hint of Catholicism,

---

27. Sanecki, "Protestant Christian Missions," 126–29.
28. Wolffe, *Expansion of Evangelicalism*, 159.
29. McGrath, *Evangelicalism and the Future*, 14.

since influential African theologians did not consider AICs Christian enough to be recognized and awarded membership to the All Africa Conference of Churches (AACC) held in 1974 in Lusaka, Zambia. Similarly, the Association of Evangelicals in Africa and Madagascar (AEAM) did not recognize AICs as Christian enough.

The IMC helped to establish the Federal Theological Seminary of Southern Africa in 1963, following a resolution at its meeting held in Tambaram in 1938. Unfortunately, mainly Africans attended this institution while their non-African counterparts attended the Faculty of Theology at Rhodes University.[30] The AIM, an evangelical mission agency, helped to establish the AEAM (now Africa Evangelical Mission, AEA) in 1966 to promote evangelical ecumenism on the continent. Evangelical Churches of West Africa brought together all churches formerly led by the SIM.[31] AEA later launched a strategy to advance its work and influence by promoting the establishment of national evangelical fellowships in every nation on the continent to promote the work of AEA[32] and to enhance ecumenical unity among Evangelicals.[33] AEA established Francophone and Anglophone theological training centers and contributed to the establishment of the Association for Christian Theological Education in Africa ten years after AEA's establishment.[34] Some years later, in association with AEA, an ecumenical project contracted seventy African scholars to contribute to writing the Africa Bible Commentary.[35] For another ecumenical project involving African leaders, Oasis International and Tyndale House discussed the need of a Bible that met the needs of African Christians. These discussions led to initiating the process and production of the Africa Study Bible, which involved theologians, pastors, and leaders from different Christian traditions living in fifty African countries.[36]

The All Africa Lutheran Conference held in Murunga in Kenya in 1955 set the stage for forging continental ecumenical efforts. In the quest to formulate an African theology, the AACC was conceived in Ibadan, Nigeria (1958),[37] and established in Nairobi, Kenya (1963).[38] The AACC concret-

30. Duncan and Egan, "Ecumenical Struggle," 9–10.
31. Eregare et al., "Ecumenism and the Church," 58.
32. Li Hing, "Role of Evangelical Associations," 19.
33. Foday-Khabenje, "Unite in Partnership," 190.
34. Heliso, "Africa," 86–87.
35. Adeyemo, *Africa Bible Commentary*, xiii–xviii.
36. Adeyemo, *Africa Bible Commentary*, 28–29.
37. International Missionary Council, *Church in Changing Africa*, 59–64.
38. All Africa Conference of Churches, *Drumbeats from Kampala*, 11.

ized efforts of African theologians to promote ecumenism in the continent among Reformed churches and mainline churches, and also to prioritize the marginalized and the voiceless. The Ecumenical Association of African Theologians was also established to work towards the same objective. This was followed by the formation of the Conference of African Theological Institutions. In 1976, theologians from Asia, Africa, and Latin America met in Dar es Salaam, Tanzania, to discuss and formulate ways and approaches of doing theology outside the dominant Western influence. The delegates resolved to establish the Ecumenical Association of Third World Theologians (EATWOT) as a platform to engage theology in the context of the Third World of war, political liberation, poverty, racial discrimination, and other issues.[39] Henceforth, this association positioned theologians from non-Western countries to engage in global matters. Later, a regional movement, Ecumenical Foundation of Southern Africa, advanced ecumenism in southern Africa.[40] In 1985, the South African–based Institute for Contextual Theology (ICT) brought theologians from different churches to reflect on church-state relations under apartheid, rejected apartheid, and produced a document called the Kairos Document.[41] In 1986, a decade after the founding of EATWOT, the Belhar Confession condemned apartheid and other forms of oppression. The Rustenburg Conference, which the SACC convened in 1990, expressed the same sentiment.[42] Likewise, Evangelicals later produced a document called the Evangelical Witness of South Africa. The most exciting and commendable development was the initiative of Mercy Oduyoye to lead and to help establish an organization called the Circle of Concerned African Women Theologians (commonly known as the Circle) in 1989 to engage women's issues from a feminist theological perspective.[43]

Comity Agreements and Ecumenical Conferences in Africa

As indicated, the Roman Catholic Church clergy were the first to arrive in the eastern and western coastlands of the African continent while accompanying Portuguese traders. They were followed by the arrival of Protestant mission agencies from Europe, Scotland, England, and the United States of America, and some from South Africa. Both types of missionaries

39. Kamphausen, "Ecumenical Association," 1.
40. See Koegelenberg, *Church and Development*.
41. Duncan and Egan, "Ecumenical Struggle," 15–16.
42. National Conference of Church Leaders in South Africa, "Rustenburg Declaration."
43. Isabel Phiri, "Major Challenges," 64–65.

claimed to be custodians of the gospel and to be reaching "natives" with the gospel; they also believed that these native converts needed to be guided after their conversion.[44] Over time inevitable clashes and rivalries between the different mission agencies on the continent emerged. To resolve these, missionaries entered into some regional comity agreements. Such agreements are often based on John 17:21.

In South Africa, the LMS (established 1795 in England) and the American Board of Foreign Mission (established 1810 in the United States of America) agreed to work together from 1835.[45] When the British South Africa Company crossed the Limpopo River from South Africa and occupied Zimbabwe in 1890, many Protestant churches and mission agencies from various parts of the world also entered Zimbabwe and later entered into a comity agreement based on the 1888 London recommendations of the Centenary Conference on Protestant Mission of the World. Almost a century later (1904), these churches and mission agencies agreed to work in allocated geographical areas on Zimbabwe to avoid rivalry and conflict.[46]

Missionaries in Nyasaland (current Malawi) met in 1900 and 1904 to establish working relationships and birthed an ecumenical working relationship in the country.[47] Comity agreements were crafted between denomination situated in western Cameroon and the eastern Enugu Province of Nigeria after 1916.[48] German Protestant and Catholic missions worked together to abolish slavery in Cameroon. Consequently, "the fight against slavery and slave trade in Cameroon became a legal commitment on the part of the German colonial government and all mission agencies operating in the territory."[49]

In northern Rhodesia (current Zambia) Protestant missionary societies and Jesuit missionaries established the General Missionary Conference (GMC) to foster working relationships and entered into a comity agreement in 1922 not to encroach in one another's area of operation.[50] The GMC also opposed attempts of those in authority to place heavy taxes on indigenous people. In Kenya, comity agreements had two bases, namely, creating

---

44. Alawode, "Challenges and Prospects," 3.
45. Jele, "United Congregational Church," 13.
46. Dzobo, "Toward a New Church," 167–69.
47. Mapala, "Critical Reflection," 72.
48. Bowie, "Inculturation Debate," 81.
49. Kpughe, "Christian Mission Agencies," 6.
50. Choobe, "Encounters," 120–21.

colonial boundaries to ensure churches followed ethnicities, and avoiding confusion and rivalry among various missionary agents.[51]

In Nigeria, church-associated mission agencies met to unite and formed an evangelical organization in 1947. However, the poor working relationship that persisted between global-oriented Worldwide Evangelistic Crusade and Africa-oriented Mission Africa is noticeable today.[52]

Major global ecumenical conferences representing the two Christian traditions (Reformed and evangelical) were held on African soil. The first was the conference held at Achimota, Ghana, in 1958 to prepare for the merging of the IMC and the WCC.[53] In 1971 the Central Committee of the WCC held a meeting in Addis Ababa. EATWOT was established in Dar es Salaam, Tanzania, in 1976. The WCC held a conference in 1975 in Nairobi, Kenya.[54] This was followed by the World Alliance of Reformed Churches (WARC) holding its gatherings in Kitwe, Zambia, in 1995; in Cape Town, South Africa, in 2001; and in Accra, Ghana, in 2004.[55] These were followed by the Third Lausanne Congress on World Evangelization, comprised of Evangelicals, held in 2010 in Cape Town, South Africa. It is important to emphasize that social action is core to the former while proclamation is core to the latter. Eight years later, in 2018, a CWME conference attended by Roman Catholics, Protestants, Evangelicals, and Pentecostals was held in Arusha, Tanzania.[56]

Several continental and regional ecumenical meetings were held across the continent between 1904 and 2020. The General Missionary Conference of South Africa (GMCSA) held conferences between 1904 and 1936.[57] As discussed above, the AACC was first conceptualized in Ibadan, Nigeria (1958), and later established in Nairobi, Kenya (1963). After its inception, the AACC held four regional conferences. These were held in Kampala, Uganda (1963); Abidjan, Nigeria (1969); Lusaka, Zambia (1974); and Nairobi, Kenya (1981). Additionally, the Pan-African conference of EATWOT was held in Ghana in 1977 before the fourth conference. The last two AACC conferences raised concerns about the voices of women on the continent. This development led to the establishment of the Circle in Accra, Ghana, in 1989. After its inception, the Circle held important

51. Gathogo, "Early Attempts," 91.
52. Arthur, "Interaction," 166.
53. Botha, "From Edinburgh to Achimota," 149.
54. Mokholela, "Mission as Dialogue," 33.
55. Rust, "Historical Context," 2–5.
56. Pavel and Buda, "Conference on World Mission," 106–7.
57. Duncan and Egan, "Ecumenical Struggle," 2.

conferences, in Nairobi, Kenya (1996); in Addis Ababa, Ethiopia (2002); and in Yaoundé, Cameroon (2007), to engage and reflect on challenges ordinary women and theologians face on the continent.[58]

Regarding the future of ecumenism in Africa, Pillay cautions that factors like socioeconomic-political issues, the rise of Pentecostalism and spirit-led churches, the return to indigenous spirituality, and denominationalism threaten ecumenism.[59] To resolve this dilemma, Plaatjies proposes that ecumenism in Africa needs to refocus and move towards an Africa-transformative, receptive ecumenism.[60]

Pentecostal Mission, Comity Agreement, Ecumenism in Africa, and Reverse Mission in the Global North

Pentecostal churches also sent their missionaries to the continent. Most were sent following two Pentecostal events, namely, the 1901 Spirit baptism among students at Charles Parham's Bethel Bible School in Topeka, Kansas, and William Seymour's 1906 Azusa Street Revival, in Los Angeles. Many missionaries associated with Pentecostal churches in the United States of America, Canada, and Britain reached western and southern Africa in the quest to bring the gospel to the dark continent. To date, adherents of Spirit baptism (Pentecostalism) are found in various Christian denominations across sub-Saharan Africa and are mainly found in small churches.[61] Pentecostalism is rapidly increasing and had penetrated Western missionary-founded churches in Africa as most of these churches have embraced and are embracing Pentecostalism. In West Africa, Pentecostal teachings affected the evangelical mission agency of the Southern Baptist Convention. The work of IMB (the international mission agency of the Southern Baptist Convention) first began in Nigeria and spread to Benin, Burkina Faso, Ivory Coast, and Togo. Due the influence of Pentecostalism, great differences emerged between the Baptist Union and IMB; the two resolved the difference by entering into an agreement regarding Pentecostalism.[62]

The tendency of competition common between Roman Catholics and Protestants, and among Protestants, is also present among Pentecostals who in most cases are not eager to participate in ecumenical efforts among themselves and with other Protestant denominations. However, in the past

58. Isabel Phiri, "Major Challenges," 66–69.
59. Pillay, "Ecumenism in Africa," 635–36.
60. Plaatjies van Huffel, "From Conciliar Ecumenism," 10–11.
61. Ma, "Pentecostal Gift," 35–36.
62. Arnett, "Pentecostalization," 72.

decades, some Pentecostals have participated in ecumenical gathering globally and continentally. A significant shift related to the need to standardize theological training occurred. This shift resulted in the establishment of Association for Pentecostal Theological Training in Africa after missionaries, theologians, and pastors agreed it was needed.[63]

Some Pentecostal churches in Africa have joined global and local ecumenical movements. This development follows the efforts of David Du Plessis, known as "Mr. Pentecost," to create dialogue between Pentecostals and the Roman Catholic Church, the WCC, and the WARC (later called the World Communion of Reformed Churches).[64] In the Southern African context, classical Pentecostal churches in South Africa (Assemblies of God, Apostolic Faith Mission, Pentecostal Holiness Church, Full Gospel Church, and a few independent Pentecostal churches) are member churches of the Evangelical Alliance of South Africa, and the AFM is a member church of the South African Council of Churches (SACC). In Botswana, Pentecostal churches associate with the Evangelical Fellowship of Botswana and collaborate with the Botswana Christian Council and the Minister's Fraternal.[65] Although Nigeria has the largest numbers of Pentecostals on the continent, regrettably, ecumenism is not yet realized between the Pentecostal Fellowship of Nigeria and the Christian Association of Nigeria.[66]

Robert argued that the independence of African and Asian nations in the 1950s and 1960s demonstrated that mission is no longer a West enterprise.[67] Additionally, her argument that mission is from all parts of the world points to the emergence of independent African Pentecostal churches from Africa, mainly from Nigeria and Ghana, reaching the Global North (especially in Europe and the United States of America) through the phenomenon of reverse missions, Nigerian churches being the larger of the two.[68] Adenekan-Koevoets mentions that some studies indicate that Nigerian churches are succeeding in "reverse missions" and that other scholars are cautious about these findings. Their members who settled in Europe and the United States of America later initiated Bible study and prayer meetings among themselves.[69] Such meetings were later

---

63. See https://theaptea.org/ for more information.

64. Resane, "Pentecostal Ecumenism," 3–6.

65. Nkomazana, "Growth of Pentecostalism," 157–58.

66. Adeboye, "Pentecostal Challenges," 152–53.

67. Robert, "Mission in Long Perspective," 62.

68. Robert, "Boston, Students, and Missions," 24; Onongha, "Emergent Church," 73–74.

69. Adenekan-Koevoets, "Nigerian Pentecostal Diasporic Missions," 428.

followed by outreaches to fellow African and Caribbeans in the respective areas. Again, Nigerian Pentecostals settled in major cities in England and in Europe for the past three to four decades. However, a study involving Nigerian churches operating in London and Amsterdam shows that these churches are struggling to retain the second- and third-generation Nigerians born in these areas due to their dissatisfaction regarding the lack of contextualizing the gospel and leadership style of the church.[70]

Bibliography

Adebayo, Francis. "A Missiological History of Christian Association of Nigeria." *Journal of Philosophy, Culture and Religion* 13 (2015) 1–9. https://www.academia.edu/34563621/A_Missiological_History_of_Christian_Association_of_Nigeria.

Adeboye, Olufunke. "Pentecostal Challenges in Africa and Latin America: A Comparative Focus on Nigeria and Brazil." *Afrika Zamani* 11–12 (2003–2004) 136–59.

Adenekan-Koevoets, Bisi. "Nigerian Pentecostal Diasporic Missions and Intergenerational Conflicts: Case Studies from Amsterdam and London." *Mission Studies* 38 (2021) 424–47.

Adeyemo, Tokunboh, ed. *Africa Bible Commentary*. Nairobi: WordAlive, 2006.

Africa Study Bible. Carol Stream, IL: Tyndale, 2016.

Alawode, Akenyemi O. "Challenges and Prospects of Partnership among Local and Foreign Christian Missionaries in Nigeria." *HvTSt* 76 (Sept. 2020). https://doi.org/10.4102/hts.v76i3.5983.

All Africa Conference of Churches. *Drumbeats from Kampala: Report of the First Assembly of the All Africa Conference of Churches, Kampala 20–30 April 1963*. London: Lutterworth, 1963.

Andriatsimialomananarivo, Solomon. "The Missiological Dimensions of African Ecclesiology." ThD diss., University of South Africa, 2001.

Arnett, Randy Ray. "Pentecostalization: The Changing Face of Baptists in West Africa." PhD diss., Southern Baptist Theological Seminary, 2012.

Arthur, Edwin D. "The Interaction between the Mission Theology and the Practices and Publicity of Six British Evangelical Mission Agencies." PhD diss., University of Leeds, 2018.

Barrett, David B. *Schism and Renewal in Africa: An Analysis of Six Thousand Contemporary Religious Movements*. Nairobi: Oxford University Press, 1968.

Bediako, Kwame. *Christianity and Identity: The Impact of Culture upon Christian Thought in the Second Century and Modern Africa*. Regnum Studies in Mission. Oxford, UK: Regnum, 1992.

———. *Christianity in Africa: The Renewal of Non-Western Religion*. Studies in World Christianity. Edinburgh: Edinburgh University Press, 1995.

Bosch, David J. *Transforming Mission: Paradigm Shifts in Theology of Mission*. American Society of Missiology Series 16. Maryknoll, NY: Orbis, 1991.

---

70. Adenekan-Koevoets, "Nigerian Pentecostal Diasporic Missions," 428, 434–40.

Botha, Nico A. "From Edinburgh to Achimota: The World Mission Conferences as a Source of Missiological Knowledge in the Thinking of D J Bosch." *Studia Historiae Ecclesiasticae* 31 (2005) 129–52. http://hdl.handle.net/10500/4360.

Bowie, Fiona. "The Inculturation Debate in Africa." *Studies in World Christianity* (Apr. 1999) 67–92. https://www.euppublishing.com/doi/pdf/10.3366/swc.1999.5.1.67.

Camp, Bruce A. "Theological Examination of the Two-Structure Theory." *Missiology: An International Review* 23 (1995) 197–209. https://journals.sagepub.com/doi/abs/10.1177/009182969502300206.

Choobe, Maambo. "Encounters between Jesuit and Protestant Missionaries in Their Approaches to Evangelization in Zambia." In *Encounters between Jesuits and Protestants in Africa*, edited by Robert Aleksander Maryks and Festo Mkenda, SJ, Jesuit Studies 13, 110–31. Leiden: Brill, 2018. https://brill.com/view/book/edcoll/9789004347151/B9789004347151_009.xml.

Duncan, Graham A., and Anthony Egan. "The Ecumenical Struggle in South Africa: The Role of Ecumenical Movements and Liberation Organisations from 1966." *Studia Historiae Ecclesiasticae* 45 (2019). https://www.researchgate.net/publication/331737267_The_Ecumenical_Struggle_in_South_Africa_The_Role_of_Ecumenical_Movements_and_Liberation_Organisations_from_1966.

Dzobo, Samuel. "Toward a New Church in a New Africa: A Biographical Study of Bishop Ralph Edward Dodge 1907–2008." PhD diss., Asbury Theological Seminary, 2017.

Eregare, Emmanuel O., et al. "Ecumenism and the Church in the Post-Modern Era: Historical, Biblio-theological and Missiological Appraisal." *Asia-Africa Journal of Mission and Ministry* 15 (2017) 51–69.

Fiedler, Klaus. *The Story of Faith Missions.* Lynx/Regnum Studies in Evangelism, Mission, and Development. Oxford, UK: Regnum, 1994.

Foday-Khabanje, Aiah. "Unite in Partnership." In *AEA Jubilee 1966–2016: Theological Consultation Compendium*, edited by Aiah Foday-Khabenje et al., 190–207. Nairobi: AEA, 2016.

Gathogo, Julius. "The Early Attempts at Ecumenical Co-Operation in East Africa: The Case of the Kikuyu Conference of 1913." *Studia Historiae Ecclesiasticae* 36 (2010) 73–93. https://uir.unisa.ac.za/handle/10500/4636.

Heliso, Desta. "Africa and Christian Theological Education." In *AEA Jubilee 1966–2016: Theological Consultation Compendium*, edited by Aiah Foday-Khabenje et al., 86–111. Nairobi: AEA, 2016.

International Missionary Council. *The Church in Changing Africa: Report of the All Africa Church Conference, Ibadan, Nigeria, January 10–19, 1958.* New York: IMC, 1958.

Jele, Sindiso. "United Congregational Church of Southern Africa beyond 1967 into the 21st Century: A Call for a New Mission Paradigm." PhD diss., Northwest University, 2018.

Kamphausen, Erhard. "Ecumenical Association of Third World Theologians." *Religion Past and Present*, 2011. https://referenceworks.brillonline.com/entries/religion-past-and-present/*-SIM_04018.

Kato, Byang H. *Biblical Christianity in Africa: A Collection of Papers and Addresses.* Theological Perspectives in Africa 2. Ghana: African Christian, 1985.

Kim, Kirsteen. *Joining In with the Spirit: Connecting World Church and Local Mission.* London: Epworth, 2009.

Koegelenberg, Riener. A. *Church and Development: An Interdisciplinary Approach; Perspectives from Southern Africa and Europe; Report of the First Church and Development Conference*. Bellville, S. Afr.: EFSA, 1992.
Kpughe, Lang M. "Christian Mission Agencies and the Question of Slavery in German Cameroon, 1884-1916." *International Journal of Arts and Humanities* 6 (2017) 1-15.
Lee, Moojang. "Rethinking the Nature of Christian Mission: A South Korean Perspective." In *The State of Missiology Today: Global Innovations in Christian Witness*, edited by Charles E. Van Engen, Missiological Engagements, 125-39. Downers Grove, IL: IVP Academic, 2016.
Li Hing, Mario. "The Role of Evangelical Associations, National and Continental." In *AEA Jubilee 1966-2016: Theological Consultation Compendium*, edited by Aiah Foday-Khabenje et al., 18-27. Nairobi: AEA, 2016.
Ma, Wansuku A. "A Millennial Shift of Global Christianity and Mission: An Initial Reflection." *Korean Diaspora and Christian Mission* (2010) 11-23.
———. "Pentecostal Gift to Christian Unity: Its Possibility in the New Global Context." *International Review of Mission* 107 (2018) 33-48.
Mapala, Cogitator W. "A Critical Reflection and Malawian Perspective on the Commemoration of the Edinburgh 1910 International Missionary Conference." *Studia Historiae Ecclesiasticae* 41(2015) 63-78.
Mbiti, John S. *Bible and Theology in African Christianity*. Nairobi: Oxford University Press, 1986.
McGrath, Allister. *Evangelicalism and the Future of Christianity*. London: Hodder & Stoughton, 1988.
McMaster, David N., et al. "Africa." *Encyclopedia Britannica*, July 8, 1999; last updated Oct. 1, 2023. https://www.britannica.com/place/Africa.
Mekouria, Tekle Tsadik. "Christian Aksum." In *General History of Africa*, edited by G. Mokhtar, Unesco General History of Africa, 2:401-21. Berkeley, CA: Heinemann, 1981.
Mokholela, James L. "Mission as Dialogue in the Context of Religious Pluralism in South Africa: A Pentecostal-Evangelical Perspective." MA thesis, Northwest University, 2013.
Mokhtar, G., ed. "Conclusion." In *General History of Africa*, edited by G. Mokhtar, Unesco General History of Africa, 2:732-37. Berkeley, CA: Heinemann, 1981.
Moon, Steve S., and David T. Lee. "Globalization, World Evangelization and Global Missiology." In *One World or Many? The Impact of Globalization on Mission*, edited by Richard Tiplady, Globalization of Mission, 252-69. Pasadena, CA: Carey, 2003.
National Conference of Church Leaders in South Africa. "The Rustenburg Declaration." Kerkargief, 1990. https://kerkargief.co.za/doks/bely/DF_Rustenburg.pdf.
Neill, Stephen. *Creative Tension*. London: Edinburgh, 1959.
Nkomazana, Fidelis. "The Growth of Pentecostalism and Christian Umbrella Organisations in Botswana." *Studia Historiae Ecclesiasticae* 40 (2014) 153-73.
Oden, Thomas C. *The African Memories of Mark: Reassessing Early Church Tradition*. Early African Christianity Set. Downers Grove, IL: IVP Academic, 2001.
———. *How Africa Shaped the Christian Mind: Rediscovering the African Seedbed of Western Christianity*. Early African Christianity Set. Downers Grove, IL: IVP Academic, 2010.

Olayo, Fredrick K. "Anglican Church Unity: The Tension between Anglican Church Unity and Ethnic Identity in Kenya." MTh thesis, MF Norwegian School of Theology, 2015.

Onongha, Kelvin. "The Emergent Church in Africa and the Phenomenon of Reverse Mission." In *African Culture and Global Politics Language, Philosophies, and Expressive Culture in Africa and the Diaspora*, edited by Toyin Falola and Danielle Sanchez, Routledge African Studies 51, 70–84. London: Routledge, 2014.

Pavel, Aurel, and Daniel Buda. "The Conference on World Mission and Evangelism 'Moving in the Spirit: Called to Transforming Discipleship,' 8–13 March 2018, Arusha, Tanzania: Some Preliminary and Personal Reflections from an Orthodox Perspective." *RES* 10 (2018) 106–11. https://sciendo.com/pdf/10.2478/ress-2018-0008.

Phiri, Isaac. "Why African Churches Preach Politics: The Case of Zambia." *Journal of Church and State* 41 (1999) 323–47.

Phiri, Isabel Apawo. "Major Challenges for African Women Theologians in Theological Education (1989–2008)." *Studia Historiae Ecclesiasticae* 34 (2008) 63–81.

Pillay, Jerry. "Ecumenism in Africa: Theological, Contextual, and Institutional Challenges." *Ecumenical Review* 67 (2015) 635–51.

Plaatjies van Huffel, Mary-Anne. "From Conciliar Ecumenism to Transformative Receptive Ecumenism." *HvTSt* 73 (2017). https://journals.co.za/doi/abs/10.4102/hts.v73i3.4353.

Posnanski, M. "Introduction to the Later Pre-History of Sub-Saharan Africa." In *General History of Africa*, edited by G. Mokhtar, Unesco General History of Africa, 2:532–50. Berkeley, CA: Heinemann, 1981.

Resane, Kelebogile T. "Pentecostal Ecumenism: The Legacy of David Du Plessis." *Pharos Journal of Theology* 102 (2021). https://doi.org/10.46222/pharosjot.102031.

Robert, Dana L. "Boston, Students, and Missions from 1810–2010." In *2010Boston: The Changing Contours of World Mission and Christianity*, edited by Todd M. Johnson et al., 13–27. Eugene, OR: Pickwick Publications, 2012.

———. "Mission in Long Perspective from 1910 to the 21st Century." In *Edinburgh 2010 Mission Today and Tomorrow*, edited by Kirsteen Kim and Andrew Anderson, Regnum Edinburgh Centenary Series 3, 55–68. Oxford, UK: Regnum, 2011.

Ruff, Jeffrey C. Review of *Savage Systems: Colonialism and Comparative Religion in Southern Africa*, by David Chidester. *MTSR* 11 (1999) 163–69. https://www.jstor.org/stable/23555597.

Rukuni, Rugare, and Erna Oliver. "Ethiopian Christianity: A Continuum of African Early Christian Polities." *HvTSt* 75 (2019). https://doi.org/10.4102/hts.v75i1.5335.

Rust, Averrel. "The Historical Context of the Accra Confession." *HvTSt* 65 (2009). https://doi.org/10.4102/hts.v65i1.280.

Sanecki, Kim. "Protestant Christian Missions, Race and Empire: The World Missionary Conference of 1910, Edinburgh, Scotland." MA thesis, Georgia State University, 2006.

Smith, David. *Mission after Christendom*. London: Darton, Longman & Todd, 2003.

Stroope, Michael W. *Transcending Mission: The Eclipse of a Modern Tradition*. London: Apollos, 2017.

Tiénou, Tite. "Christian Theology in an Era of World Christianity." In *Globalizing Theology: Belief and Practice in an Era of World Christianity*, edited by Craig Ott and Harold A. Netland, 37–51. Grand Rapids: Baker, 2006.

Walls, Andrew F. *The Missionary Movement in Christian History: Studies in the Transmission of Faith*. Maryknoll, NY: Orbis, 1996.

Weber, Hans R. "Out of All Continents and Nations: A Review of Regional Developments in the Ecumenical Movement." In *The Ecumenical Advance: A History of the Ecumenical Movement*, edited by Harold E. Fey, 2:63–92. Geneva: WCC, 1970.

Wolffe, John. *The Expansion of Evangelicalism: The Age of Wilberforce, More, Chalmers and Finney*. History of Evangelicalism Series 2. Nottingham, UK: IVP Academic, 2006.

Young, Josiah U. *African Theology: A Critical Analysis and Annotated Bibliography*. Bibliographies and Indexes in Religious Studies 26. Greenwood, IN: Bloomsbury Academic, 1993.

9

Salvation in African Pentecostalism

JOSEPH BOSCO BANGURA

ACROSS AFRICA, PENTECOSTALISM HAS rejuvenated Christian growth. Pentecostalism continues to adapt to and fulfil spiritual aspirations in line with African contextual realities beyond what missionary Christianity had offered African converts. Emerging from the fringes of Evangelical Christianity in the 1970s, Pentecostalism grew quickly to become the single most important factor impacting and transforming Africa's Christian imagination.[1] Despite the continued dominance of instrumentalist arguments premised on the resonance with African primal spirituality, little attention has been paid to the broadening of the meaning of salvation, which lies at the center of Pentecostalism's success.

This chapter discusses this African, pneumatic broadening of salvation using three prisms: First, it offers a brief overview of the theologies that supported Protestant mission in order to identify the minimalistic and reductionist understanding of salvation that was handed down to and is still present among Western-founded missionary churches in Africa. Second, it probes the continuity, discontinuity, and disruption arguments that were suggested by early African theology protagonists to explain Christianity's relation to the African primal worldview so that the salvation it offers reflects African Christianity's communal biblical worldview. And third, it explores how Africa's newer Pentecostalism has swiftly broadened conceptions of salvation in ways that enhance the African Christian aspiration for a sacrifice of participation in the church; the physical community of the kingdom of God on earth; a restoration of the vitality of health, healing, and wholeness; and an experience of the abundant and prosperous life. The chapter contends that African Pentecostalism has moved the salvation

---

1. Clarke, *Pentecostalism*, 1; Bangura, *Pentecostalism in Sierra Leone*, 4–5; Kollman, "Classifying African Christianities."

debate from Protestant, minimalistic, propositional reduction to an African, pneumatic broadening that embraces all of life.

Protestant Mission and the Minimalistic Theology of Salvation

In Protestant missions, the doctrine of salvation not only speaks about the problem of human sin and its resulting alienation from God, it also argues that this can be resolved only if the sinner personally repents of sin and places faith in the vicarious death of Christ. But in much of the history of Protestant mission, Western missionaries often operated from a presumption of salvation that was minimalistic and reductionist. Spurred by the enthusiasm of seventeenth-century puritan and pietistic movements, early missionaries disseminated this view in the colonies.[2] Beliefs about predestination and justification were interpreted in ways that reduced salvation to a matter of individual conversion based on response to the Christian kerygma. This privatized view of salvation separated new converts from the church, which was seen only in terms of the instrumentalist role it performed in mission. But this overtly privatized view of salvation bore the hallmarks of a weak ecclesiology that resulted in the separation of "soteriology from both ecclesiology and pneumatology."[3] Consequently, a review of mission theology sources suggests that there are three broad factors influencing this individualistic understanding of salvation among Protestant missionaries.

First, Protestant mission theologies of salvation were influenced by lay mistrust against church establishment and its ordained clergy among Puritans and Pietists. For the puritan movement, which had developed among (some) Calvinist churches in England and Scotland, there was resentment of what they saw as dry theological abstractions that were developed by the clergy but that had not produced any distinct missionary impulses. To correct this imbalance in the church's clerical establishment, Puritanism developed a mission theology that emphasized various theological motifs including predestination, the glory of God, colonies as theocracies, and the supremacy of Western culture.[4] The Pietists who emerged from the Lutheran Church were also critical of the mainstream Lutheran view of mission. Preferring instead to give concepts such as repentance, conversion, the new birth, and sanctification a new meaning, Pietism opted to embrace values that emphasized the disciplined life rather than sound doctrine, subjective experience of the individual

2. Nussbaum, *Reader's Guide*, 66–67.
3. Tennent, *Invitation to World Missions*, 63.
4. Nussbaum, *Reader's Guide*, 66.

rather than ecclesiastical authority, and practice rather than theory. These characteristics became the symbols with which the movement conducted its missionary engagements in the colonies.[5] To a great extent, these two movements produced mission theologies that emphasized an individualistic and minimalistic understanding of salvation. By highlighting that the defining point of the conversion process was to be personally experienced by the individual, Puritanism and Pietism influenced much of the Protestant and evangelical involvement in world missions. Vestiges of these views are still detectable across a broad range of former Protestant missionary-founded churches across the African continent.

Second, Protestant missionary initiatives held firmly to the belief that assent to the propositional statements affirming historic biblical Christianity represented the best way for individual converts to experience salvation. While the need for individual confession of sin and repentance are central in the salvation discourse, hardly did those missionaries realize that by reducing salvation to a set of beliefs that one was expected to confess and uphold, the entire missionary enterprise would be held captive by dogmatic theologies that were developed at the height of Europe's Enlightenment period. By making such views universal and by shaping salvation discourses along those individualistic lines, the Christian faith appears to resonate more easily with Western rationalistic individualism than with southern communal living where participation in church life is as important as expressing personal faith in Christ. Timothy Tennent questions this Protestant missionary minimalistic framing of salvation when he observes:

> A theological reduction ... often gives rise to a minimalistic, individualistic emphasis, which downplays the role of the church in the final goal of missions. ... The emphasis on numerical growth in evangelism and missions has tended to focus on a minimalistic view of salvation, rather than the long-term viability and reproducibility of the church.[6]

Even if converts must confess and believe certain dogmatic facts in order to be saved, their growth towards Christlike maturity is dependent upon their integration in church life. Removed from regularly participating in the life of a vibrant faith community, their faith can be exposed to diversified circumstances that may cause it to wither and contract.

Third, the specific Protestant missionary equation of the doctrine of salvation with justification contributed to the missionary minimalistic

---

5. Nussbaum, *Reader's Guide*, 67.
6. Tennent, *Invitation to World Missions*, 377.

reduction of the Christian doctrine of salvation that was used in missionary work.[7] Obviously, a proper biblical exploration of salvation will indicate that it does include the doctrine of justification where Christ's vicarious death on the cross is primarily responsible for saving sinful humanity from the blight of sin and alienation from God (Eph 2:5). But the biblical doctrine of salvation also includes the concept of sanctification, which describes a process where the individual believer is being saved in the here and now (1 Cor 1:18). Reflecting on the sanctification part of salvation, Tennent adds:

> Salvation also inherently implies incorporation in a community. We are not just baptized *by* faith; we are baptized *into* a faith that is shared in a *community* that exists in space around the world and back through time.[8]

Besides justification and sanctification, another important aspect that this understanding of the salvation process creates is that it finds full and perfect completion only at the parousia when Christ returns to establish his kingdom's glorious reign and offer glorification to the elect saints (1 Cor 3:15). Hence, to be conscientiously biblical, the missionary formulation of the doctrine of salvation that lies at the heart of the gospel must encompass justification, sanctification, and glorification, all of which are intrinsically connected to one another. Taken together, these three formulations of the doctrine of salvation bear witness to God's salvific sending of his son Jesus to die on the cross in place of sinful humanity and reconcile alienated humanity back to God. What this means is that Protestant missionary Christianity would have been well served if it had clarified the assumption that professing right doctrine was all that was needed in the salvation process.[9]

African Theology's Continuity, Discontinuity, and Disruption Thesis

When Protestant Christian missionaries arrived in sub-Saharan Africa, they came with a Christian worldview that was not only colored by an individualistic assent to faith but was also based on a propositional understanding of the Christian doctrine of salvation. Once they arrived, Western missionaries realized that Africans too have their own religious beliefs, the strength of which led to them being described as a people who are profusely and incurably religious. Africa's religiosity meant that there is often no need to offer

---

7. Tennent, *Invitation to World Missions*, 376.
8. Tennent, *Invitation to World Missions*, 62 (emphasis added).
9. Nussbaum, *Reader's Guide*, 67.

philosophical arguments proving either the existence or power of God.[10] Not surprisingly, Mercy Amba Oduyoye, a leading female theologian and bulwark behind the Circle, proposed an argument where she observes: "The fool says in his heart 'There is no God.' In traditional Africa there are no such 'fools.'"[11] Although this dictum of Africa's *homo religiosus* has been fiercely contested,[12] the common perception that still exists is that for Africans, God is the starting point of all reality, whether visible or invisible. This God is believed to be almighty and has power to do that which is consistent with and pleases the divine nature. Such divine actions have suitably provided salvation to humanity through Christ. Africans who embrace this worldview are known to use a variety of religious manifestations to help draw humankind back to conformity with the Supreme Being where they can fully enjoy God's omnipotence and the salvation God provides. In this milieu, the function of religion transcends the anthropocentric benefits followers receive, because it serves to draw people to a closer relationship with this God and through it facilitates harmonious relationship with the Supreme Being, divinities, ancestors, spirits, and human society.[13]

At the emergence of African theology, the first generation of African Christian scholars were keen on developing theological ideas that were cooked in an African pot and bore the imprint of Africa's religious identity.[14] This was deemed necessary because African Christian initiatives as well as local cultures were marginalized by both colonial agents and missionary Christianity.[15] Spurred by this concern, one of the earliest discourses that animated African theology centered on formulating a doctrine of God and salvation that would encompass the totality of Africa's religious traditions. While this was sometimes pitched against the paleness of missionary Christianity, the positions that emerged could be divided into three camps: continuity, discontinuity, and disruption.

The first camp includes those who had argued that there is continuity between African tradition and dogmatic Christian view insofar as belief in God is concerned. John Mbiti and Bolaji Idowu—both of whom were perhaps the principal supporters of this view—saw this knowledge as a *praeparatio evangelica* that both preceded Western Christian missionaries and

---

10. Mbiti, *African Religions and Philosophy*, 1; Magesa, *African Religion*, 25.
11. Oduyoye, "African Experience of God," 494.
12. See p'Bitek, *African Religions*; Jahnel, "Maps," 138; Van den Toren et al., *Is Africa Incurably Religious?*; Platvoet and Van Rinsum, "Is Africa Incurably Religious?"
13. Ngong, "African Pentecostalism," 193.
14. See Fiedler et al., *Theology Cooked*.
15. Grillo et al., *Religions in Contemporary Africa*, 138.

prepared Africans to receive the salvation offered by the Christian gospel.[16] John Mbiti, a leading architect of this view, forcefully argues:

> When we identify the God of the Bible as the same God who is known through African religion (whatever its limitations), we must also take it that God has had a historical relationship with African people. God is not insensitive to the history of peoples other than Israel. Their history has a theological meaning.[17]

To further develop this theme, Mbiti published *Concepts of God in Africa* to show that despite the many cultural differences existing across Africa, the idea of God is a unifying factor that could support Christian beliefs, particularly those relating to salvation, so that Christianity can be in a position where it takes root in African soil.[18] For his part, the Nigerian theologian Bolaji Idowu bemoans the use of adjectives that tend to hierarchize African divinities, arguing that such conceptualization contributed to the marginalization of God in African thought and made missionary Christianity's salvation message look more Western than biblical to African Christian eyes.[19]

Second, while others recognized the possibility of scattered traces of general revelation in African tradition, they still argued that there was a clear discontinuity between traditional African and the dogmatic Christian understanding of God. For instance, in his comparison of both views, Charles Nyamiti not only recognizes the similarities but observes that "the Christian conception of God is purer and more perfect, so that, by professing the Christian faith, the African will have the occasion to purify his theistic doctrine from superstition and error."[20] Questions were further raised against arguing for the theological validity of similarities in the existence and foreknowledge of the Christian God and the salvation God provides in African tradition.[21] Such criticisms meant that the consensus that emerged favored a discontinuity, which has unequivocally rejected any possibility that Africa's religious traditions could provide a basis for experiencing either the true God or serving as a *praeparatio evangelica* that would smoothen the conversion process. As was to be expected, missionary Christianity was more sympathetic with this position than the

---

16. Mbiti, "Challenges of Language"; Magesa, *Anatomy of Inculturation*, 188; Idowu, *African Traditional Religion*, 62–65.

17. Mbiti, "The Encounter of Christian Faith and African Religion," 1980, 817–20.

18. Mbiti, *Concepts of God in Africa*, 1975.

19. Idowu, *African Traditional Religion*, 62–65.

20. Nyamiti, *African Tradition*, 19.

21. Kato, *Theological Pitfalls in Africa*, 3:44, 3:70; Sawyerr, *God: Ancestor or Creator?*, p'Bitek, *Religion of Central Luo*.

first, and sometimes used it to its advantage against the African initiatives that had begun to emerge within Christianity.

Third, dissatisfaction with the essentializing positions of both views prompted the development of new ideas that aim to bring sharpened clarity on the matter. Those who propose theologies that disrupted existing understandings of God argue that what Africa needed was not a pale copy of Western Christianity that only succeeded in drawing areas where parallels and differences existed between the two worldviews. Rather, Africa needed an appropriation of Christianity that celebrated Africa's emerging Christian identity in ways that are representative of all theologies produced by God's people everywhere. Kwame Bediako takes this identity issue to aver that where a mature African Christian identity has begun to emerge, African Christians will begin to develop theologies that are true to their authentic African identity,[22] with Emmanuel Lartey suggesting a rejection of any colonial accretions and vestiges that may have been foisted on African soil.[23] It therefore makes sense to argue that to a large extent, Pentecostalism's engagement with salvation must be understood in the context of a theological disruption that African Christians are bringing to the agenda of world Christianity discourses. The primary motivation was that existing salvific formulations prevalent in the African church were more related to the preferences of the Enlightenment Christianity that missionaries had brought to Africa during colonialization than what the African Christian imagination had begun to develop. Thus, the pushback against theologies that made little sense to the African religio-cultural and primal worldview began to gain currency. For instance, Jean-Marc Éla's insights indicate just how disruptive such views are to Christianity. Éla notes:

> If Christianity wants to reach Africans, to speak to their hearts and enter into their consciousness and the space where their soul breathes, it must change. To do so, Christianity must do violence to itself and break the chains of western rationality, which means almost nothing in the African civilisation of symbols. Without some form of epistemological break with the scholastic universe, Christianity has little chance of reaching the African.[24]

---

22. Bediako, *Christianity in Africa*.
23. Lartey, *Postcolonializing God*.
24. Éla, *My Faith as African*, 41.

African Pentecostalism's Broadening of Salvation

While the hopes expressed by earlier African theological voices had predicted that indigenous African Christianity would grow in its ability to develop theologies that are reflective of the concerns, questions, and dilemmas of Africa, there would have been little expectation that this was going to come from the newer Pentecostal and charismatic movements that began to emerge out of African university campuses in the 1970s. Despite the criticisms that were levied against earlier African initiatives in Christianity, which were described in the so-called AICs, John Mbiti was forthright in observing that "cattle are born with ears, their horns grow later."[25] This comment when assessed from an African Pentecostalism perspective would suggest that after African Christianity had grown in its intellectual appropriation of the faith (which represents the horns), the form of Christianity engendered would begin to develop theologies that would be suitable both for its local cultural contexts and dialogue with counterparts in world Christianity. This process did not come easily, as African Christians took on this role only unexpectedly as a by-product of the successes of the literacy programs that Western missionaries had implemented.[26] Nevertheless, the programs gave African Christian converts the ability to read the Bible for themselves and to draw insights and understandings from the biblical text that transcended the missionary paradigms under which they were trained. For this reason, in developing a theory that was premised on the translatability of Christianity, Lamin Sanneh reasoned that missiological analysis must move from exclusively assessing the missionary's pioneering role in the historic transmission of the gospel on African soil to the indigenous reception and assimilation by locals of that gospel. This is because when African converts received the Christian gospel they were transformed and empowered by the gospel in ways that missionaries would never have anticipated.[27] The hermeneutical approaches adopted by African Christians in general and African Pentecostals in particular represent an enlarging of the meaning of biblical themes such as salvation, which is central in the Christian story. The African appropriation of Christian doctrines goes beyond those that were merely extrapolated from the biblical text using rigorous methods of textual criticism, even if those were seen as normative. African Pentecostalism was able to offer a broadened meaning of salvation that highlighted three core issues:

25. Mbiti, "Cattle Are Born."
26. Kim and Kim, *Christianity as World Religion*, 108–13.
27. Sanneh, "Horizontal and Vertical."

Salvation as Participation in the Community of the Kingdom of God

African Pentecostalism accepts the view that Jesus's vicarious death on the cross and triumphant resurrection is "the result of a divine plan to provide a mediator between an offended God and a sinful humanity."[28] Whereas this understanding of salvation primarily refers to Christianity's central doctrine of "atonement, forgiveness of sin and reconciliation with God,"[29] Pentecostalism's reckoning of the realms of human life permeated by this salvation extends far beyond the spiritual dimensions of life often emphasized by Western-missionary Christianity. For Pentecostalism, to be "born again" requires a radical break with one's traditional past. Being born again calls on new converts to sever ties that keep one bound to traditional deities. It asks for the renouncing of sinful and demonic practices, the abandoning of old habits and unacceptable practices, and the complete surrender of one's life to Christ. This act not only ushers converts into a new relationship with Christ but brings them into full membership in the church, God's visible kingdom here on earth. While the moment of conversion can be dramatic, as new converts give up items related to their past life that are publicly burned in fire in the presence of other members of the faith community, the conversion process itself "is less of an event than an ongoing process whose underlying structure is linear and teleological."[30] As an ongoing process of sanctification, Pentecostal beliefs about salvation further show the ethical consequences that are expected to accompany conversion where the new convert gives up unacceptable behavior and purposefully makes commitments to living a life of renewal in the Holy Spirit, which results in moral uprightness and responsibility. Hence, by displaying these visible signs of personal holiness, spiritual insight, and moral transformation, the Pentecostal convert is able to reinterpret "the past, which forms an integral point of conversion, produces new starting points and prospects for the present and the future."[31] As a consequence, while African Pentecostalism believes that new converts must personally repent of sin and accept God's offer of salvation in Christ, they know that any meaningful living of the born-again life happens only by participating in the church, the earthly community of the kingdom of God. It is here that new converts are socialized and receive the spiritual nutrients that facilitate growth towards Christlike maturity. It is by participating in the body of Christ that they are prepared as a bride ready

---

28. Komolafe, "Changing Face of Christianity," 228.
29. Larbi, "Nature of Continuity," 96.
30. Marshall-Frantani, "Mediating the Global," 285.
31. Roelofs, "Charismatic Christian Thought," 219.

to receive the groom and participate in the eschatological banquet where their mortal bodies receive glorification.

Salvation as Restoration of Health, Healing, and Wholeness

It was Harvey Cox who argued that healing and deliverance are practices where African Pentecostalism has the most to offer to world Christianity.[32] This is hardly a surprising comment because in African Pentecostalism, illness and health are central practices that lubricate the ambiance of the movement's pneumatic liturgies. When conducted either in the gathered church or privately, such events emphasize Jesus as the superpower who heals every disease and delivers those who are bound by demons.[33] As early as 1981 Kofi Appiah-Kubi already argued that concern for healing is the primary causation for the rise of Pentecostalism in Africa.[34] Much later, Ogbu Kalu corroborated this argument, adding:

> Healing is the heartbeat of the liturgy and the entire religious life. It brings the community of suffering together; it ushers supernatural power into the gathered community and enables all to bask together in its warmth. It releases the energy for participatory worship that integrates the body, spirit and soul.[35]

Christianity in Africa must therefore contend with salvific theologies that take seriously healing, because "Africa, more than any other continent on earth, is in need of healing in all dimensions."[36] When Pentecostalism arose, it adopted contextual approaches that validated traditional health and healing cosmologies in ways that differed from missionary Christianity even though these approaches had complemented Christian ministry by establishing hospitals where Western medicine was dispensed. Drawn from the African primal worldview, African Pentecostalism saw the human person as a "relational being whose body, mind and spirit are conditioned by critical relationships: the family (including the ancestors), the community (including witches and diviners who can affect the body by supernatural means), spirits, divinities and God."[37] Pentecostalism argued that "evil spirits and demons exercise real power over people, which can only be combatted by

32. Cox, *Fire from Heaven*, 255.
33. Hock, "Jesus Power—Super-Power!"
34. Appiah-Kubi, *Man Cures, God Heals*, 86.
35. Kalu, *African Pentecostalism*, 362.
36. Tiénou, "Training of Missiologists," 98–99.
37. Grillo et al., *Religions in Contemporary Africa*, 178.

evoking the power of God."[38] Thus, any rupture in this web of relationships will require the faithful to undertake rituals of healing and deliverance. Although sometimes criticized for presenting paradoxical nuances that at one point preserve traditional spiritual ontologies but at the same time demonize them as sites for spiritual warfare,[39] it nevertheless offers an exciting new path in the movement's understanding of salvation where "the good news also involves instances of divine healing as externalized forms of salvation. Such a theological position enables Neocharismatics to integrate God's salvific work in the Spirit as well as in the body."[40]

Salvation as Experiencing the Abundant and Prosperous Life

Unlike other expressions of Christianity across the African continent, African Pentecostalism has been most successful in arguing that salvation represents God's primary message of good news to the poor. African Pentecostalism believes that this message lies firmly anchored in Jesus's public ministry, which they see as having a clear preference for the poor, sick, demon-possessed, and marginalized in society.[41] Salvation therefore brings the convert to an embodied place where they are able to enjoy life in all the veritable fullness God intended it to be. For this reason, African Pentecostalism perpetuates among its constituents an understanding that "material, physical, professional and relational well-being are an integral part of salvation and are a sign of true faith and of God's favourability towards the true believer."[42] Nevertheless, it must be noted that far from merely understanding this holistic appropriation of salvation as dealing principally with material things, the believer's experience of the abundant and prosperous life suggests that "prosperity within an African context goes beyond personal wealth and material things and represents harmonious living through peace, satisfaction, contentment, and maintenance of the social networks."[43] E. Kingsley Larbi's research among Ghanaian Pentecostals indicates just how expansive the experience of the abundant and prosperous life is. Larbi observes:

---

38. Grillo et al., *Religions in Contemporary Africa*, 83.
39. Robbins, "Anthropology of Religion," 160.
40. Komolafe, "Changing Face of Christianity," 229.
41. Komolafe, "Changing Face of Christianity," 230.
42. Grillo et al., *Religions in Contemporary Africa*, 81–82.
43. Clarke, *Pentecostalism*, 177.

> Evidence available indicates that suppliants attend Pentecostal prayer camps primarily in search of salvation that relates to the here and now. Supplicants' concerns include the need for healing; financial and economic problems; problems related to marriages, children, employment and family needs. Some go there because of lawsuits; others go there because they are struggling with drunkenness and they want to overcome it. Some go there because of educational issues; they go there because of accommodation needs: a place to lay their heads. Some go there because of the problem of bad or frightful dreams; some have problems with demonic and witchcraft attacks. Others go there because of social expectations, particularly the need to provide for their families.[44]

Such remarks call for new analytical perspectives that explicate the wider implications of salvation for the convert's ability to experience the abundant and prosperous life in African Pentecostalism. It is partly for this reason that Ogbu Kalu perceptively counters criticisms of the prosperity gospel when he observes:

> Pentecostal prosperity theology, when properly exegeted, is rich in its capacity to re-imagine the gospel from an indigenous idiom. Pentecostal theology does not encourage people to fold their arms and wait for manna to drop from the skies; rather, poverty-alleviation strategies in indigenous communities are far more nuanced.[45]

Hence, the claims of experiencing the abundant and prosperous life are not to be understood as wishful thinking that aimlessly seeks to bring to earth the pie in the sky. Rather, having severed all ties with their traditional past, the new convert is in a better position to reorder their life priorities in line with their newfound faith and tap into the benefits such faith accrues. Further, the new convert is able to make decisions and life choices that have wider socioeconomic implications, which bring betterment in their life and family situations. This understanding of salvation, which offers the new convert a path to experiencing the abundant and prosperous life, must then be understood as representing the "productivity gospel" in African Pentecostal Christianity.[46]

---

44. Larbi, "Nature of Continuity," 96.
45. Kalu, *African Pentecostalism*, 262.
46. Barron, "Is the Prosperity Gospel."

Conclusion

The arguments presented in this chapter are conspicuous for their brevity and cannot do justice to the interesting prospects that African Pentecostalism's broadening of the meaning of salvation brings to missiology, intercultural theology, and world Christianity. However, from the analysis given, I have argued that (1) participation in the community of the kingdom of God; (2) a restoration of the vitality of health, healing, and wholeness; and (3) an experience of the abundant and prosperous life are the key dimensions that African Pentecostalism has used to explain its understanding of salvation. Thus, in times when interest among theologians is steadily gravitating towards a fuller appreciation of emerging thoughts in the doctrine of salvation in world Christianity, one wonders whether perspectives about the debate suggested by African Pentecostalism are represented at all in such discourses.[47] In our quest to look for fresh insights, African Pentecostalism's broadening of salvation must result in a greater appreciation of the riches of Africa's religious and cultural heritage that this homegrown, pneumatic Christianity is bringing to the debate. Appreciating this indigenous embroidery will require that "although African Pentecostals seldom have an elaborate theology such as is found in most of northern Christianity, they have a distinct and considerable contribution to make."[48] Therefore, because "all theologies—including biblical ones—are contextually conditioned,"[49] it must be noted that what African Pentecostalism has done with its broadening of the meaning of salvation is to allow the form of Christianity embraced by its constituents to make sense in their cultural contexts and through it begin the process of dialoguing with Christian confessions embraced by other members of the world church. But those theologies that emerge from Africa's specific cultural context do not absolutize as the West's Protestant missionaries did when they brought their minimalistic view of salvation in the missionary message. It is imperative therefore that this broadening be understood within the overall context of an African Christianity whose desire is to contribute a compass to life that makes sense among people who have embraced Christianity and are desirous to profess that faith amid difficult sociocultural circumstances. As E. Kingsley Larbi has observed,

> For these people, the concept of salvation cannot be divorced from their existential needs. The "Saviour" in this sense . . . is not only the one that saves them from the curse and the blight

---

47. See for instance, Hick et al., *Four Views on Salvation*.
48. Anderson, "Intercultural Theology," 139.
49. Hollenweger, "Intercultural Theology," 91–92.

of sin (though this is their starting point), he is also the one who supremely helps them in their day-to-day existential needs.[50]

It must be contended that Pentecostalism's broadening of the meaning of salvation represents African Christianity's attempt to produce theologies that respond to its contexts.

Bibliography

Anderson, Allan. "Intercultural Theology, Walter J. Hollenweger and African Pentecostalism." In *Intercultural Theology: Approaches and Themes*, edited by Mark J. Cartledge and David Cheetham, 128–44. London: SCM, 2011.

Appiah-Kubi, Kofi. *Man Cures, God Heals: Religion and Medical Practice among the Akans of Ghana*. Totowa, NJ: Allanheld Osmun, 1981.

Bangura, Joseph Bosco. *Pentecostalism in Sierra Leone: Contextual Theologies, Theological Education and Public Engagements*. Hamburg: Missionshilfe, 2020.

Barron, Joshua R. "Is the Prosperity Gospel, Gospel? An Examination of the Prosperity and Productivity Gospels in African Christianity." *Conspectus: The Journal of the South African Theological Seminary* 33 1 (2022) 88–103.

Bediako, Kwame. *Christianity in Africa: The Renewal of a Non-Western Religion*. Edinburgh: Edinburgh University Press, 1997.

Clarke, Clifton R. *Pentecostalism: Insights from Africa and the African Diaspora*. Eugene, OR: Cascade Books, 2018.

Cox, Harvey. *Fire from Heaven: The Rise of Pentecostal Spirituality and the Reshaping of Religion in the Twenty-First Century*. Cambridge, MA: Da Capo, 1995.

Éla, Jean-Marc. *My Faith as an African*. Maryknoll, NY: Orbis, 1988.

Fiedler, Klaus, et al. *Theology Cooked in an African Pot*. Kachere Series. Oxford, UK: African, 2000.

Grillo, Laura, et al. *Religions in Contemporary Africa: An Introduction*. London: Routledge, 2019.

Hick, John, et al. *Four Views on Salvation in a Pluralistic World*. Rev. ed. Grand Rapids: Zondervan Academic, 2010.

Hock, Klaus. "'Jesus Power—Super-Power!' On the Interface between Christian Fundamentalism and New Religious Movements in Africa." *Mission Studies* 12 (1995) 56–70.

Hollenweger, Walter. "Intercultural Theology: Some Remarks on the Term." In *Towards an Intercultural Theology: Essays in Honour of Jan A. B. Jongeneel*, edited by Martha Theodora Frederiks et al., 89–95. Zoetermeer, Neth.: Uitgeverij Meinema, 2003.

Idowu, Bolaji E. *African Traditional Religion: A Definition*. London: SCM, 1974.

Jahnel, Claudia. "Maps Are All We Possess: Critical Terms in the Study of African Theology(ies)." *Interreligious Studies and Intercultural Theology* 5 (2021) 129–45.

Kalu, Ogbu. *African Pentecostalism: An Introduction*. Oxford: Oxford University Press, 2008.

Kato, Byang H. *Theological Pitfalls in Africa*. 5 vols. Nairobi: Evangel, 1978.

---

50. Larbi, "Nature of Continuity," 96–97.

Kim, Sebastian C. H., and Kirsteen Kim. *Christianity as a World Religion: An Introduction.* London: Zed, 2021.

Kollman, Paul. "Classifying African Christianities: Past, Present, and Future: Part Two." *Journal of Religion in Africa* 40 (2010) 118–48.

Komolafe, Sunday Babajide. "The Changing Face of Christianity: Revisiting African Creativity." *Missiology: An International Review* 34 (2004) 217–38.

Larbi, E. Kingsley. "The Nature of Continuity and Discontinuity of Ghanaian Pentecostal Concept of Salvation in African Cosmology." *Asian Journal of Pentecostal Studies* 5 (2002) 87–106.

Larty, Emmanuel Y. *Postcolonializing God: An African Practical Theology.* London: SCM, 2015.

Magesa, Laurenti. *African Religion: The Moral Traditions of Abundant Life.* Maryknoll, NY: Orbis, 1997.

———. *Anatomy of Inculturation: Transforming the Church in Africa.* New York: Orbis, 2004.

Marshall-Fratani, Ruth. "Mediating the Global and Local in Nigerian Pentecostalism." *Journal of Religion in Africa* 28 (1998) 278–315. https://www.jstor.org/stable/1581572.

Mbiti, John. *African Religions and Philosophy.* Nairobi: EAEP, 1969.

———. "Cattle Are Born with Ears, Their Horns Grow Later." *Africa Theological Journal* 8 (1979) 15–25.

———. "Challenges of Language, Culture and Interpretation in Translating the Greek New Testament." *Swedish Missiological Themes* 97 (2009) 141–64.

———. *Concepts of God in Africa.* London: SPCK, 1975.

———. "The Encounter of Christian Faith and African Religion." *Journal of the Interdenominational Theological Centre* 16 (1980) 817–20.

Ngong, David. "African Pentecostalism and Religious Pluralism." In *Pentecostal Theology in Africa*, edited by Clifton R. Clarke Jr., 193–208. African Christian Studies Series 6. Eugene, OR: Pickwick Publications, 2014.

Nussbaum, Stan. *A Reader's Guide to Transforming Mission.* New York: Orbis, 2005.

Nyamiti, Charles. *African Tradition and the Christian God.* Eldoret, Kenya: Gaba, 1978.

Oduyoye, Mercy Amba. "The African Experience of God through the Eyes of an Akan Woman." *Crosscurrents* 47 (1997/1998) 493–504.

p'Bitek, Okot. *African Religions in Western Scholarship.* Kampala: Uganda Literature Bureau, 1980.

———. *Religion of the Central Luo.* Kampala: Uganda Literature Bureau, 1980.

Platvoet, Jan, and Henk van Rinsum. "Is Africa Incurably Religious? Confessing and Contesting an Invention." *Exchange* 32 (2003) 123–53.

Robbins, Joel. "Anthropology of Religion." In *Studying Global Pentecostalism: Theories and Methods*, edited by Allan Anderson et al., Anthropology of Christianity 10, 156–78. Berkeley: University of California Press, 2010.

Roelofs, Gerard. "Charismatic Christian Thought: Experience, Metonymy, and Routinization." In *Charismatic Christianity as a Global Culture*, edited by Karla Poewe, 217–33. Columbia: University of South Carolina Press, 1994.

Sanneh, Lamin. "The Horizontal and Vertical in Mission: An African Perspective." *International Bulletin of Missionary Research* 7 (1983) 165–71.

Sawyerr, Harry. *God: Ancestor or Creator? Aspects of Traditional Belief in Ghana, Nigeria and Sierra Leone.* London: Longman, 1971.

Tennent, Timothy C. *Invitation to World Missions: A Trinitarian Missiology for the Twenty-First Century*. Invitation to Theological Studies. Grand Rapids: Kregel Academic, 2010.

Tiénou, Tite. "The Training of Missiologists for an African Context." In *Missiological Education for the Twenty-First Century: The Book, the Circle, and the Sandals; Essays in Honor of Paul E. Pierson*, edited by J. Dudley Woodberry et al., American Society of Missiology, 93–100. Eugene, OR: Wipf & Stock, 2005.

Van den Toren, Benno, et al., eds. *Is Africa Incurably Religious? Secularization and Discipleship in Africa*. Regnum Studies in Mission. Oxford, UK: Fortress, 2020.

———— Section Three ————
The Story of Christianity Encounters Twenty-First-Century Issues

10

New Kinships and Identities in Christ in Africa

Harvey Kwiyani

THE TOPIC OF IDENTITY and belonging has been central to the self-understanding of African Christians for decades. It has been phrased in multiple ways, but essentially, it asks: "How can a person be an African and a Christian at the same time?" The assumption is often that it is impossible for Africans to become Christians while retaining their African identity, and this has implications on how African Christians understand their sense of belonging and kinship. This topic is critical to African Christianity because for most Africans *to be is to belong*. Even when they become Christians, Africans need to have a sense of belonging. As a matter of fact, they need multiple belongings. They need to belong to the communities of their ancestors, relatives, and neighbors who raised and shaped them, with whom they share deep sociocultural roots. They also need wider clan and ethnic identities. In addition, as Christians, they must also belong to their newly found society of Christian brothers and sisters, local, regional, and global, with whom they enjoy spiritual fellowship and religious affiliation.

In this chapter, I will explore the subject of new kinships and identities formed in the light of the gospel in Africa. By means of a historical survey focused on the nineteenth and twentieth centuries, leading on to the twenty-first, I wish to discuss the changing forms of kinships that African Christians have negotiated since the advent of Western missionaries on the continent. I reflect on this because their very religious identities have been shaped by their cultural contexts as well as the influence of Western missionaries and colonial governments. Throughout all these changes in forms of kinships and identities, African Christians have had to engage with both local and foreign theological as well as social concerns, with their experiences and posture being shaped either by colonialism or against it. These kinships and identities, therefore, ought to be understood in the light of the wider story of the development and spread of Christianity in the continent in its many expressions. To discuss these changing kinships and identities, I need to start by painting an image of Christianity in Africa in the twenty-first century.

Exploring African Christianity in the Twenty-First Century

Today, as we stand in the early years of the third decade of the twenty-firs century, Africa has more Christians than both Europe and Latin America. As a matter of fact, there are more than 150 million more Christians in Africa today than there are in Europe. Africa's overtaking of Europe and Latin America to be the most Christian continent must be one of the greatest *miracles* of twentieth century. To a great extent, it has taken us all by surprise. Nobody really expected this to happen, and if anyone did, they did not expect it to happen so soon. Back in 1900, when the European Scramble for Africa was in full gear, most of the people in sub-Saharan Africa had never heard of Jesus Christ. Those African Christians who lived on the African continent were either in the Coptic Church in Egypt or in the Ethiopian Orthodox Tewahedo Church in Ethiopia. A much smaller number of Christians lived around the mission stations that were emerging in Kenya, Uganda, Malawi, Zimbabwe, South Africa, Nigeria, Ghana, and many other countries in the southern two-thirds of the continent. There was no promise at all that Africa would turn to Christianity.

To get a fair understanding of the religious condition of Africa in the first decade of the twentieth century, we have to explore one of the most important events in mission in the 1900s—the World Missionary Conference that took place in Edinburgh in June 1910 with the stated purpose of considering missionary problems in relation to the non-Christian world. On official records, there was not even one black African delegate in attendance. Africans were not invited because, as it was understood back then, they were not ready. In his book on the conference, Brian Stanley notes:

> If African churches were deemed to be insufficiently "advanced" to merit their own representatives, it was not simply because these churches were young in years, but also because their members were thought to be starting from much further back in the process of human development than were Christian converts in Asia. The inhabitants of Africa were still in 1910 regarded as *primitive, childlike,* and *at the bottom of the evolutionary hierarchy, relatively unimportant for the future of the world church.*[1]

---

1. Stanley, *World Missionary Conference*, 13 (emphasis added).

The conference's deliberations on Africa were extremely pessimistic. Participants were reminded that "two and a half times as many people await the Gospel in China as make up the entire population of Africa."[2] Chapter 2 of commission 4 of the conference (coming after a brief general introduction that comprised chapter 1) was dedicated to discussing what they called "Animistic Religions." Of course, this was a chapter on the hindrances to conversion mainly in Africa but also in other parts of the world, especially the Pacific Islands. Animism was a term reserved for Africa because what existed in the continent back then was thought to be not a religion at all, for "nothing deserves the name of religion which is false and unethical."[3] Chapters on China and Japan have their names mentioned in their titles, "Chinese Religions" and "The Religions of Japan," respectively. Chapters on Islam and Hinduism are simply entitled "Islam" and "Hinduism" as well. Africa, however, appears to have been synonymous with animism. This emphasis on animism was to encourage more missionaries to go to Africa. They believed that Africa would be an easy mission field—animistic societies could not sustain resistance against Christianity. However, both Christianity and Islam were noted to be the two forces contending for the soul of Africa. The conference deliberations suggest that it was believed that Islam was "in many respects the more aggressive" of the two, as "the absorption of native races into Islam is proceeding rapidly and continuously in practically all parts of the continent," and concluded that "if things continue as they are now tending, Africa may become a Mohammedan continent."[4] At that time of the Edinburgh Conference, when Africa had about 9 million Christians, there were 34.5 million Muslims in the continent, and Islam was expanding along the Sahel as well as in the interior of Tanzania. In East Africa, Arabic Muslim slave traders had taken advantage of improved transportation and commercial opportunities being created by colonialism, which jihads could not have accomplished. Following the conference, Western mission agencies would invest most of their energy in Asia, sending their best missionaries to India, China, Korea, the Philippines, and other parts of Asia, because in their eyes, Asians had advanced and sophisticated religious systems and could, therefore, convert to Christianity with less hesitancy. European missionary agencies had never, as a rule, devoted their best resources or sent their finest and brightest to Africa.[5]

2. World Missionary Conference 1910, *Report on Commission 1*, 84, 204.
3. World Missionary Conference 1910, *Report on Commission 4*, 6.
4. World Missionary Conference 1910, *Report on Commission 1*, 21.
5. Walls, *Cross-Cultural Process*, 117.

The story of the rise of Christianity in Africa could startle even the most informed of missionaries of the past century. The unprecedented pace at which sub-Saharan Africa has converted to Christianity has been so dramatic that some call it the fourth age of Christian expansion. Todd Johnson of Gordon-Conwell Theological Seminary in Boston has done a brilliant job following the trends in world Christianity for the past two decades. His *Atlas of Global Christianity 1910–2010* revealed a massive jump in the number of Christians in Africa from 113 million in 1970 to 494 in 2010.[6] In the atlas, Johnson also anticipated that there would be 630 million Christians in Africa in 2025. Later, in 2016, Johnson's world Christianity report indicated that there were 555 million Christians in Africa, up from 494 in 2010 (with Latin America and Europe having more Christians, 581 million and 559 million respectively). In 2017, Africa had 582 million Christians (while Latin America still had more Christians at 591 million, and Europe had started a downward trajectory and was now at 554 million). This was the first time in centuries that Africa had more Christians than Europe. It was in the 2018 report that the table finally changed. Africa emerged to have 598 million Christians while Latin America had 596 million and Europe had 549 million. For the first time, Africa was reported to have more Christians than either Europe and Latin America. In 2019, the margin had gotten wider, as Africa had 618 million while Latin America came second at 600 million and Europe was third at 549 million. In 2021, Johnson reported that Africa had 684 million Christians while Latin America had 617 million and Europe had 564 million Christians. If Johnson is right, African Christians will double in number between now in the first half of the 2020s and 2050, when Africans will account for more than 40 percent of world Christians in 2050.[7] Today, in 2022, about 52 percent of Africa's population identifies as Christian. In sub-Saharan Africa, that percentage goes up to somewhere about 70 percent.[8]

Christian Kinship and Identity in Precolonial Africa

Contemporary African Christianity has come about as a result of the work of Western missionaries who started to respond to God's call to

---

6. Johnson et al., *Atlas of Global Christianity*, 57.

7. Todd Johnson, Gina Zurlo, and others produce a report of the trends in world Christianity every year. They are all published in the January issue of the *International Bulletin of Mission Research* (https://journals.sagepub.com/home/ibm).

8. See Zurlo and Johnson, "Religious Demographies of Africa."

go and serve in the continent in the final decades of the eighteenth century.[9] While the majority of the impetus for that missionary movement arose from Protestant Europe, it was not long before Roman Catholic missionaries outnumbered Protestant ones in the interior of Africa. Between Protestant and Catholic missionaries, various methods were used to convert Africans, but the goal was always the total Christianization of African communities. This Christianization of Africa could be evidenced, for the most part, by Africans adopting aspects of European culture and civilization. Of course, the spread of European civilization was part of the missionaries' agenda as their culture was taken to be the embodiment of the Christian life. Converts were expected to embrace the European way of life—their *civilization*—as a manifestation of their commitment to the Christian faith. Consequently, many missionaries, both Protestants and Catholics, sought not only to convert Africans to Christianity but also to teach them European culture, and in the process, to Europeanize them. This, for many early missionaries, was the definition of success.

This overwhelming desire to Christianize and civilize Africans (and, indeed, every evangelized people group) to European culture was justifiable, because in the Europeans' eyes, Europe was Christianity itself. Up until the mid-twentieth century, Europe was Christendom—Christianity geographically defined—and, therefore, European culture was the embodiment of Christianity. Back then, to be born a European was to be a Christian, and of course, to be a Christian was to be a European. As a result, European culture was the yardstick used to measure the civilizations of the peoples of the world, and Christianity (which was also understood to be the standard for all religions in the world) was the standard against which other religions were assessed. In this grand scheme of life, Africa was everything that Europe was not, and African religion was the exact opposite of Christianity. Everything African was defined as primitive, barbarous, and unholy. To be an African was to be a fraction of a human (and the European was the measure of what it means to be human); or to be a *race of children*,[10] at the beginning of human evolution; or, indeed, to be an animist at worst or a polytheist at best (either of which was unacceptable when Christian monotheism was the standard). African religious heritage, which many missionaries were encountering for the first time, and looked nothing like Christianity, was deemed to be a devilish religion that needed to be destroyed with haste. It

---

9. I recognize that Christianity has always been present in Egypt and parts of North Africa, Sudan, and Ethiopia throughout its history. In this chapter, I am focused on African Christian kinship and identity since the 1700s when mission agencies emerged in Europe and started sending missionaries to Africa.

10. Hegel, *Philosophy of Mind*, 41–42.

was Christianity's worst enemy, and Africans had to be delivered from its claws. Thus, right from the early decades of the nineteenth-century missionary era, Westerners were set to destroy African religion as well as African culture. They would seek to replace it with European culture and Christianity. Christianity was made to be the civilizing religion.

In addition, Africans were believed to have been created for the good of Europeans—to be dominated by and, therefore, to serve Europeans.[11] Thus, Europeans believed that Africans needed to be civilized to fulfil this destiny. They believed that both slave trade and colonialism was good for Africans as it was a way for Africans to fulfil their God-ordained destiny. To this effect, right from the start, Western missionaries made every effort to make Africans reject their own identity and to look down on things African. Converts to Christianity were often required to change their names, to drop their African names and adopt European names. For example, in Chinua Achebe's widely acclaimed novel, *Things Fall Apart*, the son of Okonkwo, the novel's protagonist, changed his name from Nwoye, the name he described as "darkness and ignorance," to become Isaac, the son of promise, when he became a Christian. In another famous African novel of the twentieth century, Ferdinand Oyono's *Houseboy*, a young man named Toundi Ondoua had his name changed to Joseph when he was baptized. In his own words, he says, "My name is Toundi Ondoua. I am the son of Toundi and of Zama. When the father baptized me he gave me the name Joseph."[12] On a practical level, the missionaries wanted their African converts to have names they could understand and pronounce. However, there was more to this requirement. For centuries, since the fourth century CE, European Christians had themselves been instructed against the use of names of heathen gods for their children. The Church of England prohibited the use of names of heathen origin in the sixteenth century.[13] Thus, the missionaries felt more confident about the names of their converts if they were European. They would be assured that they were in line with their own conventions back home and were not in honor of non-Christian deities of the Africans.

---

11. This logic provided the justification for the many generations of the European slave trade that saw millions of Africans kidnapped and shipped to the Americas for slave labor. The transatlantic slave trade was still running until the final decades of the nineteenth century, with most kidnapped Africans being shipped to Brazil. Of course, Brazil outlawed slavery in 1888. Thus, the transition from the trading of kidnapped and enslaved Africans to the colonization of the continent was swift. Some would justify slavery as something that was for the good of the Africans.

12. Oyono, *Houseboy*, 11.

13. Madubuike, *Handbook of African Names*, 57.

The act of naming or renaming a convert, especially with a foreign name, has serious implications. It requires a great deal of power and a sense of entitlement to rename a human being. Basically, to rename someone is to say that whoever named them first was wrong. Of course, to rename someone is to give them a new identity. The new name makes a new person. In taking on a new name, the convert becomes a new creature, and all the old things have passed away (2 Cor 5:17). This is especially noteworthy among those African cultures—and there are many of them—that attribute spiritual significance to names. For instance, some cultures name their children with the intention of honoring their deities, ancestors, or elders. Other cultures use names as prayers, or to tell stories of whatever is happening in their lives or communities, or to communicate with their ancestors. The new names, most of which were taken from the Bible or from significant and powerful Europeans, had no cultural connection for the converts. They took Africans away from their cultural roots, disconnected them from their spiritual genealogies, and made them whatever the Europeans wanted them to be. In a nutshell, the Europeans recreated Africans in their own image. There were, of course, some Africans who took agency and asked to be renamed so they could gain access to the benefits of the Western civilizations.

As if renaming them was not enough, the missionaries often required their converts to move from their communities to live in the Christian villages that they established. In these Christian villages, everything that looked like African religion was banned. Unfortunately for many African communities, culture and religion are two sides of the same coin, totally inseparable. Thus, to belong in those villages, converts had to leave their African cultures at the gate. In this requirement, the missionaries enforced the message that everything African was evil and that, for a person to be a Christian, they had to be culturally European. In some cases, the speaking of African languages was prohibited (as still happens in many schools in the continent today). All other aspects of African cultures—music, dances, initiation rights—were either banned or closely supervised by the missionaries. In these Christian villages, the missionaries exercised the role of Christian parents, instructing their African "children" in the ways of the faith. They disregarded and disrupted the long-standing social systems and governance structures that had held the communities together before the arrival of the missionaries.

European Colonialism and the African Christian Identity

The process of civilizing and Christianizing Africans was well underway before the partitioning of Africa took place at the Berlin Conference in 1884. Though the ideology behind this was widespread, it was well articulated in David Livingstone, who in the 1850s and 1860s maintained that his work in Africa was to Christianize and civilize the Africans and to bring them a new form of commerce (to replace the slave trade).[14] This strategy would come to be known as the three *c*'s—Christianity, civilization, and commerce. The outworking of these three key aspects of European mission in Africa inevitably resulted in the colonization of the continent. Livingstone himself argued, back in the early 1860s, that colonization of parts of Africa would enhance the spread of both Christianity and civilization in the continent and help stop the slave trade. By the late 1870s, Henry Morton Stanley, the youngish British man who had searched for and found David Livingstone in Tanzania in 1871, had colluded with King Leopold II of Belgium to take the entire Congo, a country more than seventy times bigger than Belgium, as Leopold's personal property. This would, by 1884, lead to the partition of Africa, with the next thirty years being characterized by the Scramble for Africa when European governments rushed to claim their colonies, using a violent pacification where necessary. With many Europeans living in Africa, governing Africans on behalf of their governments thousands of miles away and shaping African education systems that would inform both their sociocultural self-understanding and theological identity, a new dynamic emerged. European colonization of Africa was wildly successful in the first half of the twentieth century and, in a way, still influences Africa today because it changed the way many Africans view themselves.[15]

Before Europe's colonization of Africa, the most important part of the African identity was the people's ethnic community. One's ethnic community made it possible to locate both one's clan and family heritage, often with exact precision. Each of these ethnic communities had its own cultures, customs, traditions, languages, governance, and religious structures, as well as lands, but were also closely connected to other ethnic communities through trade, intermarriage, and other alliances as and when needed. Thus, when asked, "Who are you?," many could say, "I am from such and such an ethnic community, from this or that family in that clan." The partition of Africa changed all that by putting national identity above that of

14. See Ransford, *David Livingstone*, 159.

15. It is this continuing colonization of the African mind, especially using colonial languages, that African postcolonial thought wrestles with. See Thiong'o, *Decolonising the Mind*.

ethnic community. National identity, based on the concept of a nation-state, shaped by the European notion of statehood, was brought to Africa with the creation of colonies in the 1880s and 1890s. To create a colonial nation-state, multiple ethnic communities were often brought together.[16] On numerous occasions, national boundaries were drawn right through ethnic communities, splitting them across two or more nation-states.[17] The colonial nation-states that emerged were governed from Europe until the end of European colonialism in Africa, which, for most colonies, was in the 1960s. However, by the end of the Scramble for Africa, the identity of Africans had, to a great extent, started to shift from their ethnic communities to their newly-founded colonial nation-states. A person was not just a member of their ethnic community, they belonged with members of other ethnic communities to a nation-state, and to a great extent, they had to function together to make the state work. For example, a member of the Yoruba community of southwest Nigeria was not only a Yoruba, they were also a Nigerian together with the Fulanis, the Hausas, the Igbos, and many others. Depending on the context and the nature of colonial rule, the relationship between ethnic and national identity varied from one community to another and also from one country to another. However, generally speaking, national identity was more important.

In addition to national identity, religious labels began to gain significance. It became necessary for Christians, for instance, to self-differentiate from Muslims and from followers of traditional religion. Of course, Christianity continued to play a civilizing role. Its proximity to European colonial powers made it an accessory to colonialism. During the entire colonial era, Western churches gained more ground, courtesy not only of the evangelistic work they did, especially in education and health care, but also of colonial governments that provided some security. Mission schools and hospitals served as evangelizing outlets, and in many places, conversion to Christianity was required before admission. A religious kinship of Christians began to emerge that brought together people from different ethnic communities who shared their faith in Christ. This Christian kinship, though initially shaped around denominational banners, would eventually transcend them and make it possible for Christians of different ethnicities, nationalities, and faith traditions to belong together. Throughout the colonial era, the African Christians' identity and kinship were shaped by two key factors. First, there was a majority who submitted, whether willingly or coerced, to the Western

16. For example, the creation of Nyasaland (which later became Malawi) in 1891 brought together more than twenty ethnic communities.

17. The Chewa of Malawi, for instance, are spread across several countries, including DRC, Zambia, and Mozambique, and have a small presence in Zimbabwe.

missionaries' leadership. These would help establish mission-originated churches and take the gospel to places that the missionaries could not reach. On the one hand, they identified closely with the missionaries' agenda of civilizing Africa, while on the other hand, many of them loathed colonialism and would help bring it to an end.

The second identity was shaped by a refusal to accept the missionaries' Christianity and, of course, a suspicion of anything brought by the Westerners to Africa, for a justifiable fear of religious colonialism. These Christians would form faith communities that would be called AICs.[18] They gathered around charismatic, prophetic, healing leaders who sought to interpret the Bible without the mediation of European thought and performed miracles for them. They were labeled Zionist or Ethiopian churches and accounted for the significant growth of Christianity in parts of Africa. Professor John Mbiti and other African scholars would later credit them for their efforts at Africanizing Christianity. Their enthusiastic expression of Christianity made Christianity closely identifiable with African religion, which is also intensely spirit centered. To many in the colonial era, they were second-class African Christians whose Christianity was labeled syncretistic as it did not follow the Western standards of orthodoxy.

Needless to say, AICs were a source of major concern both to the missionaries and colonial governments. Many of their leaders were persecuted by both Western missionaries and colonial governments.[19] William Wade Harris, arguably the most celebrated leader of an AIC, was deported from Ivory Coast back to his home country of Liberia where he was placed on house arrest for many years.[20] His ministry had been so effective that both the missionaries and the French colonial government felt threatened. In Malawi, the British government, for example, killed John Chilembwe, deported many (British) missionaries, and jailed many local members of Chilembwe's and other independent churches for an uprising in 1915.[21] They established a law that prevented Africans from registering a church in the country, and this law was enforced until 1964 when Malawi gained her independence. In the Congo, Simon Kimbangu, who led a local, independent prophetic and healing ministry, was jailed in 1921.[22] He died in prison in 1951. These independent African churches were generally out

---

18. AICs are a precursor to the many Pentecostal and charismatic churches that have saturated sub-Saharan Africa since the 1970s.

19. A great resource on AICs is Anderson, *African Reformation*.

20. Bureau, "Prophète Harris."

21. Shepperson and Price, *Independent African*.

22. Mokoko Gampiot, *Kimbanguism*.

of bounds to Western missionaries and colonial agents. They grew quite rapidly, but their growth took place away from the Western gaze. They were the Christian "other" who did not count in the early statistics of African Christianity. Many of them, for instance, the Aladura Movement from Nigeria, modernized after the collapse of European colonialism and styled themselves as part of the Pentecostal and charismatic movement in Africa. Others, like the Cherubim and Seraphim Church (one of the white-garment churches in Nigeria) stayed as traditional Zionist or Ethiopian churches at the periphery of African Christianity. As marginalized Christian communities, they had a kinship and identity that were, for many reasons, different from that of mainline mission churches.

Postcolonial Christian Kinship and Identity in Africa

When Europe's colonization of Africa came to an end in the 1960s, African Christianity had also to go through a period of decolonization. Part of this process involved an in-depth look at the question of identity and kinship among African Christians. The first generation of African theologians (which included such scholars as John Mbiti, Bolaji Idowu, and Kwesi Dickson) wrestled with this question to a great depth. While they all contributed to the debate, it was John Mbiti whose works have continued to shape a great deal of how African Christians speak about their identity. Mbiti was unapologetic about his conviction that Christianity in Africa had to become African. The main theme underlying all his writing sought to answer the question "Can an African convert to Christianity without having to become a European?" Starting in 1969 when his *African Religions and Philosophy* was published, when he declared, "African peoples are notoriously religious,"[23] he sought to correct the colonial lies about the African life and, thereby, to restore identity and dignity to African Christianity. He is quoted in 1971 in a *New York Times* article as stating, "The days are over when we will be carbon copies of European Christians. Europe and America Westernized Christianity. The Orthodox Easternized it. Now it's our turn to Africanize it."[24] That Africanizing of Christianity could happen only if the theological thought in African Christianity was freed from the Western shackles that had been imposed by the missionaries. He wrote in 1968, "[The African Church] is a church that depends entirely on an imported theology from Europe and America."[25] Later, he added, "Africa

23. Mbiti, *African Religions and Philosophy*, 1.
24. Fiske, "African Christians Are Developing," para. 5.
25. Mbiti, "Ways and Means," 332.

is becoming Christian so rapidly that Christianity has hardly had time to become 'naturalized,' psychologically indigenized, and emotionally assimilated into the natural points of reference."[26] To naturalize Christianity in Africa, there was a need to develop an indigenous African Christian theology. Emerging African theologians needed to radically reinterpret the Christian faith to make sense of African cultural realities and answer African questions about the faith.

In this postcolonial Africanizing of Christianity, a kinship emerged that pulled together all manners of Christian communities and denominations of various traditions. This has been quite evident, because Christianity itself has exploded in Africa and has become the religion of the majority population of many countries. Unfortunately, looking back at the past fifty years of African Christianity, it becomes evident that as it has sought to become more African, it has also become more Western (with stronger influence from North America than from Europe). African Christians have been courageous in shaping their own expressions of Christianity, many of which are enthusiastic and spirit oriented and squarely rooted in the Pentecostal and charismatic tradition. In this sense, they have claimed their own Christian identity and, like the old AICs, refused particularly European theological leadership. However, it is also evident that their Pentecostalism is, to a considerable extent, shaped by North American Christianity. The concerns of the US evangelical global empire are also, generally speaking, the concerns of African urban Christianity. The issues at the forefront of US theological discourse are often echoed in African Christianity.[27] In this sense, their identity is still, to a considerable extent, shaped by foreign concerns.

Conclusion: Kinship and Identity in the Theology of Ubuntu

In conclusion, I wish to suggest a theology of ubuntu both as evidence of the mis-contextualization of African Christianity and as a call to reimagine what identity and kinship in African Christianity in the twenty-first century could look like. Ubuntu provides the foundational philosophy through which most people of southern Africa view themselves and the world around them. It is also one of the most important untapped theological resources of African Christianity. *Ubuntu*, which means "personhood,"

26. Mbiti, *African Religions and Philosophy*, 56.

27. For instance, the prevalence of US Christian books in African libraries and bookshops means that the concerns of US theology (e.g., politics, abortion rights, or prosperity) also dominate African Christian thought.

is an expansive philosophical, theological, and spiritual concept that puts human beings in a bonded community of life that includes God, spirits, society, and nature.[28] It describes a well-rounded philosophy of life in which to be a person—to have ubuntu—is to be at peace with oneself, the community around, God, the spirits, and nature. Archbishop Desmond Tutu's attempt at a definition of ubuntu says:

> A person with ubuntu is open and available to others, affirming of others, does not feel threatened that others are able and good, for he or she has a proper self-assurance that comes from knowing that he or she belongs in a greater whole and is diminished when others are humiliated or diminished, when others are tortured or oppressed, or treated as if they were less than who they are.[29]

It embodies the Nguni proverb "Ubuntu ngubuntu ngabantu," which translates to "A person is a person through other persons." At root, it means, "I am because I belong, I am because we all are; you are because I am, and I am because you are."[30] In this sense, ubuntu makes concrete the great communal values of solidarity, compassion, respect, human dignity, conformity to basic norms, and collective unity. It is the source, for Africans, of both identity and kinship. If anything, it is the community, and in this sense kinship, that makes identity happen. There is no individual without community. Of course, the individual then turns around and makes the community work. Ubuntu has been used to shape all spheres of life. It sustained communities long before the Europeans came to Africa. It continues to bring communities together even today, in the face of poverty, diseases, and famine. It provides a wholesome well-integrated system of support that takes care of all of life. Ubuntu takes care of the spiritual and material needs of a community, while at the same time protecting nature and honoring traditions. By reclaiming the community as a location for theological discourse, a theology of ubuntu allows African Christians to rethink and assert their sense of identity and kinship. It also makes it possible for Africans to make a uniquely African theological contribution to world Christianity.

Bibliography

Achebe, Chinua. *Things Fall Apart*. London: Heinemann, 1958.
Anderson, Allan H. *African Reformation: African Initiated Christianity in the Twentieth Century*. Trenton, NJ: Africa World, 2001.

28. See Sindima, "Community of Life."
29. Tutu, *No Future without Forgiveness*, 31.
30. Mbiti, *African Religions and Philosophy*, 152.

Bureau, René. "Le prophète Harris et la religion harriste." *Institut d'Ethno-Sociologie* 31 (1971) 31–195.

Fiske, Edward B. "African Christians Are Developing Their Own Distinctive Theologies." *New York Times*, Mar. 12, 1971. https://www.nytimes.com/1971/03/12/archives/african-christians-are-developing-their-own-distinctive-theologies.html.

Hegel, G. W. F. *Philosophy of Mind*. Revised with introduction and commentary by Michael Inwood. Translated by W. Wallace and A. V. Miller. Oxford: Clarendon, 2007.

Isichei, Elizabeth. *A History of Christianity in Africa: From Antiquity to the Present*. Grand Rapids: Eerdmans, 1995.

Johnson, Todd M., et al. *Atlas of Global Christianity 1910–2010*. Edinburgh: Edinburgh University Press, 2009.

Madubuike, Ihechukwu. *A Handbook of African Names*. Colorado Springs: Three Continents, 1976.

Mbiti, John S. *African Religions and Philosophy*. Garden City, NY: Anchor, 1970.

———. "The Ways and Means of Communicating the Gospel." In *Christianity in Tropical Africa: Studies Presented and Discussed at the Seventh International African Seminar, University of Ghana, April 1965*, edited by C. G. Baëta, 329–61. London: Oxford University Press, 1968.

Mokoko Gampiot, Aurélien. *Kimbanguism: An African Understanding of the Bible*. Translated by Cécile Coquet-Mokoko. Signifying (on) Scriptures. University Park: Pennsylvania State University, 2017.

Oyono, Ferdinand. *Houseboy*. Translated by John Reed. London: Heinemann, 1966.

Ransford, Oliver. *David Livingstone: The Dark Interior*. London: Murray, 1978.

Ross, Kenneth R. "The Centenary of Edinburgh 1910: Its Possibilities." *International Bulletin of Missionary Research* 30 (Oct. 2006) 177–79.

Shepperson, George, and Thomas Price. *Independent African: John Chilembwe and the Origins, Setting, and Significance of the Nyasaland Native Rising of 1915*. Edinburgh: Edinburgh University Press, 1958.

Sindima, Harvey. "Community of Life: Ecological Theology in African Perspective." In *Liberating Life: Contemporary Approaches in Ecological Theology*, edited by Charles Birch et al., 37–147. Maryknoll, NY: Orbis, 1990.

Smith, Edwin W., ed. *African Ideas of God: A Symposium*. Edinburgh: Edinburgh University Press, 1950.

Stanley, Brian. *The World Missionary Conference, Edinburgh 1910*. Grand Rapids: Eerdmans, 2009.

Thiong'o, Ngugi wa. *Decolonising the Mind: The Politics of Language in African Literature*. London: Currey, 1986.

Tutu, Desmond Mpilo. *No Future without Forgiveness*. New York: Doubleday, 1999.

Walls, Andrew F. *The Cross-Cultural Process in Christian History: Studies in the Transmission and Appropriation of Faith*. Maryknoll, NY: Orbis, 2002.

World Missionary Conference 1910. *Report on Commission 1: Carrying the Gospel to All the Non-Christian World*. Edinburgh: Oliphant, Anderson and Ferrier, 1910.

———. *Report on Commission 4: The Missionary Message in Relation to Non-Christian Religions*. Edinburgh: Oliphant, Anderson and Ferrier, 1910.

Zurlo, Gina A., and Todd M. Johnson. "Religious Demographies of Africa, 1970–2025." In *Anthology of African Christianity*, edited by Isabel Apawo Phiri et al., 155–69. Oxford: Regnum, 2016.

11

Christianity and Nation-State Formations

Tharcisse Gatwa

THE FORMULATION OF THE initial theme, "Christianity and Nation-State Formations," posed a problem of accuracy, if applied to Africa. It seemed like conditioning the formation of nation-states anywhere—in my case, Africa—to the expansion of Christianity. Like elsewhere, precolonial African millennial empires and kingdoms did not wait for external incursions, including Christianity, before they formed. The predominant model of Christianity in Africa arose from the third wave of missionary expansion in the eighteenth to twentieth centuries. Far from being the first disseminator of Christian faith, it is hereditary of the apostolic Christianity that forged global Christian theology on African soil. Therefore, we start from an assumption that African Christianity was introduced and developed in apostolic times from then onwards as a continuity.[1]

Christianity was silenced but not eliminated; it survived Islamic conquests in the northeast and Horn of Africa. Emerging from wars and social, political, moral and religious crises in Europe, Christianity regained the terrain empowered by the Western Europe imperial horizons; Portuguese missions settled in organized kingdoms of Kongo, Angola, and Matamba in the fifteenth and sixteenth centuries.[2] Soon afterwards, the adventure turned the missionaries into stakeholders of the transatlantic black slave trade, with greed that ruined the continent and disarticulated, dehumanized, disorganized societies. That form of Christianity ended in fiasco. When the abolition campaign in the UK and Europe slowed down the slave trade, colonialism took over. Meanwhile, free slaves from the UK and Americas, reinstalled in Sierra Leone (1792) and Liberia (1815) and the Jamaican missions, were instrumental in evangelizing their motherland.

---

1. Baur, *2000 Years of Christianity*; Walls, *Cross-Cultural Process*.
2. Scammell, *First Imperial Age*; Quenum, *Église et le commerce*.

Christianity as a stakeholder beatified both the transatlantic slave trade and colonialism. This attitude triggered the reimagining of different expressions of indigenous Christianity versus the Western Europe model.

With regard to delimitation in time and space, we take an anti-Hegelian approach; we consider Africa as a geographical and historical unified entity, a utopia in the philosophy of its existence, resilient in the management of its destiny. This chapter considers the power of the gospel that sustains Christian faith, having been present in different periods to reshape the resilience of Christians.

Christianity: Inculturation or Power of Resilience

The apostolic missionary movement in Africa cannot be understood outside its central role in the elaboration of Christian theology.[3] Among prominent figures, Athanasius, bishop of Egypt, translated the Bible and elaborated a liturgy in the local language, Coptic; Clement and Origen of the Alexandria theological school elaborated Christian teaching from seasoning the Egyptian and Graeco-Roman philosophies; Augustine, bishop of Hippo, author of the *City of God*, is considered the father of Christian theology after Paul; Anthony founded monastery life in the Egyptian deserts, nurturing custodians of the Bible. In North Africa, Christianity is reduced to a handful of congregations of foreigners in cities; yet its rich past was highlighted in a symposium organized by the High Islamic Council of Algeria on the recommendation of the Algerian president, Abdelaziz Boutefrika; the Augustinian University of Rome; and the University of Fribourg, Switzerland, in 2001.[4] On the topic "Augustine: The Algerian Philosopher," the debate aimed at bringing home the intellectual legacy of the philosopher born in 354 in Thangaste (Souk-Ahras), until recently a monopoly of Western intellectuals, the reason why he was associated culturally with "the colonial pass of imposed models."[5] Extraordinarily, Augustine now finds particular attention on his native soil, Algeria, where 99 percent of the population of forty-four million practice Islam.

Moving northeast, the Church of Egypt offers the most prolific theological contribution in matters of spiritual renewal. Its overwhelming impact on the Bible narratives, Old and New Testament, is well documented. Yet, it is also the place that originated controversies and heresies such as

---

3. Oden, *How Africa Shaped*; Baur, *2000 Years of Christianity*; Walls, *Cross-Cultural Process*.

4. The symposium's proceedings may be found in Fux et al., *Augustinus Afer*.

5. Sergel Lancel, quoted in Gatwa, "Contribution des églises," 139–40.

Arius's. Controversy, heresies, and martyrdom, though attacks against Christians, favored the edification of the Christian faith apology. The Egyptians are proud to track the origin of their faith from the Christian apostolic era. In Cairo, Christians venerate the Church of Saints Sergius and Bacchus, built in the place where the Holy Family is supposed to have settled during the exile with infant Jesus. In 1968, when the Coptic Orthodox patriarch invited the commemoration of the martyrdom of St. Mark, he wrote: "Shortly after the Lord's ascension, Mark arrived in Egypt. Of African origin, he was the author of the oldest Gospel. He founded the first Church in Africa in Alexandria, where he died a martyr in the summer of 68."[6] Without prejudging the authenticity of these stories, a reality is derived, the depth of the conviction that Christianity existed in Africa since apostolic times and that Christian faith heritage, including the Bible, was preserved by the Coptic Church of Egypt and its daughter, the Ethiopian. This firm belief plays a major role still in the propagation of the Christian faith; today, the Church of Egypt is actively engaged in preparation for the commemoration of Jesus Christ in 2033.

Egypt and Ethiopia, Cradles of Inculturation

Inculturation, this important concern for theologians in the developing world, affirming the relationship between the gospel and cultures, can be traced in the early Egyptian and Ethiopian church. While Christianity in North Africa remained a fundamentally externally oriented religion, Latin in language and liturgy, relying on a romanticized elite incapable of taking the gospel to the lives of local communities, Alexandria theologically became the beacon of the Mediterranean basin and Horn of Africa, more important than Athens, as much as it imaginatively and innovatively took root in the indigenous cultures.[7]

Egyptian and Ethiopian Christianity are two sides of the same coin. Eusebius, a great historian of the church, identified a list of bishops who followed St. Mark, believed to have died a martyr in Egypt. The first, Demerius (189–231), was the bishop of Clement and Origen. Both Egypt and Ethiopia continually changed as political realities. When Egypt fell under Islamic rule, Ethiopia became the Christian kingdom, known in the West as the "Christian

---

6. Schaff, *Apostolic Christianity*, 15.

7. Gatwa, "Contribution des églises," 142. From the third century BC, the five books of Moses and, later, the Old Testament were translated into Greek in Alexandria; the Septuagint was translated also in Alexandria. By 330 Bishop Athanasius had elaborated a liturgy and preached in the Coptic language.

Kingdom of Prester John." Between the fourth and sixth centuries AD, the Bible was translated into Ge'ez, the language of the Ethiopians. The Solomon dynasty that ruled the country up until the 1975 military coup, which ended the reign of Haile Selassie, links to the biblical tradition according to which the priest Zadok rescued the ark of the covenant and preserved it in Aksum. The fact that Philip baptized the Ethiopian eunuch and the Holy Spirit took him on mission in Ethiopia are all historical biblical memories relayed by generations of missionaries that "Ethiopia will submit its hand to God."[8] Today, when talking with an Ethiopian Orthodox priest, you realize how neither Athanasius nor Aksum are far away in history.[9] This is strengthened by the Ethiopian Orthodox Church co-custodianship of the Church of the Holy Sepulchre venerated by Catholics and Orthodox in the Christian quarter of the Old City of Jerusalem (at Golgotha hill).

A certain degree of ignorance maintains that the orthodox churches never stand in mission. The inaccuracy of such reasoning was dismissed in 1892 when the first Ethiopian missionary church was established in South Africa (by the twentieth century they were more than seventy). The move initiated a vast pan-African movement that channeled the consciousness of spiritual belonging to African roots among the populations of African descent in diasporas; it later associated with the creation of the African National Congress.[10] In 1928 the Ethiopian churches were accused of being "separatists" and mixing "political propaganda with religious teaching," then banned; they went underground.[11] As for lessons, for African Christianity to help re-evangelize the world, it will no longer be satisfied with the eighteenth- to early twentieth-century missionary legacy nor present-day theological uncertainty and omissions. Nor should it be continually on the defensive but return to its apostolic sources to learn from the models of exposures and resilience.

The "Beatified" Greed That Disarticulated Society

One of the shameful faces of Christianity is its blessing of the imperial horizons, particularly the transatlantic African slave trade. From the 1440s, Christianity was introduced in the kingdom of Kongo by the Portuguese missions; the royal family converted and was baptized. The heir to the

---

8. Gatwa, "Contribution des églises," 147.

9. See Baur, *2000 Years of Christianity*.

10. The African National Congress stood against the whites' apartheid regime supremacy and abuse of the populations of "color."

11. Gatwa, "Cross-Cultural Mission," 330.

throne took the name of Afonso I; when he inherited the throne from his father, he was the first monarch in sub-Saharan Africa to convert to the Christian religion. He took a serious interest in the theology of the Christian religion, hoping to establish viable diplomatic relations from his alliance with Portugal. His son, Prince Henrique, trained in Lisbon and Rome; he was consecrated bishop of Kongo in 1521. The king wanted his son to take control of all local ecclesiastical structures in a vast project of the evangelization. His dreams were thwarted by the transatlantic slave trade, which affected the population indiscriminately, even the royal family.[12] This chapter argues that the enslavement of the Africans, which took between fifty and one hundred million people from the continent, was an expression of the greed that imposed norms and standards of religious and cultural supremacy, beatified by the church through the *Code Noir*.

The Code Noir: A Heresy "Beatified" by the Church

The official legislation of slavery, the *Code Noir*, is "the most monstrous legal document of modern times."[13] The *Code Noir* was passed by Louis XIV, king of France, in 1685 to define the conditions of slavery in the French colonial empire. In sixty articles, the code became a universal legal instrument structuring the crime against humanity and to a lesser degree "objectifying" and dehumanizing the black people. According to Louis XIV, the legislation was inspired by the Catholic faith; indeed, his prime minister was Cardinal de Richelieu. Written by his minister of finance, Colbert, the code identified black slaves as goods, exchangeable for money, lendable or transferable to the heirs of their owners. The *Code Noir* condemned the slaves to legal and political nonexistence. A version of the decree was ratified in 1724 in Louisiana, and then in many other states of the US. Attempts at protecting slaves were never strictly enforced, lawbreaking masters were rarely prosecuted; it remained in force until 1848.[14]

The abolition movement was initiated in England following the Protestant revival by individuals converted to the message of God's love, including John Wesley (who later initiated the Methodist movement), Thomas Clarkson, and William Wilberforce, MP.[15] They stood up and formed a Committee for the Abolition of the Black Trade whose long struggle concluded in the 1807 bill voted on by parliament, engaging the UK to abolish

12. Hochschild, *Bury the Chains*; Barringer, *Creation of Atlantic World*, 23.
13. Sala-Molins, *Dark Side of Light*, 69.
14 Quenum, *Église et le commerce*, 151.
15. See Olusoga, *Black and British*.

the slave trade under the British flag. However, the Upper House, the lords (aristocracy and the royal family), were major shareholders of this largely lucrative enterprise. Only in 1833 did England extend the abolition to its dominion; France adopted the bill in 1848 and Brazil in 1888.

Colonialism and Missions: Two Faces of the Same Medal

When the transatlantic slave trade was abolished, colonialism took over. For a century, before the dismemberment of Africa by the 1884–85 Berlin colonial conference, several Protestant missionary societies had been settled in Africa. The BMS under the leadership of William Carey in 1792 and the LMS opened an era of missionary societies, a birth inspired by the Protestant revival in England. As the missionary movement expanded, Western European standards of Christianity were taken for normative, imposed, radicalized, or relaxed, according to whether the worldviews of people in various regions were judged closer to or different from European standards.[16] This theological orthodoxy resulted in two positions, hardened and softened views. For instance, to the question of the goal of the mission, a hardened view would be to transform the heathen, a softened view to share the good news. To the question of how should there be mission, a hardened view would be to transfer the standards and content of the truth, a softened view to educate and enlighten. On the basis of these attitudes in the relations of the missionaries and local populations, their cultures and religions resulted in dismissal and a tabula rasa methodology in the pastorate.

The Ambiguity of the Missionary Project

Lamin Sanneh suggests that Africa was colonized on the basis of race and white hegemony. Breed labels, tribe, ethyne, races were glued to its populations to evoke cultural and geographical frontiers on the basis that the populations had no historical repertoire written in the international diplomatic memories. Later, in the nineteenth century, Africans were qualifiers of "water tappers and wood splitters."[17] Africa was in a fragile situation; it served as an outlet for Europeans and world domination. For Sanneh, missionary Christianity purposed to uproot the African from history and a "heathen" past to give a new identity, constructed on the basis of a

---

16. Hardy, "Christian Missions," 5, 8, 9.
17. Dilk (1869); J. R. Seelye (1883); as cited in Bediako, *Theology and Identity*, 218–19.

package of Western European Christianity and standards. These assumptions of Western Christian standards justified violence and domination against the cultures and way of life of conquered nations. However, Sanneh articulated the ambivalence of the missionary project: on the one hand, it sealed alliance with imperial horizons through the propagation of race supremacy assumptions; on the other hand, it translated the Bible into vernacular languages, which helped the new converts worldwide to feel rehabilitated in their identity as they could communicate with God, in their own languages, idioms, symbolisms. While subjugated, Africa was finally being judged on the basis of the standards of democracy and freedom it never knew under European domination.[18]

The Berlin colonial conference, November 1884 to February 1885, aimed at helping the European nations "to settle the issue of common interest between nations engaged in the African trade and to resolve amiably conflict, avoiding misunderstanding and disagreement." Furthermore, the chair, Otto Bismarck, explained that the "inviting forces shared the idea of associating the indigenous populations of Africa to civilization, to open trade reaching the interior continent, motivate Christian missions in their enterprise of propagating useful knowledge and preparing the abolition of the Black slaves which was proclaimed by the Vienna 1815 congress."[19] Article 9 of the acts of the conference reaffirms the protection of the missionaries, freedom of religion, and slave trade interdiction. For Mark Boegner, member of the Paris board of mission, the general act of the conference was "the first diplomatic instrument of the international recognition of missions."[20] The Paris Mission in November 1885 noted that the association of the colonial enterprise and the mission was a door opened to missions to minister to colonization, "bringing salvation to people till then considered as 'savage' in as much it does not compromise the universality of mission." Alfred Boegner disagreed; for him, the association-colonization-Christian mission served to promote patriotism and egoist interests of states, not the universality of the gospel.[21]

---

18. Sanneh, *Encountering the West*, 70–71.
19. Zorn, *Grand siècle*, 18.
20. Zorn, *Grand siècle*, 18.
21. Zorn, *Grand siècle*, 20.

Rehumanizing Christianity: Three Models

The implementation of the abolition law needed a land to host the slaves liberated in England and Americas. Sierra Leone was created in 1792 by Britain, and Liberia in 1815 by the Americans. The first contingent of 1100 people arrived in Sierra Leone in 1792. Later, Sierra Leone emerged as the English experiment in the evangelization of Africa by the Africans called for a triple vocation: to give land to slaves; to ensure that the economy was not a pretext for the slave trade; and finally, to lay the foundations for missionary activity after abolition. For Walls, Sierra Leone "developed into a community conscious of its responsibility for evangelization and literacy of Africa."[22] Under this spirit, Sir Thomas Buxton, Wilberforce's successor as leader of the anti-slavery movement, led a mission in 1841 to the Niger basin, against the will of the British government. He concluded many anti-slavery treaties; created farms; and promoted the conditions for agricultural, technological, and commercial development for the locals. Sadly, the mission could not continue due to fever, which exterminated members of the expedition. Sierra Leone came to be known as "the tomb of the white man"; many missionaries refused to serve there, preferring India instead. It was then that a great African Christian figure, Samuel Ajayi Crowther, emerged as an adept of the evangelization of Africa by Africans.

Ajayi Crowther (1806–91)

Ajayi Crowther represents a vast record of both the achievements and pitfalls of Christian missions in Africa at once. Jeanne Decorvet presents him as the first leader in all the chains of Christian missions that were established in West Africa well before colonization. Born into the Yoruba people, Ajayi was captured as a slave at the age of fifteen; the ship carrying him was boarded by the British navy implementing the abolition law. Taken to Sierra Leone, converted, and baptized under the name Samuel Ajayi Crowther, he then enrolled and graduated from the well-known Fourah Bay College in Freetown in 1827. Ajayi became a teacher and evangelist; was ordained priest on June 11, 1843; was consecrated as the first black bishop in Canterbury Cathedral on June 29, 1864, by the Church of England and Ireland; and was sent in mission to his native Niger region.

The first missionary to acquire somewhat scientific knowledge of African cultures, with ethnography and linguistics, Ajayi harmonized oral tradition (tales, proverbs, stories) and Scriptures. He was first to set up a system to

---

22. Walls, *Cross-Cultural Process*, 123.

codify several African languages. He mastered several languages and cultures and explored the hydrography of the region. He secured the confidence and respect of the Muslim leaders in the Islamic north. He was the first to put structures aimed at improving the economic conditions of people at the heart of the mission, first to put into work liberated slaves like him. Beyond immense works, Ajayi Crowther's greatest contribution was to engineer the rebirth of the black population, and to rehabilitate the Christian faith mission tarnished by the evil transatlantic Africa slave trade, which caused the failure of the evangelization of the fifteenth to seventeenth centuries.

Ajayi Crowther based his pastoral ministry on the principles of respect for man, his culture and religion. Tireless, he taught his missionaries to strive to touch people's minds and feelings, not to act violently but to realize the truth of the gospel in its fullness. He invited them to engage in human education to roll back paganism and ignorance, irrationalism and obscurantism. However, Ajayi's pastoral ministry had an unhappy end. New leadership imbued with racial prejudices took over within the CMS in England, following the death of his mentor, the influential Henry Venn; they forced him to resign. Yet his theological heritage still stands, an essential dynamic of credible testimony among peoples, a challenge to ecumenism.[23]

David Livingstone: Facing the Evil

The LMS, a branch of the Evangelical Church and the CMS of the Church of England, had deployed missionaries, men of extraordinary vitality dedicated to fight the Portuguese and Arabic slave trade and racial segregation in southern Arica. Most prominent were Robert Moffat and Dr. David Livingstone, from Scotland; and Dr. Johannes van der Kemp, a Dutch military man, medical doctor, and philosopher for the LMS.[24]

Born in Blantyre, west of Scotland, Livingstone studied medicine in Glasgow and London, then theology, as he felt the call to missionary vocation. He served in South Africa under Robert Moffat and married Moffat's daughter. He led several expeditions and traveled from south to north, from east (Zanzibar) to the center; he explored places and rivers and lakes in South Africa, Botswana, Mozambique, Zambia, Malawi, eastern Congo (DRC), and Tanzania to Ujiji. He is credited with having established geographical knowledge and transport possibilities, and for having identified

23. Gatwa, "Contribution des églises," 156.

24. Dr. Johannes van der Kemp settled among the Xhosa in 1799 during the Xhosa's war against the Boers. Among his many acts of bravery, he rejected the segregation laws and fathered a child with a local woman.

various facts of the slave trade in southern and eastern Africa. Convinced of the unity of biblical and scientific faith, his main concern was to stop the hemorrhaging of Africa, the slave trade. Like Buxton before him, he saw in the development of agriculture and commerce the possibility of stopping this human folly. Struck by so many tests, including the death of his wife, he continued undiscouraged until his death in 1873.

Many saw in Livingstone's work the avant-gardism of Western European colonization and imperialism in the region. Let us not forget that in addition to his ardent fight against the inhuman folly of slavery, he belonged to the LMS, which was in principle opposed to apartheid, promoted by the Boers' claim of "pure Calvinism."[25] Livingstone dedicated the life of his family and his own life to Africa. According to his last will, his heart was buried in Africa. He died in Chitambo (Zambia), around May 1, 1873; members of his expedition team embalmed his body, buried his heart under a mpundu tree, and carved a simple memorial. His embalmed body was carried toward London and buried in Westminster Abbey following the offer by its dean to the president of the Royal Geographical Society.[26]

Cardinal Charles Lavigerie

Cardinal Lavigerie, bishop of Nancy, France, rejected the offer to occupy the archiepiscopal See of Lyon, which would have automatically made him a primate of the Church of France.[27] He opted for the diocese of Algiers, North Africa. Established in 1838 under the concordat between France (imperial power) and the Vatican under Pope Gregory XVI, this diocese of 187 parishes and 273 priests, plus 54 other priests in religious congregations, had been mandated to revive Christianity in North Africa and the rest of Africa that great African names like Cyprian, bishop of Carthage; Augustine, bishop of Hippo; and martyrs like Perpetua and Felicity should never be forgotten.

To support the work of evangelization, Lavigerie accepted the proposal of the Jesuit father Ducat and created in 1868 the Missionary Society of Our Lady of Africa, later known as the White Fathers. The society deployed missionaries towards Africa. Lavigerie set up rules for the company to guide the life of the missionaries, including:

---

25. Gatwa, "Contribution des églises," 158.

26. See https://www.westminster-abbey.org/abbey-commemorations/commemorations/david-livingstone.

27. Renault, *Cardinal Lavigerie*.

(a) Society was to organize itself along the lines of the apostles united around Jesus Christ during the period of his mortal life, instructing one another under divine grace in all the Christian and apostolic virtues; (b) Members of the society had to live in community of at least 3 Fathers or Brothers to support each other morally, materially and spiritually, as Europeans living in the middle of a continent they do not know. . . . (c) Whatever the commitment of the missionary, he had to adopt the life of the surrounding population, to be a member of their community as far as the Christian faith allowed him, learn the local language and speak it correctly, adopt the way of life, housing and food, clothing, in particular that of North Africa on Paul's formula (1 Cor. 9.22). Thus, the fathers opted for the white robe and the rosary, hence the name "White Fathers." He instructed his missionaries to create centers to generate human development: inviting missionaries to remain themselves while opening their doors to men and women alike whatever fouls they are for they remain children of God; they should welcome those who knock at their door, by caring for the sick and giving refuge to the abandoned. The first important thing was "to love the local populations and respect them," he instructed.[28]

To sum up, David Livingstone and Cardinal Lavigerie faced the counter-testimony from four centuries of globalized transatlantic slave trade. They took comfort at opposing the evil practice, modeling their actions to the principles of the English abolitionism movement. Yet, whatever efforts they deployed, Christianity was part of a common assumption defended by the slave trade and colonialism, "Christianizing" and "civilizing" the heathen races.[29]

Is Africa "Incurably Religious"?

Both Christianity and Africa traditional religions may be mistaken to take for granted Mbiti's view that all Africans are religious. In *À contretemps: L'enjeu de Dieu en Afrique*, the African writer Fabien Eboussi-Boulaga talks about Christianity, which, he believes, deliberately or by ignorance thwarted the African cultures, even their knowledge of God. He dismisses the idea of Christianity as a liberating force. It is a non-sense to believe that converting to Christianity is to rise from the abyss of African traditions and religions towards the God of Christianity. The conversion to Christianity

28. Hochschild, *Bury the Chains*, 201–2.

29. See further Quenum, *Église et le commerce*; Hochschild, *Bury the Chains*; Thomas, *Slave Trade*; Pakenham, *Scramble for Africa*.

was never genuine nor free, but an attempt to capture the secret of the white person. According to Mongo Beti, Christianity and colonialism are two faces of the same medal; the hero of *Le pauvre Christ de Bomba*, the white missionary, is identified by the people of Bomba with both Jesus Christ and the colonial administrators. Both Christianity and colonialism use violence against the African to obtain what they want, including conversion to Christianity. The conversion of the Africans is a challenge, says another school of thought; it never compensates what they leave behind. Forced mass conversions of Africans documented in the case of Rwanda led the present author to suggest that despite Rwanda being the birthplace of the eastern Africa spiritual revival, statistics on the Christian demography being over 90 percent of the population aren't genuine.[30]

Similarly, cases of atheism were acknowledged in African Messi Metogo's book, *Dieu peut-il mourir en Afrique?* (Can God die in Africa?). For Metogo, not all Africans believe in a unique God, Creator, remuneratory and vengeful. Cases of religious indifference, even absence of religiosity, in traditional societies were proved in legends and various other corpora of cultures, he says. Religious indifference and atheism are vastly present in society among officers in different professions. If we take Muzungu's point about tabula rasa and Eboussi-Boulaga and Metogo's rejection of the globalization of religiosity among the Africans, we conclude that mission is not accomplished!

Colonial Christianity: An African Response

Until recently, African Christianity was identified with the eighteenth- to nineteenth-century missionary movement expansion. However, since the beginning of the twentieth century, Africa has become the fertile field of another Christian sensibility, the AICs. Several names are used to designate them: new religious movements, indigenous churches, separatist churches, prophetic churches, messianic movements, millenarists, Zionists, etc.[31] Shortly before the end of the twentieth century, Rene Luneau put the statistics at between thirty and forty million members. From the 1990s, the end of the Cold War and the dysfunction of the authoritarianism regimes that controlled the consciences of citizens freed competition in all domains, even religious. Today, membership in the AICs is much higher.

---

30. See Gatwa, "Contribution des églises" and *Churches and Ethnic Ideology*.

31. Dumas-Charles Gapapa, "Les nouveaux mouvements religieux au Rwanda," in Gatwa and Rutinduka, *Histoire du christianisme*, 127–42.

For Andrew Walls the reasons behind the birth of the African indigenous churches comprise the desire to be free from foreign domination, the refusal to condemn the polygamy tolerated in the Bible, the seriousness given to issues like witchcraft and sorcery that poison social relations in communities, and the grabbing of land by white or foreign minorities, even the national bourgeois. According to Eric de Rosny, the founder's "first gesture of independence was not to rebel against a Church too Western in their eyes, or even to found a new Christian community, but to respond to a dazzling and personal call from God, perceived during a dramatic event, such as an epidemic, or through a dream."[32]

Reconfigured Christianity

René Luneau suggests that the great success of these churches has been, without asking anyone, to draw on Christianity and the African tradition of rites and expressions of faith that meet the needs of their communities.[33] Still, these men and women, as Kä Mana puts it, have something exceptional, a desire to be rooted in both the Scriptures and African societies with confidence to handle the magic and the invisible forces that do not allow life to be displayed in all its splendor, and to engage in evangelization that challenges the consciousness of Africans, with courage enough to challenge the abusers of power.[34] Clearly, observation of recent developments in Africa shows that present-day leaders may be losing the thrust of the leaders who challenged the injustices and prejudices of colonial times. While proclaiming the urgency for spiritual awakening—no longer a concern in secularized, colonial Christianity—they manifest a vivid desire to acquire power instead of opposing its abuse. They appeal to a spiritual theology of possibilities and miracles, combining all happenings of the present day with divinization of the spiritual leader, as opposed to the eschatology and theology of the established churches.[35]

Kä Mana highlights another sad side of new forms of Christianity in Africa.

---

32. Rosny, *Healers in the Night*, 16.
33. *Le Monde*, Jan. 3, 2001 (further bibliographic information unavailable).
34. See Kä Mana, *Mission de l'église Africaine.*
35. See Gatwa and Rutinduka, *Histoire du christianisme*, 211.

The "Imbecilization of Christianity"

By using the term "imbecilization of Christianity" Kä Mana implies that viable development of Christianity in Africa has been hindered by the North American arrogant Christianity of far-right trends, from the heralds of liberal ideologies and economies.[36] They spread a cheap Christianity, perpetuating fears and lies over supposed forces of demons and evils that only their prayers and prophecies can disentangle and deliver. In fact, this trend of Christianity from "America" is a strategy designed to maintain the enslavement of the people into nothingness and imbecility, while what he metaphorically calls the powers of Rome, Jerusalem, and Athens continue to expand their control and domination. The reading and interpretation of the Bible within these groups evolves in what Karamaga calls the "free market," a market of illusions that allowed the phenomenon to grow faster and bigger.[37] Theological education, reflection, and thinking are not taken seriously; self-appointed "Reverends," "Bishops," "Archbishops," "Doctors," "apostles," and "prophets" have no idea of what theological formation means for a church of God. When we talk about African Christianity, a crucial question is how and where to classify the "African Christians."[38]

The Public Role of Churches in Africa

Christianity in Africa is also always judged in relation to its attitude towards human rights abuses. Long before the states were formed, Christianity pioneered significant public services, including medical services, education, social services and development. Regarding educational institutions like St Andrew's College in Kiunguni, East Africa; Fourah Bay College in Freetown; the University of Fort Hare, Lovedale Institute, and Adams College in South Africa; and Achimota College in Ghana, despite working in segregation, in a colonial or apartheid environment, trained African cadres played a crucial role in national liberation.

In cases like South Africa and indeed in Rwanda, Christianity played a controversial role as promoters of ethnic and discrimination policies that fractured society. In South Africa, the cynical and degrading system of apartheid, claiming a hierarchy of the "white" race over the so-called "people of color," was both initiated and defeated by Christian theology. The segregationist laws were first introduced by the Boer Calvinists of

---

36. Rédaction, "Kä Mana."
37. As cited in Gatwa, *Churches and Ethnic Ideology*, 56.
38. Gatwa, "God in Public Domain."

the Dutch Reformed Church in the seventeenth century, and continually defended until the end by 1990. The defeat by Christianity occurred in the world ecumenical organizations from the 1960s. Under leadership of Archbishop Desmond Tutu and leading theologians, including Dr. Allan Boesak, Beyers Naudé, and Frank Chikane, apartheid was branded a heresy to the gospel and defending churches were excluded from ecumenical organizations in the early 1980s. Henceforth, its foundations were irreversibly undermined, particularly by the 1985 Kairos Document by over one hundred prominent theologians. After the liberation of Nelson Mandela, the churches became engines of the Truth and Reconciliation Commission chaired by Archbishop Desmond Tutu, to ensure space for repentance, forgiveness, and reconciliation.[39]

With the end of the Cold War in 1989, dictators who had interfered in politics, seized power from the leaders of independence, and imposed hard dictatorship and abuse of human rights coupled with spoliation of resources no longer commanded the unconditional support of either of the two rival blocs (West and East); the populations rose up in search for democratization; the national conferences, characterized by Eboussi-Boulaga as an *affaire à suivre* (promising affair),[40] disenfranchised the populations who found the event a therapy for the ruined, mutilated society, hoping to transition to participatory democracy, rights, and freedom. Churches, the sole institutions standing with a certain degree of credibility, hence were called to provide leadership to these forums. However, the Protestant presbyteries, due to many factors, including Protestant ecclesiology, doctrines more parochial than universal, and the history of missions established on ethnic configuration, were trapped in ethnic identities. The absence of tradition in leadership formation, denominational isolationism, and misinterpreting the Reformation doctrine on church-state relations restrained any possible national, even supranational, vocation.

A Cross-Cultural Mission

Some historians of missions have suggested that Christianity in Africa, in addition to demographic growth, has reached maturity in setting up norms and standards for world Christianity. Bediako proposes a five-point manifesto for African Christianity to help re-evangelize secularized Europe. He evokes the depth of African religions' spiritualities, which could help to

39. Gatwa, *Churches and Ethnic Ideology*, 221.

40. See subtitle of Eboussi-Boulaga, *Les conférences nationales en Afrique noire. Une affaire à suivre*.

resuscitate spiritualities like the Frisia in the northwestern Europe and the Celtic in Scotland, Wales, and Ireland. We have disputed the foundations of this claim on the basis of our experiences working with the Centre de Littérature Évangélique, Éditions CLÉ, Yaoundé (CLÉ), and the Association of Theological Seminaries of in Francophone Africa; and later, the field visits to many theological seminaries for the WCC and the AACC. Although the seminaries were created in 1963 by the Protestant churches in Africa and the AACC to promote general literature and African theology, the result remains mixed three decades later. By the year 2000, stepping into a room still open to a vast cooperation with churches and theological seminaries, we initiated a program called Réflexions Théologiques du Sud (Theological reflections from the south), which published theological books in French and English.[41] Meanwhile, during field visits to theological seminaries, we identified huge difficulties facing these institutions: the absence of strategic plan; working conditions in total impoverishment (poor infrastructures, underfunded library); pastoral and intellectual ostracism without interaction with other social sciences disciplines; financial precarity; underdeveloped curricula . . . and, last but not least, total apathy, before what some have called misleading theologies and prophecies. Twelve years after those field visits, the situation has changed; many seminars have metamorphosed into Christian universities, adding new faculties and expanding sources of funding, as well as adapting to national standards of higher education. The move was welcomed in the churches and society. However, the integration of theology into the university faces some challenges, not the least the unpreparedness of public regulatory bodies due to absence of experts to accredit and audit theological programs. A final challenge is that parish ministers are trained in foreign colonial languages, with limited room for the candidate in ministry to find resources within popular wisdoms, idioms, storytelling, proverbs, and religions and forms of expression in local cultures, raising the questions of how solid foundational leadership formation is and how committed churches are to fulfilling cross-cultural mission.

Conclusion

This chapter has tried to bring forth some narratives of a resilient Christianity in challenging contexts. It assessed some cases of deeds and misdeeds in the nation-state disfigured, disarticulated, even destroyed. As Martin Luther King is to have said, crises are factors of creativity; this was illustrated in selected examples who tirelessly tried to rehumanize Christianity in Africa. Both Catholic and Protestant religious congregations and missionary

41. By 2007 no fewer than thirty books were published in the series promoting both well-established and young African theologians.

societies took an active part in the conceptualization and justification of evil practices, including the transatlantic slave trade and colonialism. Many still maintain their financial assets in companies, banks, and even universities that caused and still cause tremendous suffering to billions of people. Others worked in synchrony and complicity with postindependence authoritarian regimes that abused human rights in so-called independent countries. Mission will not be accomplished until an ecclesiology and a pastorate of healing memory, confession, repentance, and eventually reparation are properly promoted as attitudes by churches at the highest levels for people deprived of their dignity to be rehabilitated as images of God. The time for their representatives to say *mea culpa* for past and present misdeeds is now. Tomorrow is not another day for that mandatory task, Jesus would say!

Bibliography

Ajayi, J. F. A "New Christian Politics? The Challenge of Mission-Educated Elite. Paper presented at the Yale-Edinburgh North Atlantic Missiology Project Conference, Cambridge, UK, Apr. 6–7, 1998.

Barringer, Terry. *The Creation of an Atlantic World: 1440–1531*. Paper presented at the Yale-Edinburgh North Atlantic Missiology Project Conference, Edinburgh, May 6–7, 1996.

Baur, John. *2000 Years of Christianity in Africa*. Nairobi: Pauline, 1994.

Bediako, Kwame. *Theology and Identity: The Impact of Culture upon Christian Thought in the Second Century and Modern Africa*. Regnum Studies in Mission. Carlisle, UK: Regnum, 1992.

Beti, Mongo. *Le pauvre Christ de Bomba*. Paris: Présence Africaine, 2001.

Eboussi-Boulaga, Fabien. *À contretemps: L'enjeu de Dieu en Afrique*. Paris: Karthala, 1991.

———. *Les conférences nationales en Afrique noire.:Une affaire à suivre*. Paris: Karthala, 1993.

Buck-Morss, Susan. "Hegel and Haiti." *Critical Inquiry* 26 (Summer 2000) 821–65. https://www.jstor.org/stable/1344332.

Fux, Pierre-Yves, et al., eds. *Augustinus Afer: Saint Augustin, africanité et universalité*. Fribourg, Switz.: Éditions Universitaires, 2003.

Gatwa, Tharcisse. *Churches and Ethnic Ideology in the Rwandan Crises 1900–1994*. Oxford, UK: OCMS, 2005.

———. "Contribution des églises non catholiques dans le développement du christianisme en Afrique." In *Cent ans de Christianisme en Afrique*, edited by Pierre Paré, 137–62. Montreal: Iris, 2001.

———. "The Cross-Cultural Mission: An Agenda for Theological Education in Africa." *Southern Africa Missiological Society Journal* 38 (2010) 321–42.

———. "God in the Public Domain: Life Giver, Protector or Indifferent Sleeper during the Rwandan Tragedies?" *Exchange* 43 (2014).

Gatwa, Tharcisse, and Laurent Rutinduka, eds. *Histoire du christianisme au Rwanda: Des origines à nos jours*. Yaoundé: CLÉ, 2014.

Hardy, Daniel. "Christian Missions and the 'Enlightenment' of the West: Upholding Orthodoxy." Presentation at "Missionary Encounter: Theological Issues" conference, Boston, June 21–24, 1998.

Hochschild, Adam. *Bury the Chains: Prophets and Rebels in the Fight to Free an Empire's Slaves*. Boston: Houghton Mifflin, 2005.

Kä Mana, G. *La mission de l'église Africaine: Pour une nouvelle éthique mondiale et une civilisation de l'esperance*. Bafoussam, Cameroon: CIPCRE-CEROS, 2005.

Metogo, Eloi Messi. *Dieu peut-il mourir en Afrique?* (Can God die in Africa?). Chrétiens en liberté. Paris: Harmattan, 1997.

Oden, Thomas C. *How Africa Shaped the Christian Mind: Rediscovering the African Seedbed of Western Christianity*. Early African Christianity Set. Downers Grove, IL: IVP Academic, 2010.

Olusoga, David. *Black and British: A Forgotten History*. Updated with a new chapter. London: Picador, 2023.

Pakenham, Thomas. *The Scramble for Africa: 1876–1912*. London: Abacus, 1991.

Quenum, A. *L'église et le commerce transatlantique*. Paris: Karthala, 1992.

Rédaction. "Kä Mana: 'Les brasseries en Afrique sont des structures d'imbécilisation collective de nos populations.'" *Tambour*, Sept. 27, 2018. https://tambour.agoraafricaine.info/2018/09/27/ka-mana-les-brasseries-en-afrique-sont-des-structures-dimbecilisation-collective-de-nos-populations/.

Renault, François. *Le Cardinal Lavigerie (1825–1892): L'église, l'Afrique et la France*. Paris: Fayard, 1992.

Rosny, Éric de. *Healers in the Night*. Translated by Robert R. Barr SJ. Eugene, OR: Wipf & Stock, 2004.

Sala-Molins, Louis. *Dark Side of the Light: Slavery and the French Enlightenment*. Translated by John Comteh-Morgan. Minneapolis: University of Minnesota Press, 2006.

Sanneh, Lamin. *Encountering the West. Christianity and the Global Cultural Process; The African Dimension*. World Christian Theology Series. London: Harper Collins, 1993.

Scammell, V. G. *The First Imperial Age: Europe Overseas Expansion c. 1400–1715*. London: Unwin Hyman, 1989.

Schaff, Philip. *Apostolic Christianity: A.D. 1–100*. Vol. 1 of *History of the Christian Church*. Peabody, MA: Hendrickson, 1994.

Thomas, Hugh. *The Slave Trade: The History of the Atlantic Slave Trade, 1440–1870*. London: Phoenix, 2006.

Walls, Andrew F. *The Cross-Cultural Process in Christian History: Studies in the Transmission and Appropriation of Faith*. Maryknoll, NY: Orbis, 2002.

Zorn, Jean-François. *Le grand siècle d'une mission protestante: La Mission de Paris de 1822–1914*. Paris: Karthala, 1993.

12

Christianity, Wars, and Ethnic Challenges

Georges Pirwoth Atido

The African continent has been affected by several conflicts and wars in the last decades. The Cold War divided Africa into three parts as some countries sided with the United States, others followed the Soviet Union, and one group decided to remain neutral (non-aligned). While this war ended with the collapse of the Soviet Union in late 1991, several other conflicts ignited the continent. Interstate wars remain relatively few in number, and mostly internal, so-called "insurrectionary wars" were observed. More than thirty African countries have experienced at least one civil war since 1960.

In a politico-cultural context characterized by weakness in the sharing of power, several wars have featured competing ethnic groups trying to gain control of the central economic operator represented by the state. Such a situation was observed in several countries, including the DRC, Central African Republic, Uganda, Rwanda, Burundi, Sudan, etc. There are also wars that emerged from religious radicalism, which contribute to Christian persecution.

It is important not to overinterpret the associated figures and not to see only the trait of generalized anarchy. Indeed, if the information that reaches us often imparts tragedies, we may need to note that many states, such as Senegal, Zambia, Ghana, and Botswana, have experienced relative peace. Similarly, one may also observe that some countries, like the DRC, Nigeria, and Somalia, have experienced instability in only part of their territory, when the rest was spared. Still other countries, like Angola and Rwanda, have demonstrated remarkable success after troubled periods.

In addition to these known stories of success in the African continent, the present chapter particularly voices the triumph of Christian witness and church growth that breathes new life into African Christianity amid these wars and turmoil.

Cold War in Africa

The Cold War was a conflict that opposed the United States (US) to the Soviet Union (USSR). The conflict developed after World War II. The US and the USSR were the only two superpowers. "The fact that, by the 1950s, each possessed nuclear weapons and the means of delivering such weapons on their enemies, added a dangerous aspect to the conflict."[1] These two renowned superpower rivals were afraid to engage in armed military fighting as this could lead to the use of nuclear weapons, which would destroy everything. So instead, they used words, havoc, and provocation as weapons, threatening and denouncing each other. This conflict divided the world in three main groups: "The United States led the West. This group included countries with democratic political systems. The [USSR] led the East. This group included countries with communist political systems. The non-aligned group included countries that did not want to be tied to either the West or the East."[2]

Over the years, the Cold War became the major force in world politics for about the second half of the twentieth century. Historians disagree about its length; but the majority seem to agree that relations between the US and the USSR stated to improve during the 1960s and early '70s; the Cold War started to end when the Berlin Wall was demolished in 1989; and the real end of the war occurred with the collapse of the USSR in late 1991.[3]

African nations found themselves politically caught up between two major forces. Both were trying to influence the continent to side with them. This gave Africa a great challenge. Nevertheless, most of the countries in the continent of Africa decided not to take part in the Cold War. They formed a camp known as the "non-aligned," a neutral camp, as they would not align either behind the US or behind the USSR. The non-aligned movement was "made up of countries that had gained independence from the European empires in the period after World War II, the movement tried to act as a stabilizing force between the two superpower blocs, as well as giving its members a more powerful voice through unity."[4]

But despite this, some African countries adopted a Marxist regime. These countries included Angola, under Agostinho Neto and José Eduardo dos Santos; Mozambique, under Samora Machel; Guinea Bissau, under Amilcar Cabral; Congo (Conakry), became a Marxist-Leninist state in

---

1. Forman, *Christianity in Non-Western World*, vii.
2. Forman, *Christianity in Non-Western World*, 3.
3. Forman, *Christianity in Non-Western World*, 3.
4. Munro, "Non-Aligned Movement," §1.

1970, under Marien Ngouabi; Egypt, under Gamal Abdel Nasser in 1954–69; Somalia, under Mohamed Siad Barre (allied in 1969, but soon changed sides to become violently anti-Soviet; during the Cold War period, it was the only government to do so under the same leader in Africa); Ethiopia, under Mengistu Haile Mariam, following the revolution in 1974; Uganda, briefly under Apollo Milton Obote in 1969; and Benin, declared a Marxist-Leninist state in 1974, under Mathieu Kérékou.[5]

These countries must pay heavily as they remained long in political and social instability. This has affected not only the government of these countries but also the church and mission, which were suffering from the communist philosophy as well as from the constant state of war, insecurity, and poverty as a result of their struggle to survive in a fight with powers beyond their strength.

The DRC and Africa's World War

For centuries, Congo has been undergoing deep social and political turmoil. After the atrocious occupation of the country by King Leopold II of Belgium, who owned the territory as his own property from 1885 to 1908, a period during which approximately ten million Congolese perished under the blow of forced labor,[6] in a half-century of Belgian colonization (1908–60) described as "the most abusive of almost any other colonizer in Africa,"[7] the country went into another half-century of political instability. Congo received independence in on June 30, 1960. The ensuing conflict between Joseph Kasa-Vubu (the president) and Patrice Lumumba (the prime minister) led the country to the Simba Rebellion in 1964 during which about twenty thousand Congolese lost their lives.[8] After this, Joseph-Désiré Mobutu came to power by coup d'état and ruled the country for thirty-three years (1965–97) in a severe dictatorship that deeply ruined the economy of the country.

Laurent Kabila took over in 1997 after two years of war, followed by different rebel factions who led the country to what was known as Africa's World War and the Great War of Africa. This war that Jason Stearns calls "many wars in one,"[9] the largest in modern African history, involved eight African nations, as well as about twenty-five armed groups. It began

5. Singh, "Nam," §4.
6. Hochschild, *King Leopold's Ghost*, 164.
7. Van Reybrouck, *Congo*, 13.
8. Lanotte, "Chronology," §38.
9. Stearns, *Dancing in the Glory*, 93.

in August 1998 and officially ended in July 2003 when the transitional government of the DRC took power (though hostilities continued).[10] By 2008 the war and its aftermath had killed 5.4 million people, mostly from disease and starvation, making the Second Congo War the deadliest conflict worldwide since World War II. This led the UN to send a military peace force to Congo in February 2006, known as MONUC (Mission de l'Organisation des Nations Unies au Congo).

In this confusion, Ituri District, where the Alur are found, experienced an interethnic armed conflict between the Lendu and Hema tribes from 1999 to 2004. In this conflict, more than sixty thousand people were killed, fifty thousand houses burned, and five hundred thousand people displaced.[11] Consequently, the city of Bunia became the base of one of the largest United Nations peacekeeping forces in Africa.

At the age of thirty, Joseph Kabila acceded to the presidency of the DRC on January 26, 2001, ten days after the assassination of his father Laurent-Désiré Kabila. He took the lead of a country torn since August 1998 by a regional war, involving multiple armed groups and several African countries.

An inter-Congolese peace accord was signed in Sun City, South Africa, on December 17, 2002, establishing a transitional government of national unity. Under the terms of the agreement, Kabila remained head of state for a transitional period of two years. He was assisted by four vice-presidents.

On October 29, 2006, Kabila was elected president in the second round against the former warlord and vice president Jean-Pierre Bemba. The winner thus became the first democratically elected president of the country since the country's independence in 1960.

On November 28, 2011, Kabila was reelected in single-round elections marred by violence and numerous irregularities. Historical opponent Étienne Tshisekedi rejected the results of the election and saw the police as repressing any attempt to rally his supporters. Kabila, proclaimed winner, was invested on December 20, 2011.

In May 2012, the rebellion of the March 23 movement began in the east of the country, in Kivu. This rebellion was composed, for the most part, of former Tutsi rebels integrated into the army. It led a murderous offensive at the gates of Goma for several months before being defeated at the end of 2013.

The year 2014 marked the beginning of a series of massacres of civilians in the Beni region of north Kivu. These killings are attributed to the

10. Horizon, *Congo*, 71.
11. International Crisis Group, "DR Congo," §3.

Allied Democratic Forces, the Uganda Liberation Army. Despite the high number of killings, the authorities struggle to unmask the criminals. As of this writing, the most recent is the attack on a Pentecostal church at Kasindi, killing fourteen people.[12]

In September 2016, the province of Kasaï, in the center of the country, fell into violence after the death of a customary chief killed by the security forces. This conflict left more than three thousand dead, including two UN experts, and 1.4 million displaced.

Félix-Antoine Tshisekedi was elected president of the DRC with 38.57 percent of the vote after the December 30, 2018, ballot. He was the first opponent to be elected president of the DRC since the country's independence in 1960. He was sworn in on January 24, 2019, at the Palais de la Nation in Kinshasa, in the presence of Kenyan president Uhuru Kenyatta, members of the diplomatic corps, army officials, magistrates, and some privileged Congolese who had access to the palace.

Since then, the country has been facing several armed groups. In 2020, the Congo Research Group made an inventory of 122 armed groups operating in eastern Congo provinces, namely Ituri, North Kivu, South Kivu, and Tanganyika. They are fighting over land control, minerals, or protection of their community's leaving.[13] The armed groups have caused the deaths of over two million people, an estimate of six million internally displaced, one million raped women, and hundreds of thousands of people facing extreme food insecurity. This situation has deeply affected the Congolese psychologically, morally, and spiritually. This situation has motivated several Christians to work into bringing new hope to the community. This includes Dr. Denis Mukwege who has been nicknamed "the man who repairs women."

Dr. Denis Mukwege and the Panzi Hospital

Dr. Denis Mukwege was born in Bukavu (DRC) on March 1, 1955. His father, a Pentecostal pastor, frequently went to visit his sick parishioners to support them and pray with them as Mukwege accompanied him frequently.

One day, when he was eight years old, Mukwege went with his father to a sick child and was surprised that no treatment was given to that child. His father explained to him that he is not a medical doctor but just a pastor and that his ministry would be limited to praying for the sick. Then Mukwege observed, as you pray for healing, I will need to treat effectively the sick.

---

12. Casper, "Terrorist Attack," para. 2.
13. Vogel et al., *Cartographie des groupes armées*, 45.

Mukwege then went to study medicine and was oriented to pediatrics. When he had to present his thesis towards the end of 1983, he began to work for a few months in a bush hospital run by Protestants in Lemera (DRC). He then discovered the difficult reality of the living conditions of women in the region. This pushed him to finally turn to gynecology.

Benefiting from a scholarship from the Swedish Pentecostal Mission, he went to France in 1984 to pursue a specialization in gynecology at the University of Angers. Gifted and well integrated, he was presented with several opportunities to stay in Europe. But the memory of the suffering women in his country compelled him to return to Congo as he understood that he would much more useful there. On September 24, 2015, he became a doctor of medical sciences at the Free University of Brussels after defending a thesis entitled "Etiology, Classification and Treatment of Traumatic Urogenital and Lower Genito-Digestive Fistulas in Eastern DRC."

In 1989, he chose to return to Congo to take care of the Lemera Hospital, of which he became medical director. In 1996, during the first Congo war, his hospital was brutally destroyed during the attack on Lemera. Mukwege escaped death while several patients and nurses were murdered.

He took refuge in Nairobi, then decided to return to Congo. With the help of the Pingstmissionens Utvecklingssamarbete, a Swedish charity, he founded the Panzi Hospital there in Bukavu in the suburbs of Bukavu in 1999. The United Nations estimates that some five hundred thousand people have been raped or subjected to sexual violence since the conflict erupted in 1996. Some attacks have targeted boys and men, but the vast majority of victims have been women and girls.[14]

Mukwege was then confronted with genital mutilation practiced on women. Deeply marked by this violence, he decided to make the world aware of the barbarism of which women in the east of the DRC are victims, and to act to help them. In a region where gang rape is used as a weapon of war, he specializes in caring for female victims of these sexual assaults, providing them with medical but also psychological, economic, and legal aid.[15]

Mukwege and his staff have helped to care for more than fifty thousand survivors of sexual violence. He is recognized as one of the world's specialists in the treatment of fistulas; as such, he received, among other things, two university awards in 2010. The Panzi Hospital not only treats survivors with physical wounds, but also provides legal and psycho-social services to its patients. Even patients who cannot afford post-rape medical care are treated without charge. Mukwege has been fearless in his efforts to

---

14. Persky, "Capital of Rape," 59.
15. Braeckman, *Homme qui répare*, 6.

increase protections for women and to advocate that those responsible for sexual violence be brought to justice, including the Congolese government and militia groups laying siege to eastern DRC.

On October 25, 2012, he was the victim of an attack in the center of Bukavu. The guardian of his house was shot dead after having alerted him to the danger, his car was set on fire, and Mukwege was tied up. But thanks to the intervention of local residents who came to his aid, he came out safe and sound. He then took refuge in Belgium for a few months before returning to work in Congo-Kinshasa.

In 2018, he received the Nobel Peace Prize with Nadia Murad, for their efforts to end the use of sexual violence as a weapon of war. Son of a Pentecostal pastor, Dr. Denis Mukwege, also nicknamed the Angel of Bukavu, is also a pastor like his father was in a church, the one his parents founded with Swedish missionaries. The congregation of his church from the denomination known as Communauté des Églises de Pentecôte en Afrique Centrale has thousands of participants in Sunday worship.[16] Thus in addition to his medical activity, Mukwege serves in pastor in an Evangelical Pentecostal church in Bukavu (DRC).

From his declaration in an interview granted to *La Free Newspaper*, his pastoral life is not due to the fact that he was born into a Christian family, nor to the fact of having benefited from a Christian education; it is due to his personal experience with Christ. He said that when he was thirteen, he had an experience that transformed his life: a personal encounter with Jesus. He was in a small prayer group and for the first time really felt God's love for him. He cried, and he could not explain why. He was in a joy that he could not explain. He realized how much he did not deserve this love from God. Since that day, he decided to do everything for the glory of God, as his main theme became love for God and love for others.[17]

Mukwege has treated thousands of women who were victims of rape as a weapon of war since the Second Congo War, some of them more than once, performing up to ten operations a day during his seventeen-hour working days.

Hutu-Tutsi Antagonism in Rwanda

Rwanda is generally perceived as the place where the East African revival began. It started with a wave of repentance, restoration of relationships, prayer, and Bible study in 1931 at Gahini, an Anglican mission station

16. Mukwege, *Plaidoyer pour la vie*, 24.
17. Carrel, "Dr Denis Mukwege," §3 (translation and paraphrase mine).

associated with the CMS.[18] It spread later to Kigezi in 1935 and Ankole in 1936 before expanding within Uganda, then in Kenya, Tanzania, Burundi, Sudan, and the DRC.

As a result, Rwanda was seen as one of the great "success stories" of West missionary work in Africa. It is estimated that in 1994 as many as 90 percent of the Rwandan population was Christian, with 62.6 percent identifying as Catholic, 18.8 percent identifying as Protestant, and 8.4 percent identifying as Seventh-Day Adventist.

But in 1994, the world was surprised by the civil war that took place opposing the Hutu and Tutsi, who were supposed to be mostly Christians, resulting in almost eight hundred thousand Tutsi and moderate Hutu killed by the Hutu within only one hundred days.

The tension between Hutus and Tutsis was related to ethnicity, power (the settlers had given power to the Tutsi minority), and a historical lack of trust. The ethnic conflicts took place from 1959 to 1961 and from 1972 to 1973. In the 1970s there was an attempted genocide of Hutus by Tutsis in Burundi (the neighboring country); thousands of Hutus were killed—a fact that fueled the fire of genocidal Hutus in 1994.[19]

The saddest part of the Rwanda civil war was the involvement of Christians in the killing—choosing their ethnic identity over their belonging to the family of Christ. The East African revival had arguably addressed some problems of reconciliation, but the 1994 massacres revealed that many Christians did not understand that accepting Jesu Christ as Savior and Lord and being reconciled to Christ also meant acceptance and reconciliation with "the other."

Although there were Christians on both sides who acted heroically, and stood up for those of the other ethnicity, many agree that part of the problem was that Christians were divided according to ethnicity lines with "us" and "them" considerations.

After the genocide, several refugees who returned to Rwanda refused to join existing churches that they accused of being linked with the regime that caused their exile but joined new emerging ones, including Zion Temple and the Restoration Church.[20]

---

18. Harper, "New Dawn," §3.
19. Katongole, *Who Are My People*, 70.
20. Choquette, "Rwanda," 1116.

Hutu-Tutsi Fraternity in Burundi

Burundi is a formerly German, then Belgian, colony, which became independent in 1962. Located in the region of the Great Lakes of eastern Africa, the Twa, Tutsi, and Hutu people live together in the country. In the 1960s, the fighting between the Tutsis and Hutus worsened, and the underlying conflicts continued during the '70s and '80s until they ended in the civil war that lasted from 1993 to 2005, in which between fifty thousand and one hundred thousand people died. Although many schools were closed, the Catholic Buta Seminar (province of Bururi, in the south of Burundi) remained open.

The rector, Fr. Zachary Bukuru, who was convinced that they would be safer in the seminary, convinced the students to stay. To avoid ethnic division between the seminarians, the professors set up an integration plan, using sport, music, dance, group work, meditation, and prayer, working on solidarity and fraternity to avoid polarization.[21]

On April 30, 1997, around 5:30 a.m., about a thousand rebels from a guerrilla group, led by a female combatant, arrived, fired heavy ammunition, and attacked the seminar. According to several testimonies, it was a militia group of the National Council for the Defense of Democracy, a Hutu political party.

Most of the 250 seminarians managed to get out through the windows of the second floor where the common dormitory was located, and fled across the country, but about fifty young people aged fourteen to twenty-one were unable to escape. The rebels reached the dormitories. One of the fighters asked not to hurt the young boys, but he was killed on the spot.

The leader of the group ordered the seminarians to divide into ethnic groups, Hutus on one side and Tutsis on the other. When the students realized that one of the two ethnic groups (the Tutsi) would be executed, they decided to remain united. Side by side, the seminarians raised their hands and declared: "We are all brothers, children of the same God, and of the same country, Burundi." The fighters tried to break their resistance by threatening to separate them. But the children refused to comply. Three times the militia repeated its order. Three times the students said, "No, we are all sons of God." The furious assailants massacred forty seminarians with guns and grenades. During this attack, some seminarians sang psalms and others repeated: "Forgive them Lord, for they do not know what they are doing." The seminarians remained united until the end: some of them lost their lives while helping the very first victims.

---

21. Bukuru, *Quarante jeunes martyrs*, 71.

After the massacre, the rebels left the place. Trapped in his rectory, Fr. Zachary Bukuru heard a student cry out at his door. As he opened the door, the boy stumbled in, wounded. "Father, we have won," he declared. "They told us to separate and we refused. We have won." Those were his last words.

The rector was able to leave his room and went directly to the site of the immolation. He found a grotesque scene there, with butchered bodies, and heard some of his dear students still screaming in agony. He went to them. One of them, before dying, confided to him: "Father, they tried to separate us, but they did not succeed." Another said to him with his last breath: "Death comes, but victory remains."

The Buta seminary massacre was covered by the media around the world, and the dead students were promptly remembered as the "martyrs of the fraternity." As Fr. Bukuru observed, the Buta massacre can be counted as a political failure. Despite the number of victims, which was raised to forty-three deaths, this was still minor out of four hundred people present on the site.

One had feared much heavier losses because the combatants were in excessive number (around two thousand) and had sophisticated weapons. Tactically, the attackers had planned to kill all the Tutsis and take the Hutus with them. But the attitude of the boys, who refused to separate, caught them out. The assailants were unable to separate the students of the Buta seminary, and also they failed to crate division among inhabitants of southern Burundi in general, considered to be the center of the power they were fighting. The assailants had counted on a general flare-up of violence or at least on an automatic rallying of all the Hutus to their cause. But the Hutus and the Tutsis remained united by the blood of Christ.[22]

Positive testimonies include that of Marguerite Barankitse, a humanitarian activist who works to improve the welfare of children and challenge ethnic discrimination in Burundi and who migrated to Rwanda because of persecution:

> a humanitarian who created Maison Shalom—House of Peace—out of the carnage of the Burundian genocide. In nearly 20 years of existence, Maison Shalom has grown to include schools, a hospital, agricultural cooperatives, a microfinance system and other projects... Maison Shalom has helped more than 20,000 children in the aftermath of the Burundian genocide.... Maggy Barankitse was forced to flee Burundi and find refuge in Rwanda after participating in political protests. She continues her work in exile and has built Maison Shalom

22. Bukuru, *Quarante jeunes martyrs*, 135.

Rwanda and the Oasis of Peace, a community center for refugees and the surrounding community. She also created the Mahama Elite Center in Rwanda, which works in conjunction with the Mahama Refugee Camp to give refugees, especially children, the care and resources they need.[23]

Central African Republic Chaos and Christian Witness

The Central African Republic has lived long in political instability. The country was proclaimed on December 1, 1958. On August 13, 1960, it gained its independence. After the assassination of Boganda in 1959, the father of Central African independence, it was Abel Goumba who seemed likely to be his successor, but David Dacko, supported by France, became the first president of the republic in 1960. Dacko quickly established a dictatorial regime. Then the chief of staff of the Central African army, Jean-Bédel Bokassa, overthrew his cousin Dacko and seized power in 1965 and became Emperor Bokassa I on December 4, 1976. He then set up a very repressive policy throughout the country. He was overthrown in September 1979, and David Dacko returned to power.

In September 1981, General André Kolingba, taking advantage of a period of social unrest, forced Dacko to hand over power to him. Kolingba then established a dictatorial military regime. In 1993, mutineers ended up forcing Kolingba to organize elections through which Ange-Félix Patassé was elected president in 1993. After political instability and unrest in 1996, during which the former dictator Bokassa died in Bangui, the Bangui agreements of January 1997 seemed to put an end to the conflicts. On September 19, 1999, Ange-Félix Patassé was reelected president. However, in 2003, while Patassé was abroad, rebels moved into Bangui and installed their president, General François Bozizé. In March 2013, Bozizé was ousted by rebels from the northern part of the country, who were mostly Muslim and collectively known as Seleka. Michel Djotodia, the coup leader, assumed power, suspended the constitution, and dissolved parliament. In mid-April he created a transitional national council that named him interim president. Djotodia was not able to stem the violence in the country, and CAR spiraled into chaos. Seleka rebels terrorized the community. Christian and indigenous believers in traditional power formed their own militias, the "anti-balaka," to retaliate and defend themselves. They were equally as brutal and

---

23. Faith & Leadership, "Maggy Barankitse," paras. 3, 1, 2.

committed rape, killings, and large-scale destruction. Almost one million people, in a country of five million, fled their homes.[24]

Amid the CAR crisis, Fr. Bernard Kinvi demonstrated Christian love by caring for the Muslims who could be perceived as his enemies. Director of the St John Paul II Hospital in the northwest of the Central African Republic, Fr. Kinvi welcomed, during the conflict in 2013–14 that bloodied the country, the wounded and the sick without distinction of ethnicity, community, or religion at the risk of his own life.[25]

Father Kinvi, Togolese by birth and Central African by adoption, belongs to the order founded by Saint Camillus de Lellis in the sixteenth century. Camillian monks take four vows: poverty, chastity, obedience, and care for the sick, even at the cost of contagion and life. The religious order of the Camillian vocation is to care for the sick.

When the civil war broke out in the CAR in 2013, Fr. Kinvi ran the St John Paul II Hospital (forty beds) in Bossemptélé, a town of 26,000 inhabitants lost in the middle of the bush 300 km northwest of Bangui, the capital city. Bossemptélé has no electricity, no paved road—only a hospital within 150 km around. Bossemptélé Hospital welcomes patients without distinction of faith. It treats typhoid fever and malaria. Fr. Kinvi very quickly made his mark, learning Sango, the local language, and integrating into the community.

The crisis began in March 2013, when the Seleka, Muslim militia from the north, overthrew the government and sparked a wave of violence, burning many villages and killing large numbers of people. In response to these acts, the so-called anti-balaka militias, a heterogeneous movement with an animist and Christian majority, fiercely anti-Muslim, began attacking Seleka bases as well as Muslim minorities. As Seleka leaders were ousted and forced to flee, Muslim civilians faced the wrath of anti-balaka forces. From city to city, Muslims were attacked and massacred, and their homes and mosques destroyed.

One of the deadliest attacks took place in Bossemptélé, where the anti-balaka killed more than eighty Muslims. Father Kinvi spent days searching for Muslim survivors, most of whom were children, and took them to the Catholic church to be safe from violence. While the conflict was in full swing, he sheltered hundreds of Muslims in the church despite numerous death threats from the anti-balaka. About 1,500 Muslims found refuge under their protection.

---

24. Tompté-Tom, *Nouvelles formes de spiritualité*, 94. See also https://www.infoplease.com/countries/central-african-republic.

25. Kinvi and Yegavian, *Mission*, 18.

Father Kinvi trembled, but he stood in his mission to assist those who came to seek protection and assistance at the hospital. His faith in Jesus Christ brought to him strength. More than once, he came face to face with machetes and Kalashnikovs. But, more than a physical and moral ordeal, the Central African conflict is for him a spiritual journey that his faith transcends. There were also Carmelite sisters present alongside the refugees, whose unfailing love for their neighbor was a great help to him.

In March 2014, African peacekeepers evacuated the majority of remaining Muslims from Bossemptélé in Cameroon, in addition to some one hundred thousand Muslims who had already fled the country. Around seventy people, including more than a dozen children with disabilities, were stranded in the Catholic church, far too weak to make the journey. Undeterred, Fr. Kinvi continued to care for the Muslims in his care and managed to take them back to their loved ones.[26]

For his exceptional courage, Fr. Kinvi received the Alison Des Forges Prize in December 2014, an award given each year to four human rights defenders of extraordinary courage. He intends to continue his actions, cherishing the dream of seeing the Muslims return to Bossemptélé.

Sudan in War and in Christian Servant Leadership

After independence from Britain on January 1, 1956, the southern Sudan region, mostly black, remained united with the north of the Sudan, which is Arab and Muslim. The religious presence was mixed with two large majorities, animist and Christian, and a minority (7–8 percent) of Muslims. The gradual imposition of Shari'a law by the north resulted in two long wars—one of them the longest in the world (1955–2005, with a short and fragile "peace" from 1973 to 1983)—which ended with agreements signed in Nairobi in 2005. The result of these thirty-eight years of war was more than 2.5 million people dead and the region of the south completely devastated, impoverished, and without services and infrastructure. The resulting embryonic process of democratization peaked four years later in 2011. In that year, there was the January 9–15 plebiscite referendum in favor of secession—98.83 percent of the citizens voted for independence! South Sudan got its independence on July 9, 2011, and became the 54th country in Africa and 193rd in the world. These epochal events, aiming to unite the people, were completely undermined by the 2013 outbreak of a bloody interethnic war that is still ongoing. The two major protagonists are the largest ethnic communities: the Dinka, the largest in numbers, and the Nuer. Tribal fractures

26. Aurora, "Bernard Kinvi."

and difficulties have increased in the last two years, and today there are at least nine other major ethnic rebel groups in the country.

Amid the Sudan war, Paride Taban provided sound Christian leadership as he sacrificially cared for the vulnerable Sudanese. An emeritus bishop of the Roman Catholic Church, Taban served in the diocese of Torit in southern Sudan from 1983 to 2004 in the midst of the most difficult circumstances of Sudan's civil war. As bishop, he was a spokesperson and advocate for the vulnerable Sudanese, taking food to the starving and traveling in different parts of the world to secure additional relief support. After his retirement in 2004, he moved from Torit to a remote area in the Sudan, and in 2005 he founded the Holy Trinity Peace Village Kuron, a place where people of different ethnicities and faiths live together. Taban calls the village a "small oasis of peace" in a country torn by ethnic and religious violence and hopes "to make Sudan a nation where people live as brothers and sisters, as people of God."[27]

Conclusion

With the end of the Cold War, one would have hoped that Africa would embark on a path of peace and solidarity. But the continent was quickly immersed in political violence, civil wars, border disputes, religious radicalism, social violence, and tribalism, etc. These multiple forms of violence are constant threats to peace in Africa.

Amid unrest, the church has remained relatively strong and mission focused despite war and starvation.[28] There are several people who stood in the name of Christ to bring healing, reconciliation, love, and hope in the midst of chaos. This outstanding cloud of witnesses includes Mukwege, who devoted himself to bring healing and hope for women who were raped by the rebels in the heart of violence in the DRC; the forty young martyrs of the fraternity in Burundi who died holding hands as they refused to be seen as Hutu and Tutsi but as children of God; Barankitse, a Burundian humanitarian who created Maison Shalom out of the carnage of the Burundian genocide; Fr. Kinvi of the Central African Republic who accepted risking his life as he cared for Muslims; and Bishop Taban who provided Christian leadership in the midst of the chaotic Sudan immersed in civil war. African Christianity can present even more, such as Angelina Atyam of Uganda who forgave the militia who abducted her daughter and preached to her

27. Faith & Leadership, "Paride Taban," §1.

28. See, for example, the case study of the Baptist Church of Congo (Kighoma, *Church and Mission*, 157).

countrymen to reconcile with the enemies,[29] and Professor Bungishabaku Katho who, during war, launched Université Shalom de Bunia in eastern Congo to promote peace, work, and a culture of excellence.[30] Katongole has rightly underlined that despite hardship, violence, war, and political instability, hope remains alive in Africa.[31]

Bibliography

Aurora. "Bernard Kinvi: 'La vie humaine est sacrée.'" Aurora, n.d. https://auroraprize.com/fr/faith-quells-retributive-justice.
Braeckman, Colette. *L'homme qui répare les femmes: Violences sexuelles au Congo, le combat du Docteur Mukwege*. Brussels: Versailles, 2012.
Bukuru, Zacharie. *Les quarante jeunes martyrs de Buta (Burundi 1997): Frères à la vie, à la mort*. Paris: Karthala, 2004.
Carrel, Serge. "Le Dr Denis Mukwege, Nobel de la paix 2018, évoque son engagement à la suite de Jésus-Christ." *Lafree*, Oct. 5, 2018. https://lafree.ch/info/monde/le-dr-denis-mukwege-evoque-son-engagement-a-la-suite-de-jesus-christ.
Casper, Jayson. "Terrorist Attack on Congolese Church Prompts Plea for Christian Advocacy." *Christianity Today*, Jan. 18, 2023. https://www.christianitytoday.com/news/2023/january/congo-church-attack-kasindi-kivu-drc-terrorism-adf.html.
Choquette, Robert. "Rwanda." In *The Cambridge Dictionary of Christianity*, edited by Daniel Patte, 1116–17. Cambridge: Cambridge University Press, 2010.
Faith & Leadership. "Maggy Barankitse: Builder of Hope." Faith & Leadership, n.d. https://faithandleadership.com/maggy-barankitse-builder-hope.
Faith & Leadership. "Paride Taban: Voice of the Voiceless." Faith & Leadership, Jan. 18, 2010. https://faithandleadership.com/maggy-barankitse-builder-hope.
Forman, Charles W. *Christianity in the Non-Western World*. New York, Libraries, 1970.
Harper, Michael. "New Dawn in East Africa: The East African Revival." *Christianity Today*, 1986. https://www.christianitytoday.com/history/issues/issue-9/new-dawn-in-east-africa-east-african-revival.html.
Hochschild, Adam. *King Leopold's Ghost: A Story of Greed, Terror, and Heroism in Colonial Africa*. New York: Houghton Mifflin, 1998.
Horizon, Sean. *Congo: Democratic Republic, Republic*. Exeter, CT: Bradt Travel Guide, 2008.
International Crisis Group. "DR Congo: Ending the Cycle of Violence in Ituri." International Crisis Group, July 15, 2020. https://www.crisisgroup.org/africa/central-africa/democratic-republic-congo/292-republique-democratique-du-congo-en-finir-avec-la-violence-cyclique-en-ituri.
Katongole, Emmanuel. *Born from Lament: The Theology and Politics of Hope in Africa*. Grand Rapids: Eerdmans, 2017.
———. *Who Are My People? Love, Violence, and Christianity in Sub-Saharan Africa*. Notre Dame, IN: University of Notre Dame Press, 2022.

---

29. Williamson, "As We Forgive," §1.
30. Mulatu, *Transitioning*, 153.
31. Katongole, *Born from Lament*, 264.

Kighoma, Eraston. *Church and Mission in the Context of War: A Descriptive Missiological Study of the Response of the Baptist Church in Central Africa to the War in Eastern Congo between 1990 and 2011*. Carlisle, UK: Langham, 2021.

Kinvi, Bernard, and Tigrane Yegavian. *Mission*. Paris: Cerf, 2019.

Lanotte, Olivier. "Chronology of the Democratic Republic of Congo/Zaire (1960–1997)." *SciencesPo*, Apr. 6, 2010. https://www.sciencespo.fr/mass-violence-war-massacre-resistance/en/document/chronology-democratic-republic-congozaire-1960-1997.html.

Mukwege, Denis. *Plaidoyer pour la vie*. Paris: Archipel, 2016.

Mulatu, Semeon. *Transitioning from a Theological College to a Christian University: A Multi-Case Study in East African Context*. Carlisle, UK: Langham, 2017.

Munro, André. "Non-Aligned Movement: International Organization." In *Encyclopedia Britannica*, July 19, 2013; updated June 20, 2023. https://www.britannica.com/topic/Non-Aligned-Movement.

Persky, Anna Stolley. "The Capital of Rape: Fighting Widespread Sexual Violence in the Democratic Republic of the Congo." *ABA Journal* 98 (2012) 59–60.

Singh, Surander. "Nam in the Contemporary World Order: An Analysis." *Indian Journal of Political Science* 70 (2009) 1213–26. http://www.jstor.org/stable/42744031.

Stearns, Jason K. *Dancing in the Glory of Monsters: The Collapse of the Congo and the Great War of Africa*. New York: Public Affairs, 2011.

Tompté-Tom, Enoch. *Les nouvelles formes de spiritualité dans l'espace centrafricain*. Paris: Harmattan, 2020.

Van Reybrouck, David. *Congo. Une histoire*. Translated by Isabelle Rosselin. Paris: Actes Sud, 2012.

Vogel, Christoph, et al. *La cartographie des groupes armées dans l'Est du Congo: Opportunités manquées, insécurité prolongée et prophéties auto-réalisatrices*. New York: Center on International Cooperation, 2021. https://kivusecurity.nyc3.digitaloceanspaces.com/reports/39/2021%20KST%20rapport%20FR.pdf.

Williamson, Sherry. "As We Forgive." *Faith & Leadership*, Mar. 1, 2010. https://faithandleadership.com/we-forgive.

13

Christianity and International Connections

Ecumenism, Development, and Advocacy Organizations

KUDZAI BIRI

THE INTERSECTIONALITY OF AFRICAN Christianity, international connections, development, ecumenism, and advocacy is characterized by dramatic events, different denominations, characters, and radical creative ideas. These aspects and characterizations weave into the story of African Christianity, a story that is not monolithic but diverse and defined by local cultural settings and shaped by various traditions. The forms of Christianity in Africa influence the variations. In addition, their specific traditions and the levels of indigenization dictate their expressions. The WCC has categorized the presence of Christianity on the continent as mainline, Protestant, Orthodox, Roman Catholic, AICs, and Pentecostal-charismatic.[1] The fact that Christianity has gone through indigenization and become part of African identity for centuries has opened a window of debate among African scholars and practitioners on its long-perceived status as a "foreign" religion. There is increasing awareness and contestation on labeling it a foreign religion, alongside Islam. However, that debate is outside the purview of this chapter, and what is significant is that African Christianity is unique and distinct, and its forms of expressions, transnational connections, ecumenical orientation, and advocacy have placed Africa in a spotlight on the global religious landscape. The establishment of mission churches by Western missionaries laid the foundation for AICs and newer Pentecostal-charismatic movements, with international connections varying from being headquartered in and administered from the West to establishment of headquarters on African soil and reverse evangelization beyond African borders.

I come from a family who respect traditions, a family who are members of the Anglican Church. Later, I was "born again" and I became a member

1. World Council of Churches, "Conference," 15.

of a leading transnational Pentecostal denomination. Hence, I write from the advantaged position of being firmly in touch with the realities of my country and continent, the power of culture, and the Christian religion in the livelihoods of many African people. I participated in the AACC and experienced the ecumenical quest as a member of the Evangelical Fellowship of Zimbabwe (EFZ), with an intimate knowledge of the cultural context, the complex forms of Christianity that include expansionist, arrogant ideologies; colonialism; globalization; schizophrenia; and continued invention of theologies. I draw my data mostly from the experiences of participation and belonging. To reach the conclusion, I present insights and examples from different geographical areas on the dynamics of Christianity, engagements, transnational orientation, and other entanglements. My argument on the pitfalls of African Christianity ends with prescriptions so that the vibrancy of African Christianity may usher people into abundant life (John 10:10). The section below examines mission churches as the first crop of established churches, and the AICs that emerged in response to the establishment of mission churches by Western missionaries.

Mission Churches and AICs

I do not intend to document the chronological historical perspectives of mission churches and AICs in Africa, for it is outside the purview of my focus. However, on historical perspectives, see the handbook edited by Bongmba.[2] Wuthnow and Offutt explain that "although religion exists in local communities and is distinctively influenced by a national cultural political context, it has connections with the wider world and is influenced by these relations."[3] The establishment of mission churches such as the Catholic, Methodist, and Salvation Army, among others on African soil, was also due to the contributions of locals. Local agency was crucial in establishment and expansion. Postcolonial Africa, in the increase of African-trained clergy, continues to witness expansion of these mission churches. What is significant is the African clergy being sent on mission all over the world, an avenue that has opened not only cultural exchange through exporting the gospel but also has created Afrocentric Christian identities in diaspora. The clergy and workforce constitute the migrants' transnational economic, cultural, and social connections, facilitated by emigration from the continent. While the label "migrant" is applied loosely to most foreigners in the West, some of them define themselves as missionaries on a mission of God.

2. See Bongmba, *Christianity in Africa*.
3. Wuthnow and Offutt, "Transnational Religious Connections," 209.

Hence, from their own perspectives, their call to evangelization rules out claims of being migrants. A new historical type of AICs constitutes significant expression of the dynamics of modern times, and shows how African leaders and congregants respond to the complex dynamics. The origin of AICs is located in the interface between world religions and indigenous systems of beliefs. Tapping from the wellspring of indigenous spiritualities remains important, as such spiritualities become instruments in the service of a process of enculturation. This section gives attention to mission churches and AICs because there are some differences in orientation and emphasis with the Pentecostal-charismatic churches discussed below, in terms of an approach to mission and ecumenical orientation.

Western missionaries established mainline churches during the colonial era. These churches, alongside mission schools and hospitals, were supervised from Western countries, from outside the continent. To date, mainline clergy have been part of the exodus team into diaspora. The Catholics and Anglican priests, for example, have sisters and other clergy recruited for training abroad, some funded in their studies outside the continent and assigned pastoral duties. Seeking to escape the vicissitudes of life created by political instability and poverty, the banner of evangelizing and pastorship provides an avenue of escape. Pastors jostle for postings abroad, which brings to the fore the question of divine calling and service. More important are social connections and status, which open avenues for recognition and "promotion"; and tribal and ethnic connections should not be completely ignored, for these indigenous blood ties, identities, *hukama*, totems, and ethnic ties remain very strong in postcolonial Africa. The AICs are more exclusivist in their theology, denouncing both mission churches and other new religious movements. In mission churches, this denunciation has political overtones because of the way missionaries worked hand in hand with colonialists. However, criticism of the new religious movements centers on theology and practice, as some go further to denounce the reading of the Bible, with claims of being led by the Holy Spirit.[4] While they have unquestioned numerical strength and international connections outside the borders, they are not militant in their approach to mission, in contrast to the new religious movements that have sprouted from both the missionary churches and AICs.

---

4. The theology of AICs is varied. For example, Johanne Masowe Chishanu on the continent refute the use of the Bible. They claim that Jesus promised the Holy Spirit; therefore, the Bible is condemned as archaic.

Transnational Pentecostal-Charismatic Movements and Diasporic Connections

A critical analysis below will do justice to the international connections, ecumenical thrust, and forms of advocacy that have revolutionized Christianity in Africa. The rationale for emphasizing the role of Pentecostal-charismatic Christianity is manifold: First, it has a militant approach to evangelization and seeks converts from other, older, established Christian denominations because of their puritanical stance. Second, it has transformed the face of Christianity on the African continent through a number of aspects such as liturgy and theology of salvation and praxis. Third, its sheer presence among diasporic communities is marked, and members endeavor to set up multiple satellite ministries and denominations in diaspora. This is evident in their names, which often carry the following: "International Ministries/Denominations/Church." Hence, in the light of the above, any study on African Christianity, especially with a focus on transnational connections, ecumenism, and advocacy, will not do justice if Pentecostal-charismatic Christianity has no space and attention. The vibrancy of the forms of Christianity has birthed different names and descriptions, such as African reformation,[5] African charismatic reformation,[6] African international Christian churches, and "a new form of reconstruction of Christian reality."[7] This vibrancy is accompanied by several variant themes that spark controversy, on the Bible, pan-Africanism, exegesis, plurality, nation-building, and struggles of clarifying values and practices within the African religious cultural milieu. An attempt to categorize the new religious movements in their diversities is not helpful, because they are dynamic and under constant process of change, and this complicates typologies.[8] It is important to note that regional diversity and varying historical dynamics apply to all Christian denominations in Africa. In addition to that, there is an undercurrent of a strong charismatic movement. In some cases, this undercurrent has contacts with the wider evangelical movement. Hence, Pentecostal-charismatic Christianity is complex, in spite of notable basic characteristics. Denominations and ministries vary; some are ecumenical, with a strong focus on institutional church unity, while others are evangelical and focus much on personal conversion and on the spiritual unity of all Christians, or they can be both.

---

5. Anderson, *African Reformation*.
6. Werbner, *Holy Hustlers*.
7. Ter Haar, "World Religions," 22.
8. Anderson, *African Reformation*, 94.

Their global influence is detectable in beliefs and practices and notable for international orientation.[9]

The story of African Christianity is not complete without AICs, which are many and varied, but this section focuses on the Pentecostal-charismatics who build on the achievements of older AICs, also known as Zionist, Apostolic, and other names. In order to measure the religious temperature of Africa, we need to take a look at new religious movements that have emerged and transformed and altered the face of Christianity at the local level and beyond the African borders. A contemporary trend in African Christianity is the rapid rise of neo-Pentecostalism, in testimony of vibrancy and revitalization.[10] An array of factors explains the sprouting in these churches' diversities that exude both missionary zeal and an ecumenical orientation. The fertile ground for their sprouting, growth, and establishment emanates from a plethora of factors that include the fatigue of missionary gospel and protest of missionary hospitals and colonization, all factors that play a big part in aiding their success story.

Matthew 28:19, "Go ye therefore," is at the heart of their agenda and is regarded as the first global command to evangelize. The new religious movements, from their fragile infancy, have a sense of mission to the world, and this evangelistic orientation defines their thrust. The international connections enhance a mutual flow of indigenized Christianity and in reverse ensure upward social mobility of those who are nodal power points in different Christian organizations. In new Pentecostal-charismatic movements, the transnational connections have positioned the "big men and women" in an uncontested status and an opportunity for commoditizing the gospel. These represent a shift from the traditional norm of Catholics and Protestant churches and the Salvation Army, which were established through Western missionaries and continue to have tutelage from the West. The new challenges and opportunities are complex, from contestation to growing awareness of belonging to cultivating a sense of ecumenism, which was very absent. Unity with other Christian denominations was often discouraged because of perceiving it as ungodly, partly because the new movements' concept of being "born again" disqualifies the traditional forms of Christianity that have normative theologies of salvation. However, a paradigm shift, probably necessitated by increasing globalization and the influx of other religions, especially from Asia, has cultivated a competitive spirit and created a sense of the need to unite as Christians. This is notable in the EFZ, where the theology has shifted to embrace other denominations

---

9. Ter Haar, "World Religions," 22.
10. Kroesbergen, *Neo-Pentecostalism*, 9.

and the confrontational tones have toned down, probably pushing us to consider Togarasei's observations that some theological emphases are moving towards secularization.[11] While circumventing the racial, ethnic, and cultural divisions and geographical boundaries and barriers, the frenzied, militaristic, puritanical approach loses fervor towards an all-embracing approach. In Nigeria, where there is stiff competition for clientele by Christians and Muslims, there is a tendency towards worldwide Christian unity and also an emphasis of the role of Africa in global Pentecostalism and Islamic transnationalism in Europe.[12]

One defining mark of African Christianity and its sense of mission is a convincing narrative of how it has moved beyond spirituality to become a key player in the world in welfare, education, economics, politics, and international relations. The phenomenal exodus from the continent enhances the capacity to maintain strong transnational connections. It provides modes of coping with rapid changes and spatial mobility. The dominant theology taps into political discourses, hinging on derogatory stereotyping of foreigners, especially of the West, and promoting the moral supremacy of Africa. Essentializing religion treats religion as the most important form of identity in the global space and poses the problem of religious hegemony and placing it on a pedestal, in particular when it is the most celebrated form of identity. Yet, globalization and its auxiliary forces militate against such an exclusivist approach of the gospel. While AICs recover cultural identity through religious power,[13] in Africa, the diasporic engagements can be seen as hegemonic, an attempt to reassert the denigrated African identities.

The diasporic communities have raised resources for churches at home. For, example, those Africans in diaspora have formed social groups that raise funds for building hospitals and schools, drilling boreholes, and many other needs of those at home. That is why the church in Africa remains responsible and accountable to developments on the continent. The capacity to maintain transnational ties is a result of the phenomenal exodus from the continent. The importance of the diasporic transnational connections is the ecumenical thrust. For example, the researcher observed African diasporic communities in Frankfurt and Bamberg, Germany, as conduits of fostering relationships of African communities from different geographical spaces and reinventing one of the most cherished African communal orientations through tribal lines; linguistic, totemic praise names; and geographical origin, which sometimes blur the division between migrant workers and

---

11. Togarasei, "Modern/Charismatic Pentecostalism."
12. Ter Haar, *Half-Way to Paradise*.
13. Kalu, *African Pentecostalism*, 2.

refugees. Communities from Nigeria and Ghana financed projects at home, and in the United Kingdom are communities from Zimbabwe. It is important to note that some diasporic communities have also funded opposition political parties through raising resources, as they disdain the ruling regimes at home. They understand their role as mission and not immigration, because the international connections fulfil God's mandate of evangelizing the world and showing acts of love, hence bringing the livelihoods of fellow Christians and those in abject poverty into association.

The exportation of the gospel from the continent requires a glimpse of the significance of borders, for they infringe on perspectives and attitudes of the diasporic communities and frame the images and construction of both Africans and African Christianity. Borders represent many things: boundaries, barriers, separation, insecurity, isolation, fear, anxiety, and places of challenge and conflict in a foreign land. However, part of a worldwide trend of religious transnationalism is to not be limited and defined by national boundaries. The significance of the transnational communities hinges on tearing down borders and establishing bridges. Ter Haar brings useful insights, challenging the traditional normative nomenclature based on category and growing irrelevance of the distinction between "world religions" and "traditional religions" because of how aspects of the indigenous religions are incorporated into Christianity and exported through evangelization.[14]

However, ecumenism remains one of the issues that the WCC grapples with. In 2018, in Arusha, Tanzania, I noted as a participant one of the hindrances towards unity of Christians, perceived as unwillingness by some denominations because of religious reasons that mostly hinge on doctrinal differences. Where they unite, some common aspects emerge, for example, denunciation of sexual minorities; uncritical prayers that bolster and authenticate corrupt regimes; and uncritical reading and deployment of biblical verses in politics and on gender issues. Theologies on gender and politics are found wanting.

It would be prudent to claim that Christians in Africa in generic terms have advanced a weak political theology, such that reconstruction is key and needful to reverse the woes on the continent. The theologies are not empowering, liberative, and life empowering. While notably the Catholic bishops have generally been forthcoming in defending and upholding a Christian ethos, such as in Zimbabwe, Malawi, and South Africa, the majority seem to collaborate with oppressive politicians because of being beneficiaries of state resources parceled out through the patronage system. Gifford has noted the

---

14. Ter Haar, "World Religions," 7.

high levels of corruption in East Africa,[15] and tribalism takes center stage as a tool for exclusion and marginalization. While the politicians engineer this, religious leaders are not empowered to confront it because some are beneficiaries, co-opted in the system. The mercenary political ethos is also a mercenary religious ethos whereby religious power has become an ethos of accumulation. I noted in gatherings that whenever a paper on these forms of Christianity came up, dialogue and intense debate followed, and criticisms ranged in all spheres of social, political, and economic aspects. However, new forms of Christian expression have remained a decided theological and social factor with which to reckon. They are religions of transformation, and their efforts to re-religionize are seen as a sign of the global breakdown of modernity. African Christian churches have given Africans a sense of belonging and moral strength in European contexts that can be hostile and exclusionary supporting drives to evangelize what are cast as decadent, old, imperial centers and to rejuvenate dwindling congregants.[16]

The ambivalence and excess meaning of the sacred creates the need to interpret the demonic not only in terms of individual moral failures, but also as part of the global struggle between evil and good. This provides the ground for the violent assertion of identity through images of spiritual warfare that extend outwards from the individual to the entire globe—at the heart of salvation, an ongoing, permanent engagement with the demonic.[17]

The perceived undemocratic nature of Pentecostal-charismatic churches could probably explain the sharp inequalities that are inherent in the Christian movement. In the Nigerian context, Marshall describes the violent encounters between Islam and Pentecostalism while intolerance on the continent is expressed in violent denunciation of homosexuality and ethnic chauvinism. In most cases, such as in the Ugandan and Zimbabwean contexts, where Robert Mugabe and Taguta Museveni patronized churches, religious and political discourses mutually support the exclusion and marginalization of the minorities and extend to race and ethnicity, where both discourses insinuate exclusion in subtle ways. This exclusion is enshrined in the discourses of empowerment of the black race and indigenization of the economy. Mobility and religion not only connect through social dynamics in global host lands, but diasporic communities are affecting religious messages and beliefs in the homeland as well.[18] Their attention to social, political, and economic consequences represents a shift influenced by global encounters

15. Gifford, *Ghana's New Christianity*.
16. Biri, "Migration, Transnationalism."
17. Marshall-Fratani, "Mediating the Global," 279.
18. McGregor and Primorac, *Zimbabwe's New Diaspora*.

and competition and includes borrowing from the West and other countries, in particular China, because of her heavy infiltration and presence on the African continent. The flow of people, money, and social remittances within these spaces is so dense, thick, and widespread that nonimmigrants' lives are transformed even though they do not move.[19]

The construction of immigration as temporary sojourn and an opportunity to invest in the homeland has created a picture of the West as a symbol of wealth and upward social movement. Thus, many Christians see exit as God's grace and favor to escape the challenges on the African continent. Significantly, the quest to escape the challenges and at the same time the negative picture of the West based on moral grounds presents a contradiction in theology. It unravels the challenge and failure by both the religious and political elites to redeem the resources of the wealthy African continent. This raises the question on the relevance of Christian liberation and empowerment theologies. There is domination of the economies by the Asians, especially the Chinese, who fill the gap to replace the mass exodus and brain drain through economic deals with politicians to loot resources. In spite of the setback, the formation of diasporic communities across the globe has raised the international profile of African Christianity, not only in religious circles but also in academia, and has given it economic and social stamina amid crises. Nevertheless, the vibrancy and emergence of new churches increase competition for clientele, which at times jeopardizes unity in the body of Christ and subsequently the ecumenical quest.

Nigeria and Ghana in particular appear in the array of evil forces as places of powerful occultism. Most West African countries are perceived as having strong indigenous spiritualities and powerful occultism, confirmed by mass exodus to its cities and villages, from all over the continent, for consultation with indigenous sacred practitioners. The churches have not been spared from the suspicion that practices are sourced from indigenous, powerful, occult forces. This suspicion and division mar ecumenical orientation of Christianity on the African continent.

Since Africa is a massively Christian continent, one questions why there are ever sprouting new churches. The dramatic expansion, the sheer presence of African communities, and the reaching out to European natives have been described by Anderson as an "African Reformation of Christianity,"[20] a response of coming to grips with the wider national and international processes and contexts of global capitalism and state formation.[21]

19. Levitt and Jaworsky, "Transnationalism Migration Studies," 138.
20. Anderson, *African Reformation*, 5.
21. Van Dijk, "From Camp to Encompassment," 140.

The claims of commoditizing the gospel have been confirmed, as the gospel has emerged as one of the "businesses" to make money and increase social status by the religious elites. In addition, it negates the extreme idealization of the continent over and above other continents—Africa as a morally superior continent. The theology of deliverance complements the gospel/theology of prosperity, and both seem intelligible in most contexts of poverty, deprivation, and gross inequalities, emanating also from within the church. This theology has also raised the profile of Mugambi on the theology of liberation and reconstruction in Africa.[22]

Pilgrimages represent a key component of transnational religious life, upholding Christian centers and maintaining Christian boundaries.[23] The attempt to re-evangelize Europe has received different designations, which include reverse proselytization and reverse flow,[24] to go back to the drawing board of preaching the puritanical gospel neglected by Europe. This attempt represents cultural hegemony in reverse, whether consciously or not. This cultural hegemony is equivalent to dominance. However, a survey that I carried out shows that most of the African diasporic communities are mostly evangelizing people from their specific homelands. Thus, the thesis of converting and preaching gospel to the whites becomes questionable.

In most mainline churches, the African pastors carry out duties alongside their counterparts in the host country. With strong historical connections with headquarters in the West, they often pastor with Western church leaders. The new Pentecostal-charismatic movements are different. While most of them have mentors in North America and other parts of the world, they have asserted their independence from Western control and tutelage, including the control and management of resources. Most of the churches have members from the countries of origin or other African communities or membership. They have played an important role in challenging missionary theologies and denominational structures and revitalizing the vibrancy of the early church through militant evangelism and an unrestrained effort to transcend the African borders. The use of modern technologies for communication and networking, and appropriating electronic media and new media outlets for worldwide broadcasting and disseminating their teachings, has enhanced publicity and connection with the outside world. Modern technology is a platform to advance advocacy, and such innovation in domesticating Christianity is a source of vitality

---

22. Mugambi, *From Liberation to Reconstruction*.

23. Wuthnow and Offutt, "Transnational Religious Connections," 223.

24. See for example, Kalu, *African Pentecostalism*, 270; Adogame, *African Christian Diaspora*; and Hunt, "Neither Here nor There," 165.

for the church in Africa. Hackett sees it as a "tool of expansion, a reflection of globalising aspirations but is also part of an attempt to transform and Christianise popular culture so that it is safe for consumption by born again Christians."[25] Religion is bipolar, addressing the physical and transcendental realities that are at times not synonymous with facts. Pentecostal-charismatic Christians on the continent have sourced from the traditional paradigm, in emphasizing transcendental realities more than any form of Christianity in Africa. This partly explains its attraction of large clientele, establishment of powerful transnational connections, and penetration of the political space, on the forefront of activism and advocacy.

Advocacy, Development, and Social Activism

Churches have become big partners with government in entrepreneurship programs. The new religious movements' establishment of hospitals, schools, and universities, to complement old mission schools and hospitals, has become the hallmark of African Christianity. Some denominations have been proactive in dealing with and responding to natural disasters. This is notable in East Africa, where drought and hunger affected some communities. In southern Africa, Cyclone Idai in Zimbabwe and Mozambique and persistent natural disasters in Mozambique have seen not only Christian denominations coming on the stage to help, but also other religions like Islam.

However, the major criticism emanates from the perceived weak political theology that avoids confrontation with corrupt dictatorial regimes. Often churches have become silent on human rights abuses, translating to complicit. Jean-François Bayart aptly describes the politics of the belly that drives political leaders through chicanery, patronization, and promotion of tribalism for political gain and deployment of political rhetoric that demonizes the West by holding on to the evils of the colonial era.[26] In the same vein, religious leaders have also denounced the West as the worst example of moral degradation and championed the moral supremacy of the African continent. The issue of rights come to the fore as religious organizations unite to denounce, for example, LGBTQ rights, women's rights, and minority rights. The significance of this lies in the uniqueness of African communal orientation where politics is at the center of socioeconomic life. The cycle of poverty and deprivation can thus be explained by poor political governance and the failure of the churches to be critical of unjust leadership styles that deprive, oppress, and exploit the masses. In addition,

25. Hackett, "Charismatic/Pentecostal Appropriation," 260.
26. Bayart, *State in Africa*.

this failure has raised questions and the need to probe the nexus between religiosity and poverty. The fervency of Christianity on the continent, the increasing inequalities and disparities, have become a cause of concern. They require serious attention in scholarship in order to weave in details that explain the significance of African versions of Christianity within the settings of poverty and deprivation.

In addition, there is a failure to embark on empowering, life-giving, and liberative theologies that are redemptive to the masses trapped in poverty. In fact, it would not be an overexaggeration to claim that some forms of Christianity are modeled on capitalist lines and promote the worst forms of capitalism, through exploiting the congregants. The irony of the gospel of prosperity is that, on the one hand, it has enabled churches without Western tutelage to embark on developmental projects and entrepreneurship, so that they have become leading partners with the governments in establishing educational and health facilities in their respective countries. Although they fund missions outside the continent, they also provide leaders an opportunity to "reap" from innocent believers, to accumulate massive wealth, and to live obscenely luxurious lives. Online connections are key for the success of international connections and partnership, maintaining the relationships and connections.

While Pentecostal-charismatic Christianity champions online media outlets for the consumption of their clientele, the mainline churches, such as the Methodist, United Methodist, Anglican, and some AICs, have also mastered the game. Advertising denominations, advocating for specific moral obligations and ethical expectations, and collaborating with some civic organizations, their role has influenced and affected the socioeconomic and political attitudes and practices within their countries. The churches as healing communities advocate peace within volatile political situations and give people hope, thus journeying with the distraught in a continent of varied challenges. The spirit fostered by churches keeps the hopes of many people alive and gives them the strength to face life's hardships, in the midst of crushing poverty and deprivation and other vicissitudes.

In 2013, the EFZ in Zimbabwe were active during the run-up to the new constitution. Their advocacy centered on mobilizing the nation to resist ethical issues such as same-sex partnerships, polygamy, and abortion, considered as evil. They advocate the breakdown of ethnic identity, commitment to national welfare, and a concern for the black race and Mother Africa. Thus, they exhibit both racial and political awareness, which at times can be termed racism in reverse as extreme theologies demonize the other races. However, they appear selective on rights because abuse of rights is also in the church, for example, children's rights, in particular girls and women. In extreme cases, they have advocated certain political leaders through deployment of selected biblical Scriptures that are misinterpreted and wrongly deployed in political discourses.

The transnational religious movements shows how Christianity has moved beyond spirituality to become a key player in the affairs of the world, in areas like economic, politics, education, and international relations. However, this does not sit well with critical minds who see advocacy, and international connections, and transnational orientations as embodying a negative hegemonic element—the essentializing of religion, treating religious identity as the most important form of identity. The creation of binaries runs against ecumenical effort, especially where lines are drawn and exclusivist, marginalizing approaches dominate.

Women and Evangelization

The story of Christianity in Africa is not complete without factoring in the agency of women and their role in propping up and expanding the gospel, both within and without African borders. The role, status, and experience of women in Africa represents a fundamental missiological issue. Their power and agency have often been overlooked; nevertheless, the churches tap their resources. It is prudent to acknowledge that women have broken barriers and enacted their personal and collective agency to engage social, cultural, organizational, and spiritual power in their communities and contexts. Some women have initiated ministries and organizations breaking and circumventing traditional gender barriers. In addition, women who flex their spiritual stamina to evangelize and draw congregants demonstrate leadership capabilities. The appeal of women as mothers, sisters, and custodians of culture means that women are in a position to carry out mission from family to societies. Hence, it seems fair to claim that the expansion of the gospel on African soil, in both colonial and postcolonial Africa, is largely the work of women.

The AACC

The AACC has focussed much on problems that torment the continent. The issues of political instability, poverty, abuse of human rights in churches and politics, and other forms of waywardness in some denominations are ignored in most AACC meetings but are important in demonstrating a united effort to deal with challenges on the continent. Churches are encouraged to participate during events like the World Day of Prayer, born in 1927, to foster worldwide unity of Christians and their institutions. The issue of terrorism gave birth to the Program for Christian Muslim Relations because of the menace of terrorism in North and West Africa. The quest to bring dialogue between Christians and Muslims is part of the AACC's emphasis on evangelizing and promoting peace for the purpose of peaceful coexistence. Religious and political leaders are identified key players in changing the socioeconomic and political life of the continent through dialogue and cooperation on key political and economic issues. Thus, advocacy of Christian denominations on the continent has varied dimensions at both local and international levels.

Challenges, Dilemmas, and Future Prospects

Mugambi calls Africa a continent of "hot peace."[27] The rosy narratives of success are not without their own challenges and dilemmas. While prophetic frenzy and evangelism are notable and commendable, probing an emancipatory role remains key, including whether such expressions promote servitude and, in some instances, compromise the biblical truths of the gospel.

Apart from the capitalization of the gospel in Africa, a number of challenges have also emerged. Preaching salvation from a continent plagued with widespread tragedy has setbacks. The abuse of power and resources attributed to men and women of the collar runs similar to the abuse of power by the political elite who see transnational connections as avenues for looting resources and investing for their families. This has blurred the division between God's blessings and greed, especially amid abject poverty and deprivation, where the masses languish in poverty. Most religious leaders do not expose and confront corruption and injustices. The nexus between Christianity and poverty requires attention, because ecumenism and advocacy are not intelligible within the matrix of inequalities and abuse of human rights, identified in both the church and public spaces, especially in politics.

The major setback that African evangelism faces is how to promote unity among world Christian churches, for closer relations, when there is no set example at home. Werbner notes the moral crisis that divides the church between the young and the elders in Botswana,[28] and this observation applies to most quarters of the continent.

---

27. See subtitle of Mugambi, *From Reconstruction to Reaffirmation: African Christian Theology in an Era of Hot Peace.*

28. Werbner, *Holy Hustlers.*

This division goes beyond the generational gap to embrace other elements that the church grapples with. I call most African nations "bruised and troubled nations" because they need forgiveness, healing, and reconciliation. The Rwandan genocide, 1985 Gukurahundi (ethnic cleansing) in Zimbabwe, apartheid in South Africa, and ethnic clashes in Kenya all have dimensions of ethnic rivalry and divisions that have spilled into the church.

Terrorism in mainly West, East, and North Africa is another monster that has faced Christians: the destruction of church buildings, abduction of boys and men for recruitment into the army, and abduction of girls and women.

The variety of Christianity, denominational ethos, orientation, and structure all determine the quest for ecumenism. The WCC has pointed out their struggle to foster and convince churches to join, for some see the WCC as an unequal union.

Mission is a challenge because leaders have not diversified theological education.[29]

History shows a failure to construct a redemptive, empowering theology, a Christian identity and practice that could have alleviated pauperization; and this failure is indissolubly linked to the postcolonial state to redeem the promises of democracy and development while at the same allowing a few to enjoy the facets of modernity to an obscene state.

I would not want these failures to overshadow the achievements and contributions of African Christianity on a global scale. African Christianity has indeed influenced the continent and the world in different ways such that it has forced stakeholders to rethink the reconstruction of theologies and new methodologies and proffer ways for future engagement with Africa in relation to multidisciplinary issues and approaches. Hence, Africa remains the richest continent in terms of wealth and religious commitment and orientation, and has potential such that it would not be an overexaggeration to say that the future of the world lies in Africa and that Africa will probably become the hotbed of Christian revivalism.

Recommendations and Conclusion

Religiosity and the sheer magnitude of violence, destruction, and suffering demand rethinking of African Christianity, theology, and priorities. Churches should have the priority of promoting abundant life (John 10:10). Leaders should resist the temptation to be co-opted by regimes and have the nerve to counter destructive narratives. African Christianity must set

29. All Africa Conference of Churches, *The Church in Africa*, 7.

priorities right, address the situations that deny full life, and liberate the Africans. This is achievable upon questioning the structures, beliefs, and attitudes of inequality to promote justice and peace for sustainable living. In diaspora, African rhythms, music, and art pervade the environments where communities have reached out or established themselves. There are both threats and promises, and it is only when they participate in the pilgrimage of peace and justice that African Christianity will touch lives in a more meaningful way.

Bibliography

Adogame, Afe. *The African Christian Diaspora: New Currents and Emerging Trends in World Christianity*. London: Bloomsbury Academic, 2013.
All Africa Conference of Churches. *The Church in Africa: Opportunities, Challenges and Responsibilities*. Geneva: WCC, 2012.
Anderson, Allan H. *African Reformation: African Initiated Churches in the 20th Century*. Asmara, Eritrea: Africa World, 2001.
Bayart, Jean-Francois. *The State in Africa: Politics of the Belly*. London: Polity, 1997.
Biri, Kudzai. "Migration, Transnationalism and the Shaping of Zimbabwean Pentecostal Christianity." *African Diaspora* 7 (2014) 139–64.
Bongmba, Elias Kiffon, ed. *Routledge Companion to Christianity in Africa*. Routledge Religion Companions. New York: Routledge, 2016.
Gifford, Paul. *Ghana's New Christianity: Pentecostalism in a Globalising African Economy*. London: Hurst, 2004.
Hackett, Rosalind I. J. "Charismatic/Pentecostal Appropriation of Media Technologies in Nigeria and Ghana." *Journal of Religion in Africa* 28 (1998) 258–77.
Hunt, Stephen. "Neither Here nor There: The Construction of Identities and Boundary Maintenance of West African Pentecostals." *Sociology* 36 (2002) 147–69.
Kalu, Obgu. *African Pentecostalism: An Introduction*. Oxford: Oxford University Press, 2008.
Kanyoro, Musimbi R. A., and Nyambura J. Njoroge, eds. *Groaning in Faith; African Women in the Household of God*. Nairobi: Acton, 2006.
Kroesbergen, Hermen, ed. *Neo-Pentecostalism in Southern Africa*. Wellington, New Zealand: CFL, 2017.
Levitt, Peggy, and Nadya Jaworsky. "Transnationalism Migration Studies: Past Developments and Future Trends." *Annual Review of Sociology* 33 (2007) 129–56.
Marshall-Fratani, Ruth. "Mediating the Global and Local in Nigerian Pentecostalism." *Journal of Religion in Africa* 28 (1998) 278–315. https://www.jstor.org/stable/1581572.
McGregor, JoAnn, and Ranka Primorac. *Zimbabwe's New Diaspora: Displacements and Cultural Politics of Survival*. New York: Berghahn, 2010.
Mugambi, Jesse N. K. *From Liberation to Reconstruction: African Christian Theology after the Cold War*. Nairobi: East African, 1995.
———. *From Reconstruction to Reaffirmation: African Christian Theology in an Era of Hot Peace*. Routledge Handbook of African Theology. Routledge Handbooks, 2020. https://www.routledgehandbooks.com/doi/10.4324/9781315107561-13.

Ter Haar, Gerrie. *Half-Way to Paradise: African Christians in Europe*. Cardiff: Cardiff University Press, 1998.

———. "World Religions and Community Religions: Where Does Africa Fit In?" Occasional Paper, Centre of African Studies, University of Copenhagen, 2000.

Togarasei, Lovemore. "Modern/Charismatic Pentecostalism as a Form of 'Religious' Secularisation in Africa." *Studia Historiae Ecclesiasticae* 41 (2015) 56–66.

Van Dijk, Rijk A. "From Camp to Encompassment: Discourses of Transsubjectivity in the Ghanaian Pentecostal Diaspora." *Journal of Religion in Africa* 27 (1997) 135–59. https://www.jstor.org/stable/1581683.

Werbner, Richard. *Holy Hustlers, Schism, and Prophecy: Apostolic Reformation in Botswana*. Anthropology of Christianity. Berkeley: University of California Press, 2011.

World Council of Churches. "Conference on World Mission and Evangelism, 8–13 March 2018, Arusha, Tanzania." Oikoumene, 2018. https://www.oikoumene.org/sites/default/files/File/Handbook_AppendixG_warshas_WEB.pdf.

Wuthnow, Robert, and Stephen Offutt. "Transnational Religious Connections." *Sociology of Religion* 69 (2008) 209–32.

14

Christianity Encounters the Gospel of Health and Wealth

A Ghanian Case Study

SAMPSON M. TIEKU

PENTECOSTALISM HAS SUCCEEDED IN accruing compliments for its unbeatable versatility and capacity to inhabit the contextual realities of the Global South. This strand of faith is a top-notch attraction for African Christians for reasons that have filled scholarly discourses in recent years. In countries like Ghana, charismatics are found to be the innovators of religious ideals centered on "the translation of salvation into practical everyday achievements in business, education, economics, and family life."[1] In general, what has come to be known as the prosperity gospel, fronted by these churches, has drawn intense backlash in academia as unbiblical and defaming the precepts of the true gospel. While the plethora of views against prosperity theology are admissible, are these doctrines merely heretic, or do they offer discernment into a critical need of the African church and its proclivity for a practically based religion? How do we respond to an ideology that is inexorably shaping the future of African Christianity? Thus, is there a need to rethink our scholarly approach to addressing the ills of this sweeping dogma in Ghana's Christianity?

This chapter argues that a careful analysis of the issues that have been the primary focus of the prosperity theology (health and wealth) in Ghana prompts a robust study that must examine the feasibility of "holistic mission"[2] as a framework for discipleship in local congregations. The chapter briefly surveys the issues of health and wealth in Ghana and

---

1. Asamoah-Gyadu, *African Charismatics*, 231.

2. Woolnough argues, "The good news Christians are to take to the world is indeed a holistic mission, catering for all the needs of the world: spiritual, the emotional, the psychological and the physical" ("Good News for Poor," 5).

proposes a study that ascertains a practical vision for a holistic mission in African Pentecostalism.

Heaven on Earth

In his 2022 lecture commemorating the Theta Phi Series at Asbury Theological Seminary, N. T. Wright tackled an intriguing topic, "The Coming of God and the New Creation," which argues that Christian hope is not as most people envision—going to heaven; instead, it is participation in the resurrection life in God's new creation. Wright asserted that "the point of Christianity is not that we should go to heaven, but that heaven should come to earth—an understanding which is premised on the biblical construal of 'thy kingdom come.' The great story that the Bible tells us from Genesis to Revelation is about God's intention and promise to come and live with us. We are not to look away from the earth to heaven, we must rather recognize that the earth is already the place where the Creator reveals his glory and love and wants to do so more."[3]

Indeed, Vinson Synan has shown how the growth of the Pentecostal faith in the last century has been marked by significant shifts in emphasis regarding its message. In contrast to Wright's viewpoint, Synan has shown how the "fivefold gospel,"[4] which became the first theological manifesto of world Pentecostalism, culminated in the "imminent return of Christ,"[5] an emphasis that was deeply ingrained in a heaven-oriented pursuit of Christianity. Primarily, Pentecostals were attuned to otherworldly pursuits, as heaven became the principal goal for being a Christian, and thus all other concerns of life were nonessential.

On the flip side, in their studies on Pentecostalism and social engagements across the globe, Donald E. Miller and Tetsuna Yamamori discovered that Pentecostals started to show ardent interest in development projects at some point. For example, in places in the Global South, they are leading some of the most innovative development projects. They note

---

3. Wright, "Coming of God."

4. Synan unpacks the theologies that undergirded what he noted as the "Pentecost message" as it evolved through the different phases of the movement. He shows how Pentecostals at different times emphasized justification by faith, which is the "new birth"; entire sanctification—as an instant experience that gave the believer victory over sin and perfect love toward God and man; then the baptism of the Holy Spirit with tongues speaking as initial evidence; and the last two pieces were divine healing through Christ's atonement and the imminent coming of Christ. Everything taken together, Synan calls the "fivefold gospel" (Synan, *Century of Holy Spirit*, 456).

5. Synan, *Century of Holy Spirit*, 456.

that "this development points to a paradigm shift from the well-known otherworldly nature of Pentecostal movement and projects to a rather new movement whose growing social sensitivity has implications for national development."[6]

Aside from a proven interest in social engagement, the Pentecostal vigor and its concomitant prosperity theology in Ghana incite an inquiry into what might have prompted the paradigm shift from otherworldly matters to this-worldly affairs. Could it be a doctrinal awakening regarding Wright's viewpoint that "the earth is already the place where the Creator reveals his glory and love and wants to do so more"?[7] In her analysis of the motif of the American prosperity gospel, Kate Bowler points out that "Pentecostal believers accepted what the theologian Miroslav Volf dubbed the *materiality of salvation*, that the work of redemption begins here and now. Historically, Pentecostals have set themselves apart by their expectation that 'signs and wonders' accompanied evangelism as anticipation of God's reign. Authentic Christianity bore witness to itself not only by the truth of its teachings but also by the supernatural trail following in its wake."[8] Without a shadow of a doubt, Volf's materiality of salvation has found expression in African Pentecostalism much more than in many other places.

Despite the huge problems that have accompanied prosperity theology, and the self-aggrandizement displayed by its heralds, does an embodied vision of the new-creation reality upheld by Pentecostals urge us to rethink the phenomenon? Ron Sider expands the idea by arguing that "Jesus never said the kingdom was fully present. Rather, he taught that the messianic kingdom is already present, but is not yet complete."[9] What is the nexus between a practical view of salvation in African Christianity and the Christian vision of "thy kingdom come"? David Martin and Asamoah-Gyadu have shown that Pentecostals in Africa understand salvation in practical terms in connection with everyday life and existential needs. For instance, in charismatic churches in Ghana, "salvation is perceived as something to be experienced, so the key soteriological view, therefore, includes the realization of 'transformation and empowerment,' 'healing and deliverance,' and 'prosperity and success in the lives of believers.'"[10] John Wimber and Kevin Springer, in their *Power Evangelism*, have argued that the inbreaking of God's kingdom on earth means power and authority for the believer. Thus,

6. Miller and Yamamori, *Global Pentecostalism*, 2.
7. Wright, "Coming of God."
8. Bowler, *Blessed*, 78.
9. Sider, "What if We Defined," 19.
10. Asamoah-Gyadu, *African Charismatics*, 133.

the appropriation of such power in Christ reinforces the victory Christ has won over death, hell, and the grave. Therefore, "we preach the gospel of the King and His Kingdom and demonstrate God's presence through supernatural insights and power in other people's lives."[11]

In African Pentecostalism, one does not miss the vignette of Pentecostal functionaries embodying an attempt to cast out demons, heal the sick, and perform signs and wonders to prove the presence of the kingdom of God. Thus, one crucial motif of prosperity theology, especially in the African context, has been shown to be the explicit embodiment of a ministry targeted at ushering in God's rule as preachers assume a posture to enact signs and wonders in contemporary times just "as they were part of the daily life of the early believers and expected by the church."[12] At the Action Chapel International in Ghana, Asamoah-Gyadu observed how Pentecostals prayed and concluded that "Pentecostal prayer is participatory, experiential, and a pragmatic spiritual practice used to harness the power of the Holy Spirit to effect progress, success, mobility, and healing; thus, opening heavenly doors to provide solutions to earthly problems."[13] So, it is not uncommon to come across Pentecostal prayer meetings in which concrete objects and materials are employed as points of contact to transmit God's power for material effects—whether concerning jobs, childbirth, travel, family life, health, or financial situations. Likewise, David Bosch's view of salvation may be supportive of the African posture. He writes, "The integral character of salvation demands the scope of the church's mission to be more comprehensive than has traditionally been the case. Salvation is as coherent, broad, and deep as the needs and exigencies of human existence."[14]

One would wonder if African Pentecostals have been on the pathway to actualizing in part the ideals of resurrection life in God's new creation as a way of objectifying the kingdom of God in the earthly realm vis-à-vis the notion of "thy kingdom come." Indeed, the essentials of Pentecostal social engagements or its prosperity orientation are markers of this-worldly attainments in which faith ideas form the core of various rituals, practices, and values employed. Also, an African worldview that upholds whole-person transformation facilitates the Pentecostal posture towards salvation. John Mbiti explains, "Religion is found in all areas of human life. It has dominated the thinking of African people to such an extent that it has shaped their cultures, social lives, political organizations, and economic activities. We can say,

---

11. Wimber and Springer, *Power Evangelism*, 32.
12. Wimber and Springer, *Power Evangelism*, 200.
13. Dzokoto, "Sighs and Signs," 128.
14. Bosch, *Transforming Mission*, 410.

therefore, that Religion is closely bound up with the traditional way of life, while at the same time, this way of life has shaped Religion as well."[15]

Therefore, we can discern the future of African Christianity in its persistence in maintaining an all-inclusive view of life. That said, despite the many criticisms against prosperity theology, the phenomenon continues to snowball in Africa and grows ever more powerful and pervasive. According to Simon Coleman, "The tendency of indigenous religions to treat the material and the spiritual as inextricably linked and to expect the indigenous spirits to enter into contracts to deliver worldly goods creates very fertile ground for a prosperity gospel."[16] The case is the same in Ghana, and prosperity tendencies are no longer exclusive to Pentecostal churches. Historic mission churches and Catholics have joined in the chorus. It is common to behold mainline traditions holding revival meetings focused on healing, deliverance, and prosperity to restrain the exodus of their members to the Pentecostal arenas. The big question is "What does the popularity of prosperity theology tell us about the world in which we live? Before we condemn it, we should see it as a sign of the times. We must not get fixated on the sign, the idea as such. We must not think that combatting the idea solves everything. Rather, we must respond to what the sign points to—a world so unequaled and unjust that even the most undiluted forms of prosperity theology are widely popular. Perhaps we need to see it as the sigh of the oppressed, the heart of a heartless world."[17] Asamoah-Gyadu has argued that the widespread influence of prosperity theology, even in mainline traditions, divulges the condition of African Christianity and its pressing need. "In rethinking the prosperity gospel, it is worth acknowledging that in the Ghanaian context, Pentecostal churches have been able to articulate a message that addresses people's situations and circumstances in a relevant manner as they stress the idea that becoming a Christian is a transformational experience."[18]

At this juncture, N. T. Wright's view of the new-creation reality, the Pentecostal vision of "thy kingdom come," and the African practical view of salvation should thrust us into a deeper reflection on the prosperity theology in Africa not merely as a problem to be dismissed but more importantly as a corruption that needs redemption. Paul Foreston puts forward a radical but meaningful proposition: "So, we are proposing a radically

15. Mbiti, "Christianity and Traditional Religions," 432; quoted in Pachuau, *World Christianity*, 113.

16. Coleman, *Globalisation of Charismatic Christianity*, 20.

17. Freston, "Prosperity Theology," 95.

18. Asamoah-Gyadu, *African Charismatics*, 231.

different prosperity theology. The reward mechanism that we are familiar with (where we obtain great plenty because the Almighty is bound to us) goes hand in hand with great social benefits; self-interest is eliminated. This would avoid what is most scandalous in prosperity theology, the two-way relationship between the preacher and hearer is replaced by a triangular relationship in which the needy person is introduced. The preacher is no longer the interested party since he is no longer the recipient of the donation."[19] We may consider a paradigm shift from our methodical polemic of prosperity theology focused on self-conceited preachers to investigating the phenomenon to unearth a discipleship framework that targets the well-being of African Christians amid challenging contextual issues of life, including health and wealth. This chapter acknowledges that the grievous problems facing Ghanaian Christians in the areas of health and wealth are complex. "So much and yet it seems so little has been written about these important issues both by Africans and non-Africans because often the accounts overlook the complexity and the multilayered contexts of the African religio-cultural dimensions of both the problems and their relative solutions."[20] Thus, this discussion explores the complications in the areas of health and wealth in the Ghanaian context, which necessitates the redemption of the prosperity theology through a holistic framework for doing ministry in Pentecostal congregations. Indeed, the real outlook of this framework may become discernible after a robust study of Pentecostal churches in Ghana in this subject area.

Health and Well-Being in African Experience

The development and well-being of any nation are partly contingent on its healthcare systems, and thus a country that is slothful in this matter plunges its citizenry into danger. At a fundamental level, good health is crucial to the well-being of every human being alive—it is a necessity for survival. "A vast majority of people living in Africa have yet to benefit from advances in medical research and public health. The result is an immense burden of death and disease that is devastating for African societies."[21] In the wake of the Coronavirus pandemic in 2020, the popular concern in Africa was how African nations with some of the poorest healthcare systems and inadequate medical resources would stand the test of time if

19. Asamoah-Gyadu, *African Charismatics*, 96.

20. Esther Acolatse, in Ilo, *Wealth, Health, and Hope*, ix.

21. Sambo and World Health Organization Regional Office for Africa, *Health of the People*, 127.

the pandemic wreaked havoc in the same manner it did in countries in the West. Indeed, the ill health that afflicts most Africans is probably unlike many places in the world—whether it is malaria, tuberculosis, HIV/AIDS, or pregnancy-related conditions that take the lives of babies and mothers. In Ghana, the gravity of healthcare challenges depends on whether one lives in a city or rural community.

In their assessment of Ghana's healthcare capability during the recent pandemic, Dzando et al. found that not only is accessibility to healthcare in rural communities a challenge, but also primary healthcare systems, which are expected to offer affordable healthcare to Ghanaians, are not well equipped.[22] It is clear that the pandemic amplified the weaknesses of Ghana's healthcare system and thus showed that the nation, like many of its counterparts on the continent, would have been ravaged uncontrollably if the disease had hit as it did in the West. The researchers also discovered:

> Ghana currently has a total of 113 adult and 36 pediatric ICU beds, which are unevenly distributed throughout the country. Out of the 16 administrative regions of the country, 10 regions with a total population of about 10 million had no ICU beds when covid-19 emerged in Ghana. There are an inadequate number of competent workers, a lack of essential medicines and supplies, poor health financial structures, and its accompanying failure in the National Health Insurance Scheme (NHIS).[23]

Now, anyone who has experienced healthcare in the West would be dumbfounded to read these facts about the prevailing conditions in Ghana. While spelling out many shortfalls in Ghana's healthcare system, including its inability to meet international benchmarks, Paul Elihu, in his thesis "A Moral Assessment of Ghana's Healthcare Delivery System," argues that "compared with some countries in Africa, Ghana does not fare too badly in its overall health worker to patient ratio."[24] This only goes to show how grievous the situation is in some African contexts. Why is this information vital for this discourse? Here, we are confronted by an insidious contextual reality in which Ghanaian Christianity is thriving and growing in numbers. Asamoah-Gyadu does not mince words when he asserts that the massive growth of Pentecostalism in Ghana is partly because "Pentecostal churches have been able to articulate a message that addresses people's situations and

---

22. Dzando et al., "Healthcare in Ghana," 2.
23. Dzando et al., "Healthcare in Ghana," 2.
24. Elihu, "Justice, Human Dignity."

circumstances in a relevant manner as they stress the idea that becoming a Christian is a transformational experience."[25]

What this means is that, for many Ghanaians, Pentecostalism provides agency for navigating such deficiencies in health systems as they resort to divine intervention for healing. Of course, the abuses in Pentecostals' response to health issues have not gone without backlash. That some Pentecostal preachers engage in economic exchanges to administer divine healing is problematic. Cephas Omenyo shows how "the contemporary Ghanaian prophets use anointing oil profusely, but they have also introduced the use of lime juice, toilet soap, and handkerchief which they consecrate and sell to clients."[26] In some Pentecostal circles, the eccentric and unbiblical nature of the healing practices and rituals is conspicuous. This is because "there is a flux of sham pastors of Pentecostal churches who are involved in crimes of extortion, religious-impersonation, murder, drug, and human trafficking, and thus abusing the name of the church and the gifts of the Holy Spirit."[27]

On the flip side, David Banda's work based on the Zimbabwean context advances a piercing viewpoint that proposes a transition from mere disapproval of prosperity theology towards a pragmatic pursuit of an antidote to what is a big problem in African Christianity today. He argues:

> Armchair criticism of the prosperity gospel is neither sufficient nor necessary. The sub-Saharan average citizenry is under the siege of many tragedies and health failures, a situation that renders them vulnerable and desperate. Anything that appears to work stands for something concrete that our people desperately need. Therefore, if there is anything wrong with the prosperity gospel as a healing approach, then alternatives must be put in place. If they are not handling it well, then concerned minds should handle it well; otherwise, it is honorable to forever keep their peace.[28]

While Banda's viewpoint in response to arguments against the prosperity theology as it pertains to health is hard hitting, his proposition that "concerned minds should handle it well" is notable. Every African scholar who has witnessed the healthcare realities of the continent in recent times may be fully aware that the prevailing healthcare conditions in many African countries have gone from bad to worse post-pandemic. Additionally, according to an African Union report on Africa's healthcare status, the brain drain in the

---

25. Asamoah-Gyadu, *African Charismatics*, 231.
26. Omenyo and Atiemo, "Claiming Religious Space," 66.
27. Majawa, "Pentecostal and Charismatic Renewal," 110.
28. Banda, "Jesus the Healer," 57.

medical field in many countries is profound. "The growing shortage of doctors and nurses across parts of Africa region is one of the greatest obstacles to tackling the heavy burden of disease."[29]

Given this, Pentecostals have been hard pressed with the need to rethink approaches to tackling health issues among their adherents. In this way, one is thrust into reflection on this question: How vital were the healing or healthcare initiatives of nineteenth-century missionaries in the Gold Coast? Apart from building hospitals at various mission posts in Ghana, "they also healed the sick through prayer and preaching of the gospel and trained those with the gift of healing to do likewise."[30] Would Pentecostalism and its prosperity dogma be any different in Ghana if healthcare systems were first-rate as those in the West?

Kate Bowler discovered in her research in the American context that healing is a counteraction to Satan's activity wherein the power of God is manifested in a decisive triumph over the forces of darkness. She recognizes that "almost two-thirds of American Pentecostals report that they have been healed or have seen another person healed, and divine healing lies at the core of what captured prosperity believers' hearts. At the same time, most faith teachers grew to accept a positive attitude toward medicine, leaving behind the antimedical rhetoric that characterized the postwar healing revivals. A minority, however, shunned hospitals and doctors and nurtured divine health only by spiritual disciplines such as prayer, fasting, and deliverance."[31] The point here is that the quest for bodily healing is ubiquitous and a universal human need regardless of geographic location. Yet, what is intriguing about Bowler's observation is how some American Pentecostals who believe in divine healing through faith shunned science and medicine. The situation in Ghana may be relatively intricate because the healthcare systems are not even dependable in the first place. Thus, for most Christians in Ghana, when all access to medical care has proven futile, faith in divine healing becomes the only option for survival. In certain circles, some Ghanaians resort to indigenous healthcare whereby "the traditional healer undertakes both physical and spiritual diagnosis to ascertain the cause of the ailment."[32]

---

29. Sambo and World Health Organization Regional Office for Africa, *Health of the People*, 118.

30. Sambo and World Health Organization Regional Office for Africa, *Health of the People*, 118.

31. Bowler, *Blessed*, 140.

32. Awuah-Nyamekye, "Role of Religion," 41.

As a matter of fact, it is essential to mention that the quest for healing through faith finds an abode in the worldviews of Ghanaians, in which diseases, especially chronic ones, are noted as having some mystical origins. The question that arises is, what should Pentecostal churches do to find a balance between responding to a debilitated healthcare system and the administration of supernatural healing as a convincing triumph over the forces of darkness—a crucial marker of the inbreaking of the reign of God on earth? Should Pentecostal congregations begin to apply themselves to practical healthcare issues aside from administering divine healing through holistic mission initiatives?

Wealth and Prosperity in African Flourishing

In his work *The Prosperity Paradox*, Clayton Christensen ponders the meaning of the prosperity of nations in relation to the "well-being of members of society through gainful employment and upward social mobility. Thus, prosperity is the process by which more and more people in a region improve their economic, social, and political well-being."[33] The recent dismal performance of Ghana's cedi against the American dollar only goes to show the intensity of the economic hardship facing the nation and its citizenry. Like many on the continent, a compendium of factors subsuming "poor macroeconomic conditions, unemployment, corruption, defective energy, low income, and poor infrastructure,"[34] among other things, have contributed to the hardship that confronts the average Ghanaian today. How does such a phenomenon shape the lives of millions of Christians, primarily Protestants, who constitute approximately 71.3 percent of the country's population?

Unfortunately, the issue of wealth and prosperity in African Pentecostalism has often been discussed through a lopsided lens that focuses on the flamboyant lifestyle of some preachers while neglecting the stories of millions of adherents seeking answers. This may be deemed as one of the subtle weaknesses of the polemics against the prosperity theology of wealth. Ghanaian Christianity is predominantly youthful, and many of these devotees have a survival syndrome—they are looking for jobs and a decent salary to manage families and care for children. Nathaniel Soede writes about African peoples and money. He asserts that, for the African, "money provides individuals with a master's power over situations of destitution, lack, misery, and suffering at

---

33. Christensen, *Prosperity Paradox*, xii.

34. Zakari, "Development Challenges in Africa," in Cox and Ter Haar, *Uniquely African*, 81.

the social, economic, political, and religious levels. It is the means without which no one can live today. It is a sign and symbol of the fruit of labor, the power required to meet human needs, grow, communicate with others, improve one's living conditions and quality of life in one's environment and the world, promote development in all cultural, economic, political, scientific, technological, spiritual, and religious areas."[35]

It is not surprising that the mission model of early missionaries in Ghana included economic empowerment such that "both the Wesleyan and Basel Missions encouraged their converts to become economically self-reliant by engaging in agricultural activity. To this end, they introduced a new range of cash and food crops to members of their congregation . . . thus, the cultivation of coffee and mangoes spread rapidly among Christian congregations in the Eastern Region of Ghana."[36] For the most part, a study of prosperity tendencies among members of Pentecostal congregations will show that despite the abuses in some Pentecostals arenas, "what many African Pentecostal preachers talk about is merely in reference to a life of dignity marked by one's ability to afford the necessities of life."[37]

Furthermore, the African interpretation of wealth is somehow different than the Western. When one attempts to examine prosperity theology in the African context using Western paradigms of wealth, an accurate picture is not attained. It also inhibits any progress in understanding the problem and its possible solution. Jim Harris has shown how the "Luo people of Kenya understand money and other sources of prosperity to come from God as a result of beseeching him. The failure to prosper is either someone's fault (juok) or the fault of the person who is not prospering (chira)."[38] This same understanding of wealth and prosperity undergirds the worldviews of many Ghanaians today. Hence, the shift in the discourse toward the prosperity imaginations of adherents rather than the flamboyant lifestyle of prosperity preachers may offer a good deal of insight into the phenomenon. In the North American context, Bowler situates her argument at the heart of what she considers to be the controversial dimension of the prosperity gospel: "The radical claim to transform invisible faith into financial rewards. Its prophets proclaim a palpable gospel, one that could be clearly seen and measured in the financial well-being of its participants."[39] In Africa, Levi Nkwocha has explored the application of faith to ideologies such as "giving money to the

35. Soede, "African Peoples and Money," 160.
36. Cox and Ter Haar, *Uniquely African*, 195.
37. Kroesbergen, *In Search of Health*, 80.
38. Harries, "Place of Money," 181.
39. Bowler, *Blessed*, 77.

pastor which makes it possible for one to control their future" and "sowing of seed syndrome which takes a variety of formats depending on the charisma of the pastor," adding, "It is obvious that many poor members of these churches are forced out of a sense of shame or guilt and emotional pressure to eke out an offering even if it means borrowing or as the preacher says 'give until it hurts' to show how much they love God."[40]

In the broader scheme of things, the abuse of wealth doctrines in Pentecostalism can also be said to be a manipulation of the worldview of Africans about money and flourishing. One is always taken aback by why many Christians remain gullible to the abusive ploy of some Pentecostal pastors. The answer is simple; the African church has a quest and a need—because of its contextual realities, it has nurtured a pursuit of wholeness and a need for hope. How to meet this challenge authentically has been a challenge for African Christianity and, particularly, Pentecostalism. Emmanuel Kwesi Anim has argued that "prosperity teaching in Ghanaian Pentecostalism is not just a clone of the American Prosperity Gospel, but Ghanaian Charismatics have creatively reconstructed the Prosperity Gospel in response to iniquitous socio-economic and cultural conditions to offer symbols of hope and optimism."[41] In what sense can Ghanaian Pentecostals apply the gospel in its authentic and unadulterated forms through pragmatic discipleship to tackle the economic issues of their ardent followers who believe God is vitally interested in their financial matters and well-being? For instance, do the economic initiatives of the Basel Mission in Ghana during the nineteenth century offer holistic mission lessons for the contemporary church in Ghana?

Conclusion and Implications for Future Research

In *Holistic Mission: God's Plan for God's People*, Brian Woolnough argues that "the good news Christians are to take to the world is indeed a holistic mission, catering for all the needs of the world: spiritual, the emotional, the psychological and the physical."[42] It is not difficult to see that issues of health, wealth, employment, family, and other exigencies of life are encapsulated in the ramifications of the human depravity that the Christian gospel must seek to address. The challenge for Christianity has been methodology—how to articulate God's heart in these areas of relevance to human existence. It is also discernible that the issues that concern holistic mission are the same

40. Nkowcha, "African Church," 228.
41. Anim, "Analysis of Prosperity Teaching," 39.
42. Woolnough, "Good News for Poor," 5.

matters on which the prosperity theology preys—but for differences in terminology and approaches to theologizing. "In the North American experience, the prosperity gospel hermeneutic has been deemed 'unacceptable,' its ethics branded 'heresy.' However, given the intercultural interpretation of Pentecostal history, any critique of the prosperity gospel needs to be considered in the light of what it means in the peculiar religious and sociocultural circumstances, and thus the theology within which Ghanaian charismatics articulate such a message. In the African context generally, as we have noted, religion serves practical soteriological ends."[43]

Based on this frame of reference, understanding the prosperity theology problem for what it truly is in Africa is a matter of great concern. An uncharitable attempt to relegate the phenomenon to the background due to the extravagant lifestyle of a Pentecostal preacher will deprive us of the opportunity to understand the signs of the times. It is a problem that cannot be taken for granted because it is seemingly shaping the future of African Christianity. The brief exploration of the complications in health and wealth matters in Ghana is a harbinger of many problems that Ghanaian Christians will continue to grapple with in the future.

The fact is that Pentecostalism in Ghana has taken a stand to be relevant to the people's existential life in the context of poverty, unemployment, disease, and squalor, among other issues. In effect, the Pentecostal vision of "thy kingdom come," Africans' practical view of salvation and desire for wholeness, and N. T. Wright's imagination of the new-creation reality drive us to critically seek an interpretation of what is going on in African Pentecostalism with the prosperity gospel. George Hunter, in describing Celtic Christianity of the fourth century, argues that "when Christianity ignores or does not help people cope with middle-level issues, we often observe 'split-level Christianity' in which people go to church so they can go to heaven, but they also visit, say, the shaman or astrologer for help with pressing problems that dominate their daily lives. Celtic Christians did not need to seek out a shaman because Celtic communities addressed life as a whole."[44] While this chapter does not justify the ills of the prosperity gospel but considers them problematic, it is detectable that the problem has not been well problematized with a longing for an antidote due to a lack of robust research and understanding of the phenomenon. Hence, it's been ignored. More significant to the problem is that the prosperity theology will continue to grow and shape Christianity in Africa because it has apparently found expression in the African worldview and speaks to fundamental

---

43. Asamoah-Gyadu, *African Charismatics*, 222.
44. Hunter, *Celtic Way of Evangelism*, 15.

health and wealth issues. Having a resemblance to holistic mission in terms of the issues it addresses, this chapter recommends that future research envision holistic mission as a means for redeeming the theology and praxis of the prosperity gospel in Pentecostal congregations in Ghana.

Bibliography

Anim, Emmanuel Kwesi. "Who Wants to Be a Millionaire? An Analysis of Prosperity Teaching in the Charismatic Ministries (Churches) in Ghana and its Wider Impact." PhD diss., Open University (UK), 2003. https://www.proquest.com/dissertations-theses/who-wants-be-millionaire-analysis-prosperity/docview/305235519/se-2?accountid=13316.

Asamoah-Gyadu, J. Kwabena. *African Charismatics: Current Developments within Independent Indigenous Pentecostalism in Ghana*. Studies of Religion in Africa 27. Leiden: Brill, 2005.

Awuah-Nyamekye, Samuel. "The Role of Religion in Indigenous Healthcare Practice in Ghana's Development: Implication for Ghanaian Universities." *Journal of Theology for Southern Africa* 138 (2010) 30–45.

Banda, Devison Telen. "Jesus the Healer." In *In Search of Health and Wealth: The Prosperity Gospel in African, Reformed Perspective*, edited Hermen Kroesbergen, 49–58. Eugene, OR: Wipf & Stock, 2014.

Bosch, David J. *Transforming Mission: Paradigm Shifts in Theology of Mission*. American Society of Missiology Series. Maryknoll, NY: Orbis, 2018.

Bowler, Kate. *Blessed: A History of the American Prosperity Gospel*. Oxford: Oxford University Press, 2013.

Christensen, Clayton. *The Prosperity Paradox: How Innovation Can Lift Nations out of Poverty*. New York: HarperBusiness, 2019.

Coleman, Simon. *The Globalisation of Charismatic Christianity*. Cambridge Studies in Ideology and Religion 12. Cambridge: Cambridge University Press, 2000.

Cox, James L., and Gerrie Ter Haar. *Uniquely African? African Christian Identity from Cultural and Historical Perspectives*. Religion in Contemporary Africa Series. Trenton, NJ: Africa World, 2013.

Dzando, Gideon, et al. "Healthcare in Ghana amidst the Coronavirus Pandemic: A Narrative Literature Review." *Journal of Public Health Research* 11 (2022) 1–8.

Dzokoto, Vivian. "Sighs and Signs of the Mind? Pentecostalism, Renewal, and a Ghanaian Mind Folk Theory." In *African Pentecostalism and World Christianity: Essays in Honor of J. Kwabena Asamoah-Gyadu*, edited by Nimi Wariboko and Adeshina Afolayan, African Christian Studies 18, 123–36. Eugene, OR: Pickwick Publications, 2020.

Elihu, Paul. "Justice, Human Dignity, and the Capabilities Approach: A Moral Assessment of Ghana's Healthcare Delivery System." MA thesis, Duquesne University, 2021.

Freston, Paul. "Prosperity Theology: A Largely Sociological Assessment." In *Prosperity Theology and the Gospel: Good News or Bad News for the Poor*, edited by J. Daniel Salinas, Lausanne Library, 87–111. Lausanne Library. Peabody, MA: Hendrickson, 2017.

Harries, Jim. "The Place of Money in Mission between Africa and the Rest: A Personal Theological Narrative." In *Wealth, Health, and Hope in African Christian Religion: The Search for Abundant Life*, edited by Stan Chu Ilo, 181–200. London: Lexington, 2018.

Hunter, George C., III. *The Celtic Way of Evangelism: How Christianity Can Reach the West . . . Again*. 10th anniv. ed., revised and updated. Nashville: Abingdon, 2010.

Ilo, Stan Chu. *Wealth, Health, and Hope in African Christian Religion: The Search for Abundant Life*. London: Lexington, 2018.

Kroesbergen, Hermen. *In Search of Health and Wealth: The Prosperity Gospel in an African, Reformed Perspective*. Eugene, OR: Wipf & Stock, 2014.

Majawa, Clement. "Pentecostal and Charismatic Renewal." In *Wealth, Health, and Hope in African Christian Religion: The Search for Abundant Life*, edited by Stan Chu Ilo, 103–29. London: Lexington, 2018.

Mbiti, John. "Christianity and Traditional Religions in Africa." *International Review of Mission* 59 (1970) 430–40.

Miller, Donald E., and Tetsuna Yamamori. *Global Pentecostalism: The New Face of Christian Social Engagement*. Berkeley: University of California Press, 2007.

Nkowcha, Levi. "The African Church and the Impact of Contemporary Fundraiser and Sustainability." In *Wealth, Health, and Hope in African Christian Religion: The Search for Abundant Life*, edited by Stan Chu Ilo, 219–40. London: Lexington, 2018.

Omenyo, Cephas N., and Abamfo O. Atiemo. "Claiming Religious Space: The Case of Neo-Prophetism in Ghana." *Ghana Journal of Religion and Theology* 51 (2006) 42–66.

Pachuau, Lalsangkima. *World Christianity: A Historical and Theological Introduction*. Nashville: Abingdon, 2018.

Sambo, Luis Gomes, and World Health Organization Regional Office for Africa. *The Health of the People: What Works; The African Regional Health Report 2014*. World Health Organization, 2014. https://iris.who.int/handle/10665/137377.

Sider, Ron. "What if We Defined the Gospel the Way that Jesus Did?" In *Holistic Mission: God's Plan for God's People*, edited by Brian Woolnough and Wonsuk Ma, Regnum Edinburgh 2010, 17–30. Eugene, OR: Wipf & Stock, 2010.

Soede, Nathaniel. "African Peoples and Money, Yesterday and Today." In *Wealth, Health, and Hope in African Christian Religion: The Search for Abundant Life*, edited by Stan Chu Ilo, 157–80. London: Lexington, 2018.

Synan, Vinson. *The Century of the Holy Spirit: 100 Years of Pentecostal and Charismatic Renewal 1901–2001*. Nashville: Nelson, 2001.

Wimber, John, and Kevin Springer. *Power Evangelism*. Rev. ed. with study guide. London: Hodder & Stoughton, 1992.

Woolnough, Brian. "Good News for the Poor—Setting the Scene." In *Holistic Mission: God's Plan for God's People*, edited by Brian Woolnough and Wonsuk Ma, 3–16. Regnum Edinburgh 2010, Eugene, OR: Wipf & Stock, 2010.

Wright, N. T. "The Coming of God and New Creation." Lecture, Asbury Theological Seminary, Wilmore, KY, Nov. 15, 2022.

15

Transtemporal Connections

African Christian History as Intellectual History

WANJIRU M. GITAU

Introduction: Imaginative Retrieval of Intellectual History

CONTEMPORARY AFRICANS ARE CAUGHT in crosscurrents of social change. Africans must navigate plural lifeworlds simultaneously—remnants of tradition; metropole worlds of school, polity, and commerce; and global cosmopolitan publics. For most, the fluidity required to navigate these worlds presents a psychologically, spiritually, and socially disorienting fragmentation, which translates into dissonance at the societal level and dysfunction in individual life. The global cultural turn to which Africa is enjoined via technology is only accelerating this sense of fragmentation. On the other hand, Christianity is thriving in twenty-first-century Africa. The question is not whether it belongs there. The question is to what degree Christianity reflects Africans' agency to act on their destiny amid the dissonance. This question cannot be addressed without tackling the growing historical and cultural amnesia, despite overflowing churches. Among other things, contemporary Christian vision must lay claim to a vital intellectual tradition to counter the historical and cultural amnesia at the heart of social and cultural fragmentation.

Hindsight from the process of Christian transmission across time and space reveals that Africa is already enjoined in, interlinked in, a chain of collective memory and shared traditions in a rich, universal (ecumenical), theological tradition. This chapter focuses on how the long history of Christianity in Africa might be synthesized as intellectual history.

Christianity is a faith shaped by the Book. To be a Bible-based faith is to be a literate and reflective faith—notwithstanding that the majority of adherents across time never had access to an actual Bible, the ability to read, or mastery of theological vocabulary. Yet all have a native sense of religion—the nature of God and creation, the meaning of worship, the need for mediation, notions of divine providence and retribution.[1] While most people encounter Christianity as a lived experience, over the long duration, the transmission process requires that it is learned, interpreted, and translated, thus participating in knowledge production and even solving problems that have to do with sustaining itself as a tradition. It cannot be abstracted; its historicization must be rooted in institutions that perpetuate learning, however rudimentary. Of necessity, it must use language creatively to recreate the cultural categories of its communities. Additionally, the reflective dimension carries weight as a theological idea whose provenance is revelatory. Sources of cultural diffusion such as music, art, ritual, and other symbols of identity forged through memory, performance, and imagination require rational judgment. These ideas converge on the notion that African Christianity through time constitutes intellectual history, as much as it consists of a moral code and mystical imagination.

Intellectual history is chiefly concerned with how people make sense of their world, particularly their past. It also includes the sphere of human thought in all disciplines. Ideas of any kind, including religious ones, take root in concrete historical settings, shaped by and shaping the societies with which they interact.[2] The concept of "intellectual" is applied to a wide range of inquiries dealing with the articulation of ideas, especially those crafted at a fairly sophisticated or reflective level. The Christian faith is a sophisticated religious system, comprising transcendent and material dimensions. Transcendence constitutes the core of theological ideas by which a religion represents the deity and the deity's relationship with the material world. Materiality includes historically mediated mythos, rituals, institutions, art, architecture, and practicing communities. From this perspective, religion, especially one dependent on a text, is a complex system that must be articulated with a degree of intellectual sophistication. Intellectual history is also concerned with tracing ideas within broader histories of the societies which they emerged. Attention to the formulation, circulation, and reception of ideas has always been understood as what makes intellectual history historical.[3]

The historical study of Christians as thinking agents is not a conventional subject. The standard approach to the "history of ideas" primarily focused on the "great texts" of Western society, largely relating to

1. See Orobator, *Theology Brewed*.
2. Chapman et al., *Seeing Things Their Way*.
3. Whatmore and Young, *Intellectual History*, 171.

philosophy and literature, and secondarily texts from elsewhere ruled the field. The idealistic coherence imposed on "great texts" is now seen as a hegemonic reductionism.[4] Intellectual historical inquiry is also absent in reference to faith because faith is primarily thought of in spiritual, otherworldly terms, only secondarily in material and cultural terms. Historians have often treated religious ideas as things that need to be reduced to secular meaning. Religious truth claims are also seen as irrationalities, a consequence of suppressing rational doubts.[5] Chapman invites intellectual historians to explore the religious dimensions of ideas using methods of general intellectual history.

The association of African historical experience with intellectual history is not new. Major steps in formalization of the African past were taken in 1948 in the University of London's School of Oriental and African Studies, through the "lectureship in the history of the tribal peoples of East Africa."[6] Journals, university departments, and postgraduate publications of hundreds of dissertation monographs created a sustained trend from the 1960s to the 1980s. A related legacy concerns archeology. In 1959, *The East Africa Standard* ran a headline, "Leakey Discovers the Missing Link," in reference to Darwin's theory of evolution from ape to man.[7] The origins of the human species came to be linked with the Olduvai Gorge in Tanzania, the site of early hominid fossils. Shortly, Kenya and Ethiopia reinforced Africa's claim as the cradle of human civilization. With radiocarbon dating of archeological and geological finds, Africa acquired status as the pioneer of Paleolithic origins.[8] Writing in the context of the heightened historical curiosity of the 1980s, African historian Ali Mazrui referred to Africa as a "cultural bazaar," "where a wide variety of ideas and values, from diverse civilizations compete for the attention. Among the items in the bazaar is the triple heritage of indigenous, Semitic, and Greco-Roman influences on Africa."[9] From a long historical gaze, there is an opportunity to reclaim the Christian dimension of that heritage as constituting its own intellectual viewpoint.

A related strand of intellectual ideas associated with Africa constitutes the rich legacy of colonial and postcolonial literary renaissance, a reassertion of black worth and achievement. Linked to Negritude and Pan-Africanist movements, African writers championed black consciousness through vast

4. Kelley, *Descent of Ideas*.
5. Chapman et al., *Seeing Things Their Way*.
6. Bentley, *Companion to Historiography*, 311.
7. Bentley, *Companion to Historiography*, 687.
8. Davidson, *Old Africa Rediscovered*, 22.
9. Mazrui, *Africans*, 99.

literary production. African academic theology was born amid the crosswinds of this cultural renaissance.[10] Literary writers, previously lay Christian graduates of mission schools, castigated missionary Christianity alongside colonialism, with Christianity seen as an iconoclastic force of disruption of people's self-identities. African theological scholars such as John Mbiti, Idowu Bolaji, Harry Sawyer, Laurenti Magesa affirmed the vitality of African religious heritage as fertile ground for theological reflection. A significant theological output emerged from these interpretations of African cultural symbols into Christian nuance. While a bigger project is required to give the subject a just treatment, this present interpretation is in some measure a contribution to that earlier debate by African theologians.

Dimensions of African Christian History as Intellectual History

As a caveat, there exists a continuous history of Christian presence on the African continent. Beginning with its foundations in Alexandria, the church flourished in North Africa, as well as Ethiopia, for some six hundred years. After Carthage, the last Christian stronghold, fell to Arabs in 697, King Mecurios of Nubia built up a Christian kingdom that stretched from the Aswan to the Blue Nile. When that kingdom succumbed to Turkish-Islamic attacks in 1270, the nine-hundred-year-old Ethiopian church was revived in the mountains of Ethiopia under Yikunno Amlak and Takla Haymanot. By the 1520s, Afonso, king of Kongo, in tropical Africa, had embraced Christianity and established a Christian kingdom that sustained links with Rome for three hundred years. By 1792, Moravian Protestants established a mission station in South Africa, while repatriated slaves established a church in Sierra Leone with intent to evangelize the interior. From there the flow of modern missions established Christianity throughout the continent.[11] The interest of this chapter is in conceptualizing this presence in intellectual terms. Three interlinked concepts converge at this task: ideas, the social and material contexts of historical experience, and the cultural milieu of reflective practitioners.

---

10. Stinton, *Jesus of Africa*.

11. Shaw and Wanjiru, *Kingdom of God*; Baur, *2000 Years of Christianity;* Sundkler and Steed, *History of the Church*.

Christian Ideation as Intellectual History

Linguistically, there is a specific semantic domain to which Christian ideas, along with their translation, appropriation, and reinterpretation belong, and that is theology. Theology can refer to any act of meaning-making of religious experience. Alternatively, theology is a rigorous methodological practice of arriving at religious or philosophical conclusions. In the first sense, theology occurs wherever there are religious people. In the second sense, theology is an academic discipline. As tautological as this sounds, to say Christianity is a theological idea is to say that it makes certain claims on truth, is embedded in spiritual practice, and forms certain kinds of eschatological communities. The essential uniqueness of Christianity on the continent is not primarily to be limited to some ontological notion, rather, it is in the narrative of how Africans have owned the Christian story, just as a similar story can be told of how other regions have owned the story. The reception of that story was dependent on historical transmission, application, and dialectical reciprocity within the cultural matrix of the world that the story encountered. Intellectual historical inquiry is centrally placed to locate African agency in any given historical era, into what is at heart a theological story.

Theologically, Africa forms a core part of the biblical imagination, so much so that it does not get special treatment—Africa simply cohabits the Judeo-Christian world. Thus, the creation account in Gen 2:10–14 names one of the four rivers as Gihon, winding through the land of Cush, alongside Tigris and Euphrates. Cush as a region appears more than fifty times in the Old Testament, Egypt even more. Inhabitants of Cush are taken for granted by prophets such as Isaiah and Jeremiah (Isa 18:2; Jer 13: 23). Famously, Egypt and Cush come alongside the kingdoms of the earth to worship in Jerusalem in Ps 68:31. When Jesus appears in the New Testament, Africans are integrated among the cosmopolitan peoples as easily as everyone else. Matthew 27: 32; Mark 15: 21; and Luke 23: 26 mention Simon from Cyrene as compelled to carry Jesus's cross, and an editorial note that he was the father of Alexander and Rufus suggests these two men belonged with the early church community. In Acts 8, the traveling official of the candace, the royal queen mother, was reading the scroll of Isaiah as though Africans traveling international highways while reading Scriptures were a quotidian practice.

Beyond the formative encounter, African Christianity nurtured the intellectual subtlety and substance that shaped historic Christian orthodoxy. Early Christian memory, argues Thomas Oden, was formed in Africa as much as it was formed in Palestinian, Syrian, and Mediterranean worlds.¹² The church in Africa faced the same questions about its core beliefs, including heresies, that challenged the church at large. Boundaries of what became orthodox versus heresy were solidified at later stages of ecumenical councils between 325 and 787.¹³

While the common misperception is that intellectual insight moved from the north to the south, African theological intellect blossomed so much that it was sought and widely emulated by Christians of the northern and eastern Mediterranean shores. Africans instructed Syriac, Cappadocian, and Greco-Roman teachers. St Augustine (354–430), the bishop of Carthage, influenced religious thought throughout the Christian world.¹⁴ Tertullian, Cyprian, Arnobius, Optatus, and Augustine came from the Magreb. Optatus, who wrote in the century preceding the Councils of Ephesus and Chalcedon, had considerable influence on the conception of Christian doctrine via St. Augustine. As the historian with firsthand contact with Donatism, his writings were scrutinized by Ambrose and Jerome. His treatise against the Donatists shaped Augustine's ideas on the doctrinal significance of the church, especially the marks of the church.¹⁵

The Coptic Church produced theologians like Athanasius (293–373), Cyril (412–44), and Anthony (251–356), founder of monasticism. In time, Christian ideas and practices flowed north to Europe from the Nilotic and Numidian traditions and with rigorous debates and councils matured into an ecumenical consensus on how to interpret sacred Scripture. In the context of bustling pluralist metropolises, Africans figured out how to read the law and prophets meaningfully, to think philosophically, and to teach the ecumenical rule of triune faith cohesively before these patterns became normative elsewhere.

Alongside spirituality, theological ideas require language and literacy for articulation. Religious literacy—the ability to use language to read, write, use vocabulary, grammar, and syntax—frames the basic building blocks of religious traditions, including symbols, doctrines, narratives.¹⁶ Like other forms of literacy, religious literacy is more a fluid than a fixed feature. Yet the ability to participate in Christian faith, even for nonliterate participants, depends on knowing and articulating basic tenets in relation to self and community. It is a celebrated fact that print and schooled literacy, along with translation, have mediated the recent phase of Christian expansion in

12. Oden, *How Africa Shaped*, 14.
13. Wilhite, *Ancient African Christianity*, 3.
14. Page, *Encyclopedia of African History*, 1:47.
15. Optatus of Mileve, *Work of St. Optatus*, iv.
16. Prothero, *Religious Literacy*, 11.

Africa.[17] Yet, early on, wherever Christianity took root, some social imaginary had capacity not only to read, but also to cite, interpret, comment on, and critique texts.[18] Origen, for example, elaborated the theory of meaning in the fourfold meaning of Scripture, the quadriga, in which the text had four layers of meaning: the literal (plain, obvious meaning), the moral (meaning for human behavior), the allegorical (meaning for human faith, belief, and doctrine), and the anagogical (meaning for the future).

Unusual vocabulary shows the comparative independence of the African documents. The oldest Latin translation of the Bible, Itala, the basis of Jerome's Vulgate, was made in Africa and for Africa, not in Rome and for Rome, but exercised profound impact on church language. Augustine considered it more faithful in its renderings and more intelligible. Latin theology was not born in Rome but in Carthage. Tertullian was the father of Latin theology, with Felix, Arnobius, and Cyprian as witnesses to the activity of African theology in the third century. The character of the African manuscripts differed from Latin texts in language and the underlying Greek texts.

Literacy transcends language. Inscribed objects from archeological excavations like commercial coins, public monuments, and worship sites reveal theological ideas alongside material and cultural ones. There is underlying heuristic value of cultural art, iconography, and architecture from particular sociohistorical contexts.[19] In the case of Ethiopian Christianity, the advanced art form of the churches of Lalibela was built to transcend the limits of time. The iconic perceptions of Jesus with notably prominent eyes convey a peculiar imagination not found elsewhere. The vision behind their construction, combined with artistic, architectural, and literary forms, bears a powerful message for posterity. The relation of art and beauty to spirituality became axiomatic to cultural identity in Aksum and remains so to Ethiopians to date. Not to be lost is the intellectual symbolism of the location of the churches in the mountains that are seen to mediate the sacred and otherworldly. Iconography in sketch paintings has acquired renewed currency through the inculturation motifs of recent theological reflection.[20]

Social and Material Conditions as Framing Intellectual Ideation

Second, African Christian history is linked to significant social histories that constitute material and political dimensions. Recent social history of

17. Sanneh, *Translating the Message.*
18. Johns, *Nature of the Book.*
19. Johnson and Parker, *Ancient Literacies.*
20. Healey and Sybertz, *Towards African Narrative Theology.*

Africa has predominated debate on Christianity's relevance in Africa and skewered it towards what Emmanuel Katongole refers to as prescriptive haste.[21] The burden of a Western legacy places Christianity's competency in the spiritual realm, largely acquiescent to distressed conditions of the temporal reality. In fact, long history demonstrates African Christianity's dynamic interface with material history, including politics and economics. Accordingly, retrieval of intellectual history includes reclamation of social contexts that shaped its trajectory.

Intellectual pursuits arise within and bear the marks of their sociohistorical worlds. Case in point, Christianity's rapid spread in North Africa was tied to Rome's rule. Rome divided the province of Africa Proconsularis from Numidia to the west and Cyrenaica to the East. Emperor Diocletian (284–305) subdivided it into seven provinces. Always, Africans equally thought of themselves as Carthagians, Numidians, or some other expression of a local identity, and could still lay claim to *Romanitas*, Roman citizenship. Despite Roman colonization, African languages like Lybian and Punic survived and even thrived. Africans also participated in various levels as *Romanitas*.[22] Tertullian wrote from Africa with a distinct African identity, and could equally occupy multiple identities: Christian, male, educated, Roman citizen, while still African.

Beyond the claims to cosmopolitan citizenship, material history matters as part of the intellectual claim of Christianity's growth to a faith embraced by kings and their whole nations. Notwithstanding theological differentiation from Latin Christianity, successive generations of Christians matured with degrees of sophistication in the valleys and cities around inland river systems up and down the Nile. Social and material dimensions also include trade and communication, conquest and migration. A case in point is the massive archeological dig that was commissioned on fifty-nine sites by UNESCO in the 1950s, which revealed an extraordinary culture buried in the sands of time in what was once the Nubian kingdom. The Nubian church was founded by traders, monks, and refugees who sailed down the Nile. It became a court religion with status as an institution that mediated the planning and building of impressive ecclesiastical monuments and artistic works. In the thousand years that followed, various expressions of the faith would thrive in the kingdoms of Nobatia, Makouria, and Alodia along the Nile.[23]

---

21. Katongole, *Future for Africa*, 41.
22. Wilhite, *Ancient African Christianity*, 15.
23. Sundkler and Steed, *History of the Church*, 30.

Ethiopia, a well-organized and prosperous civilization, was reached through the Red Sea route and up the plateau to the capital, Aksum. Frumentius and Aedesius were on their way to India, but after a shipwreck were brought to the official court at Aksum during the reign of Ousanas. They tutored two royal princes, Ezana and Zazana. Frumentius was ordained by Athanasius, patriarch of Alexandria, to establish the church in Ethiopia. He is venerated as *Abuna Salama* (father of salvation). Coins based on the Roman monetary system, which were necessary for trade, have been found in all parts of the Aksumite territory. Coinage was needed for purposes of trade. It placed Aksum on a par with other coin-issuing states and underscored the empire's status among other powers.[24]

Explorers form the parts of material culture that shape African Christianity. Before 1543, Rome, Constantinople, and Alexandria had maintained links with the church in Africa via the Mediterranean and Red Sea belt. After 1543, Portuguese and Spanish seafarers, motivated by trade and commissioned by the medieval Catholic Church, sailed southwards, establishing Christian outposts along tropical coasts down to the Cape of Good Hope and up to East Africa. The search for a king to convert in these places—ostensibly a mythical Prester John—connected the idea of Christian conquest, a spiritual crusade, with political and trade conquest. From a material perspective, later associations between national and ecclesiastical enterprises yield fraught histories of exploitation, slave trade, and imperialism. Yet that does not invalidate the profound rational, spiritual, and material energies it took foreigners to create a church in what were unfamiliar territories. Sundkler observes that the enormous activity and daring exploration, comparable to exploits of the space in our time, was inspired by the *Zeitgeist* of the period. Out of this milieu there emerged the special *conquista* idea of Christian mission as a new and unique phenomenon, different from any concept heretofore. An empire with Portuguese place-names dotted the coastlines of Africa and India.[25] The Dutch, French, and British would eventually follow with extractive trade and imperialism, with missionaries the civilizing cause of Christianity, commerce, and trade.

Material culture and politics are interlinked with spirituality. In the Kongo kingdom Dona Kimpa Vita (1684–1706) shows up as a type of Saint Anthony, the great Franciscan revered by the Capuchins. The narrative around Kimpa Vita, alongside that of kings of the kingdom in their dalliance with the Portuguese, suggests a sophisticated level of theological ideation, albeit wrapped with African cosmology. While denounced as a

---

24. Henze, *Layers of Time*.
25. Sundkler and Steed, *History of the Church*, 45–49.

witch and burned at the stake, Kimpa Vita's death encouraged her followers to venerate her and spread her message of liberation of the Kongo kingdom. Likewise, Queen Nzinga of the Dongo kingdom, Angola, baptized Donna Ana de Souza by Portuguese Jesuits and Italian Capuchins, cleverly used the foreigners' religion to strategize diversions on slave-trading incursions into her lands.[26] Sadly, in 1760, the slave traffic to Brazil destroyed two hundred years of Christian mission in Angola. Kimpa and Nzinga are seen as forerunners of charismatic movements by such as Simon Kimbangu, Isaiah Shembe, and William Wade Harris who have led spiritual protests as a response to material oppression. While charismatic leaders mobilized spiritual activism, their grievances were rooted in a rational assessment of oppressive material and cultural conditions, and that itself provides a cache of intellectual ideas whose provenance is in a biblically shaped imagination.

Slightly later in 1787, free blacks from Nova Scotia and Jamaica, inspired by evangelical religion and American utopianism, moved to Sierra Leone as the first black colony. The Krio church, built by Africans uprooted from coherent societies without the means of rediscovering their former cohesion, adopted and adapted the only viable alternative open to them, the package of Christianity and European civilization, to start a new nation and a new culture.[27] European and African elements were blended and adopted for an African context and transformed by it, writes Andrew Walls. The colony was littered with English place-names, dress, and houses and English as the language of administration and learning. The Krio community, as it was known, developed a new lingua franca, an English vocabulary with an African syntax, the Krio (Creole) language.

The Milieu of Cultural Custody of Intellectual Ideation

The third strand of intellectual history must be considered in terms of the cultural milieu of cultural custody of Christian ideas. The relationship between culture and Christianity is a fraught idea. Twentieth-century theological scholarship focused on reclaiming Africa's cultural heritage. A significant feature is the question of whether the Christian religion really belongs in Africa. One linked, unhappy sentiment is that Christianity is a white man's religion, with missionaries as handmaidens to imperialism, though the scholarship of Lamin Sanneh has debunked some of the misconceptions. Conversely, reclaimed traditional categories raise the question of what forms such identities, granted Western cultural, education, and

26. Hinga, *African, Christian, Feminist*.
27. Walls, *Missionary Movement*.

bureaucratic incursions in contemporary Africa. James Cox's query of what is a uniquely African identity in regards to Christianity strikes at the heart of the essentialism that blurs all else about Christianity on the continent.[28] While cultural history has offered a self-consciously reflexive understanding of the historical context of Christian appropriation, use of "culture" as the framework for idea production, diffusion, and reception has risked eclipsing not only the sociohistorical but also the patently theological. The theological is part of the intellectual, not merely because of the professional theologian, but because of the foundational source of Christian revelation, the Bible. In its entirety, the Bible is a carefully and systematically constructed account, so designed to inspire a reflexive moral response that challenges the rational and cultural order anywhere. Thus, as far as the cultural milieu is concerned, a turn to biographies rooted in particular communities might prove a more fruitful line of inquiry.

From a biographical standpoint, every African Christian community can resource intellectual insight into its era. A few examples suffice. Christianity was probably known in Ethiopia well before Frumentius and Aedesius arrived and Ezana officially adopted it. Several Christians, known as the *tsadkan* (righteous ones), possibly monks expelled from the Eastern Roman Empire after the Council of Chalcedon in AD 451, are said to have arrived to spread the gospel. A contemporary group of Nine Saints is traced to Syria, Cappadocia, Constantinople, Cilicia, and Rome, and established churches and monasteries in Adwa, northeast of Aksum, and Debre Damon, translating the Bible and organizing Christian communities.[29] Accounts of their legacies in the church of Abuna Yemata combine tales of extraordinary determination and courage alongside asceticism, though not isolation, as the work of building churches, standardizing rituals, creating the impressive body of doctrine and religious literature that defines the Ethiopian Orthodox Church requires enormous cooperation and mobilization. Further, the Ge'ez translations of the Old and New Testaments and church liturgy show affinities with Syriac in religious expressions, meaning there was a continuous communion with the outside world. King Lalibela of the Lalibela churches' fame invested all his energy into cutting rock churches in the mountains, aspiring for a would-be African Zion as the real Jerusalem was captured by the Muslim Saladin in 1189. This formidable project, twenty-four years in the making, required mobilization of Egyptian stonecutters, highly professional supervision of rock cutting, and

---

28. Cox and Ter Haar. *Uniquely Africa*, 6.
29. Henze, *Layers of Time*, 38–39.

careful planning of resources. It tells much of the intellectual skill of the king and the communities that around him.

The Kebra Negast (Glory of the kings), the Ethiopian national epic, was committed to writing early in the fourteenth century by Nebure-id Yeshak of Aksum. This sacred compilation and interpretation of the legend of the queen of Sheba and King Solomon includes Greek, Coptic, Syriac, and Arabic religious writings.[30] Copied in monasteries throughout the Middle Ages, it is still cited as foundational to the Ethiopian state, considered a work of enormous historical continuity. Likewise, archeological discoveries in Alwa illustrate a rich legacy. The southernmost of the kingdoms of Christian Nubia in Meroe, south of the Nile, had its capital, Soba, near modern-day Khartoum. Alwa came under the influence of Christianity when the Byzantine missionary Longinus baptized its king in 580. Alwa continued as a strong state until the sixteenth century. Soba was a bishopric, with six individual bishops who were identified by names. As late as the tenth century, an Arab writer described Soba as a city with fine houses and buildings, including churches. The bishop reported to the patriarch of Alexandria.[31] Eventually, repeated Arab attacks weakened it until it collapsed, but that does not invalidate its Christian history.

In the nineteenth century, events around two pioneers are illustrative. The first is the story of Samuel Ajayi Crowther. Sold as a slave boy, then liberated by the British navy, Ajayi would overcome adversity, study at the CMS College in London, publish the vocabulary of the Yoruba language, and translate the Bible and Book of Common Prayer into Yoruba. Eventually he was commissioned to open the Niger Mission, ordained as a bishop in 1864 as the first African bishop of the Anglican Church, and lead mission work for decades. His leadership was later discredited by the provinciality of young white missionaries, yet his unmatched accomplishments reflect tropical Africans' capability to achieve incomparably more on their own when equipped with resources analogous to their Western counterparts'. He lived through a transformation of relations between Africa and the rest of the world.[32]

Likewise, the complicated story of William Sheppard, known as the "Black Livingstone," is illustrative.[33] Sheppard was sent as a missionary to the Congo by the Presbyterian Church of the United States in 1890, in a larger scheme to send freed slaves as missionaries to Africa. Sheppard proved adept

---

30. Henze, *Layers of Time*, 56.
31. Page, *Encyclopedia of African History*, 2:14.
32. See Walls, *Cross-Cultural Process*.
33. See Phipps, *William Sheppard*.

and resourceful as he went into an African kingdom to which no outsider had ever penetrated, discovering the highly civilized Kuba kingdom. He recorded their history, collected their artifacts, and was eventually inducted into the Royal Geographical Society by Queen Victoria for his discoveries. He later toured Europe and America, joining one of the most important human rights campaigns as a star witness to the murderous and exploitative plunder of the Congo by the henchmen of King Leopold of Belgium. The larger and tragic story around Sheppard's missionary, explorer, and activist career reveals much about Africa's troubled interlinkage with the West but, equally, the role of the Christian faith in reversing fortunes.

Conclusion

Methodologically, it takes a particular work of retrieval to reclaim the continuous African Christian narrative as a strand of intellectual history. A rapprochement is nonetheless possible by imagining these same ideas in broader Christian record. Despite the vast geographical range, Christianity has spread throughout the world because of the three main strands broadly explored in this chapter: the ideas it consists of, primarily theological; the social and material contexts it embedded itself in successively; and the reflective practitioners and their communities, and the institutions they formed. A broader work may draw on a comparative analogy of the transtemporal vis-à-vis the transnational.[34] The transtemporal concerns linkages and comparisons in discrete moments, periods, and contexts across *time* while maintaining synchronic specificity of those contexts; transnational history deals with such connections across *space*. Transtemporal is not transhistorical; it is particularistic and time-bound, not timeless. It stresses the mechanisms of connections between moments and is therefore concerned with questions of concrete transmission, tradition, and reception materially and institutionally mediated. That seems to be how Christianity has retained its continuous connections in the wider world—not primarily in continuous transnational links (at least not until the twentieth century), but in transtemporal transmission of the same key ideas.

One thing that lends credence to this methodological approach is the trajectory of recent scholarship in African Christian history. Pioneering but recently deceased historians of African Christianity as a constituent of the field of world Christianity, in particular Ogbu Kalu, Lamin Sanneh, Kwame Bediako, and Andrew Walls, have produced a significant body of research that amounts to an intellectual tradition in the field of world

34. Armitage, "What's the Big Idea?"

Christianity, intercultural studies, mission studies. They are in continuity with the previously cited African theologians whose work goes back to the immediate postcolonial period, if only in rejoinder. It continues to be necessary that Africans assert their right to the whole story of Christianity as their own, tracing it right back to the apostolic age, then through the transtemporal encounter of two thousand years. The trajectory of the task is suggestive: framing a vital intellectual stream for African Christianity in a world that takes neither the Christian theological vision seriously nor the African continent as a serious partner in global affairs. If African Christianity's engagement with the wider world through mission and theology in the twenty-first century is to reflect its true place in the redemptive imagination, the African Christian story, its sociohistorical materiality, cultural production, and theology are not to be regarded as belonging to the margins of Christian thought. They are core to it.

Bibliography

Armitage, David. "What's the Big Idea? Intellectual History and the Long Duree." *History of European Ideas* 38 (2012) 493–507.

Baur, John. *2000 Years of Christianity in Africa*. Edited by Silvano Borruso. Updated by Agostino Bertolotti. 2nd ed. Nairobi: Paulines Africa, 2009.

Bediako, Kwame. *Theology and Identity: The Impact of Culture upon African Christian Thought in the Second Century and in Modern Africa*. Regnum Studies in Mission. London: Regnum, 2011.

Bentley, Michael, ed. *Companion to Historiography*. London: Routledge, 1997.

Chapman, Alister, et al. *Seeing Things Their Way: Intellectual History and the Return of Religion*. Notre Dame, IN: University of Notre Dame, 2009.

Cox, James L., and Gerrie Ter Haar. *Uniquely Africa? African Christian Identity from Cultural and Historical Perspectives*. Trenton, NJ: Africa World, 2003.

Davidson, Basil. *Old Africa Rediscovered*. London: Gollancz, 1964.

Healey, Joseph, and Donald Sybertz, eds. *Towards an African Narrative Theology*. Faith and Cultures. Maryknoll, NY: Orbis, 1996.

Henze, Paul B. *Layers of Time: A History of Ethiopia*. New York: Palgrave, 2000.

Hinga, Teresia Mbari. *African, Christian, Feminist: The Enduring Search for What Matters*. Maryknoll, NY: Orbis, 2017.

Johns, Adrian. *The Nature of the Book: Print and Knowledge in the Making*. Chicago: University of Chicago Press, 1998.

Johnson, William A., and Holt N. Parker, eds. *Ancient Literacies: The Culture of Reading in Greece and Rome*. New York: Oxford University Press, 2009.

Kalu, Ogbu. *African Christianity: An African Story*. Trenton, NJ: Africa World, 2007.

Katongole, Emmanuel. *A Future for Africa: Critical Essays in Christian Social Imagination*. Scranton, PA: University of Scranton Press, 2005.

Kelley, Donald R. *The Descent of Ideas: The History of Intellectual History*. New York: Routledge, 2002.

Mazrui, Ali A. *The Africans: A Triple Heritage*. London: Little, Brown, 1986.

Oden, Thomas C. *How Africa Shaped the Christian Mind: Rediscovering the African Seedbed of Western Christianity.* Downers Grove, IL: InterVarsity Press, 2007.
Optatus of Mileve. *The Work of St. Optatus: A Catholic Church History, Wherein a Saint and Early Church Father Condemns the Donatist Schism after the Persecution of Christians by Roman Emperor Diocletian.* Translated by Oliver Rodie Vassal-Phillips. Paris: Muséum National d'Histoire Naturelle, 1917.
Orobator, Aghbonkhianmeghe E. *Theology Brewed in an African Pot.* Maryknoll, NY: Orbis, 2008.
Page, Willie F., ed. *Encyclopedia of African History and Culture.* 5 vols. New York: Learning Source, 2001.
Parratt, John, ed. *An Introduction to Third World Theologies.* Introduction to Religion. London: Cambridge University Press, 2004.
Phipps, William. *William Sheppard: Congo's African American Livingstone.* Louisville: Geneva, 2002.
Prothero, Stephen. *Religious Literacy: What Every American Needs to Know—and Doesn't.* New York: Harper Collins, 2009.
Sanneh, Lamin. *Translating the Message: The Missionary Impact on Culture.* American Society of Missiology Series 42. Maryknoll, NY: Orbis, 1991.
Shaw, Mark, and Wanjiru Gitau. *The Kingdom of God in Africa: A History of African Christianity.* Rev. ed. Carlisle, UK: Langham, 2020.
Stinton, Diane. *Jesus of Africa: Voices of Contemporary African Christology.* Nairobi: Paulines, 2004.
Sundkler, Bengt, and Christopher Steed. *A History of the Church in Africa.* Studia Missionalia Upsaliensia 74. Cambridge: Cambridge University Press, 2004.
Thornton, John K. *The Kongolese St. Anthony: Dona Beatriz Kimpa Vita and the Anthonian Movement, 1684–1706.* Cambridge: Cambridge University Press, 1998.
Walls, Andrew F. *The Cross-Cultural Process in Christian History.* Maryknoll, NY: Orbis, 2002.
———. *The Missionary Movement in Christian History: Studies in the Transmission of Faith.* Maryknoll, NY: Orbis, 1996.
Whatmore, Richard, and Brian Young, eds. *Palgrave Advances in Intellectual History.* Palgrave Advances. New York: Palgrave Macmillan, 2006.
Wilhite, David E. *Ancient African Christianity: An Introduction to a Unique Context and Tradition.* New York: Routledge 2017.

Timeline: Africa

BRETT KNOWLES

AMERICAN CHURCH HISTORIAN MARTIN Marty has aptly commented that (in religion as elsewhere) "both hurricanes and glacial forces leave altered landscapes."[1] The hurricane represents sudden, drastic change, the product of clearly identifiable catalytic events such as, for example, the arrival of Vasco da Gama in India in 1498. By contrast, the glacier represents a process of gradual, subtle change, which may not be attributable to any specific causative event or series of events. These glacial forces therefore symbolize slow, cumulative progressions of attitudes and orientations, which cannot always be placed within a timeline of dates in the same way as catalytic hurricane events.

Nevertheless, events are significant markers of historical process, and the entries in this timeline cover the history of African Christianity from the second century CE up to the present day. Country locations are placed in bold type at the end of each entry and are derived from the website of the United Nations, Department of Economic and Social Affairs, Statistics Division;[2] those territories not listed in that website are enclosed in parentheses, e.g., (**Canary Islands**), (**Ceuta**), and (**Somaliland**). Continental entries, with no specific country location, are cited in brackets, e.g., [**Africa**].

Two additional categories have been included. Where the entry refers to an event in the Greco-Roman world (which comprised parts of Asia, Africa, and Europe, up to the end of Justinian's reign in 565), this is indicated by the annotation [**Greco-Roman World:** ...] preceding the country entry. Similarly, if the geographical location of the entry is in the Middle East (and is included in *Surviving Jewel: The Story of Christianity in the Middle East*,

---

1. Marty, "Introduction," 1.
2. See http://unstats.un.org/unsd/methodology/m49/.

the first volume in the Global Story of Christianity series[3]), this is indicated by the annotation [**Middle East: ...**] preceding the country entry.

Year and Event

ca. 120–60 Basilides (fl. ca. 120–145), a teacher in Alexandria, begins to expound gnostic ideas, interpreting Christianity through a dualistic mindset that focusses on the acquisition of gnōsis (secret esoteric knowledge); this interpretive framework is further spread in Egypt by his disciple Valentinus (fl. ca. 136–60), gaining numbers of adherents. [**Greco-Roman World, Middle East: Egypt**]

180 The first persecution in the province of Africa Proconsularis takes place under the proconsul Saturninus, in which twelve Christians (the martyrs of Scilli) are brought to trial and executed at Carthage. [**Greco-Roman World: Tunisia**]

ca. 190 Clement of Alexandria succeeds Pantaenus as the head of the catechetical school at Alexandria and lays the foundation for the integration of philosophy and Christian belief in the formulation of theology. [**Greco-Roman World, Middle East: Egypt**]

ca. 197 Tertullian, the first important Christian writer in Latin, addresses his *Apology* to the imperial governors and magistrates, arguing that persecution of Christians is contrary to justice and to Roman legal precedence, and demonstrating the reasonableness of Christianity. [**Greco-Roman World: Tunisia**]

203 The Roman authorities arrest several Christians, including Perpetua and Felicitas, but fail to persuade them to sacrifice to the emperor; these women are martyred by being exposed to wild beasts in the arena at Carthage. [**Greco-Roman World: Tunisia**]

207 Tertullian leaves the Catholic Church and joins the Montanists; this indicates that the latter are broadly doctrinally orthodox, despite their opponents' accusations to the contrary. [**Greco-Roman World: Tunisia**]

---

3. Raheb and Lamport, *Surviving Jewel*.

ca. 220–230   Origen writes *De principiis* (On first principles), the first Christian systematic theology. [**Greco-Roman World, Middle East: Egypt**]

231   The church of Caesarea ordains Origen as a presbyter, but this ordination is held to be invalid because he had made himself a eunuch (based on his literal interpretation of Matt 19:12); consequently, he is excommunicated by his home church of Alexandria. [**Greco-Roman World, Middle East: Egypt**]

250–251   The emperor Decius launches the first official, empire-wide persecution of Christians (previous persecutions had been sporadic outbreaks of local mob violence, rather than the product of imperial policy); records of this persecution come from Rome, Jerusalem, Antioch, and, especially, Carthage. [**Greco-Roman World**]

251   Cyprian, bishop of Carthage, writes *De unitate catholicae ecclesiae* (On the unity of the Catholic Church), insisting that schism violates the essential nature of the church, the unity of which is focused on its bishops; this episcopal network guarantees the cohesion of the whole diverse body. [**Greco-Roman World: Tunisia**]

258   Although he had fled to lead his church from hiding during the Decian persecution (249–51), Cyprian of Carthage is arrested and martyred in the later persecution under Valerian. [**Greco-Roman World: Tunisia**]

ca. 270   Antony of Egypt goes into the desert as an ascetic hermit, laying the foundations for the monastic movement; this solitary asceticism develops into an organized community by 305. [**Greco-Roman World, Middle East: Egypt**]

311–312   The election of Bishop Caecilian of Carthage leads to the rise of the Donatists as a "church of the pure," who had maintained a steadfast testimony in persecution, in contrast to those African Catholics who had handed over their copies of the Scriptures to be burned. [**Greco-Roman World: Algeria, Tunisia**]

318   Arius, a presbyter of the church of Alexandria, takes issue with a sermon by its bishop, Alexander, and questions whether the Son could be said to be God in the same way that the Father

was; this local dispute escalates into the empire-wide Arian controversy by 324. [**Greco-Roman World, Middle East: Egypt**]

320s Pachomius founds a new type of community in the Thēbaïd desert in southern Egypt, patterned on cenobitic monasticism (the Christian life lived in community, rather than in ascetic isolation). [**Greco-Roman World, Middle East: Egypt**]

328 Athanasius, the steadfast defender of the Creed of Nicaea against its Arian opponents, becomes bishop of Alexandria. [**Greco-Roman World, Middle East: Egypt**]

Before 356 Following his shipwreck in the Red Sea while returning from a missionary journey to India with his guardian, Frumentius becomes an official in the Aksumite court of King Ella Amida, where he converts members of the king's household; after going back to Egypt some years later he is consecrated in Alexandria and returns to Ethiopia as bishop of Aksum. [**Eritrea, Ethiopia**]

367 Athanasius sets out the canonical books of the New Testament, the first such list that exactly matches our current canon. [**Greco-Roman World, Middle East: Egypt**]

385 Augustine of Hippo abandons Manichaeism (a dualistic religion that saw the world as a cosmic warfare between the eternal principles of light and darkness, both conceived in material terms), although elements of this might have continued to influence his views on the transmission of original sin. [**Greco-Roman World: Tunisia**]

395 Augustine becomes a coadjutor bishop at Hippo and sole bishop the following year. [**Greco-Roman World: Tunisia**]

412 Cyril becomes the bishop of Alexandria and begins to ruthlessly suppress dissent (e.g., his nonintervention in the murder of the Neoplatonist teacher Hypatia by a mob in 415 and his attacks on Nestorius, whose condemnation by the Council of Ephesus in 431 is largely due to Cyril's machinations). [**Greco-Roman World, Middle East: Egypt**]

418	The Council of Carthage condemns Pelagianism (an emphasis on the role of human works in the obtaining of salvation). [Greco-Roman World: Tunisia]
452–457	A theological revolt in Egypt in 452 leads to the establishment of Coptic monophysite/miaphysite (one nature) churches in Egypt and Ethiopia; five years later, the Chalcedonian dyophysite (two nature) patriarch of Alexandria is killed in a street riot. [Greco-Roman World, Middle East: Egypt]
Before 480	A group of Dyophysite Syrian monks known as the Nine Saints arrives in Aksum, where they convert its inhabitants, set up monasteries, and translate the Bible into Ge'ez. [Eritrea, Ethiopia]
520	Kaleb, the king of Aksum, invades Yemen, where the Ḥimyarite king Dhū Nuwās is persecuting Christians; Kaleb defeats him, leading to southern Arabia becoming a Christian territory under Ethiopian hegemony for the next fifty years. [Eritrea, Ethiopia]
527–565	The emperor Justinian seeks to restore the Roman Empire in the West, abolish the last remnants of paganism, and strengthen the Orthodox Church; he achieves these aims by building splendid churches such as the Hagia Sophia (holy wisdom), by codifying its liturgy, and by consolidating Roman law on a Christian basis (the Code of Justinian). [Greco-Roman World: Algeria, Libya, Morocco, Tunisia]
543	The monophysite monk Julian (sent by the Byzantine empress Theodora) arrives in the kingdom of Nobatia, where he converts the royal court to monophysitism and facilitates Christianity's spread throughout the kingdom. [Sudan]
569	Makouria, the central and smallest African Nubian kingdom, converts from monophysitism to Chalcedonian Christianity. [Sudan]
580	The Egyptian bishop of Philae converts Alwa/Alodia, the southernmost Nubian kingdom, to monophysite Christianity. [Sudan]

640–670   The Arab takeover of Egypt and North Africa extends along the Mediterranean coast to Tunis; but further south, two attacks on northern Nubia are driven back by Nubian archers (known as the "pupil-piercers" because of their accuracy), leading to a *baqt* (pact) recognizing Nubia's independence. [Middle East: Egypt, Libya, Sudan]

665–689   The Arabs extend their conquests of North Africa from Tunis to Morocco, thus bringing all coastal North Africa under Muslim control. [Algeria, Morocco, Tunisia]

By 701   Makouria annexes its northern neighbor Nobatia, with the enlarged state adhering to monophysite Christianity. [Sudan]

739   The inscriptions of the monk Theophilus on the walls of his cave dwelling near Faras include the famous Rotas-Sator palindrome, indicating Nubia's ongoing links with the wider Christian world. [Sudan]

836   King Georgios I of Makouria visits Baghdād and reaffirms the *baqt* of ca. 650 with the 'Abbasid Caliphate; under his rule, Makouria becomes powerful, with a strong alliance between the Nubian church and the Nubian state. [Sudan]

969–1171   The Isma'ili Shi'a Fatimid Caliphate conquers Egypt, eventually extending the territory from the Red Sea to the Atlantic Ocean; it adopts a largely tolerant attitude toward Christians and Jews. [Middle East: Egypt]

1009–1016   Abu 'Ali al-Ḥākim bi-'Amr-Allāh (the "Mad Caliph") persecutes the Coptic Church in Egypt. [Middle East: Egypt]

1076   A letter from Pope Gregory VII notes that Bishop Cyriacus of Carthage is the last remaining bishop in Africa; the last Christian epigraphy in North Africa also dates from this time. [Tunisia]

1114   Despite an almost total Muslim dominance in North Africa, a Christian community survives at Al Qal'a of Beni Hammad, the first capital of the Hammamid emirs. [Algeria]

1176   The *Liber Censuum Romanae Ecclesiae* (Census book of the Roman Church), the authoritative financial record of the real

	estate revenues of the papacy from 492 to 1192, makes the last reference to Carthage as an episcopal see; no further Carthaginian bishops are known after this date. [**Tunisia**]
1219	St. Francis of Assisi goes to Egypt on a peacemaking mission, crossing the Crusader-Saracen battle lines at Damietta to preach to Sultan al-Malek al-Kāmel Nāṣer-al-dīn of Egypt, but without success. [**Middle East: Egypt**]
1220	Berard of Carbio OFM and four other Franciscan friars go to Spain, Portugal, and North Africa to preach to the Muslims, but are martyred in Marrakesh, Morocco. [**Morocco**]
1250	The Mamlūks, a non-Arab knightly "slave soldier" caste, seize power in Egypt from the Ayyubid dynasty, adopting a hostile stance toward the Coptic Christians and decisively advancing the Islamization of Egypt. [**Middle East: Egypt**]
1272	Dawud I, the Christian king of Makouria, launches an unwise attack on the Egyptian Red Sea seaport of Aidhab (despite the terms of the *baqt* treaty with its rulers), leading to a retaliatory invasion under Mamlūk Sultan Baybars. [**Sudan**]
1279	Mamlūk repression intensifies toward the Coptic Christians, with forty-four churches being destroyed in Cairo alone between 1279 and 1447. [**Middle East: Egypt**]
1293	The Catalan mystic and poet Ramon Llull makes the first of his missionary journeys to Tunis. [**Tunisia**]
1315	The Muslim government of Egypt installs a Nubian Muslim as King Saif ad-Dīn 'Abdullah Bershambo of Makouria, thus making the country officially Muslim. [**Sudan**]
1317	The conversion of the cathedral in Dongola, the capital of Makouria, into a mosque contributes to the extinction of Christianity there. [**Sudan**]
1337	The Ethiopian church begins a period of aggressive evangelization by force of arms as part of a pursuit of cultural hegemony by the Ethiopian warrior king Amda-Simon. [**Djibouti, Ethiopia, (Somaliland)**]

1415	The Portuguese make a surprise assault across the Straits of Gibraltar to seize Ceuta, thereby gaining their first foothold in Africa, which is later taken over by Spain; this attack marks the beginning of European colonialism in Africa. [(**Ceuta**)]
1416	The Portuguese prince Henry ("the Navigator") initiates voyages of exploration down the coast of West Africa; these are made possible by the invention of the caravel, a newer, lighter, and more maneuverable sailing vessel with lateen sails, which could travel further and faster, as well as sail "into the wind." [**Cabo Verde, Gambia, Guinea, Guinea-Bissau, Mauritania, Senegal, Sierra Leone, Western Sahara**]
1432	The Portuguese king Afonso V begins his reign; he is known as "the African" for his military campaigns and conquests in Morocco, which mark the beginnings of Portuguese exploration and expansion in Africa. [**Morocco**]
1434	The Portuguese explorer Gil Eanes reaches Cape Bojador on the coast of West Africa, a significant milestone in the European exploration of Africa. [**Western Sahara**]
1435	Pope Eugene IV's papal bull *Sicut dudum* forbids the enslavement of the native peoples in the Canary Islands, but this is ignored by the Spanish colonizers. [(**Canary Islands**)]
1436	The emperor Zara' Ya'eqob reforms the Ethiopian Church and attempts to resolve its long-running Sabbatarian controversy, although this schism does not end until 1450. [**Ethiopia**]
1439	Pope Eugene IV invites the Coptic patriarch John XI to attend the ecumenical Council of Florence, attempting to reestablish contact between the Catholic and the Coptic churches. [**Middle East: Egypt**]
1482	A Portuguese expedition under Diogo de Azambuja constructs the Castelo of São Jorge da Mina (the castle of St. George of the mine), the oldest European building south of the Sahara, at Elmina on the Gold Coast, as a fortified base for trading with the whole of West Africa; although this base also has a missionary focus, its resident chaplains are primarily concerned with the European enclave, and have little impact on African peoples. [**Ghana**]

1483	Portuguese ships arrive off the coast of Kongo, beginning a Catholic mission that survives, in indigenized form, until the late nineteenth century. [**Angola, Congo, DRC**]
1491	The baptisms of Nzinga a Nkuwu (who takes the title of King João I of Kongo) and of his son, Mvemba a Nzinga (who becomes King Afonso I in 1506), lead to their patronage of the Catholic mission in Kongo until 1543. [**Angola, Congo, DRC**]
1494	The Portuguese explorer Pero da Covilhão arrives in Ethiopia and claims its Emperor Eskender as Prester John; however, Da Covilhão is not permitted to leave Ethiopia and dies there thirty years later. [**Ethiopia**]
1500	Despite the eclipse of Christianity in neighboring Makouria 183 years earlier, the Christian kingdom of Alwa appears to have survived until about 1500, although a successor Islamic state is founded in 1504. [**Sudan**]
1515	The first missionaries reach the kingdom of Benin, where accounts of a distant chief monarch to the East, who had sent the newly crowned king of Benin a cross, lead them to believe that they have at last found Prester John. [**Benin**]
1517	The Ottoman Turks occupy Egypt, cutting off contacts between the Coptic Church and the West for more than a century. [**Middle East: Egypt**]
1520	Dom Henrique, the brother of King Afonso I of Kongo, becomes the titular bishop of the province of Utica (Tunisia) and, as such, the first African Catholic bishop. [**Angola, Congo, DRC**]
1530s	Both Sao Tome and Cabo Verde become independent Catholic dioceses and for several centuries provide priests at irregular intervals for the African mainland. [**Cabo Verde, Sao Tome and Principe**]
1531	Vicente Pegado, captain of the Portuguese river garrison of Sofala in Mozambique, records accounts of the ruined city of Great Zimbabwe, which apparently had been abandoned about 1450. [**Zimbabwe**]

1531–1543   Islamic jihāds from the neighboring state of Adal destroy monasteries, churches, and libraries in Ethiopia, but Portuguese help arrives in 1541, leading to the defeat of the Muslim general Imām Aḥmad ibn Ibrāhim al-Ghāzi. [**Ethiopia**]

1534   Despite its vigorous growth under the patronage of the Kongolese Christian king Afonso I (Mvemba a Nzinga), the pope places the church in the Kongo under the bishopric of Sao Tome, thus maintaining Portuguese rights of control under *patronado* (system of patronage); despite the steady export of Kongolese slaves to Sao Tome, this episcopal control would remain in place until 1596. [**Angola, Congo, DRC, Sao Tome, Principe**]

1540   A group of plotters (including some Portuguese residents) attempt to assassinate King Afonso I at an Easter Day service, in response to his opposition to the Portuguese-controlled slave trade. [**Angola, Congo, DRC**]

1543   Although half of Kongo's population of four million has by now become Christian, a large Portuguese-controlled trade continues in slaves (many of whom also were Christian) with the Americas. [**Angola, Congo, DRC**]

1553   The Jesuits found a new mission at Luanda (Angola), after being expelled from Kongo following tensions with its King Diogo I Nkumbi a Mpudi. [**Angola, Congo, DRC**]

1568   Roving bands of Yaka Jaga warriors invade Kongo, destroying San Salvador and burning churches, the king regaining his capital only with Portuguese aid. [**Angola, Congo, DRC**]

1570s   Christianity arrives in the Niger Delta kingdom of Warri and survives until the end of the eighteenth century, despite long periods without missionaries. [**Nigeria**]

1571   Under the leadership of Bartolomeu Dias's grandson, the Portuguese establish Angola as a private proprietary colony, in a format like that of the Virginia colony later set up by the British in the Americas. [**Angola**]

1596	Rome makes San Salvador (Kongo) a see in its own right to break the Portuguese monopoly on religion in the area. [Angola, Congo, DRC]
1604	The Jesuit mission in Cabo Verde begins, partly through the urging of Balthasar Barreira, a Portuguese-African layman who had previously worked with the Jesuits for thirteen years in Angola. [Cabo Verde]
1622	The Ethiopian emperor Susneyos converts to Catholicism through the influence of the Spanish Jesuit missionary Pedro Paez. [Ethiopia]
1632	The emperor Susneyos abdicates in favor of his non-Catholic son Fasildas to end hard-line Catholic demands and to avoid a civil war; this leads to the expulsion of the Jesuits and other Catholic missionaries, two centuries of closure to all Europeans, and an enduring heritage of distrust. [Ethiopia]
1644	The French Capuchins start a mission in Whydah but are later expelled by English and Dutch slave traders; the area becomes (with neighboring Togo) the center of the slave export trade in the 1670s and known as "the Slave Coast." [Benin, Togo]
1645	Pope Innocent X creates a prefecture apostolic for Kongo and puts this in the hands of the Italian Capuchins (a strict Franciscan rule). [Angola, Congo, DRC]
1652	The Dutch establish a settlement at the Cape of Good Hope to safeguard their trade routes to India and the East Indies; this settlement has significance for Christian mission only to the extent that the Khoikhoi local people became "Dutchified," adopting Dutch ways of living, including their Protestant religion. [South Africa]
1665	The Angolan invasion of Kongo weakens Kongolese Christianity, leading to the later emergence of several women prophets, the most significant of these being Dona Beatriz Kimpa Vita. [Angola, Congo, DRC]
1686	Black Catholic Lourenço da Silva de Mendouça (who, although a layman, claims descent from the kings of Kongo and

Angola) petitions the Vatican against perpetual slavery and the cruelty that accompanies it. [**Angola**]

1700s Both the Kongo nation and the Kongo church begin a long period of decline that will extend throughout the eighteenth century. [**Angola, Congo, DRC**]

1710–1711 Two Franciscan friars, Carlo Maria de Genova and Severino da Silesia, cross the Sahara from Tripoli to contact Christians reported to be among the Kwararafa people, but die of sickness in Katsina, northern Nigeria. [**Libya, Niger, Nigeria**]

1738 German Moravian missionary Georg Schmidt builds a farm at Genadendal (Valley of Grace) near Cape Town and preaches to his Khoikhoi farmhands, baptizing some of them; despite this success, the Dutch Reformed Church in the Netherlands nevertheless expels him as a heretic in 1744, claiming that he had been improperly ordained and that only Dutch Reformed ministers had the authority to baptize. [**South Africa**]

1742 Former Ghanaian slave Jacobus Capitein presents his doctoral dissertation to Leiden University, defending the slave trade as compatible with Christianity; he later becomes a Dutch Reformed minister in Ghana. [**Ghana**]

1742 The Nubian servant of a Franciscan friar in Cairo reports that a single isolated Christian community still exists, despite persecution, in the Third Cataract region of Nubia. [**Sudan**]

1752 The Anglican SPG sends its first missionary, Thomas Thompson, to the Cape Coast (Ghana), where he concentrates on ministry to the local people, rather than on a chaplaincy to the expatriate enclaves. [**Ghana**]

1765 After being taken to England as a child for his education by an Anglican SPG missionary, Fante Christian Philip Quaque studies theology and becomes the first ordained African priest in the Church of England; as such, he succeeds Thomas Thompson as chaplain at Cape Coast Castle (a transfer station for the slave trade) in 1766 and works there for the next fifty years. [**Ghana**]

1772   French-born Philadelphia Quaker and abolitionist Anthony Benezet publishes his pamphlet *Some Historical Account of Guinea* attacking the slave trade and the institution of slavery; he also founds one of the first anti-slavery societies, the Society for the Relief of Free Negroes Unlawfully Held in Bondage in 1775. [**Guinea**]

1787   The British Crown founds a settlement in Sierra Leone for freed slaves and the dregs of London society, but this is not initially successful as a local chieftain burns it to the ground two years later, necessitating its rebuilding in 1791. [**Sierra Leone**]

1787   The Fante abolitionist Ottobah Cugoano publishes his *Thoughts and Sentiments on the Evil and Wicked Traffic of the Slavery and Commerce of the Human Species, Humbly Submitted to the Inhabitants of Great-Britain*, calling for the abolition of slavery and the immediate emancipation of all slaves. [**Ghana**]

1789   Well-known freed Igbo slave Olaudah Equiano (aka Gustavus Vassa) publishes his book, *The Interesting Narrative of the Life of Olaudah Equiano, or Gustavus Vassa, the African*, an articulate, intelligent, English-speaking African voice against slavery. [**Nigeria**]

1792   A party of Nova Scotians (i.e., black Canadians whose ancestors had fled the colonial United States as slaves or freemen) arrives in Sierra Leone, with Bibles in hand and singing hymns; their arrival represents a refounding of the Sierra Leone settlement. [**Sierra Leone**]

1792   Moravian missionaries return to South Africa and find that the converts of the pioneer missionary Georg Schmidt had not only survived despite official opposition, but also continued to meet under the same tree where he had taught them to read the Bible and pray fifty-five years earlier. [**South Africa**]

1799   The Dutch LMS missionary Johannes van der Kemp arrives in Cape Town to begin missionary work, initially among the Xhosa, but later among the Khoikhoi. [**South Africa**]

1806	The British set up the Cape Colony at the Cape of Good Hope, superseding the Dutch, who had maintained a colony there for much of the previous 150 years; Protestant missions in southern Africa begin in earnest from this new starting point. [**South Africa**]
1807	Following its abolition of the slave trade, the British Parliament sends a naval squadron to patrol the West Coast of Africa, intercept transatlantic slave ships, and repatriate the freed slaves to Sierra Leone. [**Sierra Leone**]
1810	The Dutch LMS missionary Johannes van der Kemp proposes the holding of a world missionary conference in Cape Town; this eventually takes place (one hundred years later) in Edinburgh, Scotland. [**South Africa**]
1811	The British war with the Xhosa leads to the emergence of several prophet leaders with differing responses to the injustices that the Xhosa faced; these include Makhanda Nxele, who encourages war against the whites, and Ntsikana, who advocates a retreat into a mystical indigenous form of African Christianity. [**South Africa**]
1811	The German LMS missionary Heinrich Schmelen begins his missionary work among the nomadic Nama tribes of South Africa and Namibia, trekking with them to |Ui‡gandes near the Atlantic Coast, where he builds a mission station which he names Bethanie; his cottage there, erected in 1814, is long regarded as the oldest surviving building in Namibia (although the ruined fortifications at ǁKhauxa!nas predate European settlement).[4] [**Namibia**]
1816	The creation of the Zulu Empire under Shaka contributes to the Mfecane (Zulu: lit. "grinding," i.e., the mass migration of tribes fleeing Zulu expansion from 1820 on), and ultimately to the wider spread of Christianity across southern Africa. [**South Africa**]
1817	Scottish LMS missionary Robert Moffat arrives in South Africa to begin fifty-three years of missionary work; four years after his arrival, he sets up a mission station at Kuruman,

---

4. The symbols |, ‡, ǁ, and ! represent "click" sounds in the Khoikhoi language.

which becomes a flourishing oasis (due to the local springs and to Moffat's models of irrigation) and a model for other mission stations, although the Christian community there remains small. [**South Africa**]

1819   A group of St. Joseph of Cluny sisters, the first group of women missionaries in Africa, settle on Gorée Island, Senegal; however, Mother Javouhey, their foundress, stays only four years, being invalided home to France in 1823, where King Louis Phillipe pays her the highest praise he can think of: "Madame Javouhey! Mais c'est un grand homme!" (Madame Javouhey! But she's a great man!).[5] [**Senegal**]

1820   LMS Missionaries arrive in Madagascar at the invitation of its King Radama I and establish a mission enterprise that flourishes in the decades that follow, despite persecution after Radama's death in 1828. [**Madagascar**]

1820   Scottish missionary Dr. John Philip becomes the LMS superintendent at the Cape Colony, remaining in this role until his death, but attracting enduring hostility from the settlers for his sustained opposition to their oppression of the natives. [**South Africa**]

1822   The American Colonization Society, established in 1816 by Presbyterian minister Robert Finlay and other influential figures in the white community to facilitate the transporting of freeborn blacks and emancipated slaves from America to the West Coast of Africa, sets up a colony at Cape Mesurado, Liberia. [**Liberia**]

1828   Four Swiss Basel Mission missionaries come to Ghana in response to African invitations; three of them soon die due to the unhealthy environment in which they set up their mission, with the survivor, Andreas Riis, being saved only by the administrations of an African herbalist. [**Ghana**]

1829   Khoikhoi settlers at the Kat River choose the LMS missionary James Read as their minister, thus forming the first independent black church (as distinct from mission) in South Africa. [**South Africa**]

---

5. Curtis, *Civilizing Habits*, 260.

1830s	A Swiss Basel Mission missionary, Samuel Gobat, working under the auspices of the CMS, makes two brief sojourns in Ethiopia, where he seeks to reform Ethiopian religion to bring it more in line with Protestantism. [**Ethiopia**]
1833	The Bamokoteli chieftain Moshoeshoe invites members of the Paris Evangelical Missionary Society to Lesotho, although this is largely for economic and diplomatic, rather than religious, reasons; he finally seeks baptism on his deathbed in 1870. [**Lesotho**]
1834–35	The Cape frontier war highlights differences in missionary attitudes toward the Xhosa, with Wesleyan missionary William Shrewsbury advocating driving back the Xhosa "invasion," and LMS superintendent John Philip opposing the war. [**South Africa**]
1835	Black Brazilians (i.e., repatriated Afro-Brazilian freed slaves) become influential in the growth of West African Christianity (a female example being Venossa de Jesus, who builds a church in Agoué, Benin). [**Benin**]
1835–1840	The first waves of the "Great Trek" of Boer pastoralists and Cape Dutch citizens leave the British-controlled Cape Colony and move north into the interior of what is now South Africa, taking the Dutch Reformed faith with them. [**South Africa**]
1835–1861	The reigning chieftainess Ranavalona I, the widow of King Radama I, leads a hostile reaction against foreigners and Christians, apparently perceiving them as a subversive fifth column; nevertheless, the church survives during these years of persecution as a growing, self-propagating church, being led entirely by Malagasy Christians. [**Madagascar**]
1838	The Catholic Church consecrates Antony Dupuch as the first Catholic bishop of Algiers in modern times. [**Algeria**]
1838	Methodist Eurafrican missionary Thomas Birch Freeman arrives in Ghana, where he sets up churches and schools; he also visits Togo and Benin, and later begins a mission in Nigeria. [**Benin, Ghana, Nigeria, Togo**]

1839   Two Catholic missionaries, French Lazarist Justin de Jacobus and Italian Capuchin Guglielmo Massaja, begin work in Ethiopia. [**Ethiopia**]

1841   The Glasgow Missionary Society founds the Lovedale Missionary Institute, an important educational institute in the development of African education, in Lovedale, Ciskei. [**South Africa**]

1841   The Niger Expedition sends three British vessels to the Niger River as part of a grandiose New Africa policy to make treaties with the native peoples, to introduce Christianity, and to promote increased trade. [**Nigeria**]

1841–1842   The Congregation of the Sacred Heart of Mary, founded as a mission to newly freed slaves in the French colonies, sends missionary Fathers Jacques-Desire Laval and Frédéric Le Vavasseur to Mauritius, and Father Eugene Tisserant to Réunion; their success in these Indian Ocean islands secures a base for Catholic mission in Madagascar and throughout the whole of East Africa. [**Mauritius, Réunion**]

1842   The Ethiopian emperor expels all missionaries, including the German CMS missionary and explorer Johann Ludwig Krapf; as a result, Krapf transfers his activities to Zanzibar and Kenya two years later. [**Ethiopia**]

1842   The first Protestant missionaries (from the ABCFM) arrive in Gabon; the first French Catholic missionaries (the Holy Ghost Fathers) follow them two years later. [**Gabon**]

1843   The Anglican Church ordains Samuel Ajayi Crowther, previously well known for his role in the 1841 Niger Expedition, in England as its first African priest; he then returns to Africa to work in Yorubaland. [**Benin, Nigeria, Togo**]

1844   German mission pioneer Johann Ludwig Krapf arrives in Zanzibar and eventually sets up base in Mombasa but has little missionary success (although he leaves a legacy in the study of the Swahili language). [**Kenya, United Republic of Tanzania**]

1846   Black and white Christians from Jamaica, led by Scottish Missionary Society missionary Hope M. Waddell, found the

United Presbyterian mission in Calabar; this mission later becomes famous for Mary Slessor's long residence there. [**Nigeria**]

1846   The Vatican appoints the Maltese prelate Annetto Casolini as the first apostolic vicar of Central Africa; following his appointment, Casolini leads a mission to the Sudan, reaching the Nile Valley and Khartoum in 1848. [**Sudan**]

1846   The Vatican subdivides Ethiopia into two apostolic vicariates, with the Lazarists receiving the responsibility for Abyssinia and the Capuchins for Galla. [**Ethiopia**]

1847   Liberia achieves political independence from America as the first African country to gain independence from the colonial powers. [**Liberia**]

1847   Seven years after first arriving in Africa, David Livingstone reaches Kolobeng, Botswana, his third and final mission station; while here, he converts his only African convert, Sechele I, the Kgosi (hereditary leader) of the Bakwena tribe, to Christianity. [**Botswana**]

1847   The high church Anglo-Catholic Robert Gray becomes the first bishop of Cape Town, but later clashes with the low church evangelical bishop of Natal, John Colenso, over the issue of biblical criticism. [**South Africa**]

1853–1856   David Livingstone, the first European to cross the African continent, begins his explorations of the African interior; however, this transcontinental journey had been attempted fifty years previously by two African *pombeiros* (agents of Portuguese merchants). [**Angola, DRC, Malawi, Mozambique, United Republic of Tanzania, Zambia, Zimbabwe**]

1855   The *dajazmach* (commander of the gate) Kasa seizes the imperial throne, taking the messianic name Tewodros (Theodore, or "gift of God") and (in his words) seeking to "reform Abyssinia, restore the Christian faith and become master of the world."[6] [**Ethiopia**]

1856   After walking west to east across Africa from Luanda to Quelimane, David Livingstone returns to England, fueling immense

6. Hill, *History of Christianity*, 388.

excitement about opportunities for "commerce and Christianity" in Africa. [**Angola, Mozambique, Zambia, Zimbabwe**]

1857   After several decades of persecution in Madagascar (during which time Christians are forced to go into hiding, to flee to the Malagasy countryside, or to take refuge on the neighboring islands of Mauritius, Réunion, and Nosy-Bé), oppression of the Christians begins to diminish, finally ending in 1861. [**Madagascar, Mauritius, Réunion**]

1857   Despite sharing a similar Reformed faith, white Boer Christians now require the coloreds (i.e., the Griquas) to worship in separate chapels from the Europeans. [**South Africa**]

1857   Samuel Ajayi Crowther becomes the leader of the Niger Mission, but this later declines when a committee of Europeans undercuts his authority and takes over the mission's "temporalities" in 1879; it becomes effectively defunct by the time of Crowther's death in 1891. [**Nigeria**]

1857   The publication of David Livingstone's best-selling book *Missionary Travels and Researches in South Africa* reinforces his public reputation as a heroic explorer, who had made contributions to geography, medicine, and science, as well as to missionary work and the abolition of the slave trade. [**South Africa**]

1858   Livingstone's influence helps to create the UMCA, an Anglican enterprise having as its initial objective Lake Nyasa and the Shiré Valley; this mission field comes to be known as "Livingstonia." [**Malawi**]

ca. 1860   A German LMS missionary baptizes Kgama, who later becomes Kgosi Kgama III of the Ngwato, founding a Christian state with a well-organized, well-funded, independent government dominated by Christians. [**Botswana**]

ca. 1860   The circulation of Bibles in Eritrea by the British and Foreign Bible Society leads to the emergence of an Eritrean religious movement like a Protestant Reformation. [**Eritrea**]

1861   The establishment of a CMS native pastorate marks the first step toward a self-governing national church and the "euthanasia" of mission in Sierra Leone. [**Sierra Leone**]

1861	The recently enthroned king Radama II proclaims religious freedom, releases imprisoned Christians, and enables LMS missions to return to Madagascar; Catholics, Anglicans, Norwegian Lutherans, and Quakers also arrive to begin missionary work. [**Madagascar**]
1863	Bishop Robert Gray of Cape Town deposes his colleague, Bishop John Colenso of Natal, for his liberal views on biblical criticism, but the Privy Council overturns this decision on an appeal. [**South Africa**]
1864	The Anglican UMCA relocates to Zanzibar after a disastrous failure to establish a mission in Malawi in 1861, later founding new missions on the mainland from this base. [**Malawi, United Republic of Tanzania**]
1864	Two French priests (Holy Ghost Fathers Edward Blanchet and Joseph Koeberle), together with an Irish lay brother, arrive in Freetown, Sierra Leone, to begin Catholic missions. [**Sierra Leone**]
1864	Yoruba clergyman and linguist Samuel Ajayi Crowther, already well known as the leader of the Niger Mission, becomes bishop of the Niger, the mother diocese of the Church of Nigeria and, as such, the first black Anglican bishop in West Africa. [**Nigeria**]
1868	All of the LMS-associated Protestant congregations in Madagascar combine to form the Madagascar Congregational Union (the *Isan-enim-bolana*; lit. "every six months," a reference to their half-yearly meetings) as a step toward an autonomous Malagasy church. [**Madagascar**]
1868	French archbishop Charles Lavigerie of Algiers (later to become cardinal archbishop of Carthage and the primate of Africa) founds the Society of Missionaries of Africa (the White Fathers) in Algeria. [**Algeria**]
1868	Ranavalona II (widow of King Radama II, murdered in 1863) becomes the queen of Madagascar and approves Protestant missionary work in her country. [**Madagascar**]

1871	Welsh explorer and journalist Sir Henry Morton Stanley encounters Livingstone (who had been out of contact with the outside world for six years) at Ujiji on the shores of Lake Tanganyika, with the famous phrase "Doctor Livingstone, I presume?"[7] [**United Republic of Tanzania**]
1873	David Livingstone dies, from malaria and hemorrhoids, at Chitambo, Zambia, where his two coworkers, Susi and Chuma, remove his heart and viscera, burying these under a tree close to the location of his death, preserve the remainder of his body, and carry it on foot to the coast (a journey of nine months), at last carefully laying it on the porch of the church in Bagamoyo with the simple words "Mwili wa Daudi" (David's body);[8] it is then returned to Britain for eventual burial in Westminster Abbey. [**Zambia**]
1874	Sir Henry Morton Stanley returns to Uganda, teaching the principles of the Christian faith to King Mutesa I Walugembe Mukaabya of Buganda, thereby creating opportunities for later missionaries. [**Uganda**]
1877	The CMS establishes Protestant missions in Buganda (a subnational kingdom in Uganda), and the success of these marks the turn of the tide for East African missionary work. [**Uganda**]
1878	The Council of Boru-Meda, under the new emperor Yohannes IV, attempts to resolve the long-standing christological divisions in the Ethiopian church, bring about Muslim conversions, and rebuild Ethiopia. [**Ethiopia**]
1878	The English Baptists set up a chain of mission stations extending along fifteen hundred kilometers of the Congo River from Lake Malebo to Kisangani. [**Congo, DRC**]
1879 on	Intense missionary rivalry emerges between the Protestant CMS missionaries and the Catholic White Fathers in the Bugandan royal court, as well as between the embryonic Bugandan congregations; issues include the misuse of the Bible by inexperienced catechumens and the place of the title "Mary, Mother of God" in prayer and worship. [**Uganda**]

7. See the fuller story in Stanley, *How I Found Livingstone*.
8. Sundkler and Steed, *History of the Church*, 458–59.

1880s	The Church of Ethiopia makes several short-lived attempts to come into union with the Russian Orthodox Church, partly from religious motives and partly to offset the encroachment of French, British, and Italian imperialism. [**Ethiopia**]
1883	Evangelist Nehemiah Tile leaves the Wesleyan mission in the eastern Cape and sets up the Thembu National Church, the first independent African church and a forerunner of the AICs. [**South Africa**]
1884	French occupation of Tunisia creates a favorable environment for the establishment of a Catholic hierarchy, leading to the revival of the ancient archbishopric of Carthage. [**Tunisia**]
1885	Belgium's King Leopold II appropriates the Congo Free State as his personal possession, initiating a regime of egregious barbarity (beatings, mutilations, and the amputation of limbs being common punishments); he reinforces his colonial aspirations by permitting only Belgian Catholic missionaries to enter the country. [**DRC**]
1886	Following the amalgamation of the LIM's and the BMS's Congo missions two years earlier, a significant revival breaks out under Henry Richards at Banza Manteke, an awakening known as the "Pentecost on the Congo." [**DRC**]
1886	The Ganda king Mwanga begins a violent local persecution of Christians in Buganda, resulting in several Catholic and Anglican martyrdoms; most of the victims are pages at the king's court, who had refused to submit to his desires for sodomy and who suffered either maiming or burning to death. [**Uganda**]
1890	Capt. Fredrick Lugard occupies Buganda for the Imperial British East Africa Company to preempt German influence in the area and to quell local disturbances between animists, Muslims, Protestants, Catholics, and the nominal *kabaka* (king of Buganda) Mwanga II; Lugard's influence leads to Uganda becoming a British protectorate in 1893. [**Uganda**]
1892	After receiving a series of visions that lead him to seek out an Arabic Bible, Muslim Shaikh Zakaryas of Begemdir begins to preach the necessity of reforming and renewing Islam, using the Bible to point out the shortcomings in the Qur'an;

although he is strongly opposed by the local Muslim population, his message becomes more and more focused on conversion to Christianity, and eventually he and three thousand of his followers receive baptism in 1910. [**Ethiopia**]

1892　Methodist minister Mangena Maake Mokone founds an independent, intertribal Ethiopian church, in South Africa, marking the beginning of African-led urban churches, in contrast to the earlier rural-based independent churches; these Ethiopian churches later amalgamate with the African Methodist Episcopal Church in the United States, thus internationalizing the movement. [**South Africa**]

1893　Charismatic Irish layman George Pilkington (a classical scholar and translator as well as an adherent of the Keswick movement) inspires a major revival in Buganda and Nyasaland (Malawi); an immediate fruit of this revival is the spread of Ganda evangelists into other tribal areas of Uganda and among the Pygmies of the DRC. [**DRC, Malawi, Uganda**]

1895　The number of Roman Catholics increases in Egypt, partly through immigration and partly by conversion of the Copts; this results in the formation of the Coptic Uniate Church and the appointment of a patriarch of Alexandria. [**Middle East: Egypt**]

1896　Ethiopia's King Menelik II defeats an Italian army at the battle of Adowa, recognized throughout the entire African continent as a major victory against colonialism. [**Ethiopia**]

1898　The defeat of the Mahdī Muḥammad Ahmad bin Abd Allah in the Mahdist War leads to Sudan effectively becoming a British colony and to an influx of Christian missions; these have greater success in South Sudan than in the north. [**South Sudan, Sudan**]

1900　After working in Buganda for thirteen years, Alsatian missionary Bishop Jean-Joseph Hirth leads a group of White Fathers, together with twelve Ganda auxiliaries, into Rwanda to found a Catholic mission; however, their work there contains a strongly militaristic element due to their experience of more than a decade of violence in Buganda. [**Rwanda**]

1901	The White Fathers under Father Guillaume Templier arrive in Burkina Faso, establishing their base in the center of the capital, Ouagadougou; however, despite building Catholic missions there and at Koupéla, and performing their first baptisms, they have only moderate success in the country. [**Burkina Faso**]
1903	Petrus Louis Le Roux, a former Dutch Reformed missionary to the Zulus, founds the Zionist Apostolic Church, integrating African cultural features and Pentecostal spirituality; this is one of the first AICs and expands to become a large network. [**South Africa**]
1905	After twenty-four years of unproductive work by Plymouth Brethren missionaries, the outbreak of a religious awakening, remembered as *Mwaka wa Lusa* (the year of love), leads to the creation of important mission networks in Shaba and beyond. [**Angola, DRC, Zambia**]
1908	The fiery radical Anglo-Catholic priest and educator Frank Weston becomes bishop of Zanzibar; he has a particular concern for the traditional teaching and practice of the Church of England, and especially for the principle of episcopacy, which he sees as a defining characteristic of this Church as the English section of the universal Catholic Church. [**United Republic of Tanzania**]
1910	During a three-year period of increasing tensions between Copts and Muslims (1908–11), a Muslim member of the nationalist Waṭanī Party assassinates Egypt's only Coptic Christian prime minister, Pasha Boutros-Ghālī; his grandson Boutros Boutros-Ghālī would become the sixth secretary-general of the United Nations eighty-two years later. [**Middle East: Egypt**]
1910	Self-styled prophet Isaiah Shembe founds the Church of the Nazarenes (Ibandia lama Nazaretha, an important example of a Zionist, African-initiated prophetic church), building a community at Ekuphakameni. [**South Africa**]
1912	Anglican Garrick Sokari Braide receives several visionary experiences and assumes a prophetic role, eventually preaching

to thousands of followers in the Niger Delta as well as healing and baptizing his converts. [**Nigeria**]

1913 French Lutheran polymath Dr. Albert Schweitzer (philosopher, liberal theologian, and world-class organist) arrives in Lambaréné, Gabon, as a medical missionary; while there, he conceives his ethical philosophy *Ehrfurcht vor dem Leben* (veneration for life) and later receives the Nobel Peace Prize for his hospital work, which exemplifies this philosophy, in 1952. [**Gabon**]

1913 The Kikuyu controversy erupts in the Kenyan Anglican church following Anglican participation in an ecumenical communion at a missionary conference; Bishop Frank Weston sees their attendance as vitiating the traditional teaching and practice of the Church of England and castigates it as schismatic and heretical. [**Kenya**]

1913 The Liberian Grebo prophet William Wade Harris begins preaching campaigns, becoming the most successful missionary ever in West Africa with one hundred thousand converts in little more than a year. [**Ivory Coast, Ghana, Liberia**]

1913 The nationalist prophet John Chilembwe begins preaching in Nyasaland (Malawi) after the 1913 famine; this leads to an unsuccessful uprising against colonial rule after the outbreak of the First World War. [**Malawi**]

1915 Baptist missionaries in Ngombe-Luteta, central Congo, baptize Simon Kimbangu, later to become the founder of an influential African prophetic movement. [**DRC**]

1915 Colonial French authorities in Ivory Coast, fearing that the spectacular successes of the Grebo prophet William Wade Harris in converting whole villages to Christianity would have political implications for both the government and the Catholic Church, expel him back to his homeland of Liberia. [**Ivory Coast, Liberia**]

1916 Armed Senussi Bedouin bandits murder the French hermit priest Charles de Foucauld in the Saharan oasis of Tamanrasset, but communities of his Little Brothers of Jesus continue to follow his teaching and practice after his death. [**Algeria**]

1916	The Kalabari prophet Garrick Sokari Braide reaches the pinnacle of his influence in the Niger Delta, becoming known to his followers as Elijah II. [**Nigeria**]
1918	Simon Kimbangu begins receiving visions; several similar prophetic movements around the world also emerge, arising from the influenza pandemic that year (e.g., T. W. Rātana in New Zealand). [**DRC**]
1918	The *Aladura* (Yoruba: "owners of prayer") churches start as prayer groups within the older churches in Nigeria, expanding to become a widespread network of diverse groups throughout Africa. [**Nigeria**]
1919	Pope Benedict XV's apostolic letter *Maximum Illud* calls for a rejection of colonialist interests and for a greater emphasis on the training of indigenous clergy to take over from European missionaries in churches throughout the world; Pope Pius XI's encyclical *Rerum Ecclesiae* in 1926 reinforces Benedict's call, having a major impact on Catholic missions, particularly in Uganda. [**Uganda**]
1920	Converted criminal Sampson Oppong preaches to the Asante people in Ghana in the early 1920s; a mass movement to Christianity follows, with the Methodists being beneficiaries of these conversions. [**Ghana**]
1921	After eighteen years of mission work in Burkina Faso, French priest Johanny Thévenoud becomes vicar apostolic of Ouagadougou and, as such, combines missionary concern and farsighted practical social involvement; this helps to expand the Catholic Church and assist the national development of Burkina Faso. [**Burkina Faso**]
1921	Simon Kimbangu begins an influential AIC, the *Église de Jésus Christ sur la Terre par Son Envoyé Special Simon Kimbangu* (Church of Jesus Christ on earth by his special envoy Simon Kimbangu), but the Belgian authorities arrest him and sentence him to life imprisonment for undermining public security and disturbing the peace; despite his imprisonment, the Kimbanguist movement spreads. [**DRC**]

1922–1943   French Catholic bishop François Xavier Vogt, vicar apostolic in Yaoundé, oversees a period of extraordinary Catholic growth in Cameroon through the impetus of large numbers of well-trained Ewondo catechists. [**Cameroon**]

1924   Protestant missionaries arrive in Ivory Coast and begin to attract an influx of Christians previously converted under William Wade Harris, who had told his followers to await "teachers with Bibles." [**Ivory Coast**]

1925   Jesuit bishop Henri de Lespinasse Saune ordains nine priests, the first diocesan clergy in Madagascar; one of these, Ignace Ramarosandratna, becomes the first Malagasy bishop and apostolic vicar in 1939. [**Madagascar**]

1925   Presbyterian missionaries achieve great success among the Bulu, a major Bantu ethnic group, with more than seventy thousand converts being baptized in 1925. [**Cameroon, Equatorial Guinea, Gabon**]

1929   The Catholic White Fathers begin preaching to the Dagarti people in northwest Ghana, later receiving a highly receptive response after a dramatic answer to prayers for rain in July 1932. [**Ghana**]

1930   After ruling Ethiopia behind the scenes for a decade, Tafari Makonnen, the *ras* (duke) of Shewa, becomes the emperor Haile Selassie and, as such, reforms and modernizes the country, ruling until the Marxist coup d'état in 1974; Haile Selassie is a central figure in the Jamaican Rastafarian religion, the name of which derives from his title, Ras Tafari. [**Ethiopia**]

1930s   Independent churches grow exponentially among the Shona in Zimbabwe, partly as a response to the economic and political dominance of the white settler community, and partly from the impact of the Depression. [**Zimbabwe**]

1934   Almost all the Protestant groups in Madagascar amalgamate to form the United Protestant Church of Madagascar, although this represents a collaborative association for mission, rather than a total merger. [**Madagascar**]

| 1935 | Catholic missions in Rwanda and Burundi have considerable success, with a mass movement of Tutsi converts into the church; at the movement's peak, there are more than a thousand baptisms a week. [**Burundi, Rwanda, Uganda**] |

| 1935 | The Italian *duce* Benito Mussolini launches an invasion of Ethiopia and subjects the country to annexation and military occupation; this results in the expulsion of non-Italian missionaries, the Italianization of the Ethiopian church and its detachment from its centuries-old relationship with the See of Alexandria, and the execution of its Abuna (the leader of the church). [**Ethiopia**] |

| 1939 | Ugandan prelate Joseph Kiwánuka becomes the apostolic vicar of Masaka and the titular bishop of Thibica (an obsolete see in modern Tunisia), and thus the first indigenous African Catholic bishop since 1520. [**Uganda**] |

| 1945 | The discovery of the Nag Hammadi manuscripts in Upper Egypt provides a catalyst for a major reevaluation of the nature of Gnosticism and of early Christian history. [**Middle East: Egypt**] |

| 1946 | The king of Rwanda, Mutara III Rudahigwa, converts to Catholicism in 1943 and ceremonially dedicates his country to Christ three years later, effectively making Christianity the state religion of Rwanda-Urundi (the name by which the territories of Rwanda and Burundi were then jointly known). [**Burundi, Rwanda**] |

| 1950 | Hendrik Verwoerd's apartheid (separate development) regime utilizes biblical models to maintain the uniqueness of peoples, thereby theoretically giving each distinct group the right to determine its own separate destiny. [**South Africa**] |

| 1950 | Under the Population Registration and Group Areas Acts, the South African authorities deport colored (i.e., mixed race) Christian communities en masse from Cape Town to remote areas without churches. [**South Africa**] |

| 1953 | The Zambian prophetess Alice Lenshina experiences visions and begins preaching, becoming the focus of a revival |

movement at the Lubwa mission, where she had been baptized. [**Zambia**]

1955 — Conflict between Christians and Muslims erupts in the Sudan and continues until 1972; this breaks out again in 1983 over the imposition of Shari'a law by President Nimeiri. [**Sudan**]

1955 — Two years after the 1953 Lubwa revival, followers of the prophetess Alice Lenshina form the independent Lumpa Church, combining Christian and traditional African values but disallowing practices such as polygamy and idolatry; this church later becomes more radical, rejecting all secular authority and refusing to pay taxes, resulting in armed confrontations with the Zambian government in 1964. [**Zambia**]

1956 — After working for thirteen years in Sophiatown, South Africa, as a much-loved priest and vigorous anti-apartheid campaigner, English Anglican bishop Trevor Huddleston publishes his seminal book *Naught for Your Comfort*. [**South Africa**]

1956 — President Ğamāl Abdel Nāsser nationalizes the Suez Canal, provoking the retaliatory invasion of the Egyptian Sinai by Israel, together with Britain and France; Nāsser also declares Islam the religion of the state, leading to an exodus of Coptic Christians. [**Middle East: Egypt**]

1957 — Kwame Nkrumah leads Ghana to self-government, later becoming the first African head of state to promote Pan-Africanism; this movement takes concrete form in the Organization of African Unity in Addis Ababa, Ethiopia, in 1963, set up to consolidate the independence of the increasing number of postcolonial African states in the 1960s. [**Ghana**]

1958 — A major schism emerges in the Kenyan church, resulting in the formation of the Church of Christ in Africa; members of this group oppose revivalist emphases, but paradoxically name themselves *Johera* (people of love). [**Kenya**]

1959 — After decades of opposition and persecution, the Belgian colonial government recognizes the *Église de Jésus Christ sur la Terre par Son Envoyé Special Simon Kimbangu* as a legitimate church; ten years later, it becomes the first such church to be received into the WCC, giving it an appreciated badge of acceptability. [DRC]

1959 Emperor Haile Selassie abolishes the Egyptian Coptic Church's traditional right of appointment of the Abuna (the head of the Ethiopian Church) and upgrades the Abuna's role to a full patriarchate. [**Middle East: Egypt, Ethiopia**]

1960 Archbishop Laurean Rugambwa of Das es Salaam, a Haya Catholic of royal descent, becomes the first African cardinal of modern times. [**United Republic of Tanzania**]

1960 Joost de Blank, the Anglican archbishop of Cape Town, calls for the expulsion of the *Nederduitse Gereformeerde Kerk* (the Dutch Reformed Church in South Africa) from the WCC because of its support of apartheid. [**South Africa**]

1960 Many of independent Africa's new rulers come from Christian backgrounds; examples include Kwame Nkrumah (Ghana), who holds a bachelor of theology degree from his university study in the United States, Leopold Senghor (Senegal), Julius Nyerere (United Republic of Tanzania), and Kenneth Kaunda (Zambia). [**Ghana, Senegal, United Republic of Tanzania, Zambia**]

1960 The massacre of sixty-nine people (mainly women) in a crowd protesting the Pass Laws at a police station in the township of Sharpeville galvanizes international opinion against apartheid. [**South Africa**]

1961 The WCC and eight South African member churches issue a declaration against the exclusion of believers from any church because of color or race. [**South Africa**]

1962 A series of apparitions to several Luo Roman Catholics of a mystic woman with messages about the incarnation of the Son of God as a black man leads to the founding of *Legio Maria* (legion of Mary); although this is an independent African-initiated Catholic church, it does have some connections with earlier apparitions such as the Apparition of Fátima. [**Kenya**]

1964 The growth of Alice Lenshina's Lumpa Church leads to several violent clashes (the Lumpa Uprising) between her followers and Kenneth Kaunda's United National Independence

Party, in which between 700 and 1500 people lose their lives. [**Zambia**]

1965 — Dictator Joseph-Désiré Mobutu places increasing restrictions on the churches, forcing their consolidation into three bodies: the United Church of Christ in Zaire, the Catholics, and the Kimbanguists. [**DRC**]

1968 — Francisco Macias Nguéma becomes the first president of Equatorial Guinea, but proves to be violently hostile to the church, banning Christian funerals and Christian names, and declaring his country an "atheistical" state. [**Equatorial Guinea**]

1968 — Renewal takes place in the Coptic Church following several apparitions of the Virgin Mary over a period of nearly a year at a church in Zeitoun, Cairo, leading to reports of miracles and healings (including among Muslims). [**Middle East: Egypt**]

1970 — Forty-six Protestant missions and churches combine to form the *Église du Christ au Zaire* (church of Christ in Zaire); it now comprises sixty-two member denominations, making it the largest United Church in the world, ahead of the Evangelical Church in Germany. [**DRC**]

1971 — John Gatu, president of the Presbyterian Church of East Africa, calls for a moratorium on Christian missionaries and funding from the West to enable the African church to develop their own mission identity; mission historians view Gatu's call as a symbolic milestone marking an end of the colonial paradigm and the beginning of the postcolonial mission era. [**Zambia**]

1971 — The Namibian struggle against the occupation of the country by South Africa and the imposition of apartheid (strongly led by the Christian churches, and channeled through the South West Africa People's Organization, the Namibian independence movement), takes a dramatic turn with the publication of a highly critical open letter on apartheid, followed by an at times heated four-hour encounter between Namibian Lutheran bishop Leonard Nangolo Auala and South African prime minister John Vorster. [**Namibia**]

1971 — Influential Coptic leader Shenouda III becomes the pope of Alexandria and the patriarch of all Africa at the Holy

Apostolic See of Saint Mark the Evangelist of the Coptic Orthodox Church of Alexandria; he would hold this office for forty-one years. [**Middle East: Egypt**]

1972 President Mobutu orders the changing of Christian names to "authentic" African ones; bans all religious broadcasting, publications, and church youth groups; and nationalizes the Catholic university. [**DRC**]

1974 Black and white Dutch Reformed ministers form the *Broederkring* (circle of brothers) to resist apartheid within the South African Dutch Reformed churches; this becomes an important ecumenical center of opposition to apartheid. [**South Africa**]

1974 The Dergue, a Marxist military junta, overthrows Haile Selassie, the last Christian emperor of Ethiopia, deposes Patriarch Abuna Tewophilos as head of the Ethiopian Orthodox Church, and begins a regime marked by terror and opposition to Christianity. [**Ethiopia**]

1976 A group of twenty-two theologians from Asia, Africa, and Latin America gather in Dar es Salaam to form EATWOT; this theological association seeks to facilitate the development of contextual and liberationist theological dialogue within grassroots and local communities. [**United Republic of Tanzania**]

1977 Steve Biko, the honorary president of the Black People's Convention and founder of the Black Consciousness movement, dies violently while in police custody, becoming a symbolic "martyr" for the anti-apartheid movement. [**South Africa**]

1978 After thirteen years of international isolation under a white minority government following its Unilateral Declaration of Independence from Britain, southern Rhodesia begins a transition to black majority rule, the first prime minister of the new Zimbabwe Rhodesia being United Methodist bishop and national leader Abel Tendekayi Muzorewa. [**Zimbabwe**]

1980s Several Marian apparitions occur during the decade in Kibého, Rwanda (1981 on); Nsimalen, Cameroon (1986); and Nairobi, Kenya (late 1980s); these are viewed as prophetic and miraculous events, with the Kibého apparition being interpreted as a forewarning of the 1994 Rwandan genocide. [**Cameroon, Kenya, Rwanda**]

1981 President Anwār al-Sādāt effectively outlaws the Coptic Church, arresting Patriarch Shenouda III and a number of other bishops and priests (who Sādāt had accused of having political ambitions and of fostering sectarianism); however, this persecution is short-lived, as an assassin kills Sādāt a month later. [**Middle East: Egypt**]

1982 Allan Boesak and the *Nederduitse Gereformeerde Sendingkerk* (the Dutch Reformed Mission Church, i.e., the black wing of the Dutch Reformed Church) persuade the World Alliance of Reformed Churches to suspend the Dutch Reformed Church for its support of apartheid. [**South Africa**]

1983 Catholic authorities remove Emmanuel Milingo, archbishop of Lusaka, from his see after criticism of his incorporation of African traditions of healing and exorcism into his ministry. [**Zambia**]

1984 Desmond Tutu, Anglican bishop of Lesotho and the first black secretary-general of the SACC, receives the 1984 Nobel Peace Prize for his opposition to apartheid; this award transforms the South African anti-apartheid struggle into an international movement. [**Lesotho, South Africa**]

1985 The ICT issues the Kairos Document, sharply criticizing the South African apartheid regime, and advocating a "preferential option for the poor" and the kairos of reconciliation. [**South Africa**]

1986 Nobel Peace Prize–winning anti-apartheid and human rights activist Desmond Tutu becomes the first black Anglican archbishop of Cape Town; he also becomes the president of the ecumenical All Africa Conference of Churches the same year, and after the end of apartheid, chairs the Truth and Reconciliation Commission, set up to investigate past human rights abuses, in 1994. [**South Africa**]

1988 South African police, on the orders of the apartheid regime, burn down the Catholic Bishops' Conference building in

Pretoria and blow up the headquarters of the SACC in Johannesburg. [**South Africa**]

1989 — Four Catholic, Anglican, and Presbyterian church leaders in Mozambique, with encouragement from the political leaders of other African countries, mediate between the government and the rebel *Resistência Nacional Moçambicana* (Mozambique national resistance). [**Mozambique**]

1989 — Frederick Willem de Klerk becomes president of South Africa and begins the unilateral dismantling of the structure of apartheid; the following year, the South African white minority parliament votes to end the segregation of public facilities. [**South Africa**]

1990 — A national conference of church leaders in issues the Rustenburg Declaration, confessing their guilt and complicity in apartheid, and calling for complete confession, forgiveness, and restitution. [**South Africa**]

1990 — Pope John Paul II consecrates the new basilica of Our Lady of Peace (believed by the *Guinness Book of Records* to be the largest church building in the world, although other sources dispute this claim) in Yamasoukro, the birthplace of the Ivory Coast president Félix Houphouët-Boigny, who had just gifted the basilica to the Catholic Church. [**Ivory Coast**]

1990 — President de Klerk legalizes the previously banned African National Congress and releases Nelson Mandela from prison after twenty-seven years of imprisonment. [**South Africa**]

1991 — A coalition of ethnic-based parties overthrows the Marxist leader Mengistu Haile Mariam and reinstates the Coptic Orthodox church as the national religion of Ethiopia. [**Ethiopia**]

1991 — After defeating long-serving President Kenneth Kaunda's United National Independence Party by a landslide majority in a snap election, Zambia's incoming president Frederick Chiluba officially declares the country to be a Christian nation. [**Zambia**]

1994 — After a sweeping 63 percent victory by his African National Congress Party in the 1994 General Election, Nelson Mandela becomes the president of South Africa as the country's first black head of state, heading a multiparty government of national unity (which includes some of his political opponents). [**South Africa**]

2005 A study by the Pew Forum on Religion and Public Life locates the current center of gravity of world Christianity in Mali, reflecting Christianity's movement toward the Global South.[9] [**Mali**]

2012 Ellinah Ntombi Wamukoya, chaplain of the University of Swaziland, succeeds Meshack Mabuza as Anglican bishop of Swaziland, thus becoming the first woman bishop in Africa. [**Eswatini (Swaziland)**]

2014 The Islamic extremist group Boko Haram kidnaps more than two hundred Christian schoolgirls from a government secondary school in Chibok and enslaves them, compelling them to convert to Islam and forcing them into arranged marriages. [**Nigeria**]

Bibliography

Badr, Ḥabīb, et al., eds. *Christianity: A History in the Middle East*. Beirut: Middle East Council of Churches, 2005.

Bowers, Paul. "Nubian Christianity: The Neglected Heritage." *African Journal of Evangelical Theology* 4 (1985) 3–23.

Curtis, Sarah A. *Civilizing Habits: Women Missionaries and the Revival of French Empire*. Oxford: Oxford University Press, 2010.

Davidson, Ivor. *The Birth of the Church: From Jesus to Constantine, AD 30–312*. Edited by John D. Woodbridge et al. Monarch History of the Church 1. Oxford, UK: Monarch, 2005.

———. *A Public Faith: From Constantine to the Medieval World, AD 312–600*. Edited by John D. Woodbridge et al. Monarch History of the Church 2. Oxford, UK: Monarch, 2005.

Hill, Jonathan, ed. *Zondervan Handbook to the History of Christianity*. Oxford: Lion, 2006.

Isichei, Elizabeth. *A History of Christianity in Africa: From Antiquity to the Present*. London: SPCK, 1995.

Jenkins, Philip. *The Lost History of Christianity: The Thousand-Year Golden Age of the Church in the Middle East, Africa, and Asia—and How It Died*. New York: HarperOne, 2008.

---

9. Johnson, "Christianity in Global Context," 1.

———. *The Next Christendom: The Coming of Global Christianity*. 3rd ed. Oxford: Oxford University Press, 2011.
Johnson, Todd M. "Christianity in Global Context: Trends and Statistics." Pew Research, May 2005. https://www.pewresearch.org/wp-content/uploads/sites/7/2005/05/051805-global-christianity.pdf.
Koschorke, Klaus, et al., eds. *A History of Christianity in Asia, Africa, and Latin America, 1450–1990: A Documentary Sourcebook*. Grand Rapids: Eerdmans, 2007.
Lamport, Mark A., ed. *Encyclopedia of Christianity in the Global South*. 2 vols. Lanham, MD: Rowman & Littlefield, 2018.
Marty, Martin E. *The Christian World: A Global History*. New York: Modern Library, 2009.
———. "Introduction: Religion in America 1935–1985." In *Altered Landscapes: Christianity in America 1935–1985*, edited by David W. Lotz et al., 1–16. Grand Rapids: Eerdmans, 1989.
McManners, John, ed. *The Oxford Illustrated History of Christianity*. Oxford: Oxford University Press, 1995.
Neill, Stephen. *A History of Christian Missions*. Edited by Owen Chadwick. 2nd ed. Pelican History of the Church 6. Harmondsworth, UK: Penguin, 1986.
Quasten, Johannes. *Patrology*. 4 vols. Westminster, MD: Christian Classics, 1983.
Raheb, Mitri, and Mark A. Lamport, eds. *Surviving Jewel: An Enduring Story of Christianity in the Middle East*. Global Story of Christianity 1. Eugene, OR: Cascade Books, 2022.
Roberts, J. M. *The Penguin History of the World*. Rev. ed. Harmondsworth, UK: Penguin, 1995.
Ross, Emma George. "African Christianity in Ethiopia." Metropolitan Museum of Art, Oct. 2000. http://www.metmuseum.org/toah/hd/acet/hd_acet.htm.
Stanley, Henry M. *How I Found Livingstone: Travels, Adventures, and Discoveries in Central Africa; Including Four Months' Residence with Dr. Livingstone*. British Library, 1872. https://www.bl.uk/collection-items/how-i-found-livingstone-by-henry-m-stanley#.
Stevenson, J., ed. *Creeds, Councils and Controversies: Documents Illustrating the History of the Church to AD 337–461*. Revised by W. H. C. Frend. London: SPCK, 1991.
———, ed. *A New Eusebius: Documents Illustrating the History of the Church to AD 337*. Revised by W. H. C. Frend. London: SPCK, 1992.
Sundkler, Bengt, and Christopher Steed. *A History of the Church in Africa*. Cambridge: Cambridge University Press, 2000.
Tilley, Maureen A. "The Collapse of a Collegial Church: North African Christianity on the Eve of Islam." *Theological Studies* 62 (2001) 3–22.

Index of Subjects and Names

Abba Garima, 36
abuna, 99, 104–5
Abwa, Daniel, 52
Abyssinia, 94
Achebe, Chinua, 120, 166
Acts of the Scillitan Martyrs, 22
Ad Afros Epistola Synodica, 21
Adenekan-Koevoets, Bisi, 136
Adulis, 99, 100
Aedesius, 99
Afonso I, 44, 179, 244
Africa as "cradle of human civilization," 243
   as "cultural bazaar," 243
Africa Evangelical Mission (AEA), 131
Africa Study Bible, 129
Africa
   evangelism, 46
   mission societies, 47
   targeted audience, 52
Africa's World War (also, the Great War of Africa), 195
African academic theology, 244
African Bible Commentary, 131
African Christian Fellowship, 82–84, 87
African Christian history as intellectual history, 241ff.
   with African historical experience, 243
   recent scholarship in, 253
African Christianity, and African Christians, 188
   as Christian continent, 217
   defining mark of, 214
   and five-point manifesto, 189
African independent churches, 63
African Inland Mission (AIM), 130
African Initiated Church (AIC), 129, 130, 148, 170, 172, 211ff.
African National Congress, 178
African Pentecostalism, 228
African Reformation of Christianity, 217
African Religions and Philosophy, 171
African slave trade, transatlantic, 178, 180
African Study Bible, 131
African theology, 145–48
African Union report on Africa's healthcare status, 233
African Zion as the real Jerusalem, 251
Africanizing Christianity, 170–72
Africans as "incurably religious," 185ff.
Aggrey, James E. K., 80
Aksum/Axum, 28–29, 30–42, 94, 96, 98, 99, 100–101, 103, 126
Aladura Movement, 171
Alexandria, 13–14, 17, 21–22, 94, 96, 97, 126
   Alexandrian Catechetical School, 16–17
   Patriarchate of, 38
Algeria, 117–19
Algerian War of Independence (1954–1962), 117
Al-Hakim (Fatimid Dynasty), 105
All Africa Conference of Churches, (AACC), 221ff., 131–32, 134

All Africa Lutheran Conference, 131
Ambrose, Bishop, 24
American Board of Commissioners for Foreign Mission (ABCFM), 128
American Board of Foreign Missions, 133
Amos, 77
Angel of Bukavu, 199
Anim, Emmanuel Kwesi and prosperity teaching in Ghanian Pentecostalism, 237
animism, "Animistic Religions," 163, 165
Anthony (251–356), 246
Antiochenes, 97
Antony the Great, 20–21, 97
apartheid, 188
Apollo, 16
Apollos, 96
Appiah-Kubi, Kofi, 151
Ares, 29
Arius, 20–21
  controversy, 97, 126
Arnobius, 246
Arrow of God, 120
Asamoah-Gyadu, 227, 228, 230
Asbeha, Ella, *see* Kaleb, King
Association for Christian Theological Education in Africa, 131
Association for Pentecostal Theological Training in Africa, 136
Association of Evangelicals in Africa and Madagascar (AEAM), 131
Association of Theological Seminaries in Francophone Africa, 190
Athanasius of Alexandiria (293–373), 19–21, 24, 33, 97, 99, 100, 103, 126, 246
Atlas of Global Christianity 1910–2010, 164
Atripe, 94
Augustine, 24, 117, 126, 176, 246
Azikiwe, Nnamdi, 80
Azusa Street Revival, 135

Banda, David, 233
Bantu, 125

Baptist Missionary Society (BMS), 46, 128
Baptist Union, 135
Barankitse, Marguerite, 202
Basil of Caesarea, 19
Beatrice, Donna, 44–45
Bediako, Kwame, 125, 148
Belhar Confession, 132
Belloc, Hilaire, 108
Benedict XV, 111
Berlin colonial conference, 181
Berlin Conference, 43, 51, 110, 128, 168
Bethel Bible School (Topeka, KS), 135
Beti, Mongo, 186
Bismark, Otto von, 110
Boegner, Alfred, 181
Boegner, Mark, 181
Boesak, Allen, 189
Bokassa I, Emperor, 203
Bolaji, Idowu, 244
Book of Common Prayer into Yoruba, 252
Bosch, David J., 127, 228
Botswana Christian Council and the Minister's Fraternal, 136
Bowen, Reverend Thomas J., 79
Bowler, Kate, 227, 233
Bridge, 83–84, 86
British South Africa Company, 133
Brown, Althea Maria, 80
Building Bridges, 87
Bujo, Benezet, 113
Bukuru, Fr. Zachary, 201, 202
Burundi, Hutu-Tutsi Fraternity, 201
Buta Seminary Massacre, 202
Buxton, Sir Thomas, 182

Caecilian, 23–24
Cairo, 94
Calderisi, Robert, 117
Can God Die in Africa?, 186
Candace (kandaké), 98
Cao, Diego, 44
Capuchin missionaries, 44–45
Carey, Lott, 78–79
Carey, William, 46, 52, 77, 128, 130, 180
Carnaedes, 14
Carthage, 13–15, 126

INDEX OF SUBJECTS AND NAMES   295

Catechetical School of Alexandria, 96
"Catholic Model of Mission," 128
Catholicae Ecclesia, 112
Centenary Conference on Protestant Mission of the World, 133
Central African Republic, 203
Centre de Littérature Évangélique, 190
Chalcedonian, 98, 101, 102
Cherubim and Seraphim Church, 171
Chikane, Frank, 189
Chilembwe, John, 170
China Inland Missions (Overseas Missionary Society), 128
Chinn, Lloyd and Jan, 83–84, 86
Christian Association of Nigeria, 136
Christian Century, 108
Christian Epoch-Makers, 73
Christian ethos in Zimbabwe, Malawi, and South Africa, 215
Christian kinship, 169–70
Christian outposts to the Cape of Good Hope, 249
Christianity in Africa, challenges, dilemmas, and future prospects, 222
Christianization of Nubia, 100
Christians in Africa, weak political theology, 215
Churches in Africa, public role of, 188
Circle of Concerned African Women (Circle), 132, 134, 145
Clark, John, 48
Clarkson, Thomas, 179
"Classical Mission," 128
Clement, 17, 96, 177
Clitomachus, 14–15
Code Noir, 179
Coker, Daniel, 79
Cold War and Africa, 193
Coleman, Simon, 230
colonial nation states, 169
colonialism and Christianity, 186
Comboni, Daniel, 111
Commission on World Mission and Evangelism (CWME), 130
Committee for the Abolition of the Black Trade, 179
commoditizing the gospel, 218

Concepts of God in Africa, 147
Conference of African Theological Institutions, 132
Congo Conference, 51
Congo Research Group, 197
Congregation of Indulgences, 113
Congregation of the Holy Ghost, 120
Constantine, 24
Constantius II, Emperor, 33, 103
Contra Celsum, 18
Coptic Orthodox Church of Egypt, 98, 99
Copts/Coptic, 94, 96, 98, 102–6, 162
Cosmas III, 104
Council of
   Carthage, 25
   Chalcedon in AD 451, 36, 96, 251
   Ephesus, 21–22
   Nicea, 26, 39, 97
Cousepel du Mesnil, Francois, 112
Cox, Harvey, 151
Crowther, Bishop Samuel Ajayi, 53–54, 61–66, 122, 182ff., 252
Cugoano, Fanti Ottobah, 70
Cush, 94
Cyprian, 23, 126, 246
Cyril of Alexandria, 22, 97, 98, 126, 246
Cyrillian Christology, 98, 101

Dacko, David, 203
de Rosny, Eric, 187
de Souza, Donna Ana, 250
Decian persecution, 23
decolonization, 171
Dei Filius, 110
Demerius (189–231), 177
Democratic Republic of Congo, 195
Dendur temple, 102
Dengel, Anna, 115
Denis Mukwege, Dennis, 197
DeYamert, Lillian Thomas, 80
dhimmis, 103
Dickens, Charles, 61
Dickson, Kwesi, 171
Dictionary of African Christian Biography, 53
Didymus the Blind, 19
Diocletian, Emperor (284–305), 247

Dionysius, 19
Djotodia, Michel, 203
Dona Kimpa Vita (1684–1706), 249–50
Donatus Magnus, 24, 126; Donatist movement, 24–25
Du Plessis, David, 136
Ducat, 184
Dutch Reformed Church, 189
dyophysite (two natures) Christology, 98

East African revival, 199ff.
Eboussi-Boulaga, Fabien, 185
Ecclesiastical History, 30
Ecumenical Association of African Theologians, 132
Ecumenical Association of Third World Theologians (EATWOT), 132, 134
Ecumenical Foundation of Southern Africa, 132
Edict of Milan, 24
Edinburgh Conference, 43
Edinburgh, 162
Éditions CLÉ, 190
Egypt, 16
  church of, 176–7
Ekechi, Felix, 115
Ela, Jean-Marc, 148
Elihu, Paul, 232
Ella Amida, 100
English Bill of 1807, 48
Epistle of Barnabas, 16
Equiano, Olaudah, 67–70
Eritrea, 106
Ethiopia, biblical references to, 39–40
Ethiopian Christianity, 177, 247
  Aksum, Frumentius and Aedesius, 248
  Ethiopian Orthodox Church. 178, 251
  proselyte, 16
Ethiopian churches, 94, 105–6, 170, 171
Ethiopian Orthodox Tewahedo Church in Ethiopia, 98, 99, 162
ethnic community, 168–69

European standards of Christianity imposed upon African Christianity, 180, 181, 184
Eusebius of Caesarea, 30, 177
Evangelical Alliance, 130
Evangelical Alliance of South Africa, 136
Evangelical Fellowship of Botswana, 136
Evangelical Fellowship of Zimbabwe (EFZ), 210
Evangelical Missionary Alliance (Global Connection), 130
Evangelical Witness of South Africa, 132
Ezana, King, 33, 39, 99, 103
  stone inscriptions, 33–34
Ezeulu, 120

Faith Mission, 128–29
Faraji, Salim, 101
Faras (Pakhoras), 101
Federal Theological Seminary of Southern Africa, 131
Fermo Proposito, Il, 108
Fidei Donum, 111, 112
First Council of Constantinople, 21
Fontaine, Darcie, 117, 119
Forster, Elizabeth, 112, 118
Franco-Prussian War, 110
Freston, Paul, 230
Frontier Fellowship, 85, 87
Frumentius, *Abuna Salama* (father of salvation), 30–33, 99, 103, 126, 249, 251, 382,
Fuller, John Jackson, 49

Gairdner, Temple, 113
Gama, da, Vasco, 45
Gantt, Lucy, 80
Garima Gospels, 36
Ge'ez language/literature, 99–100, 105
Gelasius, 30
General Missionary Conference of South Africa (GMCSA), 133, 134
Ghana, mission model of early missionaries, 236
Ghanian Pentecostals, 152–53

INDEX OF SUBJECTS AND NAMES 297

Glasgow Missionary Society (Free Church of Scotland), 128
Global Christianity, xiii; entanglement in, xviii
Goldenberg, David, 113
Goldman, David P., 108, 109,
Goodale, Harvey, 79
Gordon-Conwell Theological Seminary, 164
Goumba, Abel, 203
Grammaire Igbo, 121
Greek Gospels of Egyptians, 16
Gregory of Nazianzus, 19
Gregory of Nyssa, 19
Gregory XVI, Pope, 111, 184
Grenfell, George 51
Guinness, Henry Grattan, 51

Habesha, 94
Ham (Noah's son) curse, 113
Harris, Jim and the Luo people of Kenya, 236
Harris, William Wade, 122, 170
Hastings, Adrian, 109, 113, 122
health and wealth gospel, 226ff.
  and African Pentecostalism, 226ff.
  influenced by American prosperity gospel, 227
health and well-being in African experience, 231
Hellenistic Jews, 15
Henrique, Prince, 179
Heraclas, 18
Hexapla, 18
Hill, Robert F., 79
Himyarite kingdom (Yemen), 103
Hodgson, Dorothy, 115
Holistic Mission: God's Plan for God's People, Brian Woolnough, 237
Holy Trinity Peace Village Kuron, 206
Homily in Honour of St. Frumentius, 30
homo religiosus, 146
House Boy, 166
how Africans have narrated the Christian story, 245
Hunter, George, 238

Hutus and Tutsis, tension, 200; united by the blood of Christ, 202; antagonism in Rwanda, 199

Idowu, Bolaji, 146, 147, 171
Igboland, 120–21
"imbecilization of Christianity", 188
In Plurimis, 111
In Supremo Apostolatus, 111
Indicopleustes, Cosmas, 37
Institute for Contextual Theology (ICT), 132
International Mission Board, 135
International Missionary Council (IMC), 130, 134
International Missionary Fellowship, 130
Isaiah, 64
Islam and Pentecostalism, violent encounters between, 216
Itala (Latin translation of the Bible), 247
Italian Capuchins, 250

Jamaican Baptist Missionary Society, 48
Jenkins, Philip, 61
Jerome of Stridon, 19, 35
Jerome's *Vulgate,* 247
Jesuit movement, 127
John III, Patriarch of Jerusalem 38
Johnson, Todd, 164
Julian of Alexandria, 101–2
Justin II, 102
Justinian, 101

Kabila, Laurent, 195, 196
"Kabyle Myth," 118
Kairos Document, 132, 189
Kaleb, King, 37–38, 103
Kalu, Ogbu, 151, 153
Kasa-Vubu, Joseph, 195
Katho, Bungishabaku, launched Université Shalom de Bunia in eastern Congo, 207
Kebra Negast (Glory of the kings), 40, 252
Kendi, Ibram, 59
Khaldun, Ibn, 61
Khoikhoi, 45

Kimbangu, Simon, 170
Kingdom of Aksum, *see* Aksum
kingdom of God in the earthly realm, 229
Kingdom Strikes Back, 75
kingdoms of Nobatia, Makouria, and Alodia along the Nile, 249
Kinvi, Fr. Bernard, 204–5
Kirkland, Colonel, 77
Kolingba, General André, 203
Kongo, Kingdom of, 178
Krapf, Johann Ludvig, 49
Kuba kingdom, 253
Kulturkampf, 110
Kuriakos, 104

L'Association de la Jeunesse Algerienne pour l'Action Sociale, 119
La mission Suisse dans l'Afrique du Sud (Swiss mission in South Africa), 128
Lalibela, King, 251
Langworthy, William, 68
Lapsley, Samuel Norvell, 79
Larbi, E. Kingsley, 152, 154
Lartey, Emmanuel, 148
Latin Christianity, 248
Latourette, Kenneth Scott, 43, 53
Lavigerie, Cardinal Charles, 112, 116, 117, 184
Le Service des Centres Sociaux, 119
Lee, Moojang, 127
Lefebvre, Marcel, 118
Leo XIII, Pope, 111, 112
Leopold II, King of Belgium, 168, 195, 253
LGBTQ rights, women's rights, and minority rights, 219
liberation and empowerment theologies, 217
Liele, George, 53, 77
Life of Antony, The, 97, 100
Livingston, David, 47–51, 129, 168, 183
Livingstone Inland Mission, 51
London Missionary Society (LMS), 128, 129, 133
Longinus, Byzantine missionary, 102, 103, 252

Lords Spiritual and Temporal and the Commons of the Parliament of Great Britain, 68
Louis XIV, King, 179
Lumumba, Patrice, 195
Luneau, Rene, 186, 187
LXX, *see* Septuagint

Magdalena, 45
Magesa, Laurenti, 244
Mahrem, 29
Majorinus, 24
Mana, Kä, 187
Manicheans, 24
Mark (the Apostle), 126
Martin, David, 228
Martyrdom of Arethas, 37–38
Marxist regimes
 Angola, under Agostinho Neto and José Eduardo dos Santos, 194–5
 Congo (Conakry) became a Marxist-Leninist state in 1970, under Marien Ngouabi, 194–5
 Egypt, under Gamal Abdel Nasser in 1954–69, 194–5
 Guinea Bissau, under Amilcar Cabral, 194–5
 Mozambique, under Samora Machel, 194–5
 Somalia, under Mohamed Siad Barre, 194–5
Maryknoll Sisters, 115
material culture that shapes African Christianity, 249
Maximum Illud, 111
Mbanza Kongo, 44
Mbiti, John S., 93, 146, 147, 170, 171, 229, 244
Mecurios, King of Nubia, 244
Medical Mission Sisters, 115
Melkite, 98, 102–3
Mensurius, 23
Merkurios of Makuria, 104
Meroe, 94, 98
Merrick, Joseph, 48–49
miaphysite (united nature) Christology, 98
Miller, Donald E., 227

Minimalistic Theology of Salvation, 143–45
Mission de France, 119
Mission de l'Organisation des Nations Unies au Congo (MONUC), 195
Missionary Sisters of our Lady of Africa, 115
Missionary Sisters of the Holy Rosary, 114
Missionary Society of Our Lady of Africa, later known as the White Fathers, 184
missions paradigms, 127
Mitzraim, 94
Mobutu, Joseph-Désiré, 195
Moffat, Robert, 47–48, 50, 183
Mokhtar, G., 126
Monastery of St. Anthony, 105
monasticism, 96–97
Mongo Beti, 186
Montanus, 23
Moravians, 45
  Moravian Church, 127–28
  Moravian Protestants mission station in South Africa, 244
Moses George of Makuria, 104, 105
Mott, John R., 128, 129
Mugabe, Robert, 216
Museveni, Taguta, 216
Mystici Corporis, 111

Napoleon III, 116
National African American Missions Council, 85–86
National Council for the Defense of Democracy, a Hutu political party, 201
National Liberation Front, 119
nation-state formation and Christianity, 175
Naudé, Beyers, 189
Negritude and Pan-Africanist movements, 243
Neil, Stephen, 73
Nelson, Ron and Star, 84–86
neo-charismatics, 152
Nestorious, 97, 98
new forms of Christianity in Africa, 187

New Frontiers International, 128
New York Times, 171
Nicene Creed, 20–21
  Nicene-Constantinopolitan Creed, 97
Niger Mission, 65–66, 252
Nilotic languages, 94
Nine Saints, 35–36, 38, 100, 251
Njoku, Chukwudi, A., 116
Nkrumah, Kwame, 80
Nkwocha, Levi, 237
Nubia, 94, 96, 98, 100, 102–6, 126
  Alodia, 94–95, 100–103
  Makuria, 94, 100, 102–4
  Meroe, 94, 98
  Nobatia/Nobadia, 94, 100–104
Nuwas, Dhu, of Himyar, 37
Nwoji, Stanley, 83
Nyamiti, Charles, 147
Nylander, Gustav, 48
Nzinga, King, 44
Nzinga, Queen of the Dongo kingdom, 250

occultism in Nigeria and Ghana, 217
Oden, Thomas, 245
Oduwole, Mercy Amba, 132, 145
Okafor, Eddie, 121
Oliver, Erna, 126
On the City of God against the Pagans, see *The City of God*
Optatus, 246
Origen, 18–19, 96, 177
Overseas Missionary Society, 128
Oyono, Ferdinand, 166

Pachomius (Pakhom), 97, 100
Pantaenus, 96
Pantalewon, Abba, 38
Panzi Hospital, 197
Parham, Charles, 135
Paris Mission, 181
Partition of Africa, 168
Pastor Aeternus, 110
Patassé, Ange-Félix, 203
Patterson, Orlando, 59
Pelagius, 25–26
Pendergrass, George and Pamela, 85

300 INDEX OF SUBJECTS AND NAMES

Pentecostal Fellowship of Nigeria, 136
Pentecostal-charismatic Christianity, 212
    transnational movements and diasporic connections, 212
Pentecostalism, 135-37
Periplus of the Erythraean Sea, 28
Perrin, David, Bishop, 85
Philae, 94
Philo of Alexandria, 15, 17
Philotheos (Fīlatéwos), 104, 105
Pietism, 144
Pillay, Jerry, 134
Pingstmissionens Utvecklingssamarbete, 198
Pius IX, Pope, 110, 113, 116
Pius X, Pope, 108-9
Pius XII, Pope, 111, 112
Plaatjies van Huffel, Mary-Anne, 134
Portuguese Jesuits, 250
Postcolonial Africa, 210
praeparatio evangelica (preparation for the gospel), 125, 146, 147
Prester John, Christian kingdom of 177, 249
Price, T., 114
"productivity gospel," 153
Prolegomena to World History, 61
Propaganda Fide, 111
Protestantism, internationalism, 61; waves of, 54-55

"race of children," 165
Réflexions Théologiques du Sud (Theological Reflections from the South), 190
resilience of Christianity, 176
Rhodes University, Faculty of Theology at, 131
Richmond African Missionary Society, 78
Riebeck, Jan, van, 45
Robert, Dana L., 136
Royal Geographical Society, 253
Rufinus, Tyrannius, 100
Rufnus, 30, 32-33
Rukuni, Rugare, 126
Rustenburg Conference, 132

Rwanda, 186; civil war, 200

Sacred Congregation for the Propagation of the Faith, 119
Saker, Alfred, 49
Saladin, 251
Salisbury, Gladys, 50
Sanneh, Lamin, 114, 121, 149, 180, 250
Saunders, Linda P., 82
Sawyer, Harry, 244
Schmidt, George, 45
Scottish Missionary Society, (Church of Scotland), 128
Scramble for Africa, 168-69
Seleka, 203
Septuagint, *see* LXX, 15
Seymour, William, 135
Shanahan, Joseph, 120
Sharp, Granville, 70
Sharpe, Henry, 77
Shenoute, 22
Sheppard, William, the "Black Livingstone," 79-80, 252
Sider, Ron, 227
Sierra Leone, 182; as the first black colony, 250; Krio church, 250
Silk Road, 101
Silko of Nobadia, 101
Simba Rebellion (1964), 195
Simon from Cyrene, 16
slavery, 110-12
Society for Missions to Africa and the East (CMS), 128
Society for the Promotion of Christian Knowledge, 127
Society for the Propagation of the Gospel (SPG), 127
Society of Catholic Medical Missionaries, 115
Soede, Nathaniel, 235
Soeurs Agricoles et Hospitaliere (Sisters for agriculture and hospitals), 115
South African Council of Churches (SACC), 136
Southern Baptist Convention, 135
Sowing Seeds of Joy, 85
Soyo, Mbanza, 44

INDEX OF SUBJECTS AND NAMES   301

Springer, Kevin, 227
St. John Paul II Hospital (Bossemptélé, Central African Republic), 204
St. Mark, See of, 38
Stanley, Brian, 162
Stanley, Henry Morton, 48, 51, 168
Stepp, Eddie, 81
storytelling components, xiii, xvii
  history, contexts, and communities, xiv
  migration and global diaspora, xviv
  movement, xvix
  public theologies, xviv
  translation, xviv;
Stroope, Michael W., 127
Student Volunteer Movement, 128
Sudan in war, 205
  Dinka, 205
Sudan Interior Mission (SIM), 130, 131
Sudan United Mission, 130
survival of African Christianity, 175
Swedish Pentecostal Mission, 198
Synan, Vinson, 227

Taban, Paride, 205
Tata, Fabian, 80
technology is a platform in domesticating Christianity, 218
Tennett, Timothy, 144, 145
Tertullian, 22–23, 126, 246, 247
Thaumaturgus, Gregory, 18
The City of God, 25
The Prosperity Paradox, Clayton Christensen, 235
Theodora of Philae, 101, 102
Theodosius of Alexandria, 102
theologies for political power, especially in Africa and the Americas, xx
  influence of evangelicalism, liberation theologies, and Pentecostal practices for, xx
Things Fall Apart, 166
Third Lausanne Congress on World Evangelization, 134
Thoughts and Sentiments on the Evil and Wicked Traffic of the Slavery and Commerce of the Human Species, 70

three C's: Christianity, civilization, commerce, 168
tribalism as a tool for exclusion and marginalization, 216
triple G's: God, glory, gold, 110
Tshisekedi, Félix-Antoine, 197
Turner Henry, McNeal, 79
Tutu, Archbishop Desmond, 173, 189
Tyrannius Ru nus of Concordia, 19

Ubuntu (theology of), 172–73
unity of Christians, hindrances towards, 215
Universities' Mission to Central Africa, 50

Valerian persecution, 23
van der Kemp, Johannes, 183
Vassa, Gustavus *see* Equiano, Olaudah
Vatican Council; First, 110, 111; Second, 111
Vedder, Henry, 73
Venn, Henry, 65
Vienna 1815 congress, 181
Volf, Miroslav and the materiality of salvation, 227
Vulgate, 19

Wall, Barbara Mann, 115
Walls, Andrew F., 93, 98, 109, 129, 187
wars and ethnic challenges, 193ff.
wazungu religion, 93
Wesley, John, 179
West Africa Conference *see* Congo Conference
Western missionary work in Africa, 200, 211
Western paradigms of wealth, 236
White Fathers in Africa, 112, 116
White Monastery of Shenoute, 94, 105
Wilberforce, William, 64, 179, 182
Willingen conference, 52
Wimber, John, 227 Wimber
Winter, Ralph D., 73–75
women and evangelization, 221
Wood, Reverend J. B, 65
World Alliance of Reformed Churches (WARC), 134, 135

World Christianity versus global
    Christianity, xv
World Council of Churches (WCC),
    118, 130, 134, 136
    and Africa, 209
World Evangelical Alliance, 130
World Evangelical Fellowship, 130
World Missionary Conference in
    Edinburgh (1910), 113, 129,
    162–63
World Venture, 83–84
World's Student Christian Federation,
    128
Wright, N. T., 227, 230
Written by Himself, 69

Yamamori, Tetsuna, 227
Yaoundé (CLÉ), 190
Yared, 39
Yoruba, 169
    Bible of 1851, 65
    people, 169, 182
Young Men Christian Movement, 128

zema, 39
Zinzendorf, Ludwig von, 127–28
Zion Temple and the Restoration
    Church, 200
Zionist churches, 170, 171